Climate Change and Children's Rights in Zimbabwe

Emmanuel Ndhlovu • Clement Chipenda
Editors

Climate Change and Children's Rights in Zimbabwe

Toward Social Policy-Based Interventions

Springer

Editors
Emmanuel Ndhlovu
College of Business and Economics
University of Johannesburg
Auckland Park, South Africa

Clement Chipenda
South African Research Chair in Social Policy, College of Graduate Studies
University of South Africa
Pretoria, South Africa

ISBN 978-981-95-6004-2 ISBN 978-981-95-6005-9 (eBook)
https://doi.org/10.1007/978-981-95-6005-9

This Springer imprint is published by the registered company Springer Nature Singapore Pte Ltd.
The registered company address is: 152 Beach Road, #21-01/04 Gateway East, Singapore 189721, Singapore

Preface

Zimbabwe and the broader African continent face an unprecedented climate crisis that demands urgent attention and transformative responses. Despite contributing merely 9% of global emissions, the 33 countries classified as 'extremely high risk' on the Children's Climate Risk Index bear the heaviest burden of climate impacts. In Zimbabwe—ranked the 15th most vulnerable country globally and among the top three in Southern Africa—6.5 million children, representing 47% of the population, confront heightened risks of food insecurity, health complications, educational disruptions, and displacement. These crises are further exacerbated by limited adaptation funding, insufficient private sector investment, and policy frameworks that inadequately address child-specific vulnerabilities.

This volume emerges from the recognition that conventional climate responses, which are often designed without meaningful child participation or consideration of differentiated impacts, have proven inadequate in protecting children's rights in climate-vulnerable contexts. The disconnection between climate policy and child rights frameworks, characterised by a failure to recognise children as both rights-holders and agents of change, has resulted in largely reactive interventions that fail to address structural inequalities or promote transformative adaptation. There is, therefore, an urgent imperative to redefine how we understand and respond to the climate-children's rights nexus in contemporary Zimbabwe.

Contributions in this volume bring fresh methodological perspectives that break from traditional approaches. Rather than presenting children as a uniform demographic, the analyses benefit from interdisciplinary insights that reveal how climate impacts produce differentiated outcomes across contexts of gender, geography, indigeneity, and socio-economic status. The chapters in this volume draw from both empirical evidence gathered across Zimbabwe's diverse districts and conceptual innovations grounded in climate justice theory, multi-species justice, the capability approach, and transformative social policy frameworks, with scholars employing tools appropriate to their specific inquiries while maintaining commitment to both methodological rigour and contextual relevance.

A distinguishing feature of this collection is its commitment to centring children's voices, agency, and Indigenous knowledge systems while maintaining critical engagement with international frameworks, including the United Nations Convention on the Rights of the Child (UNCRC), the African Charter on the Rights and Welfare of the Child (ACRWC), and the African Committee of Experts' Resolution on child-rights-based climate action. Rather than merely critiquing inadequate responses, the contributors offer constructive alternatives rooted in Zimbabwean realities. Across four thematic areas—theoretical foundations and legal frameworks; climate-induced displacement and vulnerability; impacts on health, education, and welfare; and child-centred adaptation strategies—they highlight both the persistent implementation gaps between policy and practice and innovative pathways being forged by communities, children themselves, and progressive institutions.

From Lupane's 'ovens in schools' to Mbire's food insecurity interventions, from Chivi's climate-induced migration patterns to corporate social responsibility innovations in mining communities, the chapters reveal how locally grounded, rights-based approaches can deliver meaningful protection despite structural constraints. The analyses of gender-differentiated impacts, child labour dynamics, nutritional vulnerabilities, and resilience strategies demonstrate both systemic barriers and transformative possibilities.

As the editors, we view this volume not as a definitive statement but as an urgent call for collaborative action towards creating climate responses that truly protect and advance children's rights. We hope it stimulates further research, policy dialogue, and practical interventions that honour Zimbabwe's rich diversity while addressing children's shared aspirations for survival, development, and dignified futures. Most importantly, we hope it contributes to ongoing efforts to position children not as passive victims but as powerful agents of change whose participation and leadership are essential for building climate justice and sustainable development in Africa at this critical juncture in the continent's and humanity's relationship with our changing environment.

Auckland Park, South Africa — Emmanuel Ndhlovu
Pretoria, South Africa — Clement Chipenda

Acknowledgements

The editors of this book would like to extend their deepest gratitude to its contributors—firstly, for participating in this most important volume and, secondly, for their dedication and commitment throughout the writing process. Without their commitment and hard work, this book would not have been possible. The book also benefited from the hard work of colleagues who offered to anonymously review the chapters. The editors would like to extend gratitude to them for such intellectual generosity.

We would also like to acknowledge the universities of Johannesburg (UJ) and South Africa (UNISA) for affiliation support.

Many other colleagues, students, and friends also provided support, encouragement, and reference materials; to them, we say thank you. Despite the assistance of so many people and our best efforts, there are still likely to be omissions and errors.

Contents

About the Contributors

Yasin Adam is a Social Work lecturer at Reformed Church University in Zimbabwe. He holds a Bachelor's and a Master's degree in Social Work from the University of Zimbabwe. He is an avid researcher on issues relating to social work and religion, climate change, and youth and social development.

Obert Bore is a dynamic environment and climate action expert and legal practitioner. Possessing deep academic rigour and a commitment to community impact, he leverages top skills in legal and policy analysis, project management, and climate justice. His extensive portfolio spans legal and environmental litigation, humanitarian aid, natural resource management, and research as an ecological child rights expert and institutional development practitioner. He is driven by a passion for environmental justice, environmental awareness and conservation, and tangible community development.

Chipo Chaora is a lecturer at Lupane State University (LSU) in the Faculty of Built Environment and Engineering in the Department of Urban and Regional Planning. With a strong urban and regional planning background, Chipo's research interests include urban and regional planning, rural development, water governance, climate change, and public policy evaluation. She holds a Master of Science and a Bachelor of Science degree in Rural and Urban Planning (University of Zimbabwe) and a Diploma in Education in Geography and Environmental Sciences (Belvedere Technical Teachers' College). She has recently completed a Postgraduate Diploma in Geographical Information Systems and Remote Sensing (LSU).

Doris Chasokela (PhD) is a senior lecturer at the National University of Science and Technology (NUST) in Zimbabwe. She holds a Doctorate in Education, a Master of Engineering in Electrical System Control and Information Technology, a Bachelor of Technical Education in Electrical and Electronic Engineering, and a Diploma in Technical Vocational Education. She has supervised several undergraduate projects and postgraduate dissertations. She has 11 years of experience in higher education. She has published textbooks, articles, and several book chapters. Her interests are higher education, engineering education, artificial intelligence, climate change and control systems.

Anne Chawanda is a PhD candidate in Geography at the University of Witwatersrand and holds an MSc in GIS and Remote Sensing. Her research explores the intersections of spatial analysis, environmental change, and human societies. With expertise in digital geographic tools and remote sensing technologies, Anne brings innovative approaches to understanding complex environmental challenges. She is passionate about making geographic knowledge accessible and relevant, integrating cutting-edge technologies like GIS and augmented reality into her work. Her research reflects a commitment to bridging academic rigour with practical applications in understanding our changing world.

Vincent Chenzi is a lecturer of disaster management, peace building, and strategic studies at the University of Zimbabwe. Some of his publications appeared in the *Review of African Political Economy* and the *Journal of Contemporary African Studies*, among others. His areas of interest include African politics, disaster management, military history, digital media, climate science, conflict resolution, and non-violence. Furthermore, he has been consulted by various academic, media, and non-governmental institutions as an expert on contemporary African politics and media-driven unrest. Currently, he is a PhD researcher in conflict, peace, and governance at the University of Zimbabwe's Department of Peace Security and Society.

Joshua Chibvuma is a lecturer at Lupane State University, Zimbabwe, teaching development issues in sub-Saharan Africa, urban social geography and population, and environment courses. They are actively involved in community engagement in Matabeleland North Province. Their research areas cover climate change impacts, tourism geography, rural livelihoods, and internal displacement. Joshua has over 15 years of teaching experience in secondary schools before joining Lupane State University. They are currently working on a Raoul Wallenberg Institute funded research project on internally displaced persons, durable solutions, and relocation settlements in Chimanimani using a human-rights-based approach. Joshua holds the following qualifications: Msc Natural Resources Management and Environmental Sustainability (BUSE), BA 4th Year Hons Geography and Environmental Studies (GZU), BA Geography, History, Portuguese (UZ), Postgraduate Diploma in Education (ZOU), and Executive Certificate in Research Design Monitoring and Evaluation (Arrupe Jesuit University).

Philemon Chihiya is a lecturer in the Department of Social Work, University of Zimbabwe. He has a Master of Science degree in Social Work and a Bachelor of Social Work (honours) degree, both from the University of Zimbabwe. His research interests include climate change, childhood studies, and social protection.

Witness Chikoko is a chairperson and senior lecturer at the Department of Social Work, University of Zimbabwe, and is currently a senior research fellow at the Department of Social Work, University of Johannesburg, South Africa. He holds a DPhil in Social Studies, a Master's of Social Work, a Postgraduate Diploma in Project Planning and Management, and a Bachelor of (honours) degree in Social Work, all from the University of Zimbabwe. His research interests are childhood studies, social protection, and disaster management.

Clement Chipenda (PhD) is a postdoctoral research fellow at the University of South Africa's College of Graduate Studies, where he contributes his expertise to the SARChI Chair in Social Policy. He is a co-investigator in the research project *The Social Policy Dimensions of Land and Agrarian Reform in International Perspective*, as well as the *Social Policy in the Post Covid-19 Pandemic Era: Investigating a Transformative and Gender-Sensitive Framework in South Africa*. His research interests span a diverse yet interconnected range of topics, including agrarian political economy, agro-food systems, transformative social policy, children's rights and child protection, social security, urban and rural sociology, as well as youth and gender studies.

Bhekimpilo Moyo Hlabano is a lecturer at Lupane State University and is also a research fellow at the Public Policy and Research Institute of Zimbabwe. His research interests converge at international relations, governance, peace and security, and sustainable development. He has published two book chapters on China-Zimbabwe relations and Chinese-funded surveillance systems in Zimbabwe.

Tsitsi Prudence Humanikwa is a dedicated geographical information science (GIS) Specialist and lecturer at Lupane State University, Zimbabwe. She holds an MSc in Population Informatics and Analytics and a BSc in Geographical Information Science and Earth Observations from the University of Zimbabwe. Her research passion focuses on leveraging geo-technologies to address critical demographic, food security, and climate change issues for intervention initiatives and policymaking, thereby contributing to sustainable development. As she continues her academic journey, Ms. Humanikwa is eager to contribute to the advancement of GIS research and development through research, teaching, and community engagement.

Gladman Nyasha Makwenya is a lecturer in the Social Work Department at Reformed Church University (Zimbabwe). He is an advocate for climate change mitigation, smart settlements, and a social change entrepreneur.

Ernest Kudakwashe Mando is an environmental, social, and governance (ESG) specialist and consultant with progressively more than 10 years' experience in implementing and evaluating management systems and standards in industry. He is also a researcher with substantial publications in areas of environmental management, occupational safety and health, climate change, and environmental governance. To date, he has authored over ten articles and managed three research grants from international research institutes and funders. He holds a PhD in Environmental Management from the University of South Africa (UNISA).

Emerge Masiya is a distinguished legal scholar who holds a Bachelor of Laws (LLB) and a Masters in Management and Development Law. Her research dissertation focused on combating environmental crime. Her scholarly contributions include a range of published papers and attended various conferences on legal development and policy frameworks, addressing topics such as gender-based violence prevention, environmental justice, climate justice, and multi-species justice. She has also published on critical legal studies and sexual health rights. She has spearheaded environmental law units, coordinated outreach programmes, and conducted impactful radio interviews and television programmes, all aimed at empowering communities and promoting environmental rights.

Prosper Tonderai Mataruse (Ph.D) serves as a researcher and lecturer in the Department of Community and Social Development at the University of Zimbabwe. His research interests and experience span social and ecological dynamics, sustainable development, ecological resilience, climate change impacts, mitigation and adaptation, forest and landscape management, and institutional management of natural resources. Driven by a strong passion for community engagement through collaborative methods, Prosper is well positioned to advance social innovation initiatives and transformative pathways within rural communities.

Daniel F. Meyer is a professor in the College of Business and Economics (CBE) at the University of Johannesburg (UJ), South Africa. He is a National Research Foundation (NRF) rated researcher. Daniel is a development economist and a specialist in regional and local economic development analysis and policy development. He has developed various innovative measurement tools, indices, and scales to analyse regional economies. He also has a research focus on macroeconomics and the linkages with good governance. He has authored more than 150 internationally peer-reviewed research papers since 2015 and has also presented more than 60 international conference papers, including a number of keynote addresses.

Funa Moyo holds a PhD in Public and Development Management from the University of Witwatersrand, Wits School of Governance, South Africa; a Master of Science in Development Studies from the National Science and Technology; and a Master of Education in Educational Administration, Planning and Policy Studies from Zimbabwe Open University. He holds a Bachelor of Education degree from the University of Zimbabwe and a Bachelor of Arts (Hons) in HIV and AIDS Behaviour Studies from UNISA. His research interests include natural resource governance, climate change adaptation livelihoods, artisanal gold mining, irrigation and conservation farming, social capital, and livelihoods.

Mthuthukisi Ncube is a process-driven research consultant, lecturer, and development practitioner with extensive experience in climate change adaptation; environmental change and ecosystem service degradation and conservation; food security and sustainable livelihoods; natural resource governance, climate change adaptation livelihoods, and artisanal mining-irrigation nexus; and social capital and land-use conflicts, child-rights programming in environmental contexts, and land-use transformation.

Emmanuel Ndhlovu is a research fellow at the University of Johannesburg, South Africa. He holds a PhD in Development Studies. His research interests encompass a broad range of topics, including agrarian political economy, food systems, food security, land reform, agriculture and agribusiness, as well as social policy. Emmanuel has widely published in these areas and has also successfully edited over ten books. His latest authored books include *Agriculture, Autonomous Development, and Prospects for Industrialisation in Africa* and *Social Policy in Southern Africa:*

Prospects and Possibilities. Before his current role at the University of Johannesburg, Emmanuel was a research fellow at the Vaal University of Technology, South Africa.

Sithandweyinkosi Nkomo (PhD) is a dynamic environment and climate action expert and published author, currently serving as the environment and climate focal coordinator for TDH Germany AFCO. Possessing deep academic rigour and a commitment to community impact, she leverages top skills in policy analysis, project management, and climate justice. Her extensive portfolio spans humanitarian aid, natural resource management, and research as an ecological child rights expert and development practitioner. She is driven by a passion for environmental awareness and tangible community development.

Robson Pahuwa is a holder of a BSc Honours degree in Social Ecology and an MSc in Disaster Management from the National University of Science and Technology. His areas of interest include climate change activism and monitoring of land rights, and his specialisation is disaster risk reduction. He has worked with humanitarian organisations in Zambia, Botswana, and Germany. His expertise lies in various critical areas, including land management, promoting green economies, effective flood management, climate adaptation strategies, migration issues, and disaster education, among others.

Iggy Gamuchirai Saviere is a climate advocate with expertise in environmental sustainability, climate action programming, agrifood systems transformation, and science and innovation. He holds a Bachelor of Social Work (Honours) and a Master of Science in Social Work from the University of Zimbabwe. His research interests include climate change, climate-smart agriculture, indigenous knowledge systems, social policy, youth development, social innovation, and smart cities. He is also a Social Work academic and researcher at Reformed Church University in Zimbabwe.

Sydwell Zhou holds a Master of Science degree in Demography and Population Studies and two Postgraduate Diplomas in Project Planning, Monitoring, and Evaluation and in Higher and Tertiary Education, all from Great Zimbabwe University. He also earned a Bachelor of Science (honours) in Geography and Environmental Studies from the Midlands State University. He is a lecturer in the Department of Geography and Environmental Science at Gwanda State University. His research interests include disaster risk reduction, weather and climate, population and development, environmental assessment and management, and the sustainable use and conservation of natural resources.

Part I
Foundations, Theoretical Considerations, and Legal Frameworks

Chapter 1
Introduction: Children's Rights and Climate Change in Zimbabwe—Vulnerabilities, Adaptation, and Resilience

Emmanuel Ndhlovu and Clement Chipenda

1.1 Introduction

This chapter introduces the book *Climate Change and Children's Rights in Zimbabwe: Toward Social Policy-Based Interventions*. Like many Southern African nations, Zimbabwe faces acute vulnerability to climate change, exacerbated by limited adaptation funding and insufficient private sector financial flows (Madamombe et al., 2024; Mpala & Simatele, 2024). The country is ranked as the 15th most vulnerable country to climate change globally, with a high ranking (in the top 3) in Southern Africa, according to the 2021 Global Climate Risk Index (UNICEF, 2025). For children, this vulnerability is particularly significant. UNICEF's Children's Climate Risk Index (CCRI) places Zimbabwe among countries where young people face extreme exposure to climate hazards, part of a global crisis affecting nearly one billion children worldwide (UNICEF, 2023). This environmental crisis significantly undermines children's rights and well-being, affecting their health, education, access to basic needs, and participation in cultural and recreational activities.

Building on this national context, the 6.5 million children (0–18 years old) in Zimbabwe, representing 47% of the population based on the 2022 census (3,631,208 males and 3,632,908 females under 18), face significant risks from climate-induced emergencies (Gwitira et al., 2024; UNICEF, 2025). As the most susceptible demographic, children confront heightened risks of food insecurity, health complications, educational disruptions, and displacement. Up to two-thirds of preventable illness and death from environmental hazards are experienced by children, predominantly

E. Ndhlovu
College of Business and Economics, University of Johannesburg, Auckland Park, South Africa

C. Chipenda (✉)
South African Research Chair in Social Policy, College of Graduate Studies, University of South Africa, Pretoria, South Africa

E. Ndhlovu, C. Chipenda (eds.), *Climate Change and Children's Rights in Zimbabwe*, https://doi.org/10.1007/978-981-95-6005-9_1

those aged under 5 years (UNICEF, 2025). However, this vulnerability is not unique to Zimbabwe; the continental context is equally alarming, with 39 out of 49 African countries scoring in the 'extremely high' or 'high' risk class on the CCRI, where climate-induced shocks such as droughts, floods, and heatwaves disrupt education, health, and protection systems (AECRW, 2025a, 2025b; UNICEF, 2023). Within this broader African crisis affecting over 490 million children, Moyo et al. (Chap. 4, in this volume) provide important insight by examining how these continental trends manifest specifically in Zimbabwe's indigenous children's contexts. They reveal critical implementation gaps between the country's comprehensive policy frameworks and actual child protection.

One of the most devastating manifestations of this climate vulnerability is the scale of climate-induced displacement in Africa, which is deeply concerning. Out of a total of 19.7 million child displacements due to floods worldwide between 2016 and 2021, African countries, including Somalia, Ethiopia, South Sudan, Nigeria, and Sudan, featured in the top 10 countries in absolute numbers. Even more tellingly, the list of top ten countries for child displacements relative to child population includes six African countries: South Sudan, Somalia, Niger, the Republic of Congo, Sudan, and the Central African Republic. Similarly, regarding drought-induced displacement, Somalia, Ethiopia, Angola, Burundi, Madagascar, and South Sudan are listed among the top ten countries worldwide in terms of absolute numbers affected (AECRW, 2025a, 2025b).

1.2 The Climate Reality: Zimbabwe's Changing Environment

Examining the specific climate trends shaping Zimbabwe's future is essential to understanding the full scope of these vulnerabilities. Zimbabwe's climate trajectory presents alarming trends that directly threaten children's futures. The national average temperature has warmed at a rate of about 0.1 °C per decade, with the national mean surface temperature increasing by about 0.90 °C from 1900 to 2018, with the greatest warming occurring in the 1980s (GoZ, 2024). Future projections indicate very high confidence that mean daily minimum and daily maximum temperatures will continue to increase throughout 2020–2040 for most districts, with the national annual average temperature likely to increase by about 1.0–1.5 °C for this period and projected to warm by 1.3–3.5° by 2080 (GoZ, 2024). These temperature increases align with global projections showing that by 2050, almost every child on the planet will be exposed to high heatwave frequency, with those in the poorest communities facing the greatest risks (UNICEF, 2021, 2023). The warming is projected to be most significant in the western and southern sections of the country, including Masvingo, Matabeleland North, and Matabeleland South Provinces (UNICEF, 2025). Chaora et al. (see Chap. 11, in this volume) document how these temperature increases create 'ovens in schools' where learners in Lupane face new challenges that hinder effective learning and development, demonstrating the direct educational impacts of rising temperatures on rural children.

Compounding these temperature challenges, rainfall patterns reveal equally concerning trends, with average annual rainfall declining by about ±5% across Zimbabwe from 1901 to 2018 and declining by about 5% since 1901 (GoZ, 2024). Future rainfall projections indicate a decline of up to 10% of mean national annual precipitation, suggesting further decline by approximately 15% by 2060 and up to 25% by 2080, especially over the south-western parts of the country (GoZ, 2024). These patterns contribute to water vulnerability affecting children globally, with UNICEF showing that 470 million children were already facing high or extremely high levels of exposure to drought in 2022, with the top five countries being India, Niger, Sudan, Burkina Faso, and Jordan (UNICEF, 2023). Within Zimbabwe, the regions with the most significant decrease in precipitation include the south-eastern sections of the country, including Matabeleland North and Matabeleland South, Masvingo, and Manicaland provinces (Gwitira et al., 2024; Ndhlovu, 2024). In addition, intra-seasonal characteristics of the rainfall season, which include the frequency and intensity of dry spells, the length of the rainfall season, the onset and cessation dates of the rainfall season, and the number of rainy days, have been significantly modified since the 1950s (Gwitira et al., 2024). These rainfall variations have created devastating impacts in specific districts, as Chenzi and Pahuwa (Chap. 6, in this volume) demonstrate through their case study of Mashonaland Central province, Zimbabwe's agricultural hub, where climate change effects are shown as having undermined children's rights to life, education, water, health, and protection from forced labour.

Beyond gradual temperature and rainfall changes, the frequency and intensity of extreme weather events present escalating challenges. The frequency of droughts increased dramatically from 10% between 1902 and 1979 to 25% from 1980 to 2018, with notable drought episodes including 1991–1992, 1994–1995, 2002–2003, 2015–2016, 2018–2019, 2019–2020, and 2023–2024, with the El Niño-Southern Oscillation (ENSO) events modulating the droughts (Gwitira et al., 2024). The frequency and intensity of extreme weather events such as droughts, floods, and tropical cyclones are projected to increase, with Zimbabwe now lying in the paths of tropical cyclones (GoZ, 2016, 2024). These trends mirror global patterns where climate-exacerbated disasters disrupt the education of nearly 40 million children annually, which continues to increase yearly (UNICEF, 2023).

The convergence of these climate trends creates a dangerous scenario. Given that extreme weather events such as cyclones, droughts, rainfall, and heatwaves have become intense and more frequent, the projected reduction in rainfall and increase in temperature may further amplify these climate-related hazards. The increasing intensity of cyclones will result in increased flooding, exacerbating outbreaks of waterborne disease as observed during Cyclone Idai in 2019 (Gwitira et al., 2024; Ndhlovu & Dube, 2024). Global data indicate that storms and flooding are more likely to cause displacement, accounting for 95% of recorded child displacements between 2016 and 2021, with 43 million children displaced during this period (UNICEF, 2023). In addition, future projections point towards an increase in heatwaves, with dire consequences on human health, especially on children and the elderly, as well as on people predisposed to cardiovascular disease.

Furthermore, an increase in the intensity of heatwaves directly contributes to increased risk of wildfire, thereby threatening ecosystems and livelihoods in affected areas (GoZ, 2016; Gwitira et al., 2024). According to the Intergovernmental Panel on Climate Change (IPCC), the world has less than 10 years to make the transformation necessary to avoid the worst impacts of climate change (UNICEF Zimbabwe, 2023). Thus, climate change poses significant challenges to children's rights by threatening their health, education, and overall well-being, necessitating recognising and advancing their environmental rights for sustainable development.

1.3 Children's Rights Framework: International and Regional Foundations

Responding to these climate realities requires a robust legal and policy framework grounded in children's rights. The application of a child rights-based approach to the environment requires the full consideration of all children's rights under the UNCRC and the Optional Protocols thereto (UN, 2023). A clean, healthy, and sustainable environment is both a human right in itself and necessary for the full enjoyment of a broad range of children's rights. Conversely, environmental degradation, including the consequences of the climate crisis, adversely affects the enjoyment of these rights, especially for children in disadvantaged situations or children living in regions that are highly exposed to climate change (UN, 2023). Masiya and Nkomo (Chap. 3, in this volume) advance this rights framework by examining how multispecies justice concepts can better reinterpret Zimbabwe's constitutional and legal frameworks to protect children's rights to a safe environment. They demonstrate the need for decentralising human-centric approaches to recognise the interconnectedness of human and non-human beings in environmental protection. At the international level, the UNCRC addresses environmental issues in Article 24(2)(c), by which states are obliged to take measures to combat disease and malnutrition, considering the dangers and risks of environmental pollution. There is also Article 29(1)(e), by which they are required to direct the education of children to the development of respect for the natural environment (UN, 2023). Since the adoption of the Convention, growing acceptance has emerged of the wide-ranging interconnections between children's rights and environmental protection (UN, 2023).

Complementing these international instruments, regional frameworks further strengthen this foundation through the African Charter on the Rights and Welfare of the Child (ACRWC), which provides instruments for protecting children's rights in Africa. Articles 11(2) and 14(2)(b) are especially relevant for addressing climate change impacts, although they may require reinterpretation to fully address these challenges (Fokala & Muhumuza, 2024). The evolution of African policy frameworks demonstrates increasing recognition of children's climate vulnerability. Examples of progressive policy measures include Sierra Leone's National Climate Change Policy 2021, Angola's National Strategy for Climate Change of 2017, The

Gambia's 2050 Climate Vision, Benin's Climate Change Management Policy for 2030, Tanzania's National Climate Change Strategy 2021–2026, and the National Action Plan on Gender and Climate Change for Nigeria (2020). Legislative measures specifically focused on climate change include Nigeria's Climate Change Act (2021), Mauritius's Climate Change Act 2020, and Uganda's National Climate Change Act (2021) and National Environment Act (2019) (AECRW, 2025a).

Building on these policy developments, the African Committee of Experts on the Rights and Welfare of the Child (ACERWC) has provided critical guidance through Resolution No. 18/2022, adopted during the ACERWC's 39th Ordinary Session, which provides a comprehensive framework for integrating a child rights-based approach to climate change (ACERWC, 2022). The resolution outlines 12 key commitments for state parties. These include incorporating child-specific risks into climate policies and programmes; upholding the best interests of the child in all climate-related actions; mobilising adequate resources and adopting child-sensitive budgeting; ensuring meaningful participation of children in climate decision-making; establishing robust monitoring, evaluation, and accountability mechanisms; and aligning national strategies with the AU Green Recovery Action Plan (2021–2027) (AECRW, 2022, 2025a, 2025b). Underlying these frameworks is the principle of intergenerational equity, which is entrenched in both international and African regional frameworks, although not explicitly mentioned in the UNCRC or the ACRWC, serving as a tool for promoting children's rights in the context of climate change, ensuring that future generations are considered in current climate actions (Fambasayi & Addaney, 2021).

The Committee was mindful of several relevant efforts in developing this comprehensive rights framework. These include recognising the human right to a clean, healthy, and sustainable environment by the General Assembly and the Human Rights Council. The Committee also considered the framework principles on human rights and the environment. Additionally, it acknowledged the existing and evolving norms, principles, standards, and obligations under international environmental law, such as the United Nations Framework Convention on Climate Change and the Paris Agreement. Legal developments and jurisprudence at the regional level, recognising the relationship between human rights and the environment, have also been important. Finally, there has been the recognition of some form of the right to a clean, healthy, and sustainable environment in international agreements, as well as in the jurisprudence of regional and national courts, national constitutions, laws, and policies by a vast majority of states (UN, 2023).

1.4 Intersectional Vulnerabilities and Climate Justice

While the rights framework provides essential protection mechanisms, understanding how climate change differentially impacts various groups of children requires attention to intersectional vulnerabilities and justice considerations. The intersection of climate change and children's rights represents one of the most pressing yet underexplored challenges facing contemporary Zimbabwe. Climate change and environmental degradation undermine children's rights, especially the most disadvantaged (Ndhlovu, 2025). At the heart of this challenge lies a significant injustice—children who are the least responsible for climate change bear the most significant burden of its impact. This climate injustice is illustrated by the fact that the 33 'extremely high-risk' countries in the CRRI collectively emit just 9% of global CO_2 emissions, while the 10 highest-emitting countries collectively account for nearly 70% of global emissions, with only 1 of these high-emitting countries ranked as 'extremely high risk' (UNICEF, 2023). Chipenda and Chawanda (Chap. 2, in this volume) provide a critical analysis of these climate justice imperatives, demonstrating how climate-induced environmental changes create and intensify inequalities that disproportionately burden vulnerable child populations, while examining how distributive, procedural, and recognition justice principles can inform more equitable climate adaptation strategies in Zimbabwe. The scope of this crisis is staggering. The climate crisis disproportionately impacts children, and every child on earth is exposed to at least one climate and environmental hazard, such as heatwaves, cyclones, air pollution, flooding, and water scarcity (ACERWC, 2025a; UNICEF, 2023). Globally, an estimated 850 million children, 4 in 3 worldwide, live in areas where at least 4 of these climate and environmental shocks overlap, while as many as 330 million children, 1 in 7 worldwide, live in areas affected by at least 5 major shocks (UNICEF, 2021, 2023). Nearly half of the world's one billion children live in high-risk countries (UNICEF, 2023). As the most vulnerable group, children face severe threats to their rights to survival and development, health, education, and a clean, sustainable environment, with states having an obligation to act urgently, recognising the disproportionate impact of climate change on children's rights (AECRW, 2022, 2025a, 2025b).

Within this broader climate crisis, certain groups of children face compounded vulnerabilities. Children in general, and certain groups of children, face heightened barriers to the enjoyment of their rights, due to multiple and intersecting forms of discrimination. The impact of environmental harm has a discriminatory effect on specific groups of children, especially Indigenous children, children belonging to minority groups, children with disabilities, and children living in disaster-prone or climate-vulnerable environments (UN, 2023). Among these intersectional vulnerabilities, gender disparities are pronounced, with climate hazards having disproportionate impacts on girls. Loss of livelihoods, displacement, and migration from climate-related events often put girls in precarious positions, with gender-based violence and child marriage increasing following extreme weather events and disasters. For example, in Bangladesh, the number of marriages of girls ages 11–14 increased by 50% in years with heatwaves lasting longer than 30 days (UNICEF, 2023). Chipenda and Ndhlovu (Chap. 13, in this volume) examine these gendered dimensions in depth by analysing Zimbabwe's Fast Track Land Reform Programme communities in Goromonzi and Zvimba districts. They reveal how girls experience disproportionate impacts through culturally embedded responsibilities for resource collection, with climate-induced time poverty emerging as a mechanism perpetuating intergenerational inequality. Climate change exacerbates vulnerabilities, undermining children's rights to a sustainable environment and participation in decision-making processes affecting their futures (Knox, 2016; Humphreys, 2009). These challenges are further compounded by issues of climate justice, where children disproportionately bear the consequences of climate change despite contributing least to the problem. This highlights the need for equitable solutions addressing environmental and social justice concerns.

1.5 Sectoral Climate Vulnerabilities and Impacts on Children

Intersectional vulnerabilities manifest across multiple sectors of society, each presenting unique challenges for children's rights and well-being. Climate change thus manifests across multiple sectors, each presenting unique challenges for children's rights and well-being. First and foremost, water scarcity represents one of the most critical vulnerabilities, with UNICEF revealing that as of 2022, 436 million children face extreme water vulnerability globally. This includes exposure to multiple climate and environmental shocks combined with inadequate essential services such as water and sanitation, healthcare, and education (UNICEF, 2023). In the water sector, climate hazards, including increased temperature and heatwaves, extended dry spells, frequency and severity of droughts and floods, irregular rainfall patterns, and cyclones, are causing increased evaporation, flooding and water logging, increased rate of siltation of reservoirs, and decreased water table, river flows, and groundwater recharge (UNICEF, 2023). These changes result in decreased quality of surface and groundwater for human consumption, domestic use, reduced quantity of water for irrigation, electricity generation and industrial use, and increased damage to water infrastructure (GoZ, 2024). Projections for 2030 show that while coverage of basic drinking water services is expected to increase in most regions, there will still be around 225 million children without basic drinking water globally, with more than 8 out of 10 living in sub-Saharan Africa (UNICEF, 2023). Mando et al. (Chap. 10, in this volume) document how these water vulnerabilities manifest in Bikita District, Masvingo Province. They provide insight into how extreme weather conditions and underlying harsh environmental conditions compound to violate rural school children's rights to protection and health, with droughts exposing children to labour exploitation, poor nutrition, and inadequate hygiene and sanitation.

Climate change poses significant threats to farming systems that are essential for providing nutrition to children and income for families. Key vulnerabilities include extreme temperatures that harm both plants and animals, destruction of farm facilities from severe weather, higher rates of water loss through evaporation and plant transpiration, and shifting patterns in agricultural pests, plant diseases, and invasive weeds (Mirzabaev et al., 2023). Decreased surface and groundwater availability for irrigation and livestock watering, reduced soil moisture and quality, and fewer growing days are a serious challenge. The impacts manifest as increased area coverage of drier agro-ecological zones, livestock deaths and crop losses, national food and nutrition insecurity, climate-induced migration, and decreased crop and livestock productivity (GoZ, 2024). Ndhlovu and Chipenda (Chap. 11, in this volume) explore how these agricultural disruptions compel children in peasant households into survival-oriented child labour. They show how climate-induced changes in livelihoods and agricultural productivity leave households to explore various survival strategies that tap into children's labour for survival, highlighting the absence of comprehensive policies for monitoring child labour in agriculture.

Beyond water and agriculture, human settlements, both rural and urban, face increasing vulnerabilities, including increased incidence of water pollution, heat stress and related diseases, exposure to pests and diseases, and flooding of infrastructure and settlements (ACERWC, 2025a, 2025b; UNICEF, 2021). These vulnerabilities result in thermal stress-related deaths, increased dependence on artificial cooling systems, damage and destruction of property and infrastructure, including housing, drainage, water, sanitation, and hygiene (WASH), telecommunications, roads, and railways, along with increased incidence of diseases, injury and loss of life, and climate-induced mobility and unplanned relocation (GoZ, 2024). Children and adolescents in slums are especially vulnerable to extreme heat due to the urban heat island effect and limited access to water, artificial cooling, and green space, with infants and young children being more vulnerable than adults to extreme heat as they are less able to regulate their body temperature and more prone to dehydration (UNICEF, 2023).

The health consequences of these sectoral vulnerabilities are significant and far reaching. The health sector experiences increased vector-borne, airborne, and waterborne diseases, pest incidents, contamination risks, WASH and health facilities damage, and malnutrition. These vulnerabilities translate into increased loss of life due to extreme weather events; deaths due to vector-borne, airborne, and waterborne diseases; stunted growth and poor health; destruction of health facilities; and decreased access to health facilities (GoZ, 2024; Gwitira et al., 2024). Air pollution represents a significant health challenge, with children being more likely to suffer from air pollution than adults as they breathe faster and their brains, lungs, and other organs are still developing. Household air pollution from indoor cooking is responsible for over 237,000 deaths of children under five per year globally. In contrast, over 83% of children in Europe and Central Asia are exposed to ambient air pollution (UNICEF, 2023).

1.6 Multiple Dimensions of Impact: Health, Education, and Development

The sectoral vulnerabilities outlined above translate into multidimensional impacts that affect every aspect of children's lives. The current and projected warming trend and reduction in rainfall, coupled with the increasing frequency and intensity of floods, tropical cyclones, droughts, and heatwaves, threaten children's lives and destroy schools, water supply and infrastructure, healthcare facilities, and children's play spaces (UNICEF, 2023). In addition, the reduction and increased unpredictability of rainfall threaten crops critical to livelihoods and nutrition. All these impacts can result in greater poverty, increasing children's protection risks (UNICEF, 2011). Among these multiple impacts, education disruption represents a critical dimension of climate impact. Climate shocks directly and indirectly disrupt children's education, with extreme weather events damaging or destroying schools and illnesses caused by climate impacts keeping children out of school (Marin et al., 2024). In areas affected by water insecurity, droughts directly impact children's attendance, reducing their time in school due to longer times dedicated to fetching water or dropping out altogether. In Ethiopia, for example, around 20% of girls and 5% of boys miss school time to fetch water in normal circumstances, which increases significantly during droughts (UNICEF, 2023). More broadly, climate change threatens children's survival, development, nutrition, health, education, and access to basic social services—all rights enshrined in the UNCRC. In addition, Article 24 of the UNCRC mentions that 'the dangers and risks of environmental pollution' must be considered in ensuring that children's rights are fulfilled (UN, 1989). Environmental risks such as poor solid waste management, indoor and outdoor air pollution, second-hand smoke, unsafe water, lack of sanitation, and inadequate hygiene and healthcare waste management cause irreversible and lasting negative impacts on children. They affect children's health, education, and future earnings, creating an inequality cycle that affects generations (UNICEF, 2023).

Beyond physical health and education, mental health impacts are increasingly recognised as a critical concern. Children worldwide are in the frightening position of witnessing the impacts of climate change and understanding its implications for their futures while having little power to change the situation. Survey results show that over 45% of children and young people ages 16–25 in ten countries reported that 'their feelings about climate change negatively affected their daily life and functioning' (UNICEF, 2023). Extreme heat is also associated with an increase in mental health problems, including post-traumatic stress disorder and depression in children and adolescents (UNICEF, 2023; Walinski et al., 2023). More comprehensively, the climate crisis negatively impacts all aspects of adolescent well-being. This includes physical well-being through increased risk of injury, lung disease, infectious disease, and poor nutrition. It can disrupt their connectedness to family, friends, and community through its effect on forced migration (UNICEF, 2023). Mataruse and Chipenda (Chap. 5, in this volume) document these psychosocial impacts in Chivi District, Ward 32, revealing how climate-induced parental migration creates emotional distress and increased safety risks for children who remain behind, exposing them to exploitation, abuse, and educational disruptions in the absence of adequate adult supervision.

Additionally, education for adolescents is impacted by climate-related extreme weather events as evidenced by Cyclone Idai, which destroyed schools, roads, and WASH infrastructures for schools (UNICEF Zimbabwe, 2023). The vulnerability of children begins even before birth, as children are vulnerable to stress and pollution during early childhood years, when critical biological systems such as the immune and central nervous systems are developing (Framework Institute, 2025; UNICEF, 2023). Further maternal undernutrition, infection, pollution exposure, and illness during pregnancy can cause life-long damage to children, including physical stunting, neurological impairments, and immune dysfunction (UNICEF Zimbabwe, 2023).

The cumulative effect of these impacts creates cascading crises across essential services. Increasing frequency and intensity of climate shocks negatively affect basic services such as health, education, water, sanitation and hygiene, nutrition, and protection. Negative impacts of climate change erode development gains due to the disruption of education and health systems and water insecurity, which can negatively impact drinking water access and food production. Particularly concerning are the nutritional consequences. Climate change directly affects the underlying determinants for good nutrition in multiple ways, for instance, changing people's food consumption patterns and, therefore, the quality and diversity of diets by influencing local and global food availability. Seasonal food scarcity is common in Zimbabwe and is a driver of wasting (UNICEF, 2023). Saviere et al. (Chap. 9, in this volume) extensively documented these nutritional challenges by investigating food insecurity among children in Mbire, Zimbabwe. In Mbire, they evaluate child-centred interventions including the Integrated Management of Acute Malnutrition (IMAM), the Utariri Project, and the Integrated School Feeding Programme, revealing that while these programmes offer valuable support, they fall short in addressing the full scope of climate change impacts on child nutrition. In addition, a dedicated chapter on climate change's impact on children's nutrition by Ndhlovu and Chipenda (Chap. 8, in this volume) examines how climate change affects the availability of safe food and impacts child nutrition in Zimbabwe. It proposes how artificial intelligence (AI) can be leveraged to ensure safe food and healthy diets. It addresses a critical gap where an estimated 580,000 young children have been identified as living in severe food poverty and being highly vulnerable to malnutrition in 2024.

Climate change also amplifies protection risks for children, especially girls. The scarcity of resources and resulting increased poverty and stress pose a greater risk of violence against girls and women (Spotlight Initiative, 2025). This includes increased violence against children due to the stress of others, sexual violence as girls are forced to fetch water from further distances, and the risk of transactional sex due to desperation for a basic livelihood (UNICEF, 2023). Children who are displaced are at increased risk of several dangers, including becoming separated from their families and subsequently facing a greater likelihood of experiencing exploitation, trafficking, violence, or abuse. At the same time, their education and access to essential services such as healthcare are likely to be disrupted (UNICEF, 2023). In this way, climate change increases the risks to children through its immediate and sudden onset impacts and intermediate and longer-term impacts, resulting in reduced sustainability for future generations. Not only does children's lack of access to these key essential services (such as water, sanitation and hygiene, health, education, and social protection) increase their vulnerability to climate change, but climate change is likely to make it more difficult for children and adolescents to obtain access to those key essential services (Chipenda & Cochrane, 2024; UNICEF, 2023).

Specific health threats further compound these vulnerabilities. Exposure to high temperatures and heatwaves can increase deaths in children aged up to 14. Children and adolescents in slums are particularly vulnerable due to the urban heat island effect and limited access to water, artificial cooling, and green space (Janeka et al., 2025). As children and adolescents spend more time outdoors, public spaces and parks with artificial shade and heavy tree canopies can effectively reduce heat-related symptoms (UNICEF, 2023). Asthma is the commonest chronic disease in adolescents worldwide, and its severity is strongly associated with allergic sensitisation, creating a vicious cycle of perpetual poverty, inequality, and deprivation (UNICEF, 2023).

1.7 Climate Vulnerability Hotspots and Comparative Country Perspectives Across Sub-Saharan Africa

To fully appreciate Zimbabwe's climate challenges, it is essential to situate them within the broader regional context of sub-Saharan Africa. Sub-Saharan Africa, including Zimbabwe, is highlighted as one of the most affected regions globally, with 32 out of 45 countries in the CCRI (Addaney et al., 2017; Mezmur, 2023). Sub-Saharan Africa hosts several climate change hotspots where strong physical and ecological effects of climate change intersect with large populations of poor and vulnerable communities (Godfrey & Tunhuma, 2020). The scale of climate vulnerability in this region is exemplified by the devastating impact of El Niño and La Niña[1] events across Eastern and Southern Africa, where climate change-exacerbated extreme weather has created cascading humanitarian crises affecting millions of children (UNICEF ESARO, 2025).

Across this diverse region, regional variations in climate risks are significant. While children and communities in the northern part of Africa tend to be exposed to higher risks related to water scarcity and air pollution, those living in the western and eastern parts of the continent, especially in the tropical areas, are more heavily affected by the risks posed by vector-borne diseases, heatwaves, and riverine flooding (UNICEF, 2021, 2023). Recent events illustrate the intensifying severity of these regional variations. Climate-related events in these hotspots demonstrate the escalating severity of impacts on children and communities. The severe Horn of Africa drought of 2017 ravaged at least 17 million people needing assistance across Djibouti, Eritrea, Ethiopia, Kenya, Somalia, South Sudan, and Uganda (Godfrey & Tunhuma, 2020). In early 2019, Southern Africa was hit by two subsequent cyclones, namely, Tropical Cyclone Idai and Tropical Cyclone Kenneth, with Kenneth being

[1] El Niño and La Niña are opposing phases of the El Niño-Southern Oscillation (ENSO) climate pattern. El Niño occurs when Pacific Ocean surface temperatures become unusually warm, while La Niña involves cooler-than-average temperatures in the same region. Both phenomena significantly influence global weather patterns, affecting precipitation, temperature, and storm activity worldwide.

the strongest storm ever to hit Africa and the first time in recorded history that two intense tropical cyclones hit Mozambique in the same season. The cyclones affected over 1.85 million people in Mozambique, of whom one million were children, leaving more than 1300 people dead and many more missing (Godfrey & Tunhuma, 2020). Since early 2020, East Africa has battled the worst outbreak of desert locusts for decades, creating huge threats to food security and livelihoods, with studies linking hotter climates to more damaging locust swarms that disproportionately affect Africa (Godfrey & Tunhuma, 2020).

When comparing climate impacts across the region, the comparative analysis of climate impacts across Eastern and Southern Africa reveals different but interconnected patterns of vulnerability. While Southern Africa is affected by severe drought conditions, Eastern Africa faces devastating flood impacts. This regional contrast demonstrates how the same climate phenomenon (El Niño/La Niña) manifests differently across geographical zones, creating diverse but equally severe challenges for children's rights and well-being (UNICEF ESARO, 2025). What is most alarming is the interconnected nature of climate crises, which is evident in countries experiencing simultaneous disasters. In Malawi, a comparative case study reveals how 23 out of 28 districts have faced a combination of erratic rains, floods, and prolonged dry spells, decimated crops, and left nine million people, including 4.59 million children, in desperate need. This represents approximately 50% of children in the affected districts requiring humanitarian assistance (UNICEF ESARO, 2025). Similarly, Zambia's declared national emergency encompasses both drought and floods affecting 6.5 million people, including three million children, while simultaneously grappling with severe food insecurity and rampant cholera outbreaks. Zimbabwe presents a parallel case where prolonged drought has crippled food and water supplies, intensifying risks of violence and disease amid cholera and polio outbreaks (UNICEF, 2025; UNICEF ESARO, 2025). These comparative cases demonstrate how climate variability creates compound vulnerabilities that disproportionately impact children's rights across national contexts.

The frequency of climate-related disasters has increased dramatically, with the East Asia and the Pacific region in recent years experiencing an 11-fold increase in floods, fourfold increase in storms, 2.4-fold increase in droughts, and fivefold increase in landslides over the past five decades (UNICEF, 2023). However, a comparative analysis reveals that the Eastern and Southern Africa region presents equally alarming but distinct trends. According to UNICEF in 2024, floods impacted 41 out of 47 counties in Kenya, representing 87% of the country's administrative units, displacing over 54,000 households and damaging critical infrastructure, including schools and health facilities, during the same period. Tanzania experienced concentrated but severe impacts, with floods and mudslides affecting 210,000 people and resulting in 161 deaths, while Tropical Cyclone Hidaya worsened conditions by washing away roads and bridges. Somalia presents another comparative dimension, where more than 160,000 people, two-thirds of whom were children, faced flood devastation that disrupted vital humanitarian aid delivery (UNICEF ESARO, 2025). These dynamics and their devastating impacts highlight the urgent need for robust climate change adaptation and mitigation strategies prioritising children's rights (Addaney et al., 2017; Mezmur, 2023).

Flooding represents a particular concern across Africa, with the United Nations Office for the Coordination of Humanitarian Affairs (OCHA) identifying 11 countries as flooding hotspots in 2022, including Chad, Côte d'Ivoire, and the Gambia. The Republic of Congo, Chad, Liberia, Nigeria, and Niger were among the countries most affected by floods globally in 2022 (AECRW, 2025a). A comparative analysis of flood-related health impacts reveals severe consequences for children across the region. The poor hygiene conditions during the El Niño floods of 2024 have significantly increased children's vulnerability to acute watery diarrhoea, cholera, and measles. Since 2023, over 230,000 cholera cases and 4000 deaths have been recorded across the Eastern and Southern Africa region. The demographic breakdown reveals underlying vulnerabilities as children under 15 accounted for 52% of all cholera cases, while children under 5 years old made up 40% of all fatalities, demonstrating how the youngest populations bear disproportionate mortality risks (UNICEF ESARO, 2025).

This nutritional crisis intersects with the broader pattern where climate-induced agricultural failures have created widespread food insecurity. UNICEF reports that over 20 million people across the region were expected to struggle with food access in 2025. Among these, 3.5 million children across 7 countries, namely, Angola, Malawi, Madagascar, Mozambique, Namibia, Zambia, and Zimbabwe, would desperately need life-saving nutrition treatment (UNICEF ESARO, 2025). The vulnerability is especially acute in Madagascar's Great South, where limited rainfall threatens a fresh humanitarian disaster with over 262,000 children already acutely malnourished, building upon the country's historical pattern of climate-induced malnutrition crises. In Lesotho, El Niño impacts have created severe food insecurity affecting almost 700,000 people, approximately one-third of the population in urban and rural areas (UNICEF ESARO, 2025).

The temporal dimension of climate impacts reveals important comparative patterns across affected countries. Farmers have lost half their crops in drought-affected areas, with the next harvest not expected until April 2025, creating prolonged periods of food insecurity that particularly affect child development during critical growth phases (UNICEF ESARO, 2025). This temporal lag between climate shocks and recovery demonstrates how climate change creates sustained rather than momentary disruptions to children's lives. The comparative analysis shows that recovery timelines vary significantly across countries, with some facing immediate flooding impacts. In contrast, others endure prolonged drought cycles, creating different but equally severe challenges for child welfare and rights protection (UNICEF ESARO, 2025). These extended disruptions force children to develop various coping mechanisms, which Chikoko and Chihiya (Chap. 7, in this volume) document in examining resilience strategies among rural children in Gutu District, Masvingo Province. Their research reveals how prolonged climate impacts drive children towards employment (child labour) and increased dependence on community and religious organisations. These are responses that, while demonstrating adaptability, often compromise children's rights and well-being when adequate institutional support remains absent. This pattern highlights how temporal vulnerabilities compound spatial ones, with the duration of climate shocks becoming as critical as their immediate severity in determining long-term impacts on children's development and rights.

The demographic context amplifies these concerns across the region. Nearly half of all people in Eastern and Southern Africa are children under 18, a fast-growing population expected to reach 375 million by 2050. Currently, 51 million children live through multiple overlapping crises intensified by climate-exacerbated weather patterns. These children face complex, multi-layered crises where recovery often remains a distant hope (UNICEF ESARO, 2025). Water scarcity emerges as a central driver of vulnerability across multiple contexts. In the Sahel region, water scarcity compounded by climate change, increased demand, and population growth contributes to droughts, floods, increased migration risks, urbanisation, and conflict. The burden of water collection falls mainly on women and girls, reducing time for education and exposing them to safety risks (Godfrey & Tunhuma, 2020). Water scarcity has been central to recent disasters and conflicts in Ethiopia, with a 15–20% decline in spring and summer rains since the mid-1970s. During the April 2017 drought, 95% of water points in the Ethiopian Somali region dried up, with functional points primarily sourcing from deep wells (Godfrey & Tunhuma, 2020). Madagascar faces similar challenges with no national drought monitoring system and limited data on available water resources, hindering climate adaptation efforts. These patterns demonstrate how water scarcity creates cascading vulnerabilities that disproportionately affect children and women across diverse regional contexts.

A comparative analysis of infrastructure impacts reveals how climate disasters systematically undermine essential services across different contexts. Water supplies have been contaminated, sanitation systems overwhelmed, and populations displaced in areas already burdened with weak infrastructure. The impact on educational infrastructure varies by disaster type. Flood-affected areas see schools physically damaged and made inaccessible, while drought-affected regions experience school closures due to water shortages and child hunger affecting attendance (UNICEF ESARO, 2025). National frameworks for addressing these challenges show varying degrees of effectiveness. South Africa's legislative framework demonstrates mixed compliance with international standards on children's participatory rights in climate action, with case studies from Durban and Limpopo highlighting diverse impacts from urban coastal environments to rural riverine settings, including health risks, educational disruptions, and increased vulnerability to natural disasters (Bekink, 2024; Jones et al., 2011). Kenya's adaptation policies require closer examination for their alignment with the 'best interest of the child' principle, especially as recent floods affected 41 out of 47 counties and closed over 700 schools, demonstrating how climate risks have intensified beyond the 145,000 children affected in 2018 (Boshoff, 2020; Fambasayi & Addaney, 2021; UNICEF ESARO, 2025). Nigeria similarly faces significant challenges due to climate change, substantially impacting children's rights to health, education, and development (Addaney et al., 2017; Boshoff, 2020).

The intersection of climate vulnerability with existing social inequities creates particularly acute risks for marginalised groups across all affected countries. Women, children, the elderly, and people with disabilities find themselves trapped in these complex, multi-layered crises, highlighting how climate change amplifies existing structural inequalities and creates differential impacts across social groups. Comparative analysis reveals that these intersectional vulnerabilities manifest differently across contexts. In drought-affected areas, women and children face increased water scarcity and food insecurity risks. At the same time, in flood-affected regions, displacement and disease outbreaks create different but equally severe gendered and age-related vulnerabilities (UNICEF ESARO, 2025). The scale of displacement and destruction across these countries highlights the current ferocity of climate impacts, particularly El Niño effects in Eastern Africa. It demonstrates the urgent need for coordinated humanitarian assistance tailored to the specific manifestations of climate vulnerability in each national and sub-regional context (UNICEF ESARO, 2025).

1.8 Zimbabwe's Policy Response and Implementation Gaps

Zimbabwe recognises the challenges of climate change and has developed several policies and programmes to address climate change and its impacts on children and vulnerable populations (Gwitira et al., 2024). The country has established a comprehensive policy framework building on existing instruments, including the National Climate Policy (NCP), the Child Friendly Climate Policy (CFCP), the National Climate Policy Response Strategy (NCCRS), and the revised Nationally Determined Contributions (NDC). The NCP provides strategic direction and coordination on climate change issues in Zimbabwe, including climate adaptation, as outlined in the National Adaptation Plan for Zimbabwe (GoZ, 2024). From these, the NCCRS, which was developed in 2014 and outlines Zimbabwe's strategic approach to climate change mitigation and adaptation, stands out. It highlights the need for a multi-sectoral approach and emphasises the importance of addressing climate impacts on vulnerable groups, including children and women. The NCP, launched in 2017, is equally very important. It aims to provide a framework for climate governance and recognises the specific vulnerabilities of children and women to climate change impacts (Gwitira et al., 2024).

Zimbabwe has developed an extensive legislative framework supporting climate action across multiple sectors. In agriculture, the Draft National Agriculture Policy Framework (2018–2030) promotes climate-smart agricultural practice, while the Comprehensive Agriculture Policy Framework (2012–2032) promotes food security and sustainable agriculture, aiming at increasing productivity as well as minimising risks from crop losses through the application of improved technologies to enhance national food security. The Zimbabwe Climate Smart Agriculture Framework (2018–2028) facilitates and coordinates large-scale adoption of climate-smart agriculture as a national response to climate change (GoZ, 2024). Food and nutrition security is addressed through the Food and Nutrition Security Policy (2012), which identifies irrigation development as one pillar fostering long-term food and nutrition security in the country, prioritising improvements in dam construction and WASH while providing for access to information on nutrition security and strengthening national capacity. The National Policy on Drought Mitigation promotes integration of drought preparedness, mitigation, and response activities into development programmes and projects at community, district, provincial, and national levels, providing guidelines for local-level structures to obtain financial assistance from development partners for early warning and drought monitoring (GoZ, 2024).

Water resource management and public health considerations are integrated throughout the policy framework. The National Water Policy (2013) recognises climate change as a cross-cutting issue in water resources management and acknowledges the potential impact of climate change on planning for future investments and ensuring the resilience of existing investments. The Water Act (Chap. 20:24) acknowledges the impact of climate change on water resources. In contrast, the Public Health Act (Chap. 15:17) creates a legal framework for the protection of public health in Zimbabwe under the changing climate conditions and associated impacts (GoZ, 2024). Disaster management is addressed through the Draft Disaster Risk Management Policy, which recognises the need to incorporate disaster preparedness, disaster risk reduction, and management as a priority issue in climate change adaptation, and the Civil Protection Act (Chap. 10:06), which provides an institutional framework for disaster risk management. Environmental protection is covered by the Environmental Management Act (20:27) of 2002, which provides for sustainable natural resource management through environmental impact assessments, formulation of local environmental action plans, and financing environmental protection conservation programmes. It has enabled the establishment of the Environment Fund, which supports environmental management programmes and projects. The Zimbabwe Drought Risk Management Strategy and Action Plan (2017–2025) provides a framework and guidance to support the implementation of suitable drought response practices and interventions (GoZ, 2024).

Beyond policy frameworks, Zimbabwe has implemented practical programmes targeting children and vulnerable populations. The Ministry of Primary and Secondary Education has incorporated climate change education into the national curriculum to raise awareness among children about climate change and empower them to contribute to community resilience efforts (Gwitira et al., 2024). Social protection programmes such as the Basic Education Assistance Module (BEAM) and the Harmonised Social Cash Transfer (HSCT) aim to provide financial assistance to poor households, enabling them to cope with climate-induced shocks and stresses. Clean Green Zimbabwe (CGZ) is an initiative of UNICEF implemented through the Ministry of Environment, Climate and Wildlife, meant to strengthen resilience to climate shocks by harnessing the power of children and young people as environmental stewards and change agents in communities and schools (Gwitira et al., 2024).

The institutional architecture for climate action reflects a multi-level governance approach. Zimbabwe has established a comprehensive climate change management structure comprising a cabinet committee responsible for climate change management, a ministry responsible for climate change management, and a national climate change platform serving as a multi-stakeholder platform for adaptation and mitigation. Technical sub-committees on adaptation, mitigation, capacity building, legal and transparency, advocacy, and awareness provide recommendations to the national climate change platform on issues under their purview. At the subnational level, the framework consists of provincial and district development committees serving as climate change mainstreaming working groups, chaired by the secretaries for Provincial Affairs and Devolution and District Development Coordinators, respectively. Rural and urban local authorities implement climate change-related programmes using locally generated resources and devolution funds in accordance with decisions made at the local level (GoZ, 2024). Strategic priorities guiding this framework include several key areas. Climate change adaptation should be mainstreamed into sectoral, national, and subnational development policies, strategies, plans, and activities. Climate finance for adaptation needs to be mobilised. An efficient, sustainable, and transparent investment facility for adaptation should be created. There should be enhanced research, innovation, and technology development related to climate change adaptation. Effective and efficient climate risk management is essential. Institutional arrangements and institutions' capacities in climate change adaptation and risk management should be strengthened. Climate risk information generation, utilisation, and management must be enhanced. Disaster preparedness, response, and management of climate-related hazards should be improved. Finally, climate risk management mechanisms need to be adapted and implemented (GoZ, 2024).

However, although Zimbabwe has clear policies and legislation dealing with climate change issues, there is a lack of policies specifically referring to children's concerns (Gwitira et al., 2024). Moyo et al. (Chap. 14, in this volume) examine how the private sector can bridge policy gaps. They focus specifically on the mining and manufacturing sectors. These sectors can utilise corporate social responsibility (CSR) initiatives to advance child-centred climate resilience. The authors reveal significant deficiencies in climate-responsive CSR. These deficiencies affect children's survival, development, health, and education rights. They propose innovative financial mechanisms, including green bonds and climate risk insurance. These mechanisms aim to mobilise private sector resources for child protection amid escalating climate challenges.

1.9 Critical Knowledge Gaps and Scholarly Imperative

Despite severe climate impacts on children in Zimbabwe and across Southern Africa, there exists a critical knowledge gap and a lack of scholarly engagement on the intersection of climate change and children's rights. The lack of mention of climate change in key instruments like the UNCRC and the ACRWC suggests a need for reinterpretation or additional provisions to fully protect children's rights in the face of climate change (Bulat, 2024). As UNICEF Executive Director Henrietta Fore noted, 'climate and environmental shocks are undermining the complete spectrum of children's rights, from access to clean air, food and safe water; to education, housing, freedom from exploitation, and even their right to survive' (UNICEF, 2023). The urgency of addressing this lacuna cannot be overstated, especially given Zimbabwe's position as one of the most vulnerable countries to climate-related impacts in the Southern African region. Many African countries struggle with limited resources and resilience, which hampers their ability to protect children's rights effectively, and inadequate climate financing and poor governance exacerbate these challenges (Addaney et al., 2017; Fambasayi & Addaney, 2021; Mezmur, 2023). Climate-induced migration further complicates the situation, with hazards resulting from extreme weather events causing, on average, more than 20 million people to leave their homes annually (GoZ, 2024; UNICEF, 2023). Chipenda and Ndhlovu (Chap. 15, in this volume) argue that addressing these urgent needs requires a paradigm shift towards transformative social policy that tackles structural inequalities rather than merely managing symptoms, positioning children as active agents in climate adaptation processes rather than passive victims.

This edited volume addresses the identified critical gaps by providing an interdisciplinary examination of the nexus between climate change and children's rights in Zimbabwe, integrating diverse perspectives from sociology, development studies, law, anthropology, economics, and other social science disciplines. The volume is grounded in contemporary theoretical frameworks, including climate justice theory, capability approach, ecological modernisation theory, and transformative social policy, which provide a robust conceptual foundation for understanding the dynamic relationship between climate change and children's rights. The volume recognises that children have the right to a clean, healthy, and sustainable environment, a right implicit in the UNCRC and directly linked to the rights to life, survival, and development, to the highest attainable standard of health, to an adequate standard of living, and to education (UN, 2023). While it is critical for the world to focus on emissions reduction, today's children require urgent adaptation interventions that protect their rights and enable them to survive, develop, and thrive (UNICEF, 2025).

1.10 Book Structure

The volume comprises 16 chapters organised into five parts, namely, *foundations, theoretical considerations, and legal frameworks; climate-induced displacement and child vulnerability; climate change impact on children's health, education, and welfare through a climate change justice lens; climate change impacts on children's health, education, and welfare through a climate justice lens; child-centred climate adaptation and resilience strategies in the green economy and just transitions;* and *conclusion and policy recommendations.* Each of these parts addresses critical aspects of the relationship between climate change and children's rights in Zimbabwe.

Part I comprises four chapters that establish the conceptual and legal groundwork for understanding the nexus between climate change and children's rights in Zimbabwe, drawing on different theoretical perspectives. This part integrates insights from the UN Committee's General Comment on children's rights concerning the environment. It provides a dynamic interpretation of the UNCRC, recognising the wide-ranging interconnections between children's rights and environmental protection. Part I explores how these theoretical lenses illuminate the complex relationships between environmental degradation and children's rights while more broadly examining the legal and policy landscapes governing children's environmental rights in Zimbabwe and Africa. Chapter 2 by Chipenda and Chawanda provides a critical analysis of climate justice imperatives for children's rights in Zimbabwe, employing three core justice principles—distributive, procedural, and recognition justice—to examine how climate impacts produce differentiated outcomes across Zimbabwe's diverse contexts, addressing critical gaps in mainstream climate vulnerability assessments that treat children as a uniform demographic. Chapter 3 by Masiya and Nkomo examines multispecies justice through doctrinal analysis of legal texts and comparative review of African constitutions, exploring how Zimbabwe's constitutional provisions engage with multispecies justice and its implications for children's rights to a safe environment, proposing concrete legal and policy recommendations, including integration of multispecies perspectives into statutory protections for children. Chapter 4 by Moyo et al. extends this legal analysis to examine how climate change and environmental pollution impact indigenous children's rights across Africa, focusing on Zimbabwe, where many children face climate-induced emergencies. They propose evidence-based recommendations for strengthening legal protections and integrating indigenous knowledge systems.

Part II consists of three chapters that explore the impact of climate change on child displacement and vulnerability in Zimbabwe, investigating how more than 90% of disasters are driven by weather-related factors, forcing children and their families to relocate to precarious living situations. Chapter 5 by Mataruse and Chipenda explores how climate change drives migration in Chivi District, Ward 32, demonstrating through qualitative methodology how climate-induced migration significantly affects children left behind, exposing them to increased safety risks, emotional distress, and educational disruptions. In Chap. 6, Chenzi and Pahuwa examine the implications of climate change on children's rights in Mashonaland Central province, revealing how droughts, floods, and environmental degradation have negatively impacted children's rights, including the right to life, education, water, health, and protection from forced labour. These patterns of vulnerability are further illuminated in Chap. 7 by Chikoko and Chihiya, who interrogate the resilience of children in rural Ward 39, Gutu District, documenting how rural children resort to various coping strategies including child labour, prostitution, and help from community and religious organisations, recognising both the adaptive strategies children employ and the compromises to their rights inherent in these survival mechanisms. These chapters demonstrate how physical or social displacement creates multi-layered vulnerabilities that require comprehensive policy responses.

Part III comprises five chapters that analyse how climate change affects various aspects of children's lives in Zimbabwe. The chapters examine direct and indirect impacts on children's physical and mental health, nutritional status, and ability to access education. Part III incorporates evidence that climate-exacerbated disasters disrupt children's education annually while addressing the emerging recognition that children witnessing climate change impacts with little power to change the situation experience significant climate anxiety (UN, 2023). It explores how climate change exacerbates existing socio-economic vulnerabilities, potentially pushing children into poverty and child labour. In Chap. 8, Ndhlovu and Chipenda examine the nutritional dimensions of climate vulnerability. The chapter then proposes the utilisation of AI to ensure safe food and healthy diets. Chapter 9 by Saviere et al. builds on this nutritional focus by investigating the impact of climate change on food insecurity among children in Mbire, evaluating child-centred interventions. The chapter reveals that while current programmes offer valuable support, they fail to address the full scope of climate change impacts. Chapter 10 by Mando et al. explores how rural children's safety, health, and environmental rights have been violated in Bikita District. It reveals that climate change is extending children's rights inequalities and exacerbating violations among rural school learners. Chapter 11 by Chaora et al. further explores the effects of climate change on primary school learners in rural Lupane, revealing that climate-related events such as extreme weather and water scarcity cause social, academic, and psychological effects on learners. Part III concludes with Chap. 12 by Ndhlovu and Chipenda, which explores how climate change impacts child labour in Zimbabwe's agricultural sector. The chapter demonstrates that climate change substantially worsens poverty through unpredictable weather patterns, leaving peasant households exploring survival strategies, including tapping into children's labour. These chapters collectively demonstrate how climate impacts cascade across multiple dimensions of children's well-being, from nutrition to education to protection from exploitation, revealing the interconnected nature of climate vulnerability and the need for integrated policy responses.

Part IV consists of two chapters that focus on innovative approaches to climate change adaptation that prioritise children's needs and rights, integrating the UN Committee's emphasis on children's rights to freedom of expression and their recognition as powerful global forces for environmental protection whose views add relevant perspectives to decision-making on environmental matters (UN, 2023). The chapters in this section examine child-centred strategies across various sectors, including education, agriculture, and community development, while exploring the role of indigenous knowledge systems, faith-based approaches, and environmental education in building children's resilience. Chapter 13 by Chipenda and Ndhlovu examines the intersection of climate change, children's rights, and gender inequality within Zimbabwe's Fast Track Land Reform Programme communities, revealing four critical pathways through which climate impacts systematically undermine children's rights: water insecurity creating gendered educational barriers; agricultural disruption compelling child labour; energy infrastructure deficits intensifying domestic work burdens; and health system vulnerabilities compounding climate-sensitive disease risks. Building on these structural insights, Chapter 14 by Moyo et al. examines how corporate social responsibility can advance children's rights within Zimbabwe's climate-vulnerable context, revealing significant deficiencies in climate-responsive CSR while demonstrating how innovative financial mechanisms, including green bonds and climate risk insurance, can mobilise private sector resources for child protection.

Part V concludes the book and comprises two chapters. Chapter 15 by Ndhlovu and Meyer explores climate change trends in Zimbabwe, identifies the conduits through which the impact of climate change affects food systems and children in Zimbabwe, and investigates potential and ongoing social policy-based interventions to mitigate the impact of climate change on food systems and children in Zimbabwe. Chapter 16 by Ndhlovu and Chipenda asserts that climate change vulnerabilities require a transformative social policy framework targeting deep-rooted inequities rather than symptomatic responses. The analysis in this chapter demonstrates how approaches grounded in equitable resource distribution, community engagement, and rights protection can simultaneously strengthen adaptive capacity and promote children's rights, especially within the evolving landscape of post-COVID-19 recovery and emergent development priorities beyond the Sustainable Development Goal (SDG) era.

1.11 Integration and Contribution

Together, these four themes comprehensively examine Zimbabwe's climate-children's rights nexus, moving progressively from foundational legal and theoretical frameworks through empirical documentation of vulnerabilities to forward-looking adaptation strategies. The volume's contributions demonstrate that protecting children's rights in climate change requires simultaneous attention to legal frameworks, immediate humanitarian responses to displacement and health crises, and long-term structural transformations that address underlying inequalities. The chapters reveal consistent patterns across Zimbabwe's diverse contexts. They show that climate impacts disproportionately affect the most vulnerable children; existing policies inadequately address child-specific vulnerabilities; and effective responses must integrate children's voices and agency while tackling structural determinants of vulnerability. By bridging theoretical sophistication with empirical grounding and policy relevance, the volume advances scholarly understanding and practical action on one of our time's most pressing human rights challenges, ensuring that climate action protects and advances the rights of Africa's most vulnerable citizens.

1.12 Conclusion

This chapter introduced the book *Climate Change and Children's Rights in Zimbabwe: Toward Social Policy-Based Interventions*. This introductory chapter establishes the urgent need for scholarly engagement with the intersection of climate change and children's rights in Zimbabwe. The evidence demonstrates that these are not abstract future concerns but present realities affecting millions of children. With 436 million children facing extreme water vulnerability globally, 470 million children exposed to high levels of drought, and climate-exacerbated disasters disrupting the education of nearly 40 million children annually, the scale of the crisis demands immediate and comprehensive response (UNICEF, 2023). Given current and future climate scenarios, Zimbabwe's vulnerability will increase, with projected climate changes having adverse effects on basic services such as nutrition, health, education, and WASH that are essential for human well-being, especially for women, children, youth, people with disabilities, and the elderly (GoZ, 2024). These projected changes necessitate well-coordinated approaches that promote safe responses to climate-induced challenges while ensuring children's rights remain central to all climate action.

The volume represents a timely and critical contribution to the emerging field of climate justice and children's rights, offering both theoretical insights and practical recommendations for protecting Zimbabwe's most vulnerable population in an era of unprecedented environmental change. The findings reveal a significant climate injustice. Children bear the heaviest burden of climate change impacts despite contributing least to the problem, with the most vulnerable children living in countries that emit the smallest share of global greenhouse gases. Through its four thematic sections comprising 15 chapters, the volume advances understanding, informs policy, and inspires action that places children's rights at the centre of climate responses. The contributions progress through various stages. They start with foundational theoretical and legal analyses establishing justice frameworks and constitutional provisions (Chaps. 2–4). Next, they move to empirical investigations of climate-induced displacement and child vulnerability across diverse districts (Chaps. 5–7). The focus then shifts to comprehensive examinations of health, education, and welfare impacts, demonstrating cascading effects on children's well-being (Chaps. 8–12). Finally, the contributions culminate in innovative approaches to child-centred adaptation, including gender-transformative frameworks, corporate responsibility mechanisms, and transformative social policy (Chaps. 13–15).

The diverse disciplinary perspectives in this volume, from law and sociology to development studies and environmental science, demonstrate the multifaceted nature of the climate-children's rights nexus. The empirical evidence drawn from diverse geographical contexts across Zimbabwe, including Goromonzi, Zvimba, Chivi, Mashonaland Central, Gutu, Mbire, Bikita, and Lupane districts, among others, provides a rich contextual understanding of how climate impacts manifest differently across the country's varied ecological and socio-economic landscapes. This integration of local evidence with international frameworks demonstrates the importance of context-specific approaches that nonetheless align with global commitments to children's rights and climate action. The volume charts new intellectual territory while remaining firmly grounded in the urgent practical realities facing Zimbabwe's children affected by climate-induced emergencies.

Collectively, these chapters challenge conventional approaches that treat children as passive recipients of climate impacts, instead positioning them as rights holders with agency and as essential actors in climate adaptation and resilience building. The volume thus serves multiple audiences: academics seeking theoretical and empirical insights, policymakers requiring evidence-based recommendations, practitioners implementing child-centred climate programs, and advocates working to amplify children's voices in climate governance, all united by the urgent imperative to protect and advance children's rights in an era of accelerating climate change. States are obligated to act urgently, recognising the disproportionate impact of climate change on children's rights. This volume provides a comprehensive foundation for evidence-based policy and programming prioritising child-sensitive climate action across all sectors and governance levels.

The time for action is now, as the window for avoiding the worst impacts of climate change continues to narrow, and Zimbabwe's children deserve nothing less than comprehensive. These rights-based responses protect their present and secure their future in a rapidly changing world. As Zimbabwe and the broader African continent navigate the challenges of climate adaptation and mitigation, this volume offers both a sobering assessment of current realities and a hopeful vision of what child-centred, rights-based climate action can achieve. The path forward requires not only technical solutions and policy reforms but transformations in how societies understand and respond to the climate-children's rights nexus, transformations that recognise children's inherent dignity, honour their agency, address structural inequalities, and ensure intergenerational justice in climate action and development. This volume ensures that climate action recognises children not merely as victims of climate change but as powerful agents of change whose participation and leadership are essential for building a sustainable and just future for all.

References

ACERWC. (2022). Resolution No 18/2022 of the ACERWC Working Group on Children's Rights and Climate Change to Integrate a Child Rights-Based Approach to Climate Change Action. Retrieved October 10, 2025, from https://www.acerwc.africa/en/resolutions/resolution-ndeg-182022-acerwc-working-group-childrens-rights-and-climate-change

ACERWC. (2025a). *ACERWC study on climate change & children's rights in Africa: A continental overview - 2024*. ACERWC Secretariat.

ACERWC. (2025b). Guidance note on prioritising child-rights based climate action at the Africa Climate Summit 2025. Retrieved October 11, 2025, from https://www.acerwc.africa/en/key-documents/substantive-guidelines/guiding-note-prioritizing-child-rights-based-climate-action

Addaney, M., Boshoff, E., & Olutola, B. (2017). The climate change and human rights nexus in Africa. *The Amsterdam Law Forum, 9*(3), 5–28. https://doi.org/10.37974/ALF.304

Bekink, M. (2024). The fundamental right of children to participate in climate change decision-making processes: A South African perspective. *Potchefstroom Electronic Law Journal, 27*. https://doi.org/10.17159/1727-3781/2024/v27i0a18350

Boshoff, E. (2020). The best interest of the child and climate change adaptation in Sub-Saharan Africa. In *The best interest of the child and climate change adaptation in Sub-Saharan Africa* (pp. 359–386). Palgrave Macmillan. https://doi.org/10.1007/978-3-030-27049-0_14

Bulat, D. (2024). Climate change, children's rights and the rights of future generations. *Contemporary Issues of Communication, 3*(2), 165–172. https://doi.org/10.62425/conicom.1520699

Chipenda, C., & Cochrane, L. (2024). Out of school children in the context of new policy trajectories and interlocking crises in Zimbabwe: A transformative social policy perspective. *SN Social Sciences, 4*, 131. https://doi.org/10.1007/s43545-024-00938-1

Fambasayi, R., & Addaney, M. (2021). Cascading impacts of climate change and the rights of children in Africa: A reflection on the principle of intergenerational equity. *African Human Rights Law Journal, 21*(1), 29–51. https://doi.org/10.17159/1996-2096/2021/V21N1A3

Fokala, E., & Muhumuza, N. (2024). Eroding children's rights: An analysis of the utility of the African Charter on the Rights and Welfare of the Child to Climate Action in Africa. In *The social, economic and cultural rights of children in Africa*. Brill Nijhoff. https://doi.org/10.1163/9789004685604_010

FrameWorks Institute. (2025). *Connecting early childhood development to climate change: Insights for communicators*. FrameWorks Institute.

Godfrey, S., & Tunhuma, F. A. (2020). *The climate crisis: Climate change impacts, trends and vulnerabilities of children in Sub-Saharan Africa*. UNICEF ESARO.

Government of Zimbabwe. (2016). *Zimbabwe's national climate change response strategy*. Government of Zimbabwe.

Government of Zimbabwe. (2024). *Zimbabwe national climate change adaptation plan*. Ministry of Environment, Climate and Wildlife.

Gwitira, I., Shekede, M. D., & Bhatasara, S. (2024). *Child-centred climate impact, vulnerability, and risk assessment for Zimbabwe*. UNICEF.

Humphreys, S. (2009). Introduction: human rights and climate change. In S. Humphreys (Ed.), *Human Rights and Climate Change* (pp. 1–34). introduction, Cambridge University Press.

Janeka, P., Föllmer, J., Martinez, J. A., Schrammeijer, E. A., Hertig, E., van Rompay, T., Cerrone, D., & Sawungrana, A. R. (2025). How green and blue spaces promote health among vulnerable urban populations facing climate hazards: A scoping review. *Well-being, Space and Society*. In Press, Available online 24 September 2025, 100304.

Jones, L., Martin, P., Standley, S., Kallman, K., Walker, D., Gelders, B., Mpandeli, S., Moremi, T., Laryea-Adjei, G., Viviers, A., Ferenz, M., Constabile, K., & Spalton, A. (2011). Exploring the impact of climate change on children in South Africa. Retrieved October 10, 2025, from http://reliefweb.int/sites/reliefweb.int/files/resources/SAF_resources_climatechange.pdf.

Knox, J. H. (2016). Human rights principles and climate change. In K. R. Gray, R. Tarasofsky, & C. P. Carlarne (Eds.), *The Oxford Handbook of International Climate Change Law* (online ed.). Oxford Academic. https://doi.org/10.1093/law/9780199684601.003.0011

Madamombe, S. M., Ng'ang'a, S. K., Öborn, I., et al. (2024). Climate change awareness and adaptation strategies by smallholder farmers in semi-arid areas of Zimbabwe. *International Journal of Agricultural Sustainability, 22*(1), 2293588.

Marin, S. V., Schwarz, L., & Sabarwal, S. (2024). *The impact of climate change on education and what to do about it*. World Bank.

Mezmur, B. (2023). The calm before the storm? Child rights climate change litigation in Africa. *De Jure Law Journal, 56*(1), 543–568. https://doi.org/10.17159/2225-7160/2023/v56a33

Mirzabaev, A., Kerr, R. B., Hasegawa, T., Pradhan, P., Wreford, A., Pahlen, M. C. T. V. D., & Gurney-Smith, H. (2023). Severe climate change risks to food security and nutrition. *Climate Risk Management, 39*, 100473. https://doi.org/10.1016/j.crm.2022.100473

Mpala, T. A., & Simatele, M. D. (2024). Climate-smart agricultural practices among rural farmers in Masvingo district of Zimbabwe: Perspectives on the mitigation strategies to drought and water scarcity for improved crop production. *Frontiers in Sustainable Food Systems, 7*, 129890.

Ndhlovu, E. (2024). Building farming resilience to climate change through social assistance in South-Eastern Zimbabwe. *International Journal of Research in Business and Social Science, 13*(10), 105–117.

Ndhlovu, E. (2025). Climate change: Implications for agricultural development and prospects for industrialisation in Sub-Saharan Africa. In *Agriculture, autonomous development, and prospects for industrialization in Africa* (pp. 195–217). Springer.

Ndhlovu, E., & Dube, K. (2024). Contract farming and climate change adaptation in rural Zimbabwe. *Mankind Quarterly, 64*(3), 579–594.

Spotlight Initiative. (2025). *Colliding crisis: How the climate crisis fuels gender-based violence*. Issue Brief. Retrieved October 11, 2025, from https://spotlightinitiative.org/publications/colliding-crises-how-climate-crisis-fuels-gender-based-violence

UN. (2023). *United Nations Committee on the Rights of the Child. General comment no. 26 on children's rights and the environment with a special focus on climate change*. UN.

UNICEF. (2011). *Exploring the impact of climate change on children in South Africa*. UNICEF South Africa.

UNICEF. (2021). *The climate crisis is a child rights crisis: Introducing the children's climate risk index*. UNICEF.

UNICEF. (2023). *Analysis of the CCR for least developed countries*. UNICEF.

UNICEF. (2025). *When the rains don't come: Climate change through the eyes of Zimbabwe's children*. Retrieved October 9, 2025, from https://www.unicef.org/zimbabwe/stories/when-rains-dont-come-climate-change-through-eyes-zimbabwes-children

UNICEF ESARO. (2025). *Turning climate hardship into hope in Eastern and Southern Africa*. Retrieved October 9, 2025, from https://www.unicef.org/esa/media/15181/file/UNICEF-ESA-Climate-Think-Piece-2025.pdf

United Nations. (1989, November 20). *Convention on the Rights of the Child*. Treaty Series, vol. 1577. UN.

Walinski, A., Sander, J., Gerlinger, G., Clemens, V., Meyer-Lindenberg, A., & Heinz, A. (2023). The effects of climate change on mental health. *Deutsches Arzteblatt International, 120*(8), 117–124. https://doi.org/10.3238/arztebl.m2022.0403

Chapter 2
Climate Justice Imperatives for Children's Rights in Zimbabwe: A Critical Analysis

Clement Chipenda and Anne Chawanda

2.1 Introduction

The intersection of climate change and children's rights constitutes one of the most pressing yet underexplored humanitarian challenges confronting Zimbabwe and the African continent in contemporary times. Climate change is now increasingly recognised as an emergent, unprecedented long-term threat, making the differential impacts on children an urgent area of scholarly inquiry (ACERWC, 2025). This challenge sits at the nexus of multiple Sustainable Development Goals (SDGs), especially SDG 13 (climate action), SDG 1 (no poverty), SDG 2 (zero hunger), SDG 3 (good health and well-being), SDG 4 (quality education), and SDG 10 (reduced inequalities). This highlights the interconnected nature of climate impacts on children's multidimensional well-being. This chapter examines the complex and dynamic relationship between climate change and children's rights in Zimbabwe through a climate justice lens. It engages with how climate-induced environmental changes create and intensify inequalities that disproportionately burden the nation's youngest and most vulnerable populations, who are children across varied geographic and socio-economic contexts.

The climate justice imperative gains added urgency when considered alongside Zimbabwe's demographic profile and vulnerability status. Children under 18 constitute approximately 47% of the population, totalling 7.1 million individuals according to 2022 census data (3,631,208 males and 3,632,908 females under 18) (ZimStat., 2022). UNICEF has classified Zimbabwe as being among 25 African

C. Chipenda (✉)
South African Research Chair in Social Policy, College of Graduate Studies, University of South Africa, Pretoria, South Africa

A. Chawanda
School of Geography, Archaeology and Environmental Studies, University of the Witwatersrand, Johannesburg, South Africa

E. Ndhlovu, C. Chipenda (eds.), *Climate Change and Children's Rights in Zimbabwe*, https://doi.org/10.1007/978-981-95-6005-9_2

nations at extremely high risk for children (UNICEF, 2025a). These African nations represent 75% of the 33 countries worldwide most vulnerable to climate impacts (ACERWC, 2025). This classification highlights a core climate injustice principle: populations with minimal contribution to global emissions bear the most severe climate consequences. This disparity significantly undermines the SDG principle of leaving no one behind and highlights the urgent need for accelerated action as the 2030 Agenda approaches its deadline. The disparity in carbon emissions exemplifies this injustice, as demonstrated by an average American generating 23 times more carbon than an average Nigerian (ACERWC, 2025). As the international community increasingly recognises the limitations of the current SDG framework in addressing complex, intersectional challenges like climate-induced children's rights violations, this analysis contributes to emerging discussions about post-2030 development frameworks. The chapter's findings inform the growing consensus that future global development agendas must adopt more integrated, justice-oriented approaches that centre the rights and voices of the most vulnerable populations, especially children, in climate-vulnerable contexts.

This chapter, focusing on Zimbabwe, draws from extensive secondary evidence across regional and national contexts to demonstrate how climate change functions simultaneously as an environmental and children's rights crisis. The analysis reveals how climate impacts create cascading failures across multiple SDG targets simultaneously, undermining progress towards sustainable development and highlighting the need for more holistic, rights-based approaches to climate action. The implications extend across multiple dimensions of children's well-being, protection, and developmental opportunities. The analysis identifies how the children's rights crisis manifests through interconnected challenges, including but not limited to water access, nutrition security, health outcomes, educational provision, and child protection systems. These crises can be seen to be negatively affecting children, and they constitute serious violations of children's rights as enshrined in the United Nations Convention on the Rights of the Child (UNCRC).

Current research on climate change and children's rights contains several critical gaps this chapter addresses. Mainstream climate vulnerability assessments treat children as a uniform demographic group, overlooking how climate impacts vary across geographic regions, urban-rural contexts, and socio-economic circumstances within Zimbabwe. Climate adaptation scholarship has prioritised technical and infrastructural responses while neglecting justice considerations regarding how climate risks are distributed across different children's populations. Children's rights literature has insufficiently integrated climate change as a central threat requiring specialised analytical frameworks and context-specific policy interventions. In addition, existing SDG monitoring frameworks inadequately capture the dynamic, intersectional nature of climate impacts on children's rights, often treating climate action and social development as separate rather than interconnected challenges. While international frameworks provide foundations for protecting children from climate hazards, implementation and accountability mechanisms remain inadequate, especially in Global South contexts where children experience the greatest vulnerability (Gibbons, 2014).

This chapter's contribution extends beyond a purely academic analysis to inform policy discussions about the post-SDG development agenda, advocating for frameworks that better integrate climate justice principles with children's rights protection. By demonstrating how climate change simultaneously undermines progress across multiple SDG domains, the study supports calls for more integrated, systemic approaches to sustainable development that recognise the interconnected nature of environmental and social challenges. The chapter's analytical contribution is focused on applying climate justice theory to examine how climate change produces differentiated impacts on children across Zimbabwe's diverse contexts. The investigation focuses on four critical domains, namely, educational disruption and developmental consequences, health implications and disease vulnerabilities, food security and nutritional challenges, and intersectional inequalities. The theoretical framework incorporates three core justice principles: distributive justice concerning fair allocation of climate risks and adaptation resources; procedural justice involving meaningful participation in climate decision-making processes; and recognition justice that acknowledges diverse experiences and knowledge systems. These principles align with and extend the SDG commitment to inclusive, participatory development while highlighting the need for justice-centred approaches in post-2030 frameworks. Four interconnected research questions structure this investigation. First, how do climate-induced infrastructure failures, resource scarcities, and environmental changes create differential impacts on children's rights across Zimbabwe's urban and rural settings? Second, through what specific mechanisms does climate change undermine children's rights to health, education, and development, and how do these mechanisms intersect with existing social and economic inequalities? Third, how can climate justice principles inform more equitable and child-focused approaches to climate adaptation and children's rights protection in Zimbabwe? Fourth, how can this analysis contribute to emerging discussions about post-SDG development frameworks that better integrate climate justice and children's rights considerations?

The chapter proceeds through five main sections. Following this introduction, the following section engages with a comprehensive review of literature examining existing scholarship on the theoretical framing that establishes the climate justice analytical framework, climate change and children's rights, and climate justice. The methodology section outlines this investigation's research approach and data sources. The research findings section presents the analysis across the four critical domains identified above. The discussion section synthesises these findings within the broader theoretical and policy context. At the same time, the conclusion offers recommendations for future research and policy interventions that inform both immediate SDG implementation and longer-term post-2030 development planning.

2.2 Literature Review

2.2.1 Climate Justice Theory and Children's Rights: Foundational Framework

The intersection of climate justice theory and children's rights provides the conceptual foundation for understanding how environmental degradation creates and amplifies inequalities affecting children in Zimbabwe. Climate justice theory represents an approach that integrates ethical, legal, and social dimensions to address the diverse impacts of climate change on vulnerable populations, with children constituting one of the most systematically marginalised groups in climate discourse (Puaschunder, 2020). Rather than treating climate change as a random distribution of impacts, this theoretical framework recognises that climate effects follow existing patterns of social, economic, and political marginalisation, emphasising equitable distribution of climate change burdens and benefits while considering historical responsibilities and socio-economic disparities (Pardo Buendía & Ortega, 2018). Building on environmental justice movements, climate justice theory diverges from traditional climate approaches, prioritising technological solutions. The framework is deeply rooted in principles of sustainable development and democratic citizenship. It emphasises the social and ethical dimensions while focusing on the most vulnerable populations and challenging market-oriented solutions, favouring community-based, egalitarian approaches (Tokar, 2018). Such theoretical grounding is essential for understanding children's climate vulnerabilities in contexts like Zimbabwe, where historical patterns of inequality intersect with contemporary climate risks to create significant disadvantages for young populations.

Climate justice theory operates through three interconnected core principles that form the analytical backbone for understanding children's climate vulnerabilities. Distributive justice concerns the fair allocation of climate risks, impacts, and adaptation resources across different populations. It advocates for equitable distribution while ensuring that those who have contributed least to climate change are not negatively affected (Pardo Buendía & Ortega, 2018; Puaschunder, 2020). When applied to children's rights, this principle examines how climate impacts are unevenly distributed among children, with marginalised children bearing the burden while privileged children remain relatively protected (Islam & Winkel, 2017). This becomes evident when examining how climate change affects children differently across Zimbabwe's urban-rural divide and socio-economic spectrum.

Procedural justice focuses on meaningful participation in climate-related decision-making processes, emphasising the importance of including affected communities while advocating for democratic citizenship and inclusive governance mechanisms (Pardo Buendía & Ortega, 2018). For children, this principle raises critical questions about age-appropriate participation mechanisms and the recognition of children as rights holders rather than passive beneficiaries of climate action. This is operationalised through frameworks emphasising the joint participation of children and adults in addressing climate change, as General Comment No. 26 of the UNCRC outlines. This mandates states to ensure child participation in climate-related governance and policies (Boshoff & Damtew, 2023; Staparski, 2023).

Recognition justice acknowledges the diverse experiences, knowledge systems, and cultural values of different groups affected by climate change, integrating diverse perspectives, including those of indigenous and marginalised communities, to create inclusive climate policies (Tokar, 2018). In relation to children, this principle requires acknowledging how climate impacts intersect with other forms of marginalisation based on age, gender, disability, ethnicity, and socio-economic status, creating unique vulnerabilities that require tailored responses. This gains additional relevance in Africa, where the African Charter on the Rights and Welfare of the Child (ACRWC) links children's rights to climate change, mandating states to protect children's health and well-being from climate impacts (Boshoff & Damtew, 2023).

2.2.2 Main Imperatives of Climate Justice for Children

The climate justice framework establishes several key imperatives that translate theoretical principles into actionable guidelines. Historical responsibility acknowledges the disproportionate emissions of developed countries and their responsibility to lead in mitigation efforts. There is recognition that children in the Global South bear adverse consequences despite minimal historical contribution (Vanderheiden, 2021). Common but differentiated responsibilities recognise countries' varying capabilities and responsibilities in addressing climate change, advocating for differentiated approaches based on socio-economic contexts while ensuring climate action does not marginalise vulnerable populations (Pardo Buendía & Ortega, 2018). Burden sharing calls for fair distribution of climate change burdens within and between countries, proposing mechanisms like progressive carbon taxation and burden-sharing bonds that can generate resources for child-focused climate adaptation (Puaschunder, 2020). The intersectional approach integrates diverse perspectives and experiences, recognising that children's climate vulnerabilities are shaped by multiple, intersecting forms of marginalisation, including age, gender, disability, ethnicity, and socio-economic status (Tokar, 2018). This proves essential for understanding how climate change affects different groups of children in Zimbabwe differently, requiring differentiated policy responses that address vulnerabilities.

2.2.3 International and Regional Legal Architecture

The international legal architecture addressing climate change and children's rights operates within the broader climate justice framework, but gaps remain in translating justice principles into binding legal obligations. The Paris Agreement, which was adopted on December 12, 2015, during the UN Climate Change Conference

(COP21), while universal in acceptance and establishing legally binding obligations for countries to reduce emissions, indirectly benefits children by aiming to mitigate climate change impacts. Critics argue that it insufficiently incorporates climate justice principles regarding historical responsibility and differentiated capabilities (Farber & Peeters, 2016). Despite these limitations, the Agreement's human rights reference acknowledges human rights, including children's rights, positioning climate action within a human rights context that aligns with climate justice demands (Duyck, 2015). Article 8 addresses loss and damage associated with climate impacts, obligating parties to minimise and address these effects. However, mechanisms for operationalising loss and damage remain contested and inadequate from a climate justice perspective (Amini et al., 2023).

The UNCRC provides a more direct legal basis for protecting children's rights in climate change. However, its effectiveness remains limited by implementation gaps and insufficient integration of climate justice principles. The UNCRC emphasises the child's best interests principle, which can be strategically employed in climate litigation to protect children from climate-related hazards, aligning with climate justice demands for prioritising vulnerable populations (Bulat, 2024). The Convention proves central in recognising the rights of future generations, ensuring that climate policies consider long-term impacts on children, resonating with climate justice principles of intergenerational equity and sustainable development (Bulat, 2024; Gibbons, 2014; Pardo Buendía & Ortega, 2018). Article 6 guarantees the 'right to life, survival and development', which climate impacts threaten. In contrast, Article 24 on health recognises environmental factors, requiring states to combat disease and malnutrition while considering environmental pollution dangers and mandating adequate nutrition and clean water, both of which are directly threatened by climate change (UN, 1989).

The African Charter on the Rights and Welfare of the Child (ACRWC) provides a regional framework that contextualises rights within African realities, including environmental challenges specific to the continent (OAU, 1990). Implementation, however, remains constrained by limited resources and weak enforcement mechanisms that reflect broader patterns of climate injustice. The ACRWC addresses climate change impacts through key provisions that align with climate justice principles. Article 5 (Survival and Development) requires states to ensure 'to the maximum extent possible, the survival, protection and development of the child', with climate change directly threatening this obligation through increased mortality, food insecurity, and developmental challenges. Article 14 (Health and Health Services) mandates children enjoy 'the best attainable state of physical, mental and spiritual health', which climate change undermines through increased disease burden, malnutrition, and mental health impacts. Article 11 (Education) guarantees the right to education, which climate disasters frequently disrupt through infrastructure damage and displacement (OAU, 1990). These provisions can be interpreted to require African countries to protect children from climate change impacts, although this requires stronger integration of climate justice principles in policy implementation (Fokala & Muhumuza, 2024).

The UNCRC's General Comment No. 26 represents a significant advancement in recognising the intersection of climate change with structural violence against children. The Comment explicitly incorporates climate justice principles by emphasising states' obligations to protect children's rights to a clean, healthy environment amid environmental degradation. It establishes 'justice pathways' for children to hold governments accountable for actions threatening their well-being, reflecting climate justice demands for procedural justice and meaningful participation (Bourdillon et al., 2024). However, its non-binding nature raises concerns about effectiveness in achieving climate justice outcomes, especially in contexts where political uncertainties and corporate influence hinder implementation of equitable climate policies (Staparski, 2023; Tokar, 2018). The General Comment mandates joint participation of children and adults in addressing climate change, recognising children as active agents rather than passive beneficiaries, aligning with climate justice principles of democratic citizenship and inclusive governance (Staparski, 2023). The principle of intergenerational equity is an important tool for promoting children's rights in the context of climate action in Africa, reflecting climate justice concerns about sustainable development and long-term equity (Fambasayi & Addaney, 2021).

2.2.4 *Global and Regional Climate Change Impacts on Children*

The global evidence based on climate change impacts on children reveals patterns consistent with climate justice theory's predictions about its impacts on vulnerable populations. The IPCC Sixth Assessment Report (AR6) observes with high confidence that climate risks are appearing faster and becoming more severe, with implications for vulnerable populations, including children, confirming climate justice arguments about accelerating impacts on marginalised communities (IPCC, 2023). The report emphasises that where global warming exceeds 1.5 °C, opportunities for adaptation to many climate risks are likely to be constrained, highlighting the urgency of climate justice demands for immediate and equitable climate action. UNICEF's Children's Climate Risk Index provides comprehensive evidence of global climate vulnerability that illustrates climate justice concerns about the inequitable distribution of climate impacts (UNICEF, 2021). The Index reveals that almost 1 billion children, nearly half of the world's 2.2 billion young lives, reside in countries deemed extremely high risk for climate impacts, with the majority located in the Global South despite minimal contribution to historical greenhouse gas emissions (UNICEF, 2021). The Index demonstrates that 820 million children globally are currently highly exposed to heatwaves, 330 million to riverine flooding, and 240 million to coastal flooding. Most significantly, over 99% of children globally are exposed to at least one major climate and environmental hazard, with 2.2 billion children facing multiple overlapping climate risks, exemplifying the systematic nature of climate injustice affecting children (ACERWC, 2025).

Regional evidence from Eastern and Southern Africa reveals acute climate vulnerabilities among children that reflect broader patterns of climate injustice. In Southern Africa, climate change manifests through rising temperatures (IPCC, 2023), increased rainfall variability (Nhemachena et al., 2020), and growing frequency and intensity of extreme weather events such as cyclones, floods, and droughts. Due to significant regional ecosystem variability, these climatic changes manifest differently depending on localised context, creating differentiated impacts that reflect climate justice concerns about the uneven distribution of climate risks. The region's historical experience with El Niño and La Niña weather phenomena, now intensified by climate change, creates cyclical patterns of extreme weather that negatively affect children (UNICEF, 2025b). These warming and cooling cycles, occurring every 3–7 years, are linked to trade wind strength and create an increased frequency of extreme weather events. In a region where 70% of people's lives and livelihoods rely on agriculture, shifting conditions combined with climate change create destructive weather patterns that impact children who are physically less able than adults to withstand shocks such as floods, droughts, and heatwaves (UNICEF, 2025b).

Across Eastern and Southern Africa, at least 51 million children are at the epicentre of multiple crises, including relentless climate shocks, public health emergencies, conflict, displacement, and economic instability. This demonstrates how climate change intersects with other forms of marginalisation to create significant disadvantages (Gwitira et al., 2024; UNICEF, 2025b). Specific country experiences illustrate the devastating impact on children. In 2024–2025 in Malawi, 23 out of 28 districts have faced erratic rains, floods, and prolonged dry spells, leaving 4.59 million children in desperate need. Zambia faces a similar crisis with drought and floods pushing three million children to the brink with severe food insecurity and cholera outbreaks. In Lesotho, El Niño impacts have created severe food insecurity affecting approximately one-third of the total population. At the same time, Madagascar's Great South faces limited rainfall, threatening a fresh humanitarian disaster with over 262,000 children already acutely malnourished (UNICEF, 2025b).

2.2.5 Zimbabwe's Climate Context and Governance Framework

Zimbabwe's climate change experience reflects broader regional patterns while exhibiting specific characteristics that shape children's vulnerabilities. It is a critical case study for understanding how climate injustice manifests in Southern African contexts. The country's position among the 25 African nations at extremely high risk for children, representing 75% of the 33 countries worldwide most vulnerable to climate impacts, exemplifies the climate justice principle that populations with minimal contribution to global emissions bear the most severe climate consequences (ACERWC, 2025). This classification highlights a core climate injustice where Zimbabwe's children face severe climate impacts despite the country's minimal historical contribution to global greenhouse gas emissions, with the disparity as indicated earlier exemplified by an average American generating 23 times more carbon than an average African (ACERWC, 2025).

Zimbabwe's climate projections reveal patterns that will negatively impact children and vulnerable populations. The national mean surface temperature increased by about 0.90 °C from 1900 to 2018, with the most significant warming occurring in the 1980s. There is very high confidence that mean daily minimum and maximum temperatures will continue to increase throughout 2020–2040 for most districts, with the national annual average temperature likely to increase by about 1.0–1.5 °C. Average annual rainfall declined by about ±5% across Zimbabwe over 1901–2018, with intra-seasonal characteristics including frequency and intensity of dry spells, length of rainfall season, onset and cessation dates, and number of rainy days significantly modified since the 1950s. Future rainfall projections indicate a decline of up to 10% of mean national annual precipitation, with the most significant decrease in south-eastern sections, including Matabeleland North and South, Masvingo, and Manicaland provinces. These areas already experience high poverty levels and child vulnerability (see Gwitira et al., 2024). Drought frequency has increased dramatically, exemplifying how climate change amplifies existing vulnerabilities affecting children. The frequency increased from 10% between 1902 and 1979 to 25% from 1980 to 2018, with notable drought episodes including 1991–1992, 1994–1995, 2002–2003, 2015–2016, 2018–2019, 2019–2020, and 2023–2024, with El Niño-Southern Oscillation (ENSO) events modulating the droughts. This increased frequency creates recurring crises undermining children's rights to food, water, health, and education.

While comprehensive on paper, Zimbabwe's climate change governance structure faces significant challenges in implementing climate justice principles and ensuring equitable protection for children. The governance framework is structured around a high-level committee within the Office of the President and Cabinet (OPC), ensuring cross-sectoral coordination through permanent secretaries from all ministries. The Ministry of Environment, Climate, and Wildlife (MECW) is the leading authority responsible for environmental affairs, including climate policy implementation via the National Climate Policy and the National Adaptation Plan. The Climate Change Management Department within MECW coordinates national programmes, supported by a multi-tiered institutional framework encompassing national, provincial, and local authority climate change platforms, and community-based structures like disaster risk management committees (Government of Zimbabwe, 2024).

Zimbabwe's legal and policy response is anchored in the constitutional framework and specific climate policies. The Constitution's Section 73 establishes environmental rights, guaranteeing that 'every person has the right to an environment that is not harmful to their health or well-being' and 'to have the environment protected for present and future generations'. Section 81 specifically protects children's rights, including the right to 'education, health care services, nutrition and shelter', all affected by climate change (GoZ, 2013). Zimbabwe has developed several policies, including the National Climate Change Response Strategy (NCCRS), National Climate Policy (NCP), National Adaptation Plan (NAP), education policy and curriculum reforms, and social protection programmes. However, significant implementation gaps remain, including limited integration of children's rights in climate policies, resource constraints limiting adaptation measures, lack of child participation in climate policy development, and limited coordination between climate and child protection authorities. Although Zimbabwe has clear policies dealing with climate change issues, there is a lack of policies which refer specifically to children's concerns, reflecting insufficient recognition of children's specific vulnerabilities and rights in climate policy frameworks (Gwitira et al., 2024).

2.2.6 Sectoral Analysis: Climate Impacts on Children's Rights

This section discusses how climate change undermines children's rights across four critical sectors, demonstrating how climate injustice manifests through complex pathways that create differentiated impacts on children. This applies to the Zimbabwe context.

2.2.7 Health Implications and Disease Vulnerabilities

Health implications represent a primary pathway through which climate injustice affects children's rights. Children face heightened vulnerabilities to climate-related health risks due to their physiological characteristics, including higher metabolic rates, greater surface area to body weight ratios, and developing immune systems. These biological factors make children more susceptible to heat stress, dehydration, infectious diseases, and air pollution than adults, creating inherent vulnerabilities amplified by social and economic inequalities (Ahdoot et al., 2024). Vector-borne and waterborne diseases represent specific concerns for children in climate-vulnerable regions, where rising temperatures and changing precipitation patterns alter the geographic distribution and seasonal patterns of disease vectors, potentially exposing children to new health risks or intensifying existing ones. These health impacts are not distributed equally but follow existing patterns of inequality, with children in poor communities, rural areas, and informal settlements facing the greatest risks.

Recent regional experiences provide stark evidence of these health vulnerabilities. Poor hygiene conditions during El Niño floods have significantly increased children's vulnerability to acute watery diarrhoea, cholera, and measles across Eastern and Southern Africa (UNICEF, 2025b). Since 2023, over 230,000 cholera cases and 4000 deaths have been recorded across the region, with children under 15 accounting for 52% of all cases and children under five representing up to 40% of all fatalities (UNICEF, 2025b). This alarming impact on children reflects climate justice concerns about how environmental changes amplify existing vulnerabilities among the most marginalised populations.

2.2.8 *Educational Disruption and Development Impacts*

Educational disruption constitutes another critical pathway through which climate injustice threatens children's rights. Climate change threatens children's educational access and outcomes through multiple pathways that affect marginalised populations, including infrastructure damage, displacement, health impacts, and economic pressures on families. These impacts reflect broader patterns of inequality, with children in poor communities, rural areas, and marginalised groups facing the most significant educational disruption. Extreme weather events can directly damage school infrastructure, while climate-related health impacts may reduce children's ability to attend school regularly. Economic pressures associated with climate impacts may force families to withdraw children from school to contribute to household income or care responsibilities. These decisions reflect broader socio-economic inequalities and limited adaptive capacity among poor households. Gender dimensions of educational disruption reflect intersectional climate injustice, where traditional gender roles exacerbate the vulnerabilities of girls, who may face increased exposure to risks related to water scarcity, food scarcity, and health issues (Gwitira et al., 2024). Climate disasters exacerbate existing gender inequalities, creating environments where girls are more susceptible to abuse and exploitation. Girls are notably affected by disruptions in their education due to climate-related displacement, with 70.7% experiencing this issue, demonstrating how climate change amplifies existing gender inequalities in education access (Gwitira et al., 2024).

2.2.9 *Food Security and Nutritional Vulnerability*

Food security and nutritional vulnerability represent a critical pathway through which climate injustice affects children's rights. Climate change severely threatens children's food security and nutritional status through disruptions to agricultural production, food systems, and household livelihoods (Onyeaka et al., 2024). These impacts are not distributed equally but follow existing patterns of poverty and marginalisation. Children have specific nutritional requirements for healthy growth and development. This makes them vulnerable to food insecurity and malnutrition resulting from climate impacts, especially when their families lack resources for adequate adaptation measures. Climate change has intensified food insecurity in Zimbabwe, with extreme weather events disrupting food production and supply chains. These disruptions create differential impacts based on household economic status and location (Nkrumah, 2018; Tawodzera, 2011). Urban households, especially the poor, face critical food shortages and rely heavily on purchased food, making them vulnerable to price shocks associated with climate-related supply disruptions, while wealthier households maintain greater adaptive capacity through diversified food sources and economic resources (Ruel et al., 2017; Tawodzera, 2011).

Recent evidence from the Eastern and Southern African region illustrates the severity of climate-related food insecurity affecting children. Over 20 million people across the region struggle to find enough food due to weather-induced failed harvests, with 3.5 million children across Angola, Malawi, Madagascar, Mozambique, Namibia, Zambia, and Zimbabwe desperately needing life-saving nutrition treatment (UNICEF, 2025a, 2025b). In Southern Africa alone, over 30 million people suffer from severe drought caused by extreme weather patterns, with millions at risk of acute hunger, demonstrating the regional scale of climate injustice affecting children's right to adequate nutrition (UNICEF, 2025b).

2.2.10 Intersectional Vulnerabilities and Climate Justice Dynamics

Intersectional vulnerabilities represent the fourth critical area, demonstrating how climate change intersects with multiple forms of marginalisation to create disadvantages for children. Climate change negatively impacts marginalised children, including children with disabilities, those on the move, poor children, children separated from their families, and indigenous children, reflecting climate justice concerns about how environmental changes amplify existing inequalities rather than affecting all children equally. The gendered and intersectional dimensions of climate vulnerability add complexity to Zimbabwe's child rights crisis, where girls face heightened risks due to climate change, reflecting how environmental challenges intersect with existing social inequalities to create compounded disadvantages (ACERWC, 2025).

Climate change exacerbates existing vulnerabilities among children, especially those in marginalised communities, by impacting their physical and mental health. The intersection of climate change with other global challenges, such as COVID-19, further complicates efforts to protect children's rights and demonstrates the complex, intersectional nature of climate injustice. These intersectional impacts require recognition of diverse experiences and knowledge systems, as emphasised in climate justice principles of recognition justice, calling for community-centred approaches that address the root causes of vulnerability rather than treating symptoms in isolation.

2.3 Research Methodology

This chapter employs a systematic literature methodology grounded in interpretive qualitative analysis to examine the intersection of climate change and children's rights in Zimbabwe through a climate justice lens. A systematic literature review represents a structured and methodical approach to synthesising research with predefined criteria and reproducible methods to minimise bias and errors (Brignardello-Petersen et al., 2025; Višić, 2022). This approach is valuable for examining dynamic interdisciplinary phenomena that require comprehensive evidence synthesis across environmental, social, and rights-based disciplines. The methodology's interpretive foundation acknowledges that climate impacts and children's experiences are contextually situated, enabling an analysis of how global climate phenomena manifest as localised children's rights challenges across Zimbabwe's diverse contexts. This combined approach provides an analytical and interpretive flexibility necessary to examine the differentiated impacts on children's populations.

The systematic review process followed established protocols beginning with precise research question formulation. A comprehensive search strategy employed databases including Web of Science, Scopus, Google Scholar, and institutional repositories, complemented by targeted searches of UNICEF, ACERWC, UN agencies, and civil society organisations. Key search terms included 'climate change', 'children's rights', 'climate justice', 'Zimbabwe', 'child vulnerability', 'climate adaptation', 'educational disruption', 'food security', 'health impacts', and 'intersectional inequalities'. Screening procedures followed predefined eligibility criteria, prioritising materials published between 2015 and 2025 to capture contemporary climate science and evolving children's rights discourse. Sources encompassed peer-reviewed articles, policy documents, international organisation reports, government publications, and grey literature. Quality assessment evaluated credibility, relevance, and methodological rigour to ensure that high-quality evidence informed the analysis (Arvanitis, 2024).

Data extraction employed systematic procedures capturing study contexts, methodological approaches, findings, and policy implications. The interpretive analysis was structured around three climate justice principles: distributive, procedural, and recognition justice. There was the examination of impacts across four domains, which included educational disruption, health implications, food security challenges, and intersectional inequalities. This framework facilitated integrating diverse knowledge sources, from quantitative vulnerability assessments to qualitative studies. The methodology offered important advantages, including comprehensive evidence synthesis and research gap identification (Arvanitis, 2024; Kabir et al., 2023). It enables cross-disciplinary integration across environmental science, human rights law, development studies, and policy analysis, which is essential for understanding dynamic climate impacts on children's well-being. The approach generates actionable insights for climate adaptation planning, children's rights protection, and SDG implementation while maintaining systematic rigour (Brignardello-Petersen et al., 2025).

Several limitations warrant acknowledgement. Reliance on secondary sources limits inclusion of direct children's voices, potentially constraining procedural and recognition justice analysis. The approach may reflect existing research biases towards certain geographic regions within Zimbabwe. While systematic reviews require significant resources, their quality depends on the comprehensiveness of research question formulation and search strategy (Arvanitis, 2024). These limitations highlight opportunities for future research employing primary data collection and participatory methodologies to complement this investigation's contributions.

2.4 Findings and Discussion

2.4.1 Educational Disruption and Developmental Consequences

The evidence from Zimbabwe reveals that climate change operates as a systemic disruptor of children's educational rights, creating interlocking vulnerabilities that compound existing inequalities. Infrastructure damage is a primary mechanism through which climate hazards disrupt educational provision. Recent data indicate that approximately 40% of early childhood development (ECD), primary, and secondary classrooms require minor repairs, including fixes to walls, roofs, and floors. In comparison, over 8% of classrooms in ECD and primary schools were in poor condition and needed significant repairs (Gwitira et al., 2024, p. 41). This systematic infrastructure degradation exemplifies distributive injustice where children in climate-vulnerable areas bear disproportionate educational costs. Gwitira et al. (2024) documented how climate disasters such as cyclones, floods, violent winds, and droughts have devastated educational infrastructure nationwide, frequently causing extensive damage that has significantly compromised the safety and accessibility of learning environments. Similarly, Chikoko and Chihiya (2023) found that these extreme weather events have systematically damaged school infrastructure, making it difficult for children to access education and maintain consistent attendance patterns.

The case of Cyclone Idai provides an important illustration of this pattern. The cyclone's devastating floods destroyed schools, causing increased school dropout rates and early marriages in districts such as Muzarabani, Chiredzi, and Tsholotsho (Gwitira et al., 2024). These impacts constitute clear violations of Article 28 of the UNCRC, which guarantees children's right to education, while undermining SDG 4's commitment to inclusive and equitable quality education. This pattern demonstrates how climate change transforms educational access from a development challenge into a children's rights crisis.

Chigwanda et al. (2024) provided important perspectives into the gendered dimensions of climate-induced educational disruption through their qualitative research study in Ward 25 of Chivi District, Masvingo Province, focusing on in-school adolescent girls aged 10–19 years. Their research revealed that adolescent girls were experiencing climate-induced health challenges related to physical illness and mental health disorders, which contributed to negative impacts on their education, including absenteeism, lateness to school, punishment by school authorities, difficulties concentrating and sleeping during lessons, and learning losses. This evidence highlights the dynamic and complex pathways through which climate change operates beyond infrastructure damage. It is important to demonstrate how environmental stressors infiltrate the learning process, primarily affecting girls in rural contexts.

Developing coping mechanisms reveals the tension between community resilience and systemic inadequacies in climate adaptation. Kahomwe and Muzingili's (2025) research in Ward 5, Muzarabani District, identified five primary educational coping strategies: conducting outdoor lessons, establishing temporary learning centres, leveraging technology for remote learning, migration, and resorting to child labour and marriage. They found that teaching outdoors was a common strategy when school buildings were damaged, with teachers conducting lessons under trees or temporary shade. However, this approach created significant learning challenges as outdoor learning negatively impacted students' concentration due to distractions from environmental factors such as noise, weather conditions, and nearby activities. These temporary solutions, while demonstrating adaptive capacity, simultaneously expose the inadequacy of systematic policy responses to climate-induced educational disruption.

The establishment of temporary learning centres, while demonstrating community agency, exposed critical resource gaps. Kahomwe and Muzingili (2025) documented how these centres, often constructed from plastic and sticks in safer locations during floods, enabled education continuation despite infrastructure destruction but faced significant challenges, including teacher shortages, inadequate resources, and poor working conditions. This reliance on community volunteerism rather than systematic policy responses highlights procedural injustices in climate adaptation planning, where affected communities bear primary responsibility for maintaining educational continuity without adequate state support or resources. The digital adaptation strategies revealed inequalities in technological adaptation capacities. While Kahomwe and Muzingili (2025) reported that some learners utilised WhatsApp groups facilitated by community volunteers and local teachers during disaster-related school closures, most faced insurmountable barriers, including a lack of mobile devices, poor network connectivity, and high Internet data costs. This technological exclusion demonstrates how climate adaptation strategies can exacerbate existing inequalities rather than promote inclusive development, creating new forms of educational disadvantage based on digital access.

Gender-differentiated impacts constitute an important dimension of educational disruption across the research evidence. Kahomwe and Muzingili (2025) documented how migration during disasters often results in significant educational disruptions, with girls mainly being affected, as families facing financial constraints typically prioritise the education of boys while leaving girls behind due to societal norms that undervalue the schooling of girls. This gendered educational disruption reflects more profound structural inequalities that climate change intensifies rather than creates. Chikoko and Chihiya (2023) similarly reported that climate change in Zimbabwe led to decreased school attendance as children were forced into labour or early marriages to support their families during times of food insecurity, with these patterns mainly affecting girls' educational rights. Their analysis indicated that disasters exacerbate poverty, pushing many families to withdraw girls from school and marry them off as a coping mechanism, with school closures during disasters creating opportunities for child marriage and labour. In Bikita rural area in Ward 14, evidence revealed that children were vulnerable to sexual exploitation, hunger, food insecurity, school dropout, climate change-related diseases, child prostitution, and early marriages (Chikoko & Chihiya, 2023). The comprehensive findings demonstrated that the impact of climate change had been unprecedented on the lives of children in rural Zimbabwe, encompassing hunger and food insecurity, decreased school attendance, early or forced marriages, sexual exploitation, gold panning, child labour and abuse, child prostitution, drug use and abuse, and the spread of climate change-related diseases. This evidence highlights how climate change creates cascading vulnerabilities beyond educational access to encompass children's safety and well-being.

The educational impacts generate long-term developmental consequences that extend beyond immediate disruption. Data from the Midlands Province indicated that 2.7% of students were out of school due to pregnancy and early marriage, with the child marriage rate remaining alarmingly high at 21.2% for adolescent girls aged 15–18 (Gwitira et al., 2024). Climate change amplifies these patterns as droughts and poor harvests increase financial stress on households, pushing more children, especially boys, into dangerous labour markets as a coping strategy, with Gwitira et al. (2024) documenting noticeable increases in children engaging in street vending in Bulawayo and Harare to earn income and pay school fees. This compounds an already challenging situation where the country has many children out of school (see Chipenda & Cochrane, 2024). The evidence highlighted in this section demonstrates that climate change transforms children's relationship with education from a developmental opportunity into a survival strategy, significantly altering childhood experiences and future prospects.

2.4.2 Health Implications and Disease Vulnerabilities

The analysis revealed that climate change significantly undermines children's right to health through multiple interconnected pathways that affect Zimbabwe's most vulnerable populations. These findings directly addressed the research question concerning how climate-induced environmental changes create differential impacts on children's rights across Zimbabwe's diverse contexts. The evidence from different studies indicates that health impacts manifest through both direct climate effects and indirect consequences of climate-induced social and economic disruptions, with children's immature immune systems making them vulnerable to environmental hazards including respiratory diseases, malnutrition, and infectious diseases resulting from air pollution, heatwaves, and decreased water quality (Ahdoot et al., 2024; Xu et al., 2012).

Building on this foundational understanding, disease outbreak analysis in the country reveals how climate change creates favourable conditions for vector-borne and waterborne diseases that pose significant risks to children's health and well-being. UNICEF (2025b) established a direct relationship between climate change and the frequency and severity of disease outbreaks. It was noted that increased temperatures and decreased rainfall create optimal breeding conditions for disease vectors such as mosquitoes and ticks that transmit malaria, dengue fever, and bilharzia. Children's vulnerability was found to stem from their immature immune systems and limited healthcare access, with evidence indicating that diseases like malaria and diarrhoea were expected to rise with changing climate patterns, further straining limited healthcare resources and compromising children's rights to health (Weeda et al., 2024). This pattern was exemplified in the case study of Muzarabani, where Gwitira et al. (2024) documented that waterborne diseases were the leading cause of disaster-related deaths among children, with cholera being the most widespread illness.

The systematic nature of these health vulnerabilities became evident through analysis of the 2018–2019 cholera outbreak, which exemplified how climate change amplified health risks for children. The outbreak was worsened by prolonged droughts and inadequate sanitation infrastructure, and the lack of clean water made it difficult to contain disease spread, especially in densely populated urban areas like Harare (Gwitira et al., 2024). This crisis demonstrated how climate-induced infrastructure failures created cascading health impacts that negatively affected children, highlighting the interconnected mechanisms through which climate change undermines children's rights across multiple domains simultaneously. Further evidence of systematic health system vulnerabilities emerged from Cyclone Idai's impacts, which showed how extreme weather events compromise children's health rights on multiple levels. Ray et al. (2022) documented that at least 270,000 people were affected, including 129,600 children, with more than 340 deaths, 51,000 displaced, and many missing. Manicaland health facilities initially recorded 354 cyclone-related hospital admissions, escalating to 21,952, of whom 64.3% were women. The health impacts included acute respiratory infections, malaria, dysentery, and diarrhoea cases, with trauma, injuries, multiple fractures, and lacerations constituting the main immediate health repercussions affecting women, children, and the elderly as the most vulnerable populations. This evidence, directly supported by the theoretical framework's emphasis on distributive justice, demonstrates how climate risks were not equally distributed but disproportionately burdened the most vulnerable populations, particularly children. The findings further revealed that systematic inadequacies in emergency preparedness compromised children's protection during climate-related disasters. Ray et al. (2022) found that a lack of preparedness, poor planning, inadequate resource mobilisation, and weak coordination hampered government response. Rural communities did not access early warning cyclone alerts disseminated through television, print, and social media nor did they appreciate the seriousness of events until it was too late. This preparedness failure significantly affected children, who required specialised protection during emergencies, highlighting procedural justice issues regarding meaningful participation in climate decision-making processes and demonstrating how existing inequalities were amplified during climate-related disasters.

The intersection of climate change with existing social inequalities in the Zimbabwe context is evident through analysis of gender-differentiated health impacts. These reveal how climate change intersects with traditional gender roles to create different vulnerabilities for boys and girls. Boys have been found to face specific risks through their traditional roles in livestock herding and agricultural labour, which expose them to harsh environmental conditions, including extreme heat, and this puts them at risk of heat-related symptoms and injuries associated with physical labour (Gwitira et al., 2024). In addition, the practice of boys sleeping outside to protect livestock increases their malaria risk during the rainy season, illustrating how traditional gender roles amplify climate-related health vulnerabilities. Conversely, girls have been found to experience health vulnerabilities related to their traditional roles involving collecting water, fetching firewood, and helping with farming activities. These expose them to prolonged periods under the sun and increase their risk of heat-related illnesses such as heat rashes, headaches, and fainting. Chigwanda et al. (2024) have documented changes in menstrual patterns in girls due to increased temperatures, often leading to embarrassing incidents that are further exacerbated by menstrual poverty, especially for girls in rural areas with limited access to sanitary wear.

Mental health impacts represent an underexplored but critical dimension of climate change effects on children's rights that demonstrate the comprehensive nature of climate-related health vulnerabilities. Gwitira et al. (2024) note that climate anxiety and stress related to extreme weather events have an impact on children's mental well-being, with fear and uncertainty surrounding climate change effects triggering anxiety as children worry about their communities' future, food and water availability, and family safety. Displacement compounds these mental health challenges, as the sudden loss of homes, schools, and community networks disrupts children's sense of security and belonging, resulting in stress, depression, and post-traumatic stress disorder (PTSD). This psychological trauma extends beyond individual children, as Ray et al. (2022) document psychological and post-traumatic stress among health staff working with survivors, as well as among those who have witnessed or suffered personal loss, for example, resulting from Cyclone Idai. The systematic disruption of community support systems creates lasting mental health consequences that undermine children's psychological well-being and developmental potential.

Healthcare system capacity and preparedness emerge as important factors amplifying children's health risks and compromising their right to health. This engages with and addresses the research question concerning specific mechanisms through which climate change undermines children's rights. UNICEF (2025a, 2025b) notes that climate-related disasters damage healthcare infrastructure, disrupt delivery services, and limit access to essential medicines and vaccines. The preparedness assessment by Sithole et al. (2021) reveals systemic inadequacies that affect children's health outcomes. Findings indicated that about 94% of districts in Zimbabwe had less than 50% of health workers trained to manage acute malnutrition.

Meanwhile, 26% of district hospitals and 32% of primary healthcare facilities were not admitting according to the integrated management of acute malnutrition protocol. It was established that 12 districts (63%) had none of their staff trained in infant and young child feeding, 58% had no staff trained in growth monitoring, and 63% of districts had no trained staff in the Baby-Friendly Hospital Initiative, directly compromising children's access to essential health services (Sithole et al., 2021). These capacity gaps were further contextualised by Tanyanyiwa and Muhwati's (2021) research in flood-prone Guruve, which revealed a disturbing prevalence of cardiovascular and respiratory diseases, diarrhoea, malnutrition, and waterborne and insect-transmitted diseases affecting all populations, with children being particularly vulnerable. Their findings demonstrated deep awareness of climate change among some residents, backed by observation, with most reporting that climate change made their lives worse. However, few possessed comprehensive climate literacy combining general awareness with basic knowledge about the phenomenon's origins and challenges (Tanyanyiwa & Muhwati, 2021). This finding highlights the issues of recognition justice, as it demonstrates the need to acknowledge diverse experiences and knowledge systems while building capacity for climate-informed health responses.

These findings demonstrate that climate change functions as a threat multiplier that systematically undermines children's rights to health across multiple interconnected domains. The evidence from different contexts establishes that climate-related health impacts are not randomly distributed but follow patterns of existing social and economic inequality, with the most marginalised children bearing the most significant burden of climate-induced health risks. This pattern directly supports the climate justice framework's emphasis on how populations with minimal contribution to global emissions bear the most severe climate consequences, thereby violating distributive, procedural, and recognition justice principles. The findings reveal that addressing these health vulnerabilities requires integrated approaches that address both immediate health service delivery and underlying structural inequalities that amplify children's climate-related health risks, thereby informing more equitable and child-focused approaches to climate adaptation and children's rights protection in Zimbabwe.

2.4.3 Food Security and Nutritional Challenges

Climate change significantly undermines children's right to adequate nutrition by systematically disrupting food systems and household food security. The relationship between climate change and child nutrition operates through three primary pathways identified by Gwitira et al. (2024). These include decreased diet diversity and food quality, negative impacts on child feeding practices, and impaired access to nutrition services alongside increased disease burdens. Zimbabwe's nutritional crisis reflects broader patterns of climate-induced food insecurity. Over 750,000 children between 6 months and 2 years (83%) are reportedly living in food poverty, not receiving adequately diverse diets sufficient for optimal growth and development, while over 500,000 children suffer from stunted growth, and 160,000 children suffer from wasting (Gwitira et al., 2024). These statistics represent violations of children's right to adequate nutrition as guaranteed under Article 24 of the UNCRC and directly undermine SDG 2's zero hunger commitment. Food insecurity is a significant issue, with climate change causing erratic rainfall and droughts that reduce agricultural productivity. This leads to hunger and malnutrition among children, with their nutritional status compromised, affecting their growth and cognitive development and violating their rights (Chikoko & Chihiya, 2023; Xu et al., 2012).

El Niño events demonstrate the acute impacts of climate variability on child nutrition. Zimbabwe's last major El Niño event in 2016 caused a 25% increase in children admitted for treatment of severe wasting, with similar rises in wasting admissions following the 2023/2024 El Niño event (Gwitira et al., 2024). These cyclical patterns reveal how climate variability creates predictable but inadequately addressed nutritional crises that violate children's rights to health and development. The case of Cyclone Idai illustrates the acute nutritional impacts of extreme weather events across multiple studies. Charamba et al. (2024) found that the cyclone destroyed food reserves, restricted access to basic needs, and caused unaffordable prices for many. Children were significantly affected because they relied on food from caregivers and guardians, worsening their nutritional status. This was worsened by limited social protection programs for food, especially for supplementing the nutrition of children and young individuals. Dembedza et al. (2023) conducted a mixed-methods study in Manicaland, examining the relationship between climate change and nutritional status following Cyclone Idai. Their research revealed that the cyclone negatively affected most food security indicators, with only relocated households faring better, possibly due to aid. There were variations in diet quality, and though household-level dietary diversity was adequate, this did not translate to adequate women and child dietary diversity, with food security indicators for children below acceptable levels, indicating inadequacy of relief activities for children's and women's dietary requirements (Dembedza et al., 2023).

Gender dimensions of nutritional vulnerability emerge through household food distribution practices and climate adaptation strategies. Dembedza et al. (2023) found that women, especially pregnant women and lactating mothers, suffer from malnutrition because food preference is given to men and children, with access to required and expected food diminished due to the washing away of food reserves. However, Gwitira et al. (2024) noted that malnutrition affects boys and girls differently, often depending on household food distribution practices, with some cultures giving boys larger food portions or higher-priority access to nutritious food, leaving girls more vulnerable to food shortage effects. Regional studies provide additional evidence of climate-nutrition linkages. Sithole et al. (2021) conducted qualitative research highlighting malnutrition as a significant challenge for children due to climate change-induced droughts in indigenous communities in the Save Valley area of Chipinge District. Their findings showed that climate variability heightened the frequency and intensity of shocks such as floods, with socio-economic disruptions from these shocks and slow recovery cycles in affected communities worsening their vulnerability to climate change (Sithole et al., 2021). Gwenzi et al. (2022) provide evidence from Uzumba Maramba Pfungwe (UMP) district showing how climate change led to decreased food production, resulting in fewer daily meals and causing malnutrition in households, especially among children. Their survey results showed that rainfed food production systems collapsed during droughts and severe dry spells, leading to food shortages and reduced daily meals. In contrast, food prices increased, livestock prices slumped, and pests and diseases increased, affecting breeding (Gwenzi et al., 2022).

Climate knowledge and adaptation strategies paradoxically create new nutritional risks for children. Kembo et al. (2025) found that climate change knowledge significantly influences changes in child feeding practices among rural households in Zimbabwe. Households knowledgeable about climate change were more likely to reduce the amount and diversity of food provided to children as a coping mechanism, with caregivers often limiting food quantity and diversity to one or two food groups during climate-induced stress periods such as droughts (Kembo et al., 2025). These findings highlight how well-intentioned adaptation strategies can violate children's nutritional rights. The ultra-processed food transition represents an additional climate-nutrition nexus. Gwitira et al. (2024) noted that ultra-processed foods are linked to more biodiversity loss, greenhouse gases, and plastic pollution than other food types, with the massive growth in production and marketing of cheap, nutrient-poor, ultra-processed foods becoming one of the greatest threats to child nutrition. They provide evidence showing rates of overweight rising rapidly with age, from 3% among children less than 5 years to 13% among adolescents 15–19 years and 54% among women 40–49 years.

Seasonal food insecurity patterns reflect systematic failures in climate adaptation planning. During the lean season from January to March 2024, an estimated 1.2 million children in Zimbabwe experience food insecurity, leading to potential school dropouts, particularly among girls (Gwitira et al., 2024). This seasonal vulnerability demonstrates how climate change creates predictable patterns of children's rights violations that could be mitigated through more effective adaptation planning. Regional variations in nutritional vulnerability reveal geographic inequalities in climate impacts. Districts in eastern Zimbabwe (Chipinge, Chimanimani, Mutare, Mutasa), northern Zimbabwe (Mt Darwin), and south-western Zimbabwe (Matobo, Bulilima, Beitbridge) are parts of the country which are characterised by higher stunting prevalence than other areas (Gwitira et al., 2024). These patterns reflect how climate change interacts with existing geographic and socio-economic inequalities to create differentiated impacts on children's nutritional rights.

2.4.4 Water Access and Sanitation Inequalities

Climate change undermines children's rights to water and sanitation by systematically disrupting water systems and creating new vulnerabilities around water access. The evidence reveals how water scarcity creates cascading impacts across multiple dimensions of children's well-being while exacerbating existing gender and social inequalities. Time poverty and educational impacts emerge as primary consequences of climate-induced water scarcity. Gwitira et al. (2024) documented that the worsening water crisis in Zimbabwe, marked by limited and drying boreholes in urban and peri-urban areas, has escalated competition and conflict over water resources. Children, especially girls, are the worst affected, often spending hours in long queues to fetch water. This time burden directly undermines educational rights, significantly impacting education, including increasing school absenteeism, dropout rates, and lower academic performance.

Climate change impacts children's health through increased air pollution, weather-related disasters, and food and water shortages, which are critical issues in Zimbabwe, contributing to malnutrition, infectious diseases, and mental disorders among children. These also hinder educational opportunities as children may be forced to leave school to help secure resources, violating their rights to both health and education (Chipenda & Cochrane, 2024; Xu et al., 2012). Gender-based violence around water access represents a critical intersection of climate change and child protection failures. Gwitira et al. (2024) revealed an alarming increase in abuse of girls at water points, where they are often coerced into exploitative or transactional sexual relationships to gain access to water. This phenomenon, termed 'sextortion', is prevalent in urban and peri-urban areas such as Harare, where communal boreholes have become primary water sources due to the persistent failure of local councils to provide reliable tap water. The systematic nature of water-related sexual exploitation illustrates failures in child protection systems. In high-density suburbs like Epworth, Budiriro, and Mbare, where boreholes have been drilled to address chronic water shortages, reports of harassment and exploitation at water points have become common, with men who either guard boreholes or are first in line to collect water demanding sexual favours in exchange for allowing girls access to the limited water supply (Gwitira et al., 2024).

Decreased water availability and quality due to climate change exacerbate sanitation issues, increasing the risk of waterborne diseases among children, with access to clean water being critical. Yet climate change-induced droughts and floods disrupt water supply systems and violate children's rights to water and sanitation (Xu et al., 2012). Menstrual hygiene management emerges as an important dimension of water-related gender inequalities. Drought-induced water shortages significantly hinder menstrual hygiene management and can lead to bullying and isolation that adversely affect academic focus and participation (Gwitira et al., 2024). The evidence shows approximately 60% of rural women and girls experiencing period poverty, with girls facing this issue reportedly missing up to 20% of their school life (Gwitira et al., 2024).

Waterborne disease vulnerabilities reveal how climate change amplifies existing health inequalities. Boys are more often affected by waterborne diseases such as bilharzia and cholera, which surge following floods that contaminate water sources and during droughts that force communities to use untreated water. The health risks extend beyond immediate illness to educational consequences, as children who rely on unsafe water sources during climate events face heightened risk of contracting diseases like dysentery and diarrhoea, with these health risks not only threatening well-being but also leading to increased absenteeism and declining academic performance (Gwitira et al., 2024). Sanitation system failures compound these water-related vulnerabilities. Flooding in districts such as Chimanimani often damages sanitation infrastructure, making latrines and toilets unusable, leading to open defecation and contaminating water sources, increasing the spread of waterborne diseases such as cholera, typhoid, and dysentery. These impacts affect women, especially pregnant women, who are more vulnerable to health risks associated with poor sanitation. Sithole et al. (2023) found that women are vulnerable to water and sanitation issues, which impact their menstrual hygiene and compromise their nutritional status, especially as they prioritise feeding children and men. Their research revealed that individuals with disabilities, including children, experience diverse challenges based on the type and severity of their disability. Those having hearing impairments (including children) face barriers as they lack access to essential information on disaster preparedness (triggered by climate change) and are typically the last to receive information translated into sign language (Sithole et al., 2023).

2.4.5 *Intersectional Vulnerabilities and Social Protection Failures*

The Zimbabwe context reveals how climate change intersects with multiple forms of social inequality to create compound vulnerabilities for different groups of children. These intersectional impacts demonstrate the inadequacy of universal approaches to climate adaptation and highlight the need for differentiated justice-oriented responses. Disability intersects with climate vulnerability to create disadvantages. Gwitira et al. (2024) found that children with disabilities may face challenges in mobility, communication, or self-care, making it difficult to respond to emergencies caused by climate hazards. The evidence shows differential patterns for boys and girls with disabilities. Boys with disabilities face a greater risk of injury or harm during crises due to social expectations to participate in rescue or high-risk activities, along with increased pressure to abandon education to find work and provide for family needs. For girls with disabilities, vulnerabilities include increased risk of gender-based violence during displacement due to perceived vulnerabilities, compromised health due to inadequate access to sanitary products, and high risk of early marriage as a means of securing economic or physical safety (Gwitira et al., 2024).

Geographic inequalities reveal systematic differences in climate vulnerability between urban and rural contexts. Location-based disparities highlight how rural and peri-urban children, regardless of gender, face more severe challenges than those in urban areas, with increased distance from essential services like schools and healthcare centres exacerbating vulnerability, especially when critical infrastructure is damaged during natural disasters. Rural children face additional disadvantages through limited diversity and flexibility of livelihood options, lacking assets and infrastructure critical to resilience, since poorer people tend to lose more relative to high vulnerability. Climate change in Zimbabwe significantly affects rural children, whose vulnerabilities are pronounced due to the effects of poverty and limited access to resources, with these impacts manifesting in various ways from health issues to educational disruptions and being worsened by socio-economic factors that undermine their rights (Ahdoot et al., 2024).

Age-based vulnerabilities reveal how climate impacts vary across developmental stages. Children under five are susceptible to climate-related health problems such as acute malnutrition, with younger children at higher risk of low birth weight, congenital defects, cardiovascular diseases, and developmental challenges, including poor mental health (Gwitira et al., 2024). These early-life impacts have lasting consequences, as malnutrition in the early years is often irreversible and affects school performance, earning potential, and health and nutrition in later life. Protective factors such as economic stability, access to quality healthcare, adequate infrastructure, and food security are crucial for the protection of children's rights. However, challenges in these areas in regions like Zimbabwe can worsen the impacts of climate change on health, education, food, water, and sanitation for children (Weeda et al., 2024).

Social protection system inadequacies emerge as a critical factor amplifying climate vulnerabilities. The level of child protection across the country shows that children who lack the protection of parents or family caregivers are more vulnerable to disasters, with a lack of social protection, including policies and programmes that protect children against poverty, vulnerability, and social exclusion, resulting in children becoming more vulnerable to climate change (Gwitira et al., 2024). Economic vulnerabilities intersect with climate change to create poverty traps that perpetuate children's disadvantage. Sithole et al. (2021) revealed how poverty is at the heart of vulnerability, with climate change potentially deepening inherited or intergenerational poverty as households continually living on the cusp of disaster find it challenging to prioritise building intergenerational wealth. This pattern is pronounced in Manicaland Province, which is home to the largest proportion of poor children (80.4% of children in the province live in poverty) of any province in Zimbabwe (Sithole et al., 2021).

The study by Sithole et al. (2021) on indigenous communities in the Save Valley area of Chipinge District revealed the dynamic relationship between climate change, disaster risk reduction, and socio-economic well-being. Their findings show that climate change-related shocks can disrupt family and societal cohesion if mishandled. They can do this by worsening gender-based violence, widening gender disparities, and deepening vulnerabilities of traditionally marginalised community members such as women, children, people living with disabilities, and the aged (Sithole et al., 2021). Gender disparities in climate knowledge access create additional vulnerabilities. Kembo et al. (2025) found that female-headed households were significantly less likely to know about climate change, yet women play a key role in household food security and child nutrition. This finding supports prior research demonstrating that women and girls are not only disproportionately affected by climate change but also face barriers in accessing climate-related information (Kembo et al., 2025).

2.5 Discussion

The evidence from Zimbabwe demonstrates that climate change constitutes a multidimensional children's rights crisis. It systematically compromises UNCRC provisions while undermining SDG progress through three interconnected dimensions of climate injustice. Distributive justice failures manifest through the geographic and social concentration of climate risks among Zimbabwe's most vulnerable children, where rural, impoverished, and disabled populations bear climate burdens despite minimal contribution to global emissions. The concentration of stunting in the country's eastern, northern, and south-western districts exemplifies how climate change amplifies existing inequalities rather than creating new disparities.

Procedural justice violations emerge through systematic exclusion from climate adaptation planning, where community reliance on informal coping mechanisms for education, water access, and health services shifts adaptation responsibilities to affected populations rather than systematic policy responses. The absence of child-specific early warning systems, evident in communities' failure to appreciate Cyclone Idai's severity until impact, highlights inadequate incorporation of children's vulnerabilities in climate governance structures. Recognition of justice failures manifests through treating children as a uniform demographic group, overlooking gender-specific vulnerability patterns, disability-specific challenges, and urban-rural differences that demand differentiated policy responses.

Climate change operates through existing inequality systems to create vulnerabilities that exceed individual risk factors. Gender-based violence around water access, disability-specific evacuation challenges, and age-differentiated health vulnerabilities demonstrate intersectional impacts requiring integrated responses beyond sectoral approaches. Despite Zimbabwe's UNCRC, ACRWC ratification, and SDG commitments, systematic violations of children's rights to education, health, water, sanitation, and protection persist, reflecting broader challenges in implementing rights-based approaches within contexts characterised by resource constraints and institutional weaknesses. Climate adaptation strategies paradoxically create new risks while attempting to address climate vulnerabilities. Reduced food diversity by climate-knowledgeable households, child marriage as a disaster coping mechanism, and girls' educational exclusion during family migration demonstrate how adaptation can inadvertently violate children's rights. These patterns highlight the need for rights-safeguarding approaches that consider potential negative consequences for children while addressing climate vulnerabilities.

Significant implementation gaps exist between international frameworks and local realities. While the UNCRC, ACRWC, Paris Agreement, and SDGs provide normative foundations, evidence reveals inadequate translation into effective national and local policies. The systematic unpreparedness revealed by climate-induced natural disasters and ongoing vulnerabilities across health, education, and protection systems demonstrates the need for robust accountability mechanisms and enhanced implementation support. Climate impacts create immediate rights violations and long-term developmental disadvantages through temporal complexity, requiring urgent attention. Irreversible impacts from early childhood malnutrition, educational disruption during critical development periods, and trauma from climate-induced displacement demonstrate how climate change creates predictable patterns of rights violations that could be mitigated through more effective adaptation planning. This temporal dimension necessitates climate responses addressing both immediate protection needs and longer-term prevention strategies. Market-based and technical approaches prove insufficient for addressing climate-induced rights violations, suggesting the need for transformative, justice-oriented responses. While community coping mechanisms demonstrate remarkable resilience, they remain inadequate to address systemic climate risks facing children. Digital divides, infrastructure inequalities, and healthcare system inadequacies reveal how technical solutions can exacerbate rather than reduce inequalities without attention to justice considerations.

The systematic nature of climate-induced rights violations documented across diverse Zimbabwe contexts reflects broader patterns across the Global South, indicating the need for comprehensive international support mechanisms. National-level responses prove insufficient to address climate risks that transcend boundaries and exceed national capacities, pointing to enhanced international solidarity requirements recognising climate change as a global challenge demanding collective responsibility for protecting children's rights. Post-2030 development frameworks must integrate climate justice principles with children's rights protection through more holistic approaches. The systematic undermining of multiple SDG targets demonstrates the inadequacy of sectoral approaches to addressing climate-induced rights violations. Future frameworks require integrated, justice-oriented approaches focused on children's rights, amplifying their voices while addressing root causes of climate vulnerability through transformative social and economic change. They must recognise children as rights holders rather than merely beneficiaries of climate protection efforts.

2.6 Conclusion

This chapter reveals that climate change in Zimbabwe functions as both an environmental crisis and a systematic violation of children's rights, demanding urgent justice-oriented responses. The evidence demonstrates that climate impacts are neither random nor equally distributed but follow existing patterns of inequality that burden the most vulnerable children. The failure of current approaches to adequately protect children's rights in climate-vulnerable contexts highlights the need for transformative changes in how climate adaptation and children's rights protection are conceptualised and implemented. The climate justice framework provides essential analytical tools for understanding these dynamics and developing more equitable responses. However, translating justice principles into effective policy interventions requires addressing structural inequalities that amplify children's climate vulnerabilities. This includes strengthening social protection systems, ensuring meaningful child participation in climate governance, and developing differentiated approaches recognising diverse experiences and knowledge systems.

Moving forward, post-2030 development frameworks must adopt integrated approaches that recognise the interconnected nature of climate change and children's rights. Success will depend on enhanced international cooperation, increased investment in climate-resilient infrastructure and services, and shifts towards justice-focused approaches prioritising the rights and voices of the most vulnerable children. In Zimbabwe, these proposed changes will have significant positive implications for children, primarily through improved access to climate-resilient education systems; enhanced health services that can better respond to climate-related health challenges; strengthened food and nutrition security programmes that protect children from malnutrition during climate-induced disruptions; sustainable agricultural initiatives that ensure long-term food security while teaching children environmental stewardship; and robust social protection mechanisms that safeguard children's welfare during climate emergencies. Only through such comprehensive transformation can the international community fulfil its obligations to protect children's rights in an era of climate change, ensuring that Zimbabwean children, alongside their global peers, can build resilience and thrive despite environmental challenges.

References

ACERWC. (2025). *ACERWC study on climate change & children's rights in Africa: A continental overview - 2024*. ACERWC Secretariat.

Ahdoot, S., Baum, C. R., Cataletto, M. B., Hogan, P., Wu, C. B., & Bernstein, A. (2024). Climate change and children's health: Building a healthy future for every child. *Pediatrics, 153*(3), e2023065505. https://doi.org/10.1542/peds.2023-065505

Amini, A., Abedi, M., Nesari, E., Daryadel, E., Kolahi, M., Mianabadi, H., & Fisher, J. L. (2023). The Paris Agreement's approach toward climate change loss and damage. *World Affairs, 186*(1), 46–80. https://doi.org/10.1177/00438200221147936

Arvanitis, C. (2024). Systematic literature review in five steps. *Journal of the Acoustical Society of America, 155*, A103. https://doi.org/10.1121/10.0026958

Boshoff, E., & Damtew, S. G. (2023). The potential of litigating children's rights in the climate crisis before the African Committee of Experts on the Rights and Welfare of the Child. *African Human Rights Law Journal, 22*(2), 1–34. https://doi.org/10.17159/1996-2096/2022/v22n2a1

Bourdillon, M., Driscoll, J., Myers, W., O'Kane, C., & Rink, P. (2024). Climate crisis as a form of structural violence against children and youth. *BMJ Paediatrics Open, 8*(1), e003059. https://doi.org/10.1136/bmjpo-2024-003059

Brignardello-Petersen, R., Santesso, N., & Guyatt, G. H. (2025). Systematic reviews of the literature: An introduction to current methods. *American Journal of Epidemiology, 194*(2), 536–542. https://doi.org/10.1093/aje/kwae232

Bulat, D. (2024). Climate change, children's rights and the rights of future generations. *Contemporary Issues of Communication, 3*(2), 165–172. https://doi.org/10.62425/conicom.1520699

Charamba, S., Mushunje, M., Mwapaura, K., Simango, T. G., & Risinamhodzi, N. (2024). Climate change and vulnerable groups in Zimbabwe: Implications for social work practice. *Journal of Social Development in Africa, 39*(2), 68–87. https://doi.org/10.4314/jsda.v39i2.5

Chigwanda, E., Mutopo, P., & Mutanana, N. (2024). The health-related impacts of climate change faced by in-school adolescent girls in rural Zimbabwe. *Journal of Education and Practice, 15*(6), 1–16.

Chikoko, W., & Chihiya, P. (2023). Climate change and vulnerabilities of children in rural Zimbabwe: The case of ward 14 of Bikita District, Zimbabwe. *African Journal of Social Work, 13*(2), 78–86. https://doi.org/10.4314/ajsw.v13i2.4

Chipenda, C., & Cochrane, L. (2024). Out of school children in the context of new policy trajectories and interlocking crises in Zimbabwe: A transformative social policy perspective. *SN Social Sciences, 4*, 131. https://doi.org/10.1007/s43545-024-00938-1

Dembedza, V. P., Chopera, P., Mapara, J., Muchindi, M., Chatira, A., Kembo, J., Mufunda, E., Manhanzva, T., Gombe, N. T., Juru, T. P., Shambira, G., Bangure, D., & Tshimanga, M. (2023). The relationship between climate change induced natural disasters and selected nutrition outcomes: A case of cyclone Idai, Zimbabwe. *BMC Nutrition, 9*, 19. https://doi.org/10.1186/s40795-023-00679-z

Duyck, S. (2015). The Paris climate agreement and the protection of human rights in a changing climate. *Yearbook of International Environmental Law, 26*, 3–45. https://doi.org/10.1093/YIEL/YVX011

Fambasayi, R., & Addaney, M. (2021). Cascading impacts of climate change and the rights of children in Africa: A reflection on the principle of intergenerational equity. *African Human Rights Law Journal, 21*(1), 29–51. https://doi.org/10.17159/1996-2096/2021/V21N1A3

Farber, D. A., & Peeters, M. (2016). The emergence of global climate law. In D. A. Farber, & M. Peeters (Eds.), *Climate Change Law* (pp. 687–702). Edward Elgar Publishing. https://doi.org/10.4337/9781783477616.I.56

Fokala, E., & Muhumuza, N. (2024). Eroding children's rights: An analysis of the utility of the African Charter on the Rights and Welfare of the Child to climate action in Africa. *The Social, Economic and Cultural Rights of Children in Africa*, 222–245. https://doi.org/10.1163/9789004685604_010

Gibbons, E. D. (2014). Climate change, children's rights, and the pursuit of intergenerational climate justice. *Health and Human Rights, 16*(1) Retrieved August 1, 2025, from https://www.hhrjournal.org/2014/07/01/climate-change-childrens-rights-and-the-pursuit-of-intergenerational-climate-justice/

Government of Zimbabwe. (2013). *Constitution of the Republic of Zimbabwe*. Government Printers.

Government of Zimbabwe. (2024). *Zimbabwe national climate change adaptation plan*. Ministry of Environment, Climate and Wildlife.

Gwenzi, J., Mafongoya, P. L., & Mashonjowa, E. (2022). Effects of climate change on food production in semi-arid areas: A case study of Uzumba Maramba Pfungwe district, Zimbabwe. In *Handbook of climate change across the food supply chain* (pp. 451–465). Springer. https://link.springer.com/chapter/10.1007/978-3-030-87934-1_26

Gwitira, I., Shekede, M. D., & Bhatasara, S. (2024). *Child-centred climate impact, vulnerability, and risk assessment for Zimbabwe*. UNICEF.

Intergovernmental Panel on Climate Change. (2023). *Climate change 2022: Impacts, adaptation, and vulnerability. Contribution of Working Group II to the Sixth Assessment Report of the Intergovernmental Panel on Climate Change*. Cambridge University Press. https://doi.org/10.1017/9781009325844

Islam, S. N., & Winkel, J. (2017). *Climate change and social inequality* (DESA Working Paper No 152 ST/ESA/2017/DWP/152). United Nations, Department of Economics and Social Affairs. Retrieved from https://bhekisisa.org/wp-content/uploads/2023/09/wp152_2017.pdf

Kabir, R., Hayhoe, R. P. G., Mercy Bai, A. C., Vinnakota, D., Sivasubramanian, M., Afework, S., Chilaka, M., Mohammadnezhad, M., Aremu, O., Sah, R. K., Khan, H. T. A., Messner, S., Syed, H. Z., & Parsa, A. D. (2023). The systematic literature review process: A simple guide for public health and allied health students. *International Journal of Research in Medical Sciences, 11*(9), 3498–3506. https://doi.org/10.18203/2320-6012.ijrms20232496

Kahomwe, L., & Muzingili, T. (2025). Impact of climate change disasters on access to education and coping mechanisms for rural learners in Zimbabwe. *Cogent Education, 12*(1). https://doi.org/10.1080/2331186X.2025.2517505

Kembo, G., Kairiza, T., Dembedza, M. P., Manditsera, F. A., & Macheka, L. (2025). Climate change knowledge and changes in child feeding practices in rural Zimbabwe. *Journal of Hunger & Environmental Nutrition, 1–14*. https://doi.org/10.1080/19320248.2025.2532132

Nhemachena, C., Nhamo, L., Matchaya, G., Nhemachena, C. R., Muchara, B., Karuaihe, S. T., & Mpandeli, S. (2020). Climate change impacts on water and agriculture sectors in Southern Africa: Threats and opportunities for sustainable development. *Water, 12*(10), 2673. https://doi.org/10.3390/w12102673

Nkrumah, B. (2018). Edible backyards: Climate change and urban food (in)security in Africa. *Agriculture & Food Security, 7*, 45. https://doi.org/10.1186/s40066-018-0196-y

Onyeaka, H., Nwauzoma, U. M., Akinsemolu, A. A., Tamasiga, P., Duan, K., Al-Sharify, Z. T., & Siyanbola, K. F. (2024). The ripple effects of climate change on agricultural sustainability and food security in Africa. *Food and Energy Security, 13*, e567. https://doi.org/10.1002/fes3.567

Organisation of African Unity. (1990, July 11). *African Charter on the Rights and Welfare of the Child*. OAU.

Pardo Buendía, M., & Ortega, J. (2018). Environmental justice and climate justice: The slow but irreversible path towards fair, sustainable development. *Barataria. Revista Castellano-Manchega de Ciencias Sociales, 24*, 83–100. https://doi.org/10.20932/barataria.v0i24.415

Puaschunder, J. (2020). *Governance & climate justice: Global South & developing nations*. Palgrave Macmillan. https://doi.org/10.1007/978-3-319-63281-0

Ray, S., Goronga, T., Chigiya, P. T., & Madzimbamuto, F. D. (2022). Climate change, disaster management and primary health care in Zimbabwe. *African Journal of Primary Health Care & Family Medicine, 14*(1), 1–3. https://doi.org/10.4102/phcfm.v14i1.3684

Ruel, M. T., Garrett, J. L., & Yosef, S. (2017). Food security and nutrition: Growing cities, new challenges. In *2017 global food policy report* (pp. 24–33). International Food Policy Research Institute (IFPRI). https://doi.org/10.2499/9780896292529_03

Sithole, P. K., Mawere, M., & Mubaya, T. R. (2023). Socio-economic impacts of climate change on indigenous communities in the Save Valley area of Chipinge district, Zimbabwe. *Frontiers in Environmental Economics, 2*, 1135831. https://doi.org/10.3389/frevc.2023.1135831

Sithole, Z., Nyadzayo, T., Kanyowa, T., Mathieu, J., Kambarami, T., Nemaramba, M., & Gasasira, A. (2021). Enhancing capacity of Zimbabwe's health system to respond to climate change-induced drought: A rapid nutritional assessment. *Pan African Medical Journal, 40*(113), 2–11. https://doi.org/10.11604/pamj.2021.40.113.30545

Staparski, T. (2023). Climate changes in the practice of the UN committee on the rights of a child. *Pravo - teorija i praksa, 40*(2), 101–111.

Tanyanyiwa, V. I., & Muhwati, T. (2021). Attitudes towards climate change in a rural district in Zimbabwe: Indications from Guruve District. In W. Leal Filho, J. Luetz, & D. Ayal (Eds.), *Handbook of climate change management. Research, leadership, transformation* (pp. 3561–3579). Springer International Publishing.

Tawodzera, G. (2011). Vulnerability in crisis: Urban household food insecurity in Epworth, Harare, Zimbabwe. *Food Security, 3*(4), 503–520. https://doi.org/10.1007/S12571-011-0152-1

Tokar, B. (2018). On the evolution and continuing development of the climate justice movement. In *Routledge handbook of climate justice* (pp. 13–25). Routledge. https://doi.org/10.4324/9781315537689-2

UNICEF. (2021). *The climate crisis is a child rights crisis: Introducing the children's climate risk index*. UNICEF.

UNICEF. (2025a). When the rains don't come: Climate change through the eyes of Zimbabwe's children. Retrieved from https://www.unicef.org/zimbabwe/stories/when-rains-dont-come-climate-change-through-eyes-zimbabwes-children

UNICEF. (2025b). Child rights and climate. The climate crisis is a child rights crisis, and it is happening. Retrieved from https://www.unicef.org/esa/child-rights-and-climate

United Nations. (1989, November 20). *Convention on the rights of the child* (Treaty series) (Vol. 1577). UN.

Vanderheiden, S. (2021). Justice and climate change. In T. M. Letcher (Ed.), *The impacts of climate change: A comprehensive study of physical, biophysical, social, and political issues* (pp. 491–501). Elsevier. https://doi.org/10.1016/B978-0-12-822373-4.00001-X

Višić, M. (2022). Connecting puzzle pieces: Systematic literature review method in the social sciences. *Sociologija, 64*(4), 543–569. https://doi.org/10.2298/SOC2204543V

Weeda, L. J. Z., Bradshaw, C. J. A., Judge, M. A., Saraswati, C. M., & Le Souëf, P. N. (2024). How climate change degrades child health: A systematic review and meta-analysis. *Science of the Total Environment, 920*, 170944. https://doi.org/10.1016/j.scitotenv.2024.170944

Xu, Z., Sheffield, P. E., Hu, W., Su, H., Yu, W., Qi, X., & Tong, S. (2012). Climate change and children's health—A call for research on what works to protect children. *International Journal of Environmental Research and Public Health, 9*, 3298–3316. https://doi.org/10.3390/ijerph9093298

ZimStat. (2022). *2022 Zimbabwe National Population and household census*. ZimStat.

Chapter 3
Multi-Species Justice and Children's Rights: Reinterpreting Constitutional Protections in Africa

Emerge Masiya and Sithandweyinkosi Nkomo

3.1 Introduction

3.1.1 Background of Multi-Species Justice and its Origins from Climate Justice

The glaring realities of climate change cannot be underestimated nor mythicised. The court in *VZW Klimaatzaak v. Kingdom of Belgium and Others (2021)* noted that 'climate science leaves no room for doubt that a real threat of dangerous climate change exists'. In addition, it was projected by the Climate Vulnerability Monitor (2012) that economic losses from floods, storms, and landslides alone will reach $194 billion per year by 2030. Between 80% and 90% of economic costs will fall on developing countries, where, on average, children and youth make up at least half of the population (Gibbons, 2014). The predictions indicate that by 2040, one in four children will live in areas with extreme water shortages, most of whom will be in Africa. In Zimbabwe specifically, 6.5 million children representing 47% of the population face significant risks from climate-induced emergencies, with the country ranked as the 15th most vulnerable globally to climate change impacts (see Chipenda & Chawanda, Chap. 2, in this volume).

Despite the evident victimisation of children because of climate change, the international community is only now awakening to the idea of children and youth as environmental actors and stakeholders through cases like *Future Generations v. Ministry of the Environment and Others (2018)*, *Environmental Justice Australia*

E. Masiya (✉)
Hebert Chitepo Law School, Great Zimbabwe University, Masvingo, Zimbabwe

S. Nkomo
Institute of Development Sciences, National University of Science and Technology, Bulawayo, Zimbabwe

E. Ndhlovu, C. Chipenda (eds.), *Climate Change and Children's Rights in Zimbabwe*, https://doi.org/10.1007/978-981-95-6005-9_3

(EJA) v. Australia (2021), and *Herrera Carrion* et al. *v Ministry of Environment* et al. *(2020) (Caso Mecheros)*, among others. Children are also considered in court decisions, as reflected in the *African Climate Alliance and Others v Minister of Mineral Resources and Energy and Others (2024)* (also known as the #CancelCoal case). Thus far, the court decisions have been reactive. However, these judicial responses remain insufficient in addressing the accelerating climate crisis and its disproportionate impacts on African children, who bear the most significant burden despite contributing least to global emissions (see Chipenda & Ndhlovu, Introduction, in this volume).

Environmental protection and climate change issues are imperative to children's rights today. According to the UN Special Rapporteur on human rights and the environment, a safe, clean, healthy, and sustainable development is integral to the full enjoyment of a wide range of human rights, including the right to life, health, food, water, and sanitation (United Nations Environment Programme, n.d.). Without a healthy environment, we cannot fulfil aspirations within the minimum standards of human dignity. Thus, a less nuanced understanding of the right to a safe and healthy environment and a strategic approach to interpreting the same right are necessary to implement this right effectively. In climate-vulnerable contexts like Zimbabwe, where children face extreme exposure to droughts, floods, heatwaves, and tropical cyclones, the need for robust constitutional protections becomes even more urgent. As documented across multiple districts in this volume, climate change is extending children's rights inequalities and exacerbating violations among rural school learners, affecting their health, education, and protection from exploitation (see Mando et al., Chap. 10, in this volume; Chenzi & Pahuwa, Chap. 6, in this volume).

While recent jurisprudence has begun to acknowledge children as environmental stakeholders, these efforts remain largely reactive and anthropocentric. Traditional rights frameworks often fail to account for harm's relational and ecological dimensions, thus treating children as passive victims rather than embedded participants in multi-species ecosystems (Sturman et al., 2025). For example, traditional frameworks are property focused (MacDonald, 1991). Environmental damage is often seen as property damage while sidelining cultural, spiritual, and ecological values. This conceptual gap calls for a more expansive interpretive lens that recognises the interconnectedness of human and more-than-human life. This limitation is problematic in addressing climate change impacts, where the destruction of ecosystems directly threatens children's survival, health, education, and development. These rights are fundamentally interconnected with ecological integrity.

While climate change literature increasingly acknowledges children as disproportionately affected by environmental degradation, much of this scholarship remains anthropocentric, framing children as passive victims rather than ecologically embedded actors. Existing studies, such as Sanson and Burke (2020), emphasise intergenerational justice but rarely interrogate the ontological assumptions that separate children from the more-than-human world. Constitutional interpretations of environmental rights often rely on narrow readings of 'health' and 'safety' that exclude ecological interdependence. The court acknowledged children's vulnerability in cases like *African Climate Alliance v. Minister of Mineral Resources and*

Energy (2024). However, it did not protect the multi-species networks that sustain their well-being. This reactive posture limits the transformative potential of environmental rights jurisprudence in addressing the systemic and interconnected nature of climate impacts on children's rights.

Multi-species justice (MSJ) is an approach that is not only involved in expanding the subjects of justice. It is a shift from focusing on individuals to the relational webs sustaining all life and recognising the ontological enmeshment of humans and Earth's other ecosystems (Sturman et al., 2025). A multi-species justice approach expands climate justice by decentring humanity and recognising the everyday relations that bind individuals and societies to networks of close and distant others, including others and more-than-human beings. Such an approach is essential for addressing the complex vulnerabilities, where climate impacts cascade across water, agriculture, health, and education systems, creating interconnected threats to children's well-being as argued by Moyo et al. (Chap. 4, in this volume).

This chapter examines the constitutional entrenchment of the right to a safe and healthy environment in Zimbabwe, South Africa, Uganda, and Kenya. These nations represent diverse constitutional frameworks and legal traditions within Africa, ranging from South Africa's transformative constitutionalism to Uganda's judicial activism in defence of ecological rights and Kenya's evolving human rights jurisprudence. Compared to Zimbabwe, these countries have paved the way for children's rights protection in environmental governance. Zimbabwe has similar legal frameworks but lacks jurisprudence. While countries like Kenya and South Africa face greater threats in coastal areas, their exemplary implementation of existing legal frameworks demands a comparative examination. Uganda, like Zimbabwe, borders Kenya but seems to be making more strides in general environmental protection than Zimbabwe. This diversity enriches comparative analysis, revealing how multi-species justice might be integrated or resisted in varying legal cultures.

This chapter first provides an overview of MSJ as a theoretical framework ideal for children's rights protection in environmental and climate change law. It also identifies traits within multi-species justice that have the potential to reaffirm children's rights and provide more secure protections. Lastly, it proffers different ways of interpreting the right to a safe and clean environment to protect children's rights in the face of accelerating climate change impacts.

3.2 Multi-Species Justice as a Theoretical Framework

While most scholars credit Haraway (Celermajer et al., 2021), McKibbin (2025) credits Heise, who suggested multi-species justice in framing environmentalist thinking at the Green Citizenship Symposium. MSJ calls for a more inclusive approach to addressing environmental and social challenges by considering the needs of all species and ecosystems (Winter & Schlosberg, 2023). The foundational ideas of MSJ, however, are not all new. Several of them reflect principles and understandings that have been prevalent (in multiple ways) among non-Western, indigenous cultures, and knowledge systems worldwide (Winter & Schlosberg, 2023). Willis emphasises that MSJ traces the contributions it has been gathering from disciplines and fields as diverse as STS, animal rights theories, ecofeminism, environmental justice, posthumanism, indigenous and decolonial thought, cultural anthropology, and political ecology, among others, can be found elsewhere (Houart et al., 2025).

Celermajer et al. (2021), noting the core elements of MSJ, assert that it adopts a relational ontology that rejects the hierarchical notion that humans or human individuals exist distinct from others. It also adopts an ethic of difference that rejects the idea that capacities and affordances of being human provide the ideal against which other beings ought to be evaluated, and lastly, they proclaim that it tries to understand the intersection of different manifestations of injustice among humans and against non-humans (Tschakert et al., 2021). This relational understanding is crucial for addressing climate change impacts on children, as it recognises that the degradation of ecosystems, whether through deforestation, water pollution, or biodiversity loss, directly undermines children's rights to health, nutrition, and development.

One way of approaching multi-species justice would be through a negative route, first highlighting the position it seeks to renounce. It rejects the anthropocentric view that humans occupy an important place in the moral universe for three reasons. Firstly, they are essentially distinct from other species; they are unique compared to other species, due to their possession of a set of special qualities, such as the ability to consciously reason and deliberate; and they are, therefore, worthy of superior moral consideration to other species (Thompson, 2015). MSJ invites otherwise silenced animals (and people) into the realm of justice, giving voice and recognition to those (non)humans left out of Anthropocene stories (Celermajer et al., 2021). It therefore expands justice without extending personhood.

Human exceptionalism has historically marginalised children, often equated with the non-human world. Taylor and Pacini-Ketchabaw (2019) highlight the importance of breaking with universalising traditions of 'casting children as instinctual, prerational, asocial, apolitical, and uncorrupted beings, and therefore aptly positioned alongside animals on the "nature" side of the nature/cultural divide'. MSJ enters the discussion with an appreciation of both the human and non-human worlds' value. This chapter aims to propose MSJ as an approach to constitutional interpretation of the right to a safe and healthy environment. It will also highlight court decisions that have unconsciously used this approach and thus ensured the protection of children's rights. This approach compels legal actors to consider the well-being of ecosystems, animals, and future generations as integral to realising human rights. Such an approach is relevant in Zimbabwe's climate-vulnerable context, where protecting watersheds, forests, and biodiversity is inseparable from protecting children's rights to water, food security, and health.

While some scholars have asserted climate justice as the better means to an end, scholars like Tschakert et al. (2021) have noted that climate justice is no longer adequate to address the climate crisis, based on the fact that it is insufficient to overcome the persistent silencing of voices belonging to multiple 'others'. More so, it does not question human exceptionalism and the violence it enacts. Some climate justice approaches perpetuate structural racism and intersecting traumas through resilience-building programmes among vulnerable populations (Tschakert et al., 2021). Consequently, MSJ presents a transformative approach to climate issues by actively rejecting exclusionary propensities inherent in other frameworks.

MSJ scholars argue for frameworks that are not about decentring any human per se but about decentring and deconstructing specific, dominant human ontologies, systems, and modes of relationship regarding the more-than-human world (e.g. especially those that rely on the belief in human exceptionalism and legitimise exploitation and destruction of rivers and their multi-species communities) (Houart et al., 2025). Through an intersectional approach, MSJ recognises that multiple identities and categories of difference and inequalities are simultaneous (e.g. race, age, class, gender, ability, and being) and that they intersect each other in structures and processes of oppression and injustice (Tschakert et al., 2021). MSJ does not aim to confer personhood on non-humans such as the assimilative logic disseminated by racial justice, Indigenous, crip, and queer theories. The agency of all things (living or non-living) is highlighted, and the existence and flourishing of all animals and ecosystems are rendered important. This intersectional perspective aligns with findings from across Zimbabwe's diverse districts, where climate impacts intersect with poverty, gender inequality, and rural marginalisation to create compounded vulnerabilities for children (see, e.g. Chipenda & Ndhlovu, Chap. 13, in this volume).

Although MSJ seems prima facie concerned with the injustice of Earth's other beings (who are not human), it is equally concerned with the various intra-human injustices. Multi-species injustice comprises all the human interruptions of this broad array of relations (Celermajer et al., 2021). It appreciates the interconnectedness of the different areas of injustice. MSJ must also not amount to continuing arrangements of excluding or rendering invisible specific assemblies of human actors deeply impacted by asymmetrical power relations and the global capitalist economy (Fitz-Henry, 2022). These various injustices are rooted in a set of constructed and hierarchically organised binaries centred on the ideal of a specific type of human.

A constitutional and human rights-based analysis, with a multi-species justice-based approach, can achieve greater protections for both human and non-human entities. While the constitutional and human rights-based analysis affords protections against injustices, its centralisation of humanity debilitates its approach. Critics of MSJ like Ginn (2014) remind us that focusing on connectivity, vitality, and belonging obscures as much as it reveals. It is impossible to encompass everything all at once. Desires to do so, to totalise and universalise children's multi-species relations, open the door to romanticised notions and ambiguous, depoliticised claims ('everything is relational') (Nelson & Drew, 2024). At the same time, some scholars like Robert Goordin lament the absurdity of entertaining the possibility of Earth's others participating in decision-making (Celermajer et al., 2025). Young (2000) argues for a corrective communicative theory of democracy that does not possess exclusionary tendencies based on the assumption of what is deemed 'appropriate forms of political speech'.

MSJ welcomes differences in communication and representation through various networks. Meijer (2019) advances this by examining animal vocalisations, body language, and scent marking to challenge the human-centric view that only language-based communication is meaningful. MSJ challenges us to nurture the arts of attentiveness and active listening practices (Rose, 2012). These are political because they directly relate to processes of inclusion/exclusion and of (mis)recognition of diverse subjects. MSJ has the potential to help children realise their rights. This includes the right to participation. It does not use frameworks that treat children like adults. Instead, it values children as they are. It considers children equally important.

Giving a platform to othered persons can be achieved through an inclusive and corrective communicative theory of democracy that does not possess exclusionary tendencies based on the assumption of what is deemed ‘appropriate forms of political speech’ (Young, 1996). Corrective communicative theory of democracy in today’s world, however, seems distant in the future. The suspension of three Māori MPs for their protest haka during a sitting in 2024 in New Zealand hints at the strides that adults themselves are yet to make to accept an inclusive and corrective communicative theory of democracy, not to mention the inclusion of children and non-human entities. Nixon in Willis emphasises that MSJ invites otherwise silenced animals (and people) into the realm of justice, giving voice and recognition to those (non)humans left out of Anthropocene stories (Willis, 2024). This democratic inclusivity becomes especially urgent in climate governance, where children’s voices and lived experiences of climate impacts remain systematically marginalised despite their disproportionate vulnerability.

3.3 Constitutional Entrenchment of the Right to a Safe and Healthy Environment

3.3.1 Environmental Rights and Intergenerational Justice

Though all four constitutions, South Africa, Kenya, Uganda, and Zimbabwe, recognise the right to a clean, safe, and healthy environment, how these rights are framed and to whom they apply differ significantly. In South Africa, Kenya, and Zimbabwe, the right is broadly vested in ‘everyone’ or ‘every person’, with explicit intergenerational clauses. The intergenerational justice clauses explicitly refer to the ‘present and future generations’. This suggests a constitutional openness to protecting the environment for current human inhabitants, future generations, and, by extension, all living beings affected by environmental harm. Uganda limits environmental rights to ‘every Ugandan’. It lacks an explicit intergenerational clause, which may restrict the interpretation of these rights and exclude non-citizens, including potentially vulnerable or stateless children.

Inclusive language in the constitution creates interpretive space for advancing multi-species justice, as ecological degradation impacts humans and non-human life across generations. Scholars have been advocating for climate justice through an intergenerational equity lens, and children are demanding recognition of themselves and their future (Gasparri et al., 2021). More inclusive language allows for a generous interpretation that is conscious of multi-species justice, as scholars like Moyo (2016) and Currie and De Waal (2013) often advocate. Uganda's citizen-focused language, unless read ecologically, may narrow this scope. In Zimbabwe's context, where climate change projections indicate that mean annual temperatures will increase by 1.0–1.5 °C by 2040 and rainfall will decline by up to 10%, the intergenerational framing becomes critical for protecting both present and future children from escalating climate impacts (GoZ, 2024).

Although the United Nations Framework Convention on Climate Change (UNFCCC) does not mention children, it calls for preserving the global climate for present and future generations. The UN Convention on the Rights of the Child (UNCRC) also does not explicitly mention environmental rights. However, it does recognise environment-related rights, such as Article 24, the right to health, water, environmental sanitation; Article 27, social development; and Article 29, respect for the environment. At the international level, environmental issues are transboundary, yet substantive provisions of the UNCRC are arguably not interpreted widely enough to safeguard children beyond states' national jurisdiction (Ferguson et al., 2013). The MSJ approach to interpretation can potentially turn the tide. This interpretive gap is problematic for addressing climate change, which operates across borders and generations, affecting children's rights to life, health, and development in ways that transcend national jurisdictions.

3.3.2 Children's Rights and Legal Recognition

Children's rights are affirmed in each constitution, but there are differences in age definitions and the emphasis of key rights. South Africa, Kenya, and Zimbabwe all define a child as anyone under 18, while Uganda uses a lower threshold of 16 years. Across the board, constitutional provisions guarantee the right to identity, care, education, and protection, with special provisions for the best interests of the child (South Africa and Zimbabwe) and affirmative action for youth (Kenya). Uganda's constitution emphasises education, health, care, and protection from exploitation, focusing particularly on orphans and vulnerable children. This focus on vulnerability, care, and protection, especially in Uganda, signals an opportunity to extend these principles, through a multi-species lens, to non-human dependents such as animals and ecosystems. Recognising children's vulnerability should also extend to their vulnerability to nature. The child's best interest should also be interpreted to include recognition of the child's best interest in participating actively in the climate change discourse. Ruggeri et al. (2021) note that participation is necessary to enhance children's developmental competencies, and thus, the lack thereof would not be in their best interest. In Zimbabwe's climate-vulnerable context, where children face heightened risks of malnutrition, disease, educational disruption, and displacement due to droughts, floods, and cyclones, the best interest principle must encompass protection from climate-induced harms and meaningful participation in climate adaptation strategies.

3.3.3 Youth Participation and Affirmative Action

The degree to which participation is recognised varies, depending on the state. Kenya explicitly affirms youth rights to participate and provides for affirmative action, while Zimbabwe affirms participation with implied affirmative action through section 18 that advocates for fair representation in all institutions and government agencies. Uganda does not explicitly guarantee youth participation but does include age-based affirmative action, and South Africa's provisions could be interpreted to allow for broad youth inclusion. The South African constitutional entrenchment of the right to freedom of expression, access to information, and its emphasis on accountability and openness is open ground for youth inclusion. The strong protection for youth participation in Kenya creates fertile ground for youth-led advocacy in multi-species justice. This highlights a pathway through which multi-species justice can grow from a constitutional foundation.

The UNCRC (1989) not only stipulates that children's best interests be a 'primary consideration' in all actions by public and private authorities but that children have a right to be heard and to participate in decisions which affect them. Children's voices are scarcely heard despite international laws, and their concerns are strangely invisible in climate policy dialogues. In Zimbabwe, though the state has actively taken steps to incorporate youth participation through programs like Zimbabwe's Local Conference of Children and Youth (LCOY).

3.3.4 Recognition of Vulnerability and Protection

All the constitutions distinguish children from adults, but Uganda specifically names vulnerable groups, such as orphans and disabled children, providing them with specific protections. Other jurisdictions offer general protection without naming specific groups. Uganda's approach to recognising differentiated vulnerability stands out. It could serve as a model for extending explicit constitutional protection to non-human species, especially endangered or ecologically sensitive ones. This sets a precedent for integrating the concept of vulnerability into broader frameworks of rights and protection, potentially benefiting all beings affected by environmental and social challenges. Such differentiated recognition becomes essential in the climate change context, as climate impacts disproportionately affect marginalised children. This includes those in rural areas, girls facing increased domestic burdens, and children with disabilities who face compounded vulnerabilities during climate-induced disasters.

3.3.5 Potential Impacts of Integrating Multi-Species Justice into Constitutional Interpretation

Legal frameworks tend to be adult centric (Makuch, 2019). However, multi-species justice shuns a centralisation of either intra-human or between-species. Constitutional provisions denoting the conferring of rights to 'every person' or to 'everyone' would thus be invalidated. MSJ does not extend personhood but confers rights to all species. Thus, the right to a safe and healthy environment would include children, adults, plants, and animals. The inclusion of other species would safeguard the environment and children. This holistic protection is especially relevant in Zimbabwe, where children's well-being depends directly on ecosystem health, from forests that regulate water cycles to wetlands that provide food security and biodiversity that sustains agricultural livelihoods.

Like gender quotas in parliaments, quotas for young people in national ministries and international organisations would provide young people with the opportunity to hold leadership positions. While some authors proclaim that to achieve meaningful participation, young people must understand the need for and ask for further support to sharpen their skills to analyse climate change proposals using a rights-based lens (Gasparri et al., 2021). MSJ does not expect children first to obtain the adult intellectual understanding of political or climate change challenges. It meets children halfway by trying to understand their language, not vice versa. In this light, a reinterpretation of constitutional provisions (right to access information, the right of youth to associate and be represented) would allow children to participate more easily in environmental policies. This is critical in Zimbabwe's climate adaptation planning, where children's experiential knowledge of local environmental changes and community-level impacts could significantly inform more effective and contextually appropriate responses.

MSJ would allow for a broader interpretation of 'the best interests of the child' (BIC) as contained in various constitutions. Scholars like Ippolito (2022) have noted that BIC is the primary consideration when other interests are at stake, like environmental infringement. The BIC principle encompasses the state's duty to incorporate it in all relevant environmental policies, programmes, and projects and integrate it in all legislative, administrative, and judicial proceedings. Thus, implementing the right to a safe and healthy environment should also take special notice of children's presence and disadvantage. In Zimbabwe's climate-vulnerable districts, where children face educational disruptions from droughts, health risks from waterborne diseases following floods, and increased labour exploitation due to crop failures, the BIC principle must be interpreted to prioritise climate-resilient development pathways that protect children's rights across all sectors.

MSJ also encourages children's separate rights. They are unique and face unique dangers to adults. The MSJ approach to interpretation encourages an interpretation that is aware of the innate prejudices that children face and the intersectionality of the different abuses that different children face. Existing child-specific provisions within the Zimbabwean, South African, Ugandan, and Kenyan constitutions already appreciate this reality. However, even decisions like the #CancelCoal case fall short of acknowledging the differentiated abuses that various children face. Special attention should have been given to the inherent disadvantage that children in coastal areas like South Africa face because of climate change or fossil fuels, as well as taking judicial notice of disabled children in coastal areas. Similarly, in Zimbabwe's diverse ecological zones, children in drought-prone southern regions face climate vulnerabilities different from those in flood-prone eastern districts, requiring differentiated constitutional protections and targeted adaptation measures.

Literature shows that not only have children, in their supposed undeveloped nature, been advocating for climate justice through an intergenerational equity lens (Donger, 2022), but MSJ also allows for the interpretation of the 'present and future generation' to include the rights of children born and unborn (Gasparri et al., 2021). Constitutional provisions with an intergenerational justice clause should be interpreted with an appreciation of children's dependence on nature and the fact that disregard of nature is the disregard of children's rights. MSJ interpretation appreciates such an interpretation but includes nature and other species. More precisely, MSJ interpretation appreciates the rational relationship between children, adults, and other species. This relational understanding is essential for Zimbabwe, where climate projections indicate that today's children will face increasingly severe droughts, floods, and food insecurity throughout their lifetimes, with impacts cascading across generations unless transformative action is taken now to protect both ecological systems and children's rights simultaneously.

3.3.6 Comparative Judicial Approaches to Children's Environmental Rights in Africa

Key themes that emerge from recent legal cases in Zimbabwe demonstrate that environmental protection is seen not only as a matter of ecological stewardship but also as an essential safeguard for public health and livelihoods. However, for historical context, previous environmental cases must be examined. For example, issues highlighted in the *Dora Community v Mutare City Council (2005)* and *Manyame Park Residents v. Chitungwiza Municipality (2003)* cases show the direct connection between environmental degradation and children's health, emphasising that municipal accountability, rather than solely corporate misconduct, remains central in litigation. These cases illustrate how water pollution and inadequate sanitation directly threaten children's rights to health and life. Yet courts have failed to recognise children as rights holders with unique vulnerabilities to environmental harms.

In the Manyame case, the Zimbabwe Environmental Law Association (ZELA) sought an order to compel the Chitungwiza Municipality to construct proper sewage systems. ZELA demonstrated that the municipality negligently discharges raw sewage into a public stream and a residential area in contravention of the then recently enacted Environmental Management Act (EMA) and its right to a healthy environment. The court granted the order, and the municipality admitted to the pollution but pleaded that it did not have the resources to rehabilitate the contaminated land or build proper sewage structures. Places like Chitungwiza were subsequently hit hard by the 2008–2010 cholera outbreak (Soyapi, 2020). This case starkly highlights the climate-health nexus. Poor sanitation infrastructure, exacerbated by climate-induced water stress, creates conditions for disease outbreaks that disproportionately affect children. Yet legal remedies failed to address children's vulnerabilities or prevent future harm.

In the Dora Community case, ZELA initiated a case similar to Manyame Park Residence when it approached the courts for an order compelling the Mutare City Council to stop depositing semi-treated waste into a river (which the Council controlled) and to monitor, control, and prevent the unbridled discharge of untreated industrial waste into the river in violation of the right to a healthy environment in terms of the EMA. ZELA obtained judgement by consent, after the sitting councillors had admitted to the pollution and agreed to put remedial measures in place. Again, while the case addressed community environmental rights, it failed to recognise that children, who are more susceptible to waterborne diseases and developmental impacts from pollution exposure, constitute a distinct vulnerable group requiring specific constitutional protections.

The burden of urban neglect is disproportionately felt by vulnerable communities, with children often standing as the most affected group, even though their rights are usually implied within broader community claims rather than explicitly argued in court. Children's rights in Zimbabwean environmental litigation are typically embedded rather than overtly expressed. While children are recognised as silent stakeholders, especially in cases involving exposure to unsafe water, disease, and degraded ecosystems, their welfare is usually considered through the lens of the community's well-being. Despite being at the centre of harm, children's individual rights have not yet become a focal point in environmental lawsuits, leaving a gap in the explicit legal recognition of their interests. This gap is problematic in the climate change era, where children's unique physiological, developmental, and temporal vulnerabilities to environmental harms demand explicit constitutional recognition and targeted legal protections.

A notable development in Zimbabwe is the growing recognition of the need for environmental impact assessments (EIAs). This is illustrated by the *Debshan (Pvt) Ltd. v Provincial Mining Director, Mat. South Province & Ors (2017)*. Debshan (Pvt) Ltd., a cattle ranching and wildlife safari operator, managing Shangani Ranch in Insiza District, approached the High Court seeking a declarator against mining authorities. The applicant argued that any mining licences, permits, or certificates issued for claims on its land without a valid EIA certificate under section 97 of the Environmental Management Act (EMA) were null and void. The ranch, home to over 4000 wild animals and 4200 cattle, faced threats from unregulated mining, including fire outbreaks and ecological degradation. The court granted the declaratory relief, reinforcing the primacy of environmental safeguards and procedural compliance before mining activities can commence on ecologically sensitive private land. While this case demonstrates judicial commitment to environmental protection, it exemplifies the anthropocentric and property-centred approach that fails to recognise the intrinsic value of ecosystems or the specific rights of children who depend on healthy environments for their development and well-being.

Procedural integrity and access to justice are also gaining prominence within Zimbabwean environmental cases. Decisions in matters such as *Sandawana Mines (Private) Limited v The Mining Commissioner - Midlands Province N.O and 4 Others (2023)* and *ZELA & Ors v Anjin Inv. (Pvt) Ltd & Ors (2015)* demonstrate an increasing judicial willingness to uphold procedural requirements, such as compliance with environmental impact assessments (EIAs) and ensuring meaningful public participation, even in the face of strong mining interests. The courts affirm the legitimacy of community standing and public interest litigation as effective mechanisms for promoting environmental accountability and safeguarding both human and ecological interests. However, such decisions fall short of judicial notice of children's rights infringements. These procedural advances, while important, remain insufficient in addressing climate change impacts that operate across temporal and spatial scales, requiring anticipatory and precautionary approaches that explicitly centre children's present and future rights.

In contrast, the South African context is characterised by a constitutional framing of environmental justice, with a strong focus on children's rights and climate change. The #CancelCoal case is a prime example, as it was explicitly argued around children's constitutional rights to life, dignity, and a healthy environment. The court recognised the importance of intergenerational equity and held that the expansion of coal operations violated children's rights as guaranteed by Sections 24 and 28 of the Constitution. South African litigation tends to emphasise the impacts of climate change, air pollution, and fossil fuel dependency, which are less prominent themes in Zimbabwean legal challenges. This case represents a significant advancement in linking fossil fuel extraction to children's constitutional rights. However, it still falls short of adopting a multi-species justice lens that would recognise the intrinsic value of ecosystems and the interconnected vulnerabilities of human and non-human life.

Another prominent South African case, *Green Connection & Natural Justice v Minister & Total/Shell (2025)*, concentrated on protecting marine ecosystems and the livelihoods of small-scale fishers while scrutinising procedural shortcomings in approving offshore drilling projects. The court's decision to invalidate environmental authorisations was based on failures to properly assess transboundary effects, climate impacts, and socio-economic risks. This approach reflects a more technocratic and rights-oriented judicial review than Zimbabwe's pragmatic, community-centred litigation. The case's recognition of transboundary and intergenerational impacts begins to approximate multi-species justice concerns, although it remains primarily anthropocentric in its analysis.

The Kenyan experience, as seen in *Rodgers Muema Nzioka v Tiomin Kenya Ltd (2001)*, is defined by community resistance and the promotion of environmental democracy. In this case, rural farmers opposed titanium mining in Kwale District, and the court highlighted the necessity of public participation, the precautionary principle, and intergenerational equity. While children's rights were not at the forefront, the case advanced the concept of community entitlement to clean ecosystems, aligning with Zimbabwe's focus on procedural justice and public participation. This devastating toll on children's lives highlights the urgency of centring children's rights in environmental litigation, primarily in climate-vulnerable contexts where mining and extractive industries threaten both immediate survival and long-term developmental rights.

Uganda presents another distinctive model, emphasising constitutional trusteeship and explicit governmental responsibility for climate action. *The Mbabazi & Others v Attorney General & NEMA* case was brought forward on behalf of four minors, invoking the public trust doctrine and constitutional obligations to protect natural resources for future generations. The litigation directly connects climate change to children's rights, demanding state accountability for emissions and climate mitigation planning. Although Uganda's approach is more forward-looking and rights explicit than Zimbabwe's, progress remains slow and is often seen as largely symbolic. Nevertheless, the case represents an important precedent for African jurisprudence by explicitly framing climate action as a constitutional obligation owed to children as rights holders, a framework that Zimbabwe could adapt and strengthen through multi-species justice principles.

A comparative analysis of these national contexts reveals important differences and convergences. In Zimbabwe, children's rights are implicit, often interpreted through health and sanitation claims. South Africa and Uganda adopt explicit constitutional or public trust frameworks that centre children as rights holders. Multi-species justice is emerging only in Zimbabwe, with some conceptual presence in Uganda, whereas South Africa's and Kenya's cases focus primarily on human impacts. Legal strategies differ, ranging from community-driven and pragmatic approaches in Zimbabwe to rights-based and strategic litigation in South Africa, participatory grassroots resistance in Kenya, and symbolic constitutional accountability in Uganda. Climate change, meanwhile, is a central issue in South African and Ugandan litigation but remains a peripheral concern in both Zimbabwe and Kenya. This comparative analysis reveals a critical gap across all jurisdictions. While some progress has been made in recognising children as environmental stakeholders, no African jurisdiction has yet fully embraced a multi-species justice framework that would recognise the interconnection between ecological integrity and children's rights realisation.

Both the Kenyan and Zimbabwean cases are commendable since the courts recognised the damage to the community and the potential ecological damage. However, multi-species justice would have required the court to take special recognition of disproportionate effects towards children, unlike the current judicial position in which children's recognition is implied. Moreover, a multi-species justice approach would compel courts to recognise that protecting ecosystems is not merely instrumental to human welfare but essential to maintaining the relational webs that sustain children's survival, development, and flourishing. This extends from pollination services that ensure food security to watershed protection that guarantees clean water access.

While some jurisdictions, such as South Africa and Uganda, have responded positively to environmental rights litigation brought by children, others merely acknowledge their presence in a formal sense, like Kenya, while Zimbabwe largely disregards them altogether. These varied developments across Uganda, Zimbabwe, Kenya, and South Africa highlight the significant disparity in recognising children's unique vulnerability to environmental harm. They also underscore the urgent need to centre multi-species justice within both environmental protection and children's rights frameworks. Nonetheless, all these jurisdictions fall short in taking judicial notice of children's rights within environmental litigation. It is insufficient for courts to limit their consideration to the parties' submissions alone; they must actively engage with the silent stakeholders, children, whose lives and futures are profoundly affected by judicial decisions. In the climate crisis, where today's environmental decisions will determine whether children can exercise their rights to life, health, education, and development for decades to come, judicial passivity amounts to a constitutional failure to protect the most vulnerable from foreseeable and preventable harms.

3.4 Traits Within Multi-Species Justice that Can Reaffirm Children's Rights

3.4.1 Interdependent Relationships

MSJ allows adults (particularly those in power) to understand that they depend on children and children, in turn, depend on the adults (Celermajer et al., 2025). Litigation shows that throughout the years, mankind has interfered with nature without considering the consequences on the environment (Spentzou, 2021). MSJ proposes judgements that appreciate networks of violence and injustice that result from environmental infringements (Celermajer et al., 2025, p. 1). The court in the *Green Connection NPC and Another v Minister of Forestry, Fisheries and the Environment and Others (2025)* case exemplifies an understanding of relational ontology, despite the respondent asserting that a lack of duty to assert transboundary harm. The court reiterated that the state respondents failed to consider the transboundary impacts of the proposed project, both on Namibia and on international waters. This decision echoes MSJ's understanding of one's responsibility in the greater ecological scheme. In Zimbabwe's climate context, this relational understanding becomes critical. When droughts destroy crops, children's rights to food and education are violated; when floods contaminate water sources, their health rights are compromised; when ecosystems collapse, their rights to development and an adequate standard of living are undermined. These are all connections that courts must explicitly recognise and protect.

3.4.2 Children's Rights and Participation in Environmental Decision-Making

Even though children are more vulnerable to direct and indirect effects of climate change, they were largely left out of discussions about appropriate responses to climate change (Willis, 2024). The UNCRC states that children have the right to participate in and influence decision-making processes that may be relevant in their lives (UN General Assembly, 1989). In *Minors Oposa v Secretary of the Department of Environment and Natural Resources (1993)*, the plaintiffs were minors, representing themselves and unborn generations. They requested to cancel registered permits issued based on the timber licensing agreements (TLAs) and cease issuing new ones, as they permitted deforestation. They found legal ground on the right of balanced and healthful ecology, as established in the Constitution of the Philippines. While the case was on appeal, the government passed a law to declare the remaining forests a national protected area reserved for perpetual protection for the benefit of present and future generations not yet born (Gibbons, 2014). This case demonstrates how children's participation in environmental litigation can catalyse systemic legal reforms. This is a model particularly relevant for Zimbabwe, where children possess invaluable experiential knowledge of climate impacts on their daily lives, from walking longer distances to fetching water to missing school during droughts to help with household survival strategies.

Environmental racism and participation can also be addressed with MSJ. The silencing of marginalised people, including children and activists of colour, has been widely reported. Vanessa Nakate, a youth activist from Uganda, founded the Rise Up Movement to give voice to African climate activists who were systematically silenced by the media in international settings and addressed primarily as victims of climate change (Gibbons, 2014). Nakate experienced this discrimination herself when the Associated Press removed her image from a photograph with other (white) youth climate activists participating in the 2020 Davos World Economic Forum Summit. MSJ appreciates the disproportionality in participation among youth in environmental discourse, and constitutional affirmative action provisions should ensure that not only children participate but also black children participate. In Zimbabwe, where many children face climate-induced emergencies yet remain systematically excluded from climate governance, constitutional provisions on youth participation must be reinterpreted through an MSJ lens. This will ensure meaningful inclusion of rural children, girls, Indigenous children, and other marginalised groups whose voices are most silenced yet whose experiences are most urgent.

3.4.3 Environmental Vulnerability and Justice for Children

MSJ understands the intersectional veracities of children vis-à-vis other disadvantages depending on their peculiar realities. An MSJ approach to interpretation would be cognisant, for example, of the double jeopardy of children in disadvantaged circumstances. Unless We Act Now (2015) clearly explains how climate change disproportionately affects the poorest children, deepening existing inequalities. The courts in cases like the Dora Community case and the Manyame Park Residents case in Zimbabwe should have highlighted the double jeopardy of children's rights violations to their right to food, water, and environment, especially in Zimbabwe's rural communities that depend on natural resources for sustenance. This is especially critical in Zimbabwe's climate-vulnerable districts, where children face compounded vulnerabilities. Rural children who must walk further for water during droughts, missing school and facing safety risks, girls who shoulder increased domestic burdens as climate impacts intensify resource scarcity, and children in farming communities who are drawn into exploitative child labour when crop failures threaten household survival. These are patterns that demand explicit judicial recognition and constitutional protection.

3.4.4 Legal Recognition of Non-human Entities

Contrary to assimilative logic based on hierarchical anthropocentrism that echoes sentiments of conferring personhood to non-humans, MSJ disregards anthropocentrism altogether and advocates for justice for nature despite their differences with humanity. The conferring of personhood by courts in 2013, when the government of India banned the capture of dolphins and orcas because cetaceans have been proven to be sensitive and highly intelligent, and that they should never be seen as 'non-human person'. However, MSJ champions the protection of nature by appreciating its worth, not vis-à-vis humanity but in itself. Traits of this rationale are notable in the Māori traditions and in the Waitangi Tribunal, in which the Tribunal recognised that 'a river may be a taonga (precious) as a valuable resource, its mauri of life force is another taonga' (Stewart-Harawira, 2020). This appreciation of the value of nature can potentially open avenues for legislative interpretation that gives rights to nature, not as similar to humans but as entities deserving of rights. For Zimbabwe's children, whose well-being depends significantly on ecosystem health, from the Zambezi River basin that provides water and food to the miombo woodlands that regulate climate and provide traditional medicines, recognising nature's intrinsic rights becomes inseparable from protecting children's constitutional rights to life, health, and development.

While most constitutional entrenchment of the right to a safe and healthy environment is based on anthropocentrism, a multi-species justice approach would allow for ecocentrism that confers rights to nature (Kopnina et al., 2017). Such an interpretation would allow for judgements like the *Future Generations v. Ministry of the Environment and Others (2018)* in which the Supreme Court reversed the lower court decision, recognising that the 'fundamental rights of life, health, the minimum subsistence, freedom, and human dignity are substantially linked and determined by the environment and the ecosystem'. It further recognised the Colombian Amazon as a 'subject of rights' in the same manner that the Constitutional Court recognised the Atrato River. The Supreme Court declared that the Colombian Amazon was entitled to protection, conservation, maintenance, and restoration. The Court ordered the government to formulate and implement action plans to address deforestation in the Amazon. This ecocentric approach has direct implications for Zimbabwe, where deforestation rates, wetland destruction, and biodiversity loss directly undermine children's rights. Forests regulate rainfall patterns essential for agricultural food security; wetlands filter water and prevent floods that destroy schools and health facilities; and biodiversity provides ecosystem services that sustain livelihoods and nutrition. These are all connections that courts must recognise through constitutional interpretation.

An MSJ approach to interpretation appreciates the notion that an activity based on exploiting non-renewable energies is not sustainable (Montani, 2007). Therefore, activities that allow for such exploitation would be rendered unconstitutional based on its failure 'to promote conservation and secure ecological sustainable development'. Such sentiments are echoed by *the Court in Legality of the Threat or Use of Nuclear Weapons, Advisory Opinion (1996)*, wherein it weighed the possible damage caused by nuclear weapons not only to generations afterwards but to 'all civilisation and the entire ecosystem of the planet' and the #CancelCoal case. In Zimbabwe's context, this principle has urgent implications. Coal mining expansions that accelerate climate change, wetland conversions that eliminate natural flood buffers, and deforestation that disrupts water cycles all constitute constitutional violations of children's rights to a safe environment and sustainable development, especially when these activities lock in environmental degradation that will affect children throughout their lifetimes and burden future generations with irreversible harms.

3.5 Conclusion

In Zimbabwe, the Environmental Management Agency has exercised its regulatory authority by imposing fines and issuing interdicts against municipal councils and private entities for environmental infractions. Notable examples include a US$5000 penalty levied against Bikita Minerals (Chitagu, 2024), a US$10,000 fine imposed on the Harare City Council (the Herald Online, 2016), alongside a pending matter concerning the issuance of development permits in ecologically sensitive wetlands, and the collection of US$3500 in fines from the Bulawayo City Council for various environmental violations (Nkala, 2025). While these administrative actions demonstrate regulatory capacity, they remain reactive, piecemeal, and disconnected from the systemic, intergenerational nature of climate change impacts on children's rights.

Despite these administrative actions, there remains a conspicuous absence of litigation invoking constitutional claims, particularly in cases where environmental degradation intersects with human rights concerns. Outside of proceedings narrowly focused on environmental impact assessments (EIAs), constitutional and rights-based arguments are largely underutilised. Within this gap, the framework of MSJ offers a transformative lens. MSJ reorients constitutional interpretation to recognise the interdependence of human and non-human life forms, challenging anthropocentric legal paradigms and expanding the scope of justice beyond the human subject. By integrating MSJ into environmental jurisprudence, Zimbabwean law could unlock new avenues for legislative implementation that foreground ecological integrity, interspecies ethics, and the constitutional promise of protection for all sentient life in their unique prism. Most critically, MSJ provides the conceptual tools to address climate change as a children's rights crisis. By recognising that ecosystem destruction and children's rights violations are inseparable, protecting biodiversity and children's futures are interconnected imperatives and that constitutional obligations extend across species and generations to ensure survival, dignity, and flourishing for all life.

MSJ reimagines youth participation in environmental governance. It does not require children to adopt adult reasoning but instead adapts legal interpretation to their lived realities, making rights like access to information and representation more accessible. The BIC principle gains new depth under MSJ, especially in environmental contexts. It calls for judicial and legislative recognition of children's unique vulnerabilities, including those in climate-sensitive or marginalised communities. Finally, MSJ strengthens intergenerational justice by recognising the rights of both born and unborn children and their intrinsic connection to nature. It offers a transformative lens that links ecological integrity with the realisation of children's rights and the broader ethical inclusion of all life forms. For Zimbabwe, where climate change threatens to reverse decades of development gains and condemn millions of children to lives marked by food insecurity, educational deprivation, health crises, and displacement, adopting a multi-species justice approach to constitutional interpretation represents not merely an academic exercise but an urgent constitutional imperative. This one recognises that protecting children's rights in the climate era requires protecting the multi-species ecosystems upon which their survival, development, and flourishing fundamentally depend.

References

Celermajer, D., Burke, A., Fishel, S., Fitz-Henry, E., Rogers, N., Schlosberg, D., & Winter, C. (2025). *Institutionalising multi-species justice*. Cambridge University Press.

Celermajer, D. S., Rickards, L., Stewart-Harawira, M., Thaler, M., Tschakert, P., Verlie, B., & Winter, C. (2021). Multi-species justice: Theories, challenges, and a research agenda for environmental politics. *Environmental Politics*, 119–140.

Chitagu, T. (2024). Locals slam Zimbabwe for turning a blind eye to Chinese miner's violations, *Mongabay*, https://news.mongabay.com/2024/04/locals-slam-zimbabwe-for-turning-a-blind-eye-to-chinese-miners-violations/#:~:text=Discoloration%20in%20the%20Matezva%20dam,and%20communities%20nearby%2C%20he%20said

Currie, I., & De Waal, J. (2013). *The Bill of Rights Handbook* (6th ed.). Juta.

Donger, E. (2022). Children and youth in strategic climate litigation: Advancing rights through legal argument and legal mobilization. *Transnational Environmental Law, 11*(2), 263–289.

EMA fines city council, *HeraldOnline*, (2016). https://www.heraldonline.co.zw/ema-fines-city-council/

Ferguson, K. T., Cassells, R. C., MacAllister, J. W., & Evans, G. W. (2013). The physical environment and child development: An international review. *International Journal of Psychology*, 437–468.

Fitz-Henry, E. (2022). Multi-species justice: A view from the rights of nature movement. *Environmental Politics, 31*(2), 338–359.

Gasparri, G., El Omrani, O., Hinton, R., Imbago, D., Lakhani, H., Mohan, A., et al. (2021). Children, adolescents, and youth pioneering a human rights-based approach to climate change. *Health and Human Rights, 23*(2), 95–108.

Gibbons, E. D. (2014). Climate change, children's rights, and the pursuit of intergenerational climate justice. *Health & Human Rights Journal, 16*(1), 19–31.

Ginn, F. (2014). Sticky lives: Slugs, detachment and more-than-human ethics in the garden. *Transactions of the Institute of British Geographers, 39*(4), 532–544.

GoZ. (2024). *Zimbabwe national climate change adaptation plan*. Ministry of Environment, Climate and Wildlife.

Houart, C., Hoogesteger, J., & Boelens, R. (2025). Power and politics across species boundaries: Towards multi-species justice in riverine hydrosocial territories. *Environmental Politics, 34*(1), 49–69.

Ippolito, F. (2022). The Best interests of the child: another string to environmental and climate protection'bow?. *Questions of international law, 7*.

Kopnina, H., Washington, H., Cryer, P., Taylor, B., & Piccolo, J. (2017). Why ecocentrism is the key pathway to sustainability. *Ecological Citizen, 1*(1), 35–41.

MacDonald, K. C. (1991). The recovery of restoration costs: Analytical synthesis of common-law property damages, restitution, and natural resource damages under CERCLA. *Tulane Environmental Law Journal, 5*, 255–290.

Makuch, K. E. (2019). Tomorrow's stewards: The case for the Unified International Framework on the Environmental Rights of Children. *Health and Human Rights Journal, 21*, 203–224.

McKibbin, P. (2025). Kaupapa Māori and multi-species justice: A reciprocal critique. *AlterNative: An International Journal of Indigenous Peoples, 21*(1), 11–13.

Meijer, E. (2019). *When animals speak: Toward an interspecies democracy (Vol. 1)*. NYU Press.

Montani, G. (2007). The ecocentric approach to sustainable development: Ecology, economics and politics. *The Federalist - Pavia, 49*(1), 25–44.

Moyo, A. (2016). Constitutional Analysis of the Interpretation Clause of the Zimbabwean Declaration of Rights. In *2016 National Symposium on the Promise of the Declaration of Rights under the Constitution of Zimbabwe*, held at Cresta Lodge, Harare, Zimbabwe, on (Vol. 5).

Nation, U. (1989). *United Nations Treaty series*. Retrieved September 9, 2025, from United Nations: https://treaties.un.org/doc/Treaties/1990/09/19900902%2003-14%20AM/Ch_IV_11p.pdf

Nelson, N., & Drew, J. (2024). Multi-species collaboratories: Reconfiguring children's more-than-human entanglement with colonisation, urban development and climate change. *Children's Geographies, 22*(2), 165–168.
Nkala, S. (2025). Bulawayo City Council raises a paltry US$3,5K from environment violation fines, *Southern Eye*, https://www.newsday.co.zw/southerneye/local/article/200045092/bulawayo-city-council-raises-a-paltry-us35k-from-environment-violation-fines
Rose, D. B. (2012). *Multispecies knots of ethical time. Environmental Philosophy, 9*(1), 127–140.
Ruggeri, A., Walker, C. M., Lombrozo, T., & Gopnik, A. (2021). How to help young children ask better questions?. *Frontiers in Psychology, 11*, 586819.
Sanson, A. V., & Burke, S. E. (2020). Climate change and children: An issue of intergenerational justice. In N. Balvin & D. J. Christie (Eds.), *Children and peace* (pp. 343–362). Springer.
Soyapi, B. C. (2020). The judiciary and environmental protection in Zimbabwe. In *Human Rights and the Environment under African Union Law* (pp. 349-379). Springer International Publishing.
Spentzou, D. (2021). Climate change litigation as a means to address intergenerational equity and climate change. *Queen Mary Law Journal*, 153–177.
Stewart-Harawira, M. W. (2020). Troubled waters: Māori values and ethics for freshwater management and New Zealand's freshwater crisis. *WIREs Water, 7*(4), e1464.
Sturman, A., Celermajer, D., MácDonald, F., & Verlie, B. (2025, March 13). Prefiguring multispecies justice: How communities are challenging and transfiguring care, labour, and belonging in the midst of climate catastrophe. *Environmental Politics*. https://doi.org/10.1080/09644016.2025.2467527
Taylor, A., & Pacini-Ketchabaw, V. (2019). *The common worlds of children and animals: Relational ethics for entangled lives*. Routledge.
Thompson, A. (2015). Anthropocentrism: Humanity as peril and promise. In I. S. M. Gardiner & A. Thompson (Eds.), *The Oxford handbook of environmental ethics* (pp. 77–90). Oxford University Press.
Tschakert, P., Schlosberg, D., Celermajer, D., Rickards, L., Winter, C., Thaler, M., et al. (2021). Multi-species justice: Climate-just futures with, for and beyond humans. *Wiley Interdisciplinary Reviews: Climate Change, 12*(2), e699.
United Nations Environment Programme. (n.d.). *United Nations Environment Programme.* Retrieved September 8, 2025, from United Nations Environment Programme: https://wedocs.unep.org/handle/20.500.11822/32450
UNITED NATION CONVENTION ON THE RIGHTS OF THE CHILD, (1989) *UNITED NATIONS,* https://www.ohchr.org/en/instruments-mechanisms/instruments/convention-rights-child
Willis, M.-J. (2024). Realising multi-species justice: A (dog) walk in the park? *World Leisure Journal, 66*(4), 516–537.
Winter, C. J., & Schlosberg, D. (2023). What matter matters as a matter of justice? *Environmental Politics*, 1–20.
Young, I. (1996). Communication and the other: Beyond deliberative democracy. In S. Benhabib (Ed.), *Democracy and difference* (pp. 120–135). Princeton University Press.
Young, I. M. (2000). *Inclusion and democracy*. Oxford University Press.

Chapter 4
Protecting Indigenous Children's Rights Amidst Climate Change: A Legal and Policy Analysis of Zimbabwe

Funa Moyo, Mthuthukisi Ncube, Sithandweyinkosi Nkomo, Doris Chasokela, Obert Bore, Bhekimpilo Moyo Hlabano, and Clement Chipenda

4.1 Introduction

Climate change and environmental degradation constitute not merely ecological challenges but a significant human rights crisis with devastating implications for children across Africa. Among the continent's 490 million children, mostly residing in countries highly vulnerable to climate and environmental hazards, indigenous and marginalised communities bear disproportionate burdens (ACRWC, 2025). Climate-induced shocks, including droughts, floods, and heatwaves, systematically disrupt education, health, and protection systems, threatening children's rights to survival and development, health, education, and a clean, sustainable environment. Climate change is considered to be heightening existing social and economic inequalities; it intensifies poverty and reverses progress towards children's

F. Moyo · M. Ncube (✉) · S. Nkomo
Institute of Development Sciences, National University of Science and Technology, Bulawayo, Zimbabwe
e-mail: funa.moyo@nust.ac.zw; mthuthukisi.ncube@nust.ac.zw

D. Chasokela
Faculty of Science Education, National University of Science and Technology, Bulawayo, Zimbabwe

O. Bore
Northwest University, Mahikeng, South Africa

Zimbabwe Environmental Law Association, Harare, Zimbabwe

B. M. Hlabano
Lupane State University, Lupane, Zimbabwe
e-mail: bnhlabano@lsu.ac.zw

C. Chipenda
South African Research Chair in Social Policy, College of Graduate Studies, University of South Africa, Pretoria, South Africa

E. Ndhlovu, C. Chipenda (eds.), *Climate Change and Children's Rights in Zimbabwe*, https://doi.org/10.1007/978-981-95-6005-9_4

well-being. This results in disproportionate impacts on children with disabilities, children on the move, poor children, children separated from families, and indigenous children (United Nations General Assembly, 2018).

The intersectional nature of climate vulnerability demands urgent recognition. Of the 33 countries worldwide that UNICEF ranks as 'extremely high risk' for children, 25 or 75% are in Africa (UNICEF, 2021). This stark reality becomes even more troubling when contextualised against responsibility for emissions. Africa accounts for less than 4% of global greenhouse gas emissions, yet African children suffer the most severe consequences (ACRWC, 2025). When the African Union joined the G20 in 2023, a group whose members collectively produced 77% of global emissions, its 55 member states contributed merely 5% to the group's total emissions (UNEP, 2024). This inequity highlights the urgent need to frame climate change not simply as a child rights crisis but specifically as an African child rights crisis requiring differentiated responsibility and climate justice approaches.

The climate crisis manifests through multiple, overlapping dimensions that compound existing vulnerabilities. In Eastern and Southern Africa, nearly half of all people are children under age 18, with this population segment expected to reach 375 million by 2050 (UNICEF ESA, 2025). Currently, 51 million children in this region experience multiple and often overlapping crises intensified by unpredictable climate-exacerbated weather patterns, including relentless climate shocks, public health emergencies, conflict, displacement, and economic instability. These children face interrelated crises in water, nutrition, health, education, and child protection, all rights enshrined in the United Nations Convention on the Rights of the Child (UNCRC). Zimbabwe presents an urgent case study within this regional context, exemplifying the disconnect between comprehensive policy frameworks and effective implementation. Ranked in the top three in Southern Africa on the 2021 Global Climate Risk Index (UNICEF, 2021), Zimbabwe faces continued warming through 2080, with projections indicating the most significant temperature increases in western and southern regions, precisely where indigenous communities reside (Gwitira et al., 2024). The 6.5 million Zimbabwean children confronting climate-induced emergencies position the country as the 15th most vulnerable globally to climate change. Prolonged drought has crippled food and water supplies, intensifying violence risks and further compromising children's rights (UNICEF ESA, 2025). Climate disasters such as Cyclone Idai of 2019 have destroyed schools, roads, and water, sanitation, and hygiene (WASH) infrastructures, severely disrupting educational continuity for thousands of children (UNICEF, 2025a).

In light of these dynamics, Zimbabwe has established one of the most comprehensive climate policy architectures in Southern Africa. Notably, it includes the National Climate Change Response Strategy (2015), National Climate Policy (2017), revised Nationally Determined Contributions (2021), and National Long-term Low Greenhouse Gas Emission Development Strategy (2020–2050). This paradox, consisting of extensive policy development alongside persistent implementation failures, highlights a critical knowledge gap at the intersection of climate change impacts and children's rights, especially concerning indigenous children in Africa. Existing scholarship often treats environmental degradation and children's rights as discrete domains, failing to capture how climate-induced vulnerabilities compound the pre-existing marginalisation of indigenous communities whose survival depends on natural resource access.

Environmental threats to indigenous children extend beyond climate change to encompass artisanal mining and pollution. These phenomena disrupt traditional knowledge systems, increase vulnerability to natural disasters, and expose children to severe health risks, including respiratory illnesses, waterborne diseases, and malnutrition. Artisanal mining activities involve child labour, land grabs, and environmental degradation that contaminate water sources and destroy ecosystems upon which indigenous livelihoods depend. Harmful chemicals such as mercury and cyanide in mining operations render water unsafe. In contrast, air pollution from mining dust and industrial emissions causes long-term respiratory problems for children near extraction sites. Article 24 of the UNCRC mandates consideration of the dangers and risks of environmental pollution in ensuring children's rights are fulfilled (UN, 1989), yet legal frameworks designed to protect children often fall short of addressing indigenous populations' unique vulnerabilities.

This chapter engages with these interconnected challenges through integrated rights-based analysis connecting climate science, legal scholarship, and indigenous perspectives. Central research questions guide this investigation: How do climate change, environmental pollution, and artisanal mining specifically impact indigenous and marginalised children's rights in Africa, with particular attention to Zimbabwe's experience? What gaps exist between legal frameworks spanning international treaties, regional instruments, and national legislation and their actual implementation in protecting children's environmental rights? What policy interventions are needed to align national legislation with international children's rights standards and ensure sustainable livelihoods for vulnerable children? The objectives encompass examining multifaceted impacts of climate change, artisanal mining, and environmental pollution on indigenous children's rights across Africa with specific reference to Zimbabwe; engaging international, regional, and national legal frameworks protecting children's environmental rights; identifying implementation gaps and policy fragmentation hindering adequate protection; and proposing evidence-based recommendations for strengthening legal protections while centring indigenous voices in climate adaptation strategies. Through this integrated approach combining child-centred vulnerability assessments, policy document reviews, and insights from indigenous communities, the chapter demonstrates how environmental degradation functions as structural violence against indigenous children, violating their rights under multiple international conventions while threatening intergenerational transmission of traditional knowledge and practices.

Without urgent intervention, vulnerabilities of indigenous and marginalised children will deepen, exacerbating disparities they already face. States must act decisively, recognising climate change's disproportionate impact on children's rights (ACRWC Guidance Note, 2025). By implementing sustainable practices, promoting responsible mining, addressing root causes of pollution, and harmonising legal frameworks with adequate enforcement mechanisms, we can create pathways towards protecting Africa's most vulnerable children and ensuring sustainable futures for coming generations.

4.2 Theoretical Framework

This chapter adopts a dual theoretical framework combining ecological systems theory and human rights theory. These were selected for their complementary strengths in analysing the multilayered impacts of climate change on indigenous children's rights. This integrated approach was considered appropriate as it addresses both the empirical mechanisms of environmental impacts and the normative standards for evaluating state accountability.

Bronfenbrenner's (1979) ecological systems theory provides the foundational lens for understanding how environmental factors operate across multiple, nested systems shaping indigenous children's well-being. This theory is useful as it emphasises the interconnectedness of environmental, legal, social, and cultural systems rather than treating them as isolated domains. The framework highlights how climate-induced disruptions such as drought, flooding, or mining pollution simultaneously affect family livelihoods (microsystem), community cohesion and traditional practices (mesosystem), access to resources and services (exosystem), and preservation of cultural identity and knowledge systems (macrosystem). For children whose communities rely on natural resources for survival and cultural transmission, environmental degradation significantly alters the developmental contexts within which they grow. The theory's chronosystem dimension also enables examination of how climate impacts accumulate over time, affecting both individual developmental trajectories and intergenerational equity.

Human rights theory complements this ecological perspective by providing normative frameworks for analysing state obligations and accountability mechanisms (OHCR, 2013). This approach is appropriate because it centres children as rights holders rather than merely vulnerable subjects, emphasising their agency, dignity, and entitlement to specific protections under international and national law. The rights-based approach establishes clear standards for assessing legal frameworks and policy implementation, providing analytical tools for identifying where and why implementation failures occur (Kecskés & Lux, 2023; Okonkwo, 2021). It foregrounds principles of non-discrimination, substantive equality, and differentiated responsibility. These are concepts essential for understanding why African indigenous children bear disproportionate climate burdens despite minimal contribution to global emissions.

The integration of these perspectives creates a robust framework addressing both what impacts occur (through ecological systems analysis) and what legal and moral obligations exist to prevent and remediate them (through human rights analysis). This dual approach recognises climate change and environmental degradation as structural violence that systematically violates children's rights while threatening intergenerational transmission of traditional knowledge essential for community resilience (Bourdillon et al., 2024). The framework thus enables rigorous examination of how environmental, social, legal, and cultural systems interact to protect or undermine children's rights while providing clear standards for evaluating policy effectiveness and proposing evidence-based recommendations that connect climate science, legal scholarship, and indigenous perspectives.

4.3 Methodology

The interpretivism paradigm guided the qualitative approach adopted by the study. The rights-based approach emphasises state obligations to uphold children's environmental rights through legislative, judicial, and administrative measures (Okonkwo, 2021). Effective policy requires integrating environmental justice principles into legal systems. The study employed a systematic literature review and key informant interviews with legal experts, policymakers, and indigenous rights advocates to generate rich, contextual data on the implementation and challenges of children's environmental rights in Zimbabwe.

Using a systematic literature review, relevant peer-reviewed articles, legal documents, and policy reports published between 2010 and 2024 were analysed. A multi-database search strategy was employed, utilising academic databases with search terms such as 'children's rights', 'environmental justice', 'climate change', and 'Zimbabwe' or 'Africa'. Special attention was paid to Zimbabwe-specific policy documents and child-centred vulnerability assessments. The inclusion criteria prioritised sources addressing legislative frameworks, policy implementation mechanisms, and documented cases of environmental rights violations affecting children. Grey literature, including NGO reports and government policy briefs, was included to capture practical implementation experiences.

Key informant interviews were conducted with 20 experts from diverse backgrounds. A purposive sampling technique was employed to ensure representation across relevant sectors. Semi-structured interview guides facilitated in-depth exploration of participants' experiences and perspectives while allowing flexibility for emergent themes. Thematic analysis was used to identify patterns in legal provisions, policy implementation, and rights violations. Following Braun and Clarke's (2006) six-phase framework, the analysis process involved (1) familiarisation with data through repeated reading of transcripts and documents, (2) generating initial codes, (3) searching for themes, (4) reviewing themes, (5) defining and naming themes, and (6) producing the final analysis. The analysis incorporated data from regional assessments and country-specific reports to provide both continental and national perspectives. Triangulation of data sources enhanced the credibility and trustworthiness of the findings.

4.4 Literature Review

4.4.1 Climate Change and Children's Rights: An Environmental Justice Crisis

Climate change constitutes a multifaceted phenomenon posing significant risks to children's rights globally, with severe implications for indigenous and marginalised communities in Africa. The climate crisis has cast a shadow over nearly every child globally. However, children in different parts of the world are not affected equally, with the top 50% of states by income responsible for 86% of cumulative global CO_2 emissions. In contrast, children in low- and middle-income countries bear the brunt of losses and damage to health, human capital, land, cultural heritage, local and indigenous peoples' knowledge, and biodiversity (CERI, 2022). This environmental injustice highlights that demands for climate action have become increasingly associated with children. It is linked to broader economic and social justice notions, requiring child rights-based approaches to climate change mitigation and adaptation at the intersection of human rights, climate change, development, and disaster risk reduction frameworks.

Rising temperatures, extreme weather events, and environmental degradation have direct consequences on children's well-being and development, with indigenous communities residing in vulnerable areas experiencing exacerbated inequalities and marginalisation. Research demonstrates that climate-induced environmental degradation exacerbates poverty, displacement, and health crises among indigenous populations, with indigenous children facing threats to education, health, and cultural heritage compounded by limited legal recognition of land rights (Ngugi, 2022; Smith & Jones, 2021a, 2021b). Children are disproportionately affected by climate change, ranking among the most vulnerable to heatwaves, droughts, and floods, as they may be unable to access safe shelter, clean water, and nutritious food (UNICEF, 2025a; UNICEF ESA, 2025). Climate-induced changes in weather patterns disrupt agricultural systems and livelihoods, making it increasingly challenging for families to provide for their children's basic needs. In contrast, extreme weather events such as cyclones or floods lead to loss of school days and limited access to quality education (Gwitira et al., 2024). In Zimbabwe, unreliable rainfall, increased temperatures, and extreme weather events have adversely affected agriculture and food production, which are crucial for livelihoods (Gundu-Jakarasi & Nhidza, 2021). These environmental changes have resulted in biodiversity loss and ecosystem deterioration, further compromising human livelihoods and well-being (Sango & Godwell, 2015), with children facing increased vulnerabilities such as hunger, food insecurity, and health issues, including the spread of climate-related diseases (Anderko et al., 2020; Chikoko & Chihiya, 2023).

In Southern Africa alone, over 30 million people suffer from severe drought caused by extreme weather patterns, with millions at risk of acute hunger due to El

Niño.[1] Additionally, it causes drastic rainfall deficits and record-high temperatures that push rural communities to the brink of collapse (UNICEF ESA, 2025). Rain shortfalls have critically affected crop growth, leading to widespread harvest failures and livestock deaths. Climate change directly affects underlying determinants for good nutrition in multiple ways, including changing food consumption patterns and therefore quality and diversity of diets by influencing local and global food availability. Seasonal food scarcity is common in Zimbabwe and is a waste driver. In contrast, scarcity of resources and resulting increased poverty and stress pose a greater risk of violence against girls and women, including increased violence against children due to stress, sexual violence as girls are forced to fetch water from further distances, and the risk of transactional sex due to desperation for basic livelihoods. Climate change exacerbates social issues for children. In Zimbabwe, this has included decreased school attendance, early marriages, and increased child labour and exploitation (Chikoko & Chihiya, 2023).

4.4.2 Gendered and Cultural Dimensions of Climate Vulnerability

The discriminatory effect of climate change based on sex, disability, economic and social status, and other grounds is evident through gendered vulnerabilities arising from water scarcity that manifest in different ways for boys and girls. For girls, water shortages significantly affect menstrual hygiene management. The climate crisis negatively impacts all aspects of adolescent well-being, including physical well-being through increased risk of injury, lung disease, infectious disease, and poor nutrition, while disrupting connectedness to family, friends, and community through forced migration (Gwitira et al., 2024). Increasing frequency and intensity of climate shocks negatively affect basic services, including health, education, water, sanitation and hygiene, nutrition, and protection (UNICEF, 2025b). Over half a billion children worldwide are vulnerable to the impacts of extreme weather events driven by climate change, which threaten the environment and disrupt ecosystems, leading to the emergence of infectious diseases (Williams et al., 2023).

Indigenous children in Africa possess valuable traditional knowledge and practices passed down through generations, yet with the arrival of climate change, these knowledge systems face extinction. Climate change disrupts traditional farming practices, alters the availability of certain foods, and forces communities to relocate, resulting in indigenous children losing cultural identity and ancestral connection to their land (Dervieux & Belgherbi, 2020). Climate change has precipitated loss of

[1] El Niño refers to the warm phase of the El Niño-Southern Oscillation (ENSO) climate pattern, characterised by unusually warm ocean temperatures in the equatorial Pacific Ocean. This phenomenon occurs every 2–7 years and typically brings reduced rainfall, prolonged droughts, and higher temperatures to Southern Africa, significantly impacting agricultural productivity and water availability.

traditional knowledge and practices through forced migration and climate-related mobility that tends to increase rather than decrease human social vulnerability. Increased vulnerability to natural disasters has become one of Africa's most significant challenges, as climate change increases risks of floods, droughts, and storms. Indigenous and marginalised children living in disaster-prone areas are especially vulnerable, with homes, schools, and livelihood sources potentially destroyed (Kupika et al., 2017). This leads to displacement, loss of education, and increased vulnerability to abuse, exploitation, and violence.

Environmental risks, including poor solid waste management, indoor and outdoor air pollution, second-hand smoke, unsafe water, lack of sanitation, inadequate hygiene, and healthcare waste management, cause irreversible and lasting negative impacts on children. Children are vulnerable to stress and pollution during early childhood years as critical biological systems, such as the immune and central nervous systems, develop. As children grow, their developing lungs and brains make them especially vulnerable to air pollution. Their immune systems are weaker than adults', making them more vulnerable to viruses, bacteria, and other infections, which increases the risk of respiratory infection and reduces their ability to fight it (UNICEF, 2025b). Young children breathe faster than adults and take in more air relative to their body weight, often through the mouth, which takes in more pollutants. They are also closer to the ground, where some pollutants reach peak concentrations (UNICEF, 2025b). In addition, maternal undernutrition, infection, pollution exposure, and illness during pregnancy can cause lifelong damage to children, including physical stunting, neurological impairments, and immune dysfunction (UNICEF, 2025b). During pregnancy, a woman's body can store harmful chemicals from the air, passing them to her baby during pregnancy and breastfeeding. Air pollution can seriously affect the health of the foetus, leading to adverse pregnancy outcomes such as miscarriages, early delivery, and low birth weight. It can impact the healthy development of children's brains (UNICEF, 2025b). Climate change brings a range of health risks for children, especially respiratory illnesses, malnutrition, and waterborne diseases, with indigenous and marginalised children often lacking access to adequate healthcare and clean water, making them more susceptible to these health impacts. Air pollution causes both immediate and long-term health effects in children that can be irreversible. Air pollution is linked to respiratory conditions such as pneumonia, bronchitis, and asthma. It can exacerbate underlying health conditions and harm children's physical and cognitive development. When children get sick, they might miss school, further limiting their learning and development potential. The effects of air pollution can last a lifetime, as adults who were exposed to air pollution as children tend to have respiratory problems later in life (UNICEF, 2025b).

In Eastern and Southern Africa, the impacts of El Niño and La Niña[2] are also related to devastating floods and droughts on water, sanitation, and health systems

[2] La Niña represents the cool phase of the El Niño-Southern Oscillation (ENSO) climate pattern, characterised by frigid ocean temperatures in the equatorial Pacific Ocean. In contrast to El Niño, La Niña typically brings increased rainfall and flooding to Southern Africa. However, both phe-

(UNICEF ESA, 2025). The nutritional forecast is equally severe, with widespread food insecurity and malnutrition predicted due to the impact of extreme weather events on agricultural systems across the region. Climate change-exacerbated heavy rainfall and flooding have decimated crops, contaminated water supplies, overwhelmed sanitation systems, and displaced populations in areas already burdened with weak infrastructure (UNICEF ESA, 2025). In Zimbabwe specifically, water scarcity in regions like Matabeleland, combined with mining pollution threatening water sources in areas inhabited by San and Tonga communities, has compounded these challenges (Mathe et al., 2025; Moyo et al., 2018). Climate change has reduced water resources, caused desertification, and decreased food production, significantly impacting the environment and biodiversity, resulting in poor human health outcomes, affecting women and children who are often more vulnerable to food insecurity and health issues (Kigotho & Mutuota, 2025). In the Makonde communal lands in Zimbabwe, for example, climate change has led to significant environmental degradation, including the deterioration of ecosystem productivity, diversity, and services, impacting biodiversity through altered water cycles, plant and animal growth, and increased variability in rainfall. Children are affected as food security diminishes, leading to malnutrition and health issues, while the depletion of forest resources and wildlife encroachment further exacerbate these challenges (Sango & Nhamo, 2015).

4.4.3 Artisanal Mining and Child Labour Exploitation

Artisanal mining, or small-scale mining, constitutes a significant economic activity in many African countries yet is often associated with environmental degradation and human rights violations (Chuma et al., 2024). Artisanal mining, prevalent across Africa, often occurs in remote areas where indigenous and marginalised communities reside, with unregulated and unsustainable practices resulting in environmental degradation (Benkenstein, 2012), posing significant risks to children's rights. This sector contributes significantly to land degradation, environmental pollution, and disruption of local communities, with children's access to clean water, food, and health severely compromised (Harris & Thompson, 2021). The extraction of minerals often necessitates clearing forests, destroying natural habitats, and contaminating water sources, directly impacting children's rights to a healthy environment and adequate nutrition. Methods employed in artisanal mining, including harmful chemicals, explosives, and heavy machinery, result in deforestation, soil erosion, and pollution of water sources, further endangering local ecosystems (Bauer & Liao, 2020). Exposure to these environmental hazards diminishes the availability of clean water and nutritious food essential for children's survival and development

nomena disrupt normal weather patterns and create extreme conditions that threaten food security, water systems, and children's well-being.

(UNICEF, 2018). In addition, artisanal mining generates significant air pollution by releasing dust, chemicals, and other pollutants into the atmosphere, leading to long-term health risks, including respiratory problems for children living near mining sites (White & Lee, 2019).

Water body contamination is especially alarming, with toxic substances such as mercury and cyanide often improperly disposed of, rendering water sources unsafe for consumption and increasing waterborne disease risks (Klein & Oduro, 2021). Consequently, children living in proximity to mining operations are exposed to various toxic chemicals and heavy metals, heightening vulnerability to malnutrition, developmental issues, and respiratory and other health disorders (Jones et al., 2020). Access to clean water may be challenging in mining communities where natural environments have been either degraded or polluted by mining pollutants and mining dumps. Polluted water sources are unsafe for children, leading to increased waterborne diseases and limited access to clean water for basic hygiene practices.

In addition, artisanal mining in Africa is notorious for child labour use, with children as young as five engaged in hazardous activities, including digging, transporting materials, and handling dangerous chemicals (Smith, 2019). For many indigenous and marginalised children, these exploitative labour practices are driven by poverty, displacement, and lack of access to education. This forced labour not only violates children's rights to protection and education but also exposes them to serious physical dangers, including accidents and exposure to toxic substances (Cameron & Anderson, 2021). Waste mining as a livelihood activity meant to cope with climate change challenges may also involve child labour. Children are often forced to engage in hazardous activities, such as scavenging for metal waste or working in polluted environments, which endangers their physical safety and hinders their right to education. This is in a context where artisanal mining frequently occurs on indigenous lands without consent, leading to land grabbing and displacement. These communities lose access to ancestral lands, vital natural resources, and traditional livelihoods, exacerbating food insecurity and economic vulnerability (Bauer & Liao, 2020). Community disruption not only diminishes children's access to education and healthcare but also undermines cultural identity and practices, further perpetuating marginalisation (Gibson, 2020). The detrimental effects of artisanal mining on indigenous and marginalised children in Africa are multifaceted. It ranges from environmental destruction to severe health risks and exploitation. It requires comprehensive strategies to protect children's rights, mitigate environmental damage, and empower indigenous communities to preserve lands, livelihoods, and cultural heritage (UNICEF, 2018).

4.4.4 Environmental Pollution and Biodiversity Loss

Environmental pollution constitutes a pervasive problem in Africa, threatening the well-being and rights of all children. Environmental pollution, including air and water pollution, poses significant risks to children's rights in Africa, with contamination of natural resources and ecosystems affecting children's physical health and infringing upon their rights to a clean and healthy environment (Rother et al., 2019). Air pollution from industrial activities, vehicle emissions, and burning fossil fuels has significant health implications for children, whose bodies are more susceptible to adverse effects, including respiratory diseases, allergies, and impaired brain development (UNICEF, 2025b). Children living in polluted areas are more likely to suffer from respiratory illnesses, asthma, and respiratory infections, and these are health conditions that can limit physical activities, impair cognitive functions, and increase vulnerability to diseases (UNICEF, 2025b).

Water pollution from industrial waste, sewage, and harmful chemicals poses significant risks to children's health. Some African communities lack access to clean and safe water, making them more susceptible to waterborne diseases and malnutrition (UNICEF ESA, 2025). Children who rely on polluted water sources for drinking, bathing, and washing face a higher risk of infections and illnesses (Gwitira et al., 2024; UNICEF, 2025a). Environmental pollution also results in biodiversity loss, an important component in ensuring ecological balance and climate change resilience. This is where communities rely on biodiversity for livelihoods, traditional practices, and cultural identities. Climate change and pollution further exacerbate biodiversity loss, impacting the availability of medicinal plants, food sources, and natural habitats that children use for play and recreation. In Zimbabwe's Matobo District, climate change has led to significant environmental alterations, including the disappearance of flora and fauna, which are crucial for local livelihoods. Declining precipitation and rising temperatures exacerbate food insecurity, impacting children's nutrition and health. As natural habitats diminish, biodiversity loss threatens ecological balance, further endangering the resources children rely on for sustenance and well-being, ultimately affecting their development and prospects (Dube & Phiri, 2013). Erratic rainfall, increasing temperatures, and extreme events like droughts adversely affect wildlife resources and biodiversity, threatening species survival, disrupting ecosystems, and reducing habitat quality, impacting food security and livelihoods. Consequently, children face heightened vulnerability due to diminished access to natural resources, increased human-wildlife conflict, and potential health risks from climate-related diseases (Kupika et al., 2017). Biodiversity loss exacerbates climate change effects, affecting children's health due to vulnerability. Children face increased risks from heatwaves, flooding, and diminished access to green spaces, which are crucial for their physical and mental well-being. The loss of biodiversity can also hinder the development of new medicines, further impacting paediatric health (Seastedt et al., 2024). Loss of ecosystems can also deprive children of educational opportunities, as environmental pollution disrupts children's education by affecting concentration and academic ability, with absenteeism and reduced academic performance a direct consequence. Addressing these environmental and biodiversity challenges requires comprehensive adaptation strategies, including enhancing community resilience through initiatives such as solar-powered irrigation and integrated planning, as well as multi-stakeholder engagement to develop tailored adaptation and mitigation strategies with strong governance and sustainable value chains (Gundu-Jakarasi & Nhidza, 2021). However, without immediate action, the health and well-being of current and future generations of children will be severely compromised due to these environmental challenges (Williams et al., 2023).

4.4.5 International and Regional Legal Frameworks

International legal frameworks play crucial roles in safeguarding children's rights in the context of climate change impacts and environmental pollution, establishing standards and providing mechanisms to ensure rights protection. The UNCRC, adopted in 1989 and ratified by almost all African countries, including Zimbabwe in 1990, sets out the rights of all children, affirming their right to survival, development, and protection while recognising unique cultural identities (Moyo & Dlamini, 2023). The UN Declaration on the Rights of Indigenous Peoples (UNDRIP) provides important normative guidance, with Article 29 articulating rights to conservation and protection of the environment and Article 25 protecting spiritual relationships with traditional lands and resources (Addaney et al., 2017).

Key regional instruments such as the ACRWC, ratified by Zimbabwe in 1995, recognise children's environmental rights, including Article 14 establishing the right to health, including a clean environment. Yet it lacks enforceability mechanisms (Moyo & Dlamini, 2023). National legal systems often fail to align with these frameworks, creating policy fragmentation. The principle of intergenerational equity emphasises the need to protect future generations' rights, yet its implementation remains limited in African regional frameworks (Fambasayi & Addaney, 2021). Child rights-based climate change litigation is emerging as a tool to address these challenges, although it faces significant hurdles in terms of implementation and enforcement (Mezmur, 2023). Climate change adversely impacts human rights, including food, water, and housing rights. These are important for sustainable livelihoods, with children often reliant on natural resources, facing heightened vulnerabilities due to climate-induced displacement and resource scarcity affecting well-being and prospects (Addaney et al., 2017).

Zimbabwe's 2013 Constitution provides important foundations through Section 73 (environmental rights), Section 81 (children's rights), and Section 80C (recognition of customary law), although specific provisions linking children's rights to environmental protection remain limited (GoZ, 2013). Zimbabwe has developed an extensive legislative framework supporting climate action. The Environmental Management Act (Chap. 20:27) establishes the Environmental Management Agency (EMA) and requires environmental impact assessments (EIAs). It, however, contains limited specific provisions for indigenous communities or children. The Children's Act (Chap. 5:06) provides general protection but lacks specific provisions on environmental rights for children. The Communal Land Act (Chap. 20:04) governs land in areas where most communities reside but vests control in the president rather than communities, undermining traditional land management systems.

The National Climate Change Response Strategy (NCCRS), developed in 2014, outlines Zimbabwe's strategic approach to climate change mitigation and adaptation, highlighting the need for multi-sectoral approaches and emphasising the importance of addressing climate impacts on vulnerable groups, including children and women (Government of Zimbabwe, 2014; Gwitira et al., 2024). The strategy identifies priority areas such as food security, water resources management, health, and disaster risk reduction (DRR) directly affecting children. The National Climate Policy (NCP), launched in 2017, aims to provide a framework for climate governance and guide the implementation of climate change mitigation and adaptation measures across different sectors. It recognises the specific vulnerabilities of children and women to climate change impacts and calls for targeted interventions to enhance their resilience (Government of Zimbabwe, 2017; Gwitira et al., 2024).

Zimbabwe's revised Nationally Determined Contributions (NDCs) under the Paris Agreement outline the country's climate action commitments, focusing on adaptation in the agriculture and water sectors. However, it has limited consideration of indigenous knowledge systems. The Water Act (Chap. 20:24) governs water resources management but provides limited recognition of customary water rights. In contrast, the Mines and Minerals Act (Chap. 21:05) regulates mining activities, often affecting indigenous territories, with weak provisions for community consultation (GoZ, 2024). The Ministry of Primary and Secondary Education has incorporated climate change education into the national curriculum to raise awareness among children about climate change and empower them to contribute to community resilience efforts (Gwitira et al., 2024). Also developed has been a Disaster Risk Management and Resilience Plan 2021–2025, which provides step-by-step guidelines on how climate change affects the education sector.

Zimbabwe has established a comprehensive climate change management structure that includes a Cabinet Committee responsible for climate change management and a ministry dedicated to the same. In addition, a National Climate Change Platform is a multi-stakeholder platform for adaptation and mitigation. Subnational levels consist of Provincial and District Development Committees, which function as climate change mainstreaming working groups (GoZ, 2024). However, significant implementation gaps persist. Although Zimbabwe has clear policies and legislation addressing climate change issues, there is a lack of policies referring specifically to children's concerns (Gwitira et al., 2024). The legal framework faces challenges, including limited resources for enforcing environmental regulations, inadequate consultation with indigenous communities on development projects, weak procedural mechanisms for children's participation in environmental decision-making, and insufficient recognition of indigenous knowledge systems in climate adaptation strategies.

Social protection programmes such as the Basic Education Assistance Module (BEAM) and the harmonised social cash transfer (HSCT) aim to provide financial assistance to poor households, enabling them to cope with climate-induced shocks and stresses (Gwitira et al., 2024). However, compliance with legal frameworks poses challenges, especially in rural and hard-to-reach areas where resources are scarce and implementation mechanisms are weak. Key examples of policy measures across Africa include Sierra Leone's National Climate Change Policy 2021, Angola's National Strategy for Climate Change of 2017, the Gambia's 2050 Climate Vision, Benin's Climate Change Management Policy for 2030, Tanzania's National Climate Change Strategy 2021–2026, Nigeria's National Action Plan on Gender and Climate Change (2020) and Climate Change Act (2021), Mauritius's Climate Change Act 2020, and Uganda's National Climate Change Act (2021) and National Environment Act (2019), among others (ACRWC, 2025).

4.4.6 Rights-Based Approaches and Practical Interventions

Practical strategies are essential for safeguarding children's rights in the context of climate change impacts and environmental pollution, aiming to address immediate challenges while ensuring long-term well-being. Community-based adaptation represents one successful strategy involving empowering local communities to identify and develop strategies to adapt to climate change. These include establishing early warning systems, improving water access, and diversifying livelihoods. Recognising indigenous land sovereignty and integrating indigenous knowledge into climate adaptation strategies can enhance sustainable livelihoods for indigenous children.

Promoting access to education and healthcare represents another practical strategy. Ensuring that children have access to quality education and healthcare services can help them overcome the impacts of climate change and environmental pollutants on their health, including providing scholarships, building schools, and establishing health clinics in remote areas. Collaboration among African governments, international organisations, and civil society is also essential, with joint efforts needed to promote and implement policies and strategies protecting indigenous and marginalised children's rights. Collaborative efforts between indigenous communities and stakeholders are crucial for developing effective mitigation strategies that uphold children's rights and promote sustainability. This includes supporting community-based initiatives, raising awareness, and advocating for legislation promoting their rights.

The rights-based approach emphasises state obligations to uphold children's environmental rights through legislative, judicial, and administrative measures (Kecskés & Lux, 2023; Okonkwo, 2021). Effective policy requires integrating environmental justice principles into legal systems. Environmental degradation disproportionately affects specific groups of children, including indigenous children, especially in vulnerable areas like Africa and Zimbabwe. Climate change and pollution hinder their developmental potential and violate their rights under the UNCRC, compromising access to clean water, health, and food security (Bulat, 2024). Climate change and environmental degradation, viewed as structural violence, significantly impact children's rights, including those of indigenous children in Africa and Zimbabwe. These children face health, education, and sustainable livelihood threats due to environmental harm. The UN Committee emphasises that states must ensure a clean environment to protect these rights, implying that failure to address climate issues exacerbates vulnerabilities for indigenous children, undermining their ability to sustain their communities and cultures (Bourdillon et al., 2024).

4.5 Discussion

Issues discussed in the preceding sections highlight the disconnect between comprehensive policy frameworks and their practical implementation in protecting children's rights in the face of climate change and environmental degradation. This discussion engages with the research questions posed at the outset, synthesising evidence from continental and Zimbabwe-specific analyses to demonstrate how environmental crises function as structural violence against Africa's most vulnerable children.

4.5.1 Climate Change as a Multidimensional Rights Violation

Addressing the first research question, how climate change, environmental pollution, and artisanal mining specifically impact indigenous children's rights, the evidence reveals interconnected pathways of harm that extend far beyond environmental disruption. Climate-induced shocks systematically undermine children's rights across multiple domains simultaneously. The manifestations are stark in Zimbabwe, where 6.5 million children face climate-induced emergencies, such as educational disruption through school closures and infrastructure damage, health crises from waterborne diseases and malnutrition, cultural erosion through displacement from ancestral lands, and economic vulnerability through livelihood destruction.

The gendered dimensions identified in this research deserve particular emphasis. Water scarcity affects menstrual hygiene management for girls while simultaneously increasing risks of sexual violence and exploitation for all children forced to travel greater distances for resources. This intersectionality demonstrates that climate impacts cannot be understood through single-issue frameworks; they compound existing vulnerabilities based on gender, ethnicity, geography, and socio-economic status. The disproportionate burden borne by African children, who suffer extreme consequences despite the continent contributing less than 4% of global emissions, highlights the environmental justice crisis at the heart of climate change.

Artisanal mining emerges as an insidious threat, simultaneously exploiting child labour, contaminating water sources with mercury and cyanide, degrading ecosystems upon which indigenous livelihoods depend, and displacing communities from ancestral territories. The convergence of mining pollution with climate-induced water scarcity in Zimbabwe's Matabeleland regions exemplifies how multiple environmental stressors interact to create catastrophic outcomes for indigenous children.

4.5.2 Legal Frameworks and Implementation Failures

The second research question concerning gaps between legal frameworks and implementation reveals a paradox central to this chapter's findings. Zimbabwe exemplifies extensive policy development coexisting with persistent implementation failures, a pattern replicated across much of Africa. The country has established a comprehensive legislative architecture, including the National Climate Change Response Strategy, National Climate Policy, revised NDCs, and constitutional environmental and children's rights provisions. However, these frameworks remain largely ineffective in protecting vulnerable populations.

The study reveals several critical implementation gaps. First, policy fragmentation characterises legal frameworks across jurisdictions. Environmental legislation, child protection laws, and climate policies operate in silos with insufficient coordination mechanisms. Zimbabwe's environmental, children's, and land tenure laws address relevant issues but lack integration, creating enforcement challenges when rights violations span multiple domains. Second, resource constraints severely limit implementation capacity. While Zimbabwe established sophisticated governance structures, including a Cabinet Committee on Climate Change, National Climate Change Platform, and Provincial/District Development Committees, these institutions lack adequate funding and technical capacity for effective operation. Social protection programmes like BEAM and HSCT aim to support climate-affected households, but insufficient coverage leaves millions of vulnerable children without assistance.

Third, consultation deficits with indigenous communities undermine policy legitimacy and effectiveness. This is in a context where legislation vests control in the president rather than communities, systematically excluding indigenous peoples from decision-making processes affecting their territories and livelihoods. This exclusion violates principles enshrined in UNDRIP while preventing integration of indigenous knowledge systems, which research demonstrates enhances climate adaptation effectiveness. Fourth, enforcement mechanisms remain weak, especially in rural and remote areas where most indigenous communities reside. Environmental regulations exist, but limited monitoring capacity, corruption, and competing priorities result in minimal accountability for violations. Children exposed to mining pollution or displaced by climate-induced disasters have virtually no recourse to justice.

The comparative analysis with other African nations reveals that countries like Kenya with more integrated legal frameworks demonstrate better outcomes in protecting children's environmental rights. This suggests that policy comprehensiveness alone is insufficient, and implementation requires political will, adequate resources, meaningful community participation, and robust accountability mechanisms. The disconnect between Zimbabwe's sophisticated policy architecture and persistent rights violations exemplifies what happens when frameworks remain aspirational rather than operational.

4.5.3 Towards Rights-Based Climate Justice

The third research question regarding necessary policy interventions demands approaches that transcend conventional adaptation strategies to embrace transformative rights-based frameworks. Evidence from this research demonstrates that effective protection of children requires simultaneous action across legal, institutional, community, and resource domains. Legal harmonisation emerges as foundational. National legislation must align with international treaties, including UNCRC, UNDRIP, and ACRWC, while recognising indigenous children's environmental rights. Zimbabwe's constitutional provisions provide a starting point, but amendments to sectoral legislation are essential. Legislation on land tenure requires reform to recognise traditional resource management systems and uphold customary land rights. Environmental legislation needs specific provisions protecting children from pollution and requiring child impact assessments for development projects. Child protection laws must address climate-induced vulnerabilities, including displacement, food insecurity, and exploitation.

Institutional strengthening must accompany legal reforms. Building capacity within judicial and administrative bodies to understand and enforce environmental rights requires targeted training and resources. Establishing specialised environmental courts or tribunals with expertise in children's rights and indigenous issues could enhance accountability. Critically, coordination mechanisms between climate change management structures and child protection agencies must be formalised and operationalised to address the cross-cutting nature of climate impacts. Community engagement represents not merely a procedural requirement but an ethical and practical necessity. Indigenous communities possess invaluable traditional knowledge for climate adaptation that mainstream policy frameworks systematically overlook. Research demonstrates that integrating indigenous knowledge systems enhances resilience outcomes for vulnerable populations. Meaningful participation, different from token consultation, requires recognising indigenous peoples' rights to free, prior, and informed consent regarding developments affecting their territories. Community-based monitoring systems can empower local populations while addressing state capacity constraints for environmental oversight.

Resource mobilisation requires creative approaches, given African governments' chronic budgetary limitations. Prioritising climate finance specifically targeting children's rights protection represents one avenue. Expanding social protection coverage to ensure comprehensive support for climate-affected households addresses immediate vulnerabilities while building long-term resilience. Climate-resilient infrastructure investments, including schools, healthcare facilities, and WASH systems in indigenous areas, protect essential services. International climate finance mechanisms must prioritise African children, given the significant inequity whereby the continent bears disproportionate climate burdens despite minimal contribution to global emissions.

4.5.4 Intergenerational Equity and Cultural Survival

An underlying theme throughout this research concerns intergenerational equity and cultural survival. Climate change threatens not only indigenous children's immediate well-being but the transmission of traditional knowledge, languages, and practices essential for cultural continuity. When displacement forces communities from ancestral territories, when environmental degradation destroys ecosystems upon which traditional livelihoods depend, and when pollution renders sacred sites uninhabitable, the very survival of indigenous cultures hangs in the balance.

This cultural dimension receives insufficient attention in conventional climate policy frameworks, prioritising economic metrics and infrastructure adaptation. However, for children, cultural identity and connection to ancestral lands constitute important aspects of well-being protected under international law. The UNCRC emphasises that states must ensure that environmental conditions enable children's cultural development. Climate change and environmental degradation, by systematically undermining indigenous cultures, constitute violations of children's rights under Articles 8, 29, and 30 of UNCRC alongside Article 29 of the UNDRIP.

Zimbabwe's projected warming through 2080, with the most significant temperature increases forecast for western and southern regions, threatens the existence of some communities. Traditional farming practices become impossible under altered precipitation patterns. Medicinal plants disappear as ecosystems shift. Wildlife migrations disrupt hunting practices that have developed over millennia. The erosion of biodiversity eliminates resources essential for material survival and cultural practices. Without urgent intervention addressing these cultural dimensions alongside material needs, indigenous peoples face not merely adaptation challenges but cultural extinction.

4.6 Conclusion

Climate change and environmental degradation constitute violations of children's rights across Africa, with Zimbabwe exemplifying the tragic disconnect between comprehensive policy frameworks and effective implementation. This chapter has demonstrated that environmental crises function as structural violence, systematically undermining children's rights to health, education, cultural identity, and sustainable livelihoods. It has also threatened the intergenerational transmission of traditional knowledge essential for community resilience. The evidence reveals multiple, interconnected pathways through which climate impacts manifest, from water scarcity affecting menstrual hygiene and increasing sexual exploitation risks, to mining pollution contaminating ancestral territories, to forced displacement severing cultural connections to land. These impacts disproportionately burden African children who bear extreme consequences despite the continent contributing less to global emissions, highlighting environmental injustice demanding differentiated responsibility approaches.

The analysis of legal frameworks spanning international treaties, regional instruments, and national legislation reveals significant gaps between normative standards and practical protection. Zimbabwe's sophisticated policy architecture, including constitutional provisions, policies, and legislation, coexists with persistent implementation failures rooted in resource constraints, inadequate community consultation, weak enforcement mechanisms, and insufficient integration of indigenous knowledge systems. Comparative evidence suggests that policy comprehensiveness alone proves insufficient. Effective implementation requires political will, adequate resources, meaningful indigenous participation in decision-making, and robust accountability mechanisms. Countries with more integrated legal frameworks demonstrate better outcomes, confirming that harmonisation across environmental, child protection, and climate policies enhances effectiveness while fragmentation undermines rights protection.

Addressing these challenges demands transformative rights-based approaches that recognise indigenous children not as passive victims but as rights holders entitled to specific protections under international law. The policy recommendations proposed encompass legal harmonisation, institutional strengthening, genuine community engagement, targeted resource mobilisation, independent oversight mechanisms, climate-responsive education, gender-sensitive interventions, and regional cooperation, providing evidence-based pathways towards fulfilling state obligations while building climate-resilient futures for Africa's most vulnerable populations. Future research must advance this agenda through participatory methodologies that enable indigenous children to document impacts and propose solutions. It should also include longitudinal studies tracking intergenerational climate effects, comparative case studies examining implementation successes across diverse African contexts, dedicated investigations of gender-specific vulnerabilities and effective interventions, and systematic documentation of the efficacy of indigenous knowledge systems in climate adaptation. The stakes extend beyond immediate adaptation to encompass cultural survival, as climate change threatens the very existence of indigenous knowledge systems, languages, and practices developed over millennia. Only through integrated approaches that bridge environmental, social, legal, and cultural interventions can African nations fulfil their obligations under UNCRC, UNDRIP, and ACRWC. These approaches must be grounded in meaningful partnerships with indigenous communities and informed by rigorous ongoing research. This will ensure that indigenous children inherit both habitable environments and intact cultural heritages capable of sustaining future generations.

References

ACERWC. (2025). *ACERWC study on climate change & children's rights in Africa: A continental overview - 2024*. ACERWC Secretariat.

Addaney, M., Boshoff, E., & Olutola, B. (2017). The climate change and human rights nexus in Africa. *Amsterdam Law Forum*. Retrieved from https://ssrn.com/abstract=3213391

Anderko, L., Chalupka, S., Du, M., & Hauptman, M. (2020). Climate change and reproductive and children's health: A review of risks, exposures, and impacts. *Pediatric Research, 87*(2), 414–419. https://doi.org/10.1038/S41390-019-0654-7

Bauer, L., & Liao, X. (2020). Environmental degradation and the impact of artisanal mining on local communities in sub-Saharan Africa. *Environmental Research Journal, 12*(1), 45–58.

Benkenstein, A. (2012). *Artisanal and small-scale mining in Africa: Opportunities and challenges*. Retrieved October 3, 2025, from https://saiia.org.za/research/artisanal-and-small-scale-mining-in-africa-opportunities-and-challenges/

Bourdillon, M., Driscoll, J., Myers, W., O'Kane, C., & Rink, P. (2024). Climate crisis as a form of structural violence against children and youth. *BMJ Paediatrics Open, 8*(1), e003059. https://doi.org/10.1136/bmjpo-2024-003059

Braun, V., & Clarke, V. (2006). Using thematic analysis in psychology. *Qualitative Research in Psychology, 3*(2), 77–101. https://doi.org/10.1191/1478088706qp063oa

Bronfenbrenner, U. (1979). *The ecology of human development*. Harvard University Press.

Bulat, D. (2024). Climate Change, Children's Rights and the Rights of Future Generations. *Contemporary Issues of Communication, 3*(2), 165–172. https://doi.org/10.62425/conicom.1520699

Cameron, S., & Anderson, P. (2021). Child labour and exploitation in Africa's artisanal mining sector. *International Journal of Child Labour, 34*(2), 123–136.

Chikoko, W., & Chihiya, P. (2023). Climate change and vulnerabilities of children in rural Zimbabwe: The case of ward 14 of Bikita District, Zimbabwe. *African Journal of Social Work, 13*(2), 78–86. https://doi.org/10.4314/ajsw.v13i2.4

Children's Environmental Rights Initiative (CERI) Coalition. (2022). *Incorporating Child Rights into Climate Action: CERI Position Paper for COP27 (November)*. https://ceri-coalition.org/wp-content/uploads/2022/11/COP27-Position-Paper-Incorporating-Child-Rights-into-Climate-Action.pdf

Chuma, M., Field, T.-L., & Mutemeri, N. (2024). A conceptual framework for reframing artisanal and small-scale mining: Understanding characterisation of artisanal and small-scale mining in South Africa. *Journal of the Southern African Institute of Mining and Metallurgy, 124*(6), 311–318.

Dervieux, Z., & Belgherbi, M. (2020). "We used to go asking for the rains": Local interpretations of environmental changes and implications for natural resource management in Hwange District, Zimbabwe. In *Springer* (pp. 35–54). Springer. https://doi.org/10.1007/978-3-030-37312-2_3.

Dube, T., & Phiri, K. (2013). *Rural livelihoods under stress: The impact of climate change on livelihoods in South Western Zimbabwe*. Social Science Research Network. Retrieved from https://www.aijcrnet.com/journals/Vol_3_No_5_May_2013/2.pdf

Fambasayi, R., & Addaney, M. (2021). Cascading impacts of climate change and the rights of children in Africa: A reflection on the principle of intergenerational equity. *African Human Rights Law Journal, 21*(1), 29–51. https://doi.org/10.17159/1996-2096/2021/V21N1A3

Gibson, J. (2020). Indigenous communities and Africa's struggles for land and rights: A socio-environmental perspective. *African Indigenous Studies, 28*(3), 91–108.

Government of Zimbabwe. (2013). *Constitution of the Republic of Zimbabwe*. Government Printers.

Government of Zimbabwe. (2014). *National Climate Change Response Strategy*. Ministry of Environment, Water and Climate.

Government of Zimbabwe. (2017). *National Climate Policy*. Ministry of Environment, Water and Climate

Government of Zimbabwe (GoZ). (2024). *Zimbabwe national climate change adaptation plan*. Ministry of Environment, Climate and Wildlife.

Gundu-Jakarasi, V. N., & Nhidza, J. (2021). Climate change in Zimbabwe's vulnerable communities: A case study of supporting enhanced climate action project (SECA project) in Bulilima District. In *Springer* (pp. 211–223). Springer. https://doi.org/10.1007/978-3-030-70952-5_14.

Gwitira, I., Shekede, M. D., & Bhatasara, S. (2024). *Child-centred climate impact, vulnerability, and risk assessment for Zimbabwe*. UNICEF.

Harris, D., & Thompson, R. (2021). The ecological impacts of artisanal mining in Africa: An assessment of health risks to children. *Environmental Health Perspectives, 42*(4), 77–90.

Jones, L., Patel, K., & Smith, A. (2020). Artisanal mining and environmental health risks: A case study in West Africa. *Global Health Journal, 15*(2), 214–228.

Kecskés, G., & Lux, Á. (2023). There is no plan(et) B - Environmental "crossroads" of children's rights. *Hungarian Journal of Legal Studies, 64*(1), 4–31. https://doi.org/10.1556/2052.2023.00440. Retrieved from https://ssrn.com/abstract=4679842

Kigotho, M., & Mutuota, R. N. (2025). Climate change resilience in Africa: The case of Kenya and Zimbabwe. *MAI Journal, 14*(1), 115–121. https://doi.org/10.20507/maijournal.2025.14.1.10

Klein, R., & Oduro, A. (2021). The pollution of water bodies through artisanal mining in Africa: A critical analysis of toxic waste management. *Water Resources Journal, 17*(3), 89–102.

Kupika, O. L., Gandiwa, E., & Kativu, S. (2017). *Impacts of climate change and climate variability on wildlife resources in Southern Africa: Experience from selected protected areas in Zimbabwe*. IntechOpen. https://doi.org/10.5772/INTECHOPEN.70470

Mathe, T., Ncube, M., Moyo, F., & Ncube, V. (2025). Unravelling artisanal mining land use-land cover-change nexus through remote sensing in mining areas of Filabusi, Zimbabwe. *African Journal of Public Administration & Environmental Studies (AJOPAES), 4*(1).

Mezmur, B. D. (2023). The calm before the storm? Child rights climate change litigation in Africa, *De Jure Law Journal, 56*(1), 543–568. https://doi.org/10.17159/2225-7160/2023/v56a33

Moyo, T., & Dlamini, S. (2023). Policy gaps in environmental and children's rights law in Africa. *African Journal of Law and Policy, 12*(3), 45–67.

Moyo, F., Ndlovu, T., Francis, B., & Ncube, T. M. (2018). The effects of artisanal mining on irrigation farming-the case of Umzinyathini irrigation scheme in Umzingwane District, southern Matabeleland, Zimbabwe. *African Journal of Public Affairs, 10*(2), 139–162.

Ngugi, J. (2022). *Climate justice and indigenous rights in Africa*. Green World Publications.

Office of the High Commissioner for Human Rights. (2013). *WHO WILL BE ACCOUNTABLE? Human rights and the post-2015 development agenda*. United Nations.

Okonkwo, L. (2021). The rights-based approach in environmental governance. *Journal of Environmental Law, 19*(2), 101–126.

Rother, H.-A., Wijesekera, S., & Ward, F. (2019). The impact of the environment on South Africa's child and adolescent health: An overlooked health risk. *South African Child Gauge*. Retrieved October 3, 2025, from https://ci.uct.ac.za/sites/default/files/content_migration/health_uct_ac_za/533/files/CG2019%2520-%2520%25289%2529%2520The%2520impact%2520of%2520the%2520environment%2520on%2520SA%2520child%2520and%2520adolescent%2520health.pdf

Sango, I., & Godwell, N. (2015). Climate change trends and environmental impacts in the Makonde communal lands, Zimbabwe. *South African Journal of Science, 111*, 1–6. https://doi.org/10.17159/SAJS.2015/20140266

Seastedt, H., Schuetz, J., Perkins, A., Gamble, M. V., & Sinkkonen, A. (2024). Impact of urban biodiversity and climate change on children's health and well being. *Pediatric Research*. https://doi.org/10.1038/s41390-024-03769-1

Smith, A., & Jones, B. (2021a). *Children, climate change, and human rights: An African perspective*. Global Rights Press.

Smith, K. (2019). Child labor in Africa's artisanal mining sector: A growing concern. *Children's Rights Monitor, 22*(1), 56–70.

Smith, L., & Jones, P. (2021b). Artisanal mining and environmental pollution in Africa: A dual crisis for children's rights. *Environmental Policy Review, 15*(3), 204–218.

UNEP. (2024). *Emissions Gap Report 2024: No More Hot Air ... Please! With a Massive Gap Between Rhetoric and Reality, Countries Draft New Climate Commitments*. United Nations Environment Programme. https://doi.org/10.59117/20.500.11822/46404

UNICEF. (2018). *The state of the world's children 2018: Artisanal mining and children's rights*. UNICEF.

UNICEF. (2025). *Children and air pollution*. Retrieved October 3, 2025, from https://www.unicef.org/parenting/emergencies/air-pollution

UNICEF. (2025a). *When the rains don't come: Climate change through the eyes of Zimbabwe's children*. Retrieved October 2, 2025, from https://www.unicef.org/zimbabwe/stories/when-rains-dont-come-climate-change-through-eyes-zimbabwes-children

UNICEF. (2025b). *Child rights and climate. The climate crisis is a child rights crisis, and it is happening*. Retrieved October 2, 2025, from https://www.unicef.org/esa/child-rights-and-climate

UNICEF. (2021). *The climate crisis is a child rights crisis: Introducing the Children's Climate Risk Index*. UNICEF.

United Nations. (1989). *Convention on the rights of the child*. United Nations.

United Nations General Assembly. (2018). *Report of the Special Rapporteur on the issue of human rights obligations relating to the enjoyment of a safe, clean, healthy and sustainable environment (A/73/188)*. Retrieved October 3, 2025, from https://undocs.org/A/73/188

White, C., & Lee, M. (2019). Air pollution from artisanal mining and its impact on child health in sub-Saharan Africa. *Environmental Pollution Studies, 19*(2), 78–92.

Williams, P. C. M., Beardsley, J. C., Isaacs, D. F. A., Preisz, A., & Marais, B. J. (2023). The impact of climate change and biodiversity loss on the health of children: An ethical perspective. *Frontiers in Public Health, 10*. https://doi.org/10.3389/fpubh.2022.1048317

Part II
Climate-Induced Displacement and Child Vulnerability

Chapter 5
Climate-Induced Migration and Its Effects on Children's Welfare: A Case of Chivi District, Ward 32

Prosper Tonderai Mataruse and Clement Chipenda

5.1 Introduction

Climate change presents significant global challenges and increasingly threatens human well-being, especially in marginalised communities (Almulhim et al., 2024). The effects of climate change are evident in droughts, rising temperatures, and extreme weather events, which are continually compromising ecosystems, social structures, and the functioning of communities worldwide (Clarke et al., 2022; Hoffmann, 2022; Serdeczny et al., 2017). In Africa, where many countries, including Zimbabwe, depend on rain-fed agriculture, the effects of climate change are severely felt. Zimbabwe's main staple crop, which is maise, is particularly vulnerable due to its high sensitivity to rainfall variability (Källmark, 2018; Le Roux, 2009), making agricultural production and food security highly vulnerable to changes in climate (Kwanhi et al., 2024; Onafeso, 2020).

Droughts, one of Africa's most common climate change-induced disasters, are expected to increase in frequency, devastatingly affecting food and income security in developing countries (Ogunrinde et al., 2021). Their effects can cascade to communities, resulting in multiple, complex, and intertwined challenges (Boas et al., 2019; Hoffmann, 2022). Notably, droughts resulting from climate change are destroying crops, killing domestic animals, and altering traditional livelihood strategies for most rural communities (Milán-García et al., 2021; Wesselbaum & Aburn, 2019). These effects inevitably undermine the well-being and welfare of vulnerable

P. T. Mataruse (✉)
Department of Community and Social Development, University of Zimbabwe,
Harare, Zimbabwe

C. Chipenda
South African Research Chair in Social Policy, College of Graduate Studies,
University of South Africa, Pretoria, South Africa
e-mail: chipec@unisa.ac.za

E. Ndhlovu, C. Chipenda (eds.), *Climate Change and Children's Rights in Zimbabwe*, https://doi.org/10.1007/978-981-95-6005-9_5

populations, including children in regions already facing socio-economic challenges (Fambasayi & Addaney, 2021).

As the challenges from climate intensify, several studies have demonstrated that migration has become a typical response (Mayer, 2014; Wesselbaum & Aburn, 2019), as people search for alternative livelihood strategies elsewhere (Stavi et al., 2022). Climate change-induced migration is often a direct result of extreme weather events and environmental degradation, affecting health, nutrition, and livelihoods (Stavi et al., 2022; Wesselbaum & Aburn, 2019). Thus, climate change has triggered population movements across borders and within the same countries, leading to a substantial rise in migration and displacement (Källmark, 2018; Stapleton et al., 2017). Climate change-induced migration is increasingly prevalent in developing countries where the reliance on rain-fed agriculture makes communities even more vulnerable to climate variability (Stojanov et al., 2021; Thalheimer et al., 2021). Studies estimate that the climate change and migration nexus is becoming more complex, and it is expected to be significant in developing countries (Bohra-Mishra et al., 2014; Hanna & Oliva, 2016; Ogunrinde et al., 2021; Stojanov et al., 2021), and already, many of these developing countries are overburdened by multi-layered problems (Fambasayi & Addaney, 2021).

Families often are compelled to migrate due to food insecurity and failure to adapt to climate change-induced disasters (Kaczan & Orgill-Meyer, 2020; Stavi et al., 2022). A noticeable shift and growth in human mobility has occurred as climate change disrupts livelihoods (IPCC, 2023; McLeman, 2017). According to the IFRC (2021), in 2020 alone, about 40.5 million people were forced to migrate, with 30.7 million being direct victims of climate-induced hazards and risks. The risk of climate-induced migration as a coping mechanism lies in its potential impacts on family dynamics (McLeman, 2017). The vulnerability of children is compounded by their age, fewer economic resources, less mobility, extra care needs, and their dependence on adults for their development and welfare (Hutton, 2010). Migration often necessitates family separations (Bakaki, 2016). In most cases, migrating parents temporarily or permanently leave their children under the care of extended family members (Bakaki, 2016; Lu et al., 2021). When both parents are absent for prolonged periods, children face difficulties compared to peers raised with parental support (Lu et al., 2021). The burden of caring for the household falls on the shoulders of the remaining children, who often find themselves navigating the cares and responsibilities assumed prematurely (Bakaki, 2016). Some children end up taking care of younger siblings in the absence of their parents (Bakaki, 2016). Thus, separating children and parents can lead to challenges that take different forms, and understanding them is important for developing supportive policies for vulnerable children (Lu et al., 2021).

Bakaki (2016) notes that the emergence of climate change-induced migration is complex, and its effects cannot be overstated. Although parents recognise the importance of their presence in the development and welfare of their children, the socio-economic pressures resulting from climate change often leave them with no viable alternative but to migrate (Tang et al., 2024; Wei et al., 2023). While the involvement of extended family can provide some support to left-behind children, the effectiveness of this arrangement varies significantly, and it rarely compensates fully for the absence of a parent (Haagsman & Mazzucato, 2020). Although migration has the potential to yield some economic benefits and cushion the family, its benefits come at a significant cost to the welfare of left-behind children (Fambasayi & Addaney, 2021).

While substantial research has been done on the relationship between climate change and migration, a critical gap exists in understanding the experiences of children left behind. Therefore, this study seeks to address this gap by establishing how climate change-induced migration impacts the welfare of children left behind, thus contributing valuable insights to the existing body of knowledge. This study addresses the following fundamental questions: (1) How is climate change affecting livelihoods in Ward 32 of Chivi District? (2) What patterns and trends of climate-induced migration are observed in recent years in Ward 32 of Chivi District? (3) How does climate change-induced migration affect the welfare and well-being of children left behind in Ward 32 of Chivi District? By answering these questions, the study aims to create an avenue for tailored and context-specific interventions meant to improve the welfare of children left behind due to climate change-induced migration.

5.2 Literature Review

In Zimbabwe, the intersection of climate change, migration, and child welfare presents significant challenges, particularly within its predominantly agrarian context, where rural livelihoods heavily depend on agriculture (Källmark, 2018; Tom, 2024). Climate change is seen functioning as a 'threat multiplier', especially for communities reliant on rain-fed agriculture, leading to increased migration as families seek food security (Chitongo et al., 2021; Ncube et al., 2024). Households in small-scale farming areas increasingly resort to migration as a coping strategy against extreme climatic events that disrupt agricultural productivity (Maganga & Suso, 2022). Over the past decades, the country's experience with severe socio-economic crises, including hyperinflation, erosion of savings, and inadequate social protection mechanisms, compounded the challenges posed by increasing drought frequency and rainfall unpredictability. This has made traditional farming increasingly precarious (Bushu & Kufakurinani, 2024; Kwanhi et al., 2024). These environmental pressures and existing socio-economic vulnerabilities drive many rural communities to adopt migration as an adaptation strategy. This study employs and integrates three theoretical frameworks to analyse these complex dynamics: push-pull migration theory, vulnerability and adaptation framework (VAF), and Bronfenbrenner's ecological systems theory. This section synthesises existing literature to highlight how these frameworks can be utilised in an integrated manner to enhance our understanding of climate-induced migration's effects on children's welfare, particularly in a rural Zimbabwe context, where existing socio-economic challenges strain community resilience (Fambasayi & Addaney, 2021).

5.2.1 The Push-Pull Migration Theory

The push-pull migration theory was selected as one of the frameworks for this study. This was due to its utility in offering a critical understanding of the complexities of climate-induced migration. In the context of climate change-oriented studies, this theory posits that 'push' factors such as environmental degradation and the economic repercussions of climate events drive individuals away from their homes. 'Pull', conversely, comprises factors such as the allure of improved opportunities in other regions, attracting people to new destinations (Shrestha et al., 2017; Wesselbaum & Aburn, 2019). The nexus between these 'push and pull' factors significantly influences migration patterns, and numerous studies support this phenomenon. It has been observed, for example, that adverse climate events can lead to diminished agricultural productivity, prompting individuals to seek better living conditions elsewhere. In Nepal, rainfall shocks have increased migration to India by 54%, highlighting how environmental stressors can compel households to relocate (Shrestha et al., 2017). Even wealthier individuals may find their living conditions untenable when economic decline and conflict prevail, resulting in heightened migration rates abroad (Shrestha et al., 2017). On the pull side, it has been observed that economic opportunities in sectors experiencing growth, such as manufacturing and construction, serve as powerful incentives for migration. These sectors attract individuals to regions with better job prospects, further driving migration (Shrestha et al., 2017). Social networks also play a crucial role in facilitating migration. Established connections in destination areas can ease the transition for newcomers and help them integrate into their new environments (Feleky & Gödrı, 2014).

While the push-pull theory effectively explains many migration decisions, it is essential to recognise its limitations. For example, this is important when explaining why some individuals opt to remain in their home countries despite adverse conditions. Cultural ties, family responsibilities, and perceived risks associated with migration can strongly influence these decisions (Feleky & Gödrı, 2014). The complex dynamics of climate-induced migration are further explained by Stavi et al. (2022), who note that the deterioration of traditional livelihood strategies, such as rain-fed agriculture, can serve as a significant push factor, while the promise of economic opportunities in other regions can act as a compelling pull factor. This dynamic is influenced by many factors, including economic, environmental, social, and political elements, all of which contribute to the decision-making processes surrounding migration. The push-pull framework explains how drought and agricultural failure exert immense pressures on families, compelling them to seek alternatives elsewhere. Understanding push-pull migration dynamics is crucial for formulating effective migration policies and adaptation strategies. The socio-economic, environmental, and political factors that shape climate-induced migration patterns must be considered, ultimately fostering resilience in affected communities.

5.2.2 The Vulnerability and Adaptation Framework (VAF)

The second theory that the study utilised was the vulnerability and adaptation framework (VAF). The VAF is important in showing community responses to climate-related stresses. It is relevant when examining why specific populations, especially in marginalised communities, face disproportionate impacts from climate change (Aswani et al., 2018). For the study, the VAF was considered to help explain why migration emerges as an adaptation strategy, which, unfortunately, often creates new vulnerabilities, particularly for children left behind. As a structured approach, the VAF assesses and enhances resilience against climate change impacts by evaluating vulnerability across various contexts (Hung et al., 2024). It has utility in guiding policy and planning, and this stems from its integration of diverse methodologies and stakeholder inputs to create a comprehensive understanding of climate risks and adaptive capacities (Ziervogel & Taylor, 2023). The VAF encompasses several key components. First, it distinguishes between susceptibility to harm and system resilience. This enables a deep understanding of how different systems respond to climate stressors (Shockley, 2017). Second, it emphasises participatory methods. This ensures that local knowledge and preferences inform assessments, thereby enhancing the relevance and effectiveness of adaptation strategies (Ziervogel & Taylor, 2023). Finally, it accommodates diverse contexts and data availability by promoting varied assessment depths and tools. These are crucial for effective climate adaptation responses (Ziervogel & Taylor, 2023).

This framework's selection was seen as particularly appropriate given that research consistently demonstrates vulnerability's versatile and compounded nature. As Serdeczny et al. (2017) and Clarke et al. (2022) emphasise, climate change impacts cascade through social structures, creating interconnected challenges that affect community functioning. In Zimbabwe's context, this vulnerability is particularly evident in a country highly dependent on agriculture, with many communities producing climate-sensitive crops (Källmark, 2018; Kwanhi et al., 2024). These indicate that environmental and socio-economic vulnerabilities intersect, which justifies the need for a comprehensive analytical framework, hence the decision to use the VAF.

5.2.3 Bronfenbrenner's Ecological Systems Theory

The third theory utilised in this study is Bronfenbrenner's ecological systems theory, also known as the bioecological model. This theory emphasises the relationships between individuals and their environments. This framework was seen to be valuable for understanding how climate-induced migration impacts child welfare across various systemic levels. The theory delineates several layers: the microsystem (direct interactions with family, peers, and schools), the mesosystem (connections between microsystems), the exosystem (external influences), and the macrosystem (cultural and societal norms). Each level shapes individual development and well-being (Gonzales, 2020; Kaushik & Arokkiaraj, 2023). This theory is relevant in examining the effects of parental migration on children's immediate microsystem. Research by Udrea and Guiu (2022) and Lu (2014) indicates that when parents migrate, children experience both economic advantages and social challenges. Their environments change significantly, often forcing them to take on adult responsibilities at a young age. At the mesosystem level, the theory highlights how extended family relationships strive to fill the gap left by absent parents. However, as Haagsman and Mazzucato (2020) noted, this support seldom completely mitigates the negative impacts of parental absence. At the exosystem level, Bronfenbrenner's model highlights how climate change affects local economies and agricultural systems, which in turn can influence children's welfare through their parents' employment and migration choices (Genienė et al., 2021). The framework emphasises the importance of supportive environments in fostering positive developmental outcomes for children, particularly in adverse situations.

The theory aids in understanding how migrants navigate various ecological systems, impacting their adaptation and integration processes. It also provides a lens for analysing how environmental changes affect community structures and individual resilience, especially among vulnerable populations. As it presents opportunities for examining the interactions between individuals and their environments across multiple levels, this theory offers valuable perspectives into the connections between climate change, migration, and child welfare. This motivated and justified its selection for this study.

5.2.4 Theoretical Integration and Research Application

Integrating the push-pull migration theory, the vulnerability and adaptation framework, and Bronfenbrenner's ecological systems theory provided a robust analytical foundation for the study. This foundation was important for examining the relationship between climate change, migration, and child welfare in the study area. Each theory contributed unique insights and, when combined, created a comprehensive framework that went a long way in addressing the study's objectives. To examine how climate change affects livelihoods in the study area, the vulnerability and adaptation framework provided the analytical tools for understanding the direct impacts of environmental changes and the community's adaptive capacity. This framework helped to identify the specific vulnerabilities and explain how these vulnerabilities translate into livelihood challenges. Combined with push-pull migration theory, it showed the thresholds at which environmental stressors become migration triggers.

The patterns and trends of climate-induced migration were primarily examined through push-pull migration theory. This theory provided a structured approach for analysing migration decisions in response to environmental pressures. It provided the basis for explaining why specific migration patterns emerge and persist, as documented by Wesselbaum and Aburn (2019). The vulnerability and adaptation framework could supplement this analysis by highlighting how different adaptive capacity levels influence community migration decisions. For the analysis of the effects of climate-induced migration on children's welfare, Bronfenbrenner's ecological systems theory was particularly valuable. It provided a multi-layered framework for examining how parental migration reverberates through children's social ecosystems, affecting their development and well-being. When integrated with the other theories, it revealed how environmental vulnerabilities and migration decisions cascade through family systems to affect children's lives.

The synthesis of these theories was practical and powerful as it captured both the macro-level environmental and economic forces driving migration and the micro-level impacts on family dynamics and child development. This integrated approach acknowledged that climate-induced migration's effects on children cannot be understood in isolation but must be examined within the context of broader environmental, social, and economic systems. The theoretical integration provided a framework for understanding how local cultural and social structures, such as extended family networks, mediate the impacts of climate-induced migration on children. As it employed these complementary theoretical frameworks, the study was able to move beyond simply documenting the effects of climate-induced migration to understanding the underlying mechanisms that create and perpetuate challenges for children.

5.3 Methodology

The study employed a case study design in which interpretive research philosophy, aligning with qualitative methodology, was used. The interpretive philosophy acknowledges and emphasises the subjectivity of reality, highlighting that it is socially constructed, thus placing the understanding of lived experiences and meanings within specific contexts. Using this research philosophy, the study aimed to understand children's lived experiences in the absence of their parents.

5.3.1 Study Area

The study was carried out in four villages, namely, Masvibe, Nyika, Garabwe, and Muzenda, located in Ward 32 of Chivi District. The District is located in Masvingo Province in Zimbabwe at 20.05′S; 31.37′E, with an average elevation of 890 m above sea level. Chivi District falls under agro-ecological region 5, which is characterised by highly variable and erratic rainfall. As such, Chivi is one of the driest districts in Zimbabwe and receives an average annual rainfall of 450 mm. The arid nature of the area makes it more susceptible to droughts, making rain-fed crop production and livestock rearing risky.

Chivi District was chosen because it embodies the climatic and socio-economic vulnerabilities central to the study, particularly its susceptibility to climate variability and high migration rates due to its proximity to the Zimbabwe-South Africa border. The District is characterised by subsistence farming and frequent migration patterns, which provide a suitable context for examining the effects of climate change-induced parental migration on children.

5.3.2 Study Site Selection and Sampling Methods

Ward 32 of Chivi District was purposely selected based on its accessibility, the researchers' familiarity with the area, and climatic vulnerabilities. The researchers leveraged existing networks in the District, ensuring cost-effective and logistical efficiency. These aspects were important for answering the study's research questions. The area's high incidence of migration provided a relevant background for the study's research questions.

Four villages were purposively selected for key informant interviews and in-depth interviews. Purposive sampling was also used to identify participants for key informant interviews and in-depth interviews. Participants were mainly selected community members, local leaders, and children left behind. The ages of selected community members and local leaders ranged between 35 and 65 years. Targeted participants were those who knew about climate change-induced migration and its effects on the children left behind. Left-behind children aged 8–14 years were included because they could provide detailed responses relevant to the research questions. All the participants were identified and recruited for the study with the help of village heads. Table 5.1 shows the distribution of research participants.

5.3.3 Data Sources and Collection Methods

In order to obtain data responding to the research questions, the study used key informants and in-depth interviews with selected community members, local leaders, and children. Including children in the study created a platform where they

Table 5.1 Distribution of research participants

Village	Key informant interviews (local leaders)	In-depth interviews (selected community members)	In-depth interviews (children left behind)
Masvibe	1	2	3
Nyika	1	1	2
Garabwe	1	1	3
Muzenda	1	2	3
Total	*4*	*6*	*11*

expressed their views on how climate change-induced parental migration affects their welfare and well-being. The interviews captured how climate change affects livelihoods, observed climate change-induced migration trends, and their effects on the welfare and well-being of children left behind.

5.3.4 Data Analysis Procedures

Key informant interviews and in-depth interviews were recorded with the participants' permission. The data collected from key informants and in-depth interviews were transcribed verbatim and analysed using a thematic approach. The thematic approach included identifying major and recurring themes essential for understanding climate change-induced migration and its effects on the welfare and well-being of children left behind.

5.3.5 Ethical Considerations

Ethical considerations were integral to this study, particularly given its focus on children, a vulnerable population group. The researchers ensured adherence to ethical research principles. For adult participants, informed consent was obtained after providing detailed information about the study's objectives, procedures, and voluntary nature. For children, assent was secured alongside consent from their guardians or a respected elderly community member. The researchers explained the study in age-appropriate language to ensure understanding. Participants were informed of their right to withdraw at any stage without penalty, ensuring their autonomy and comfort throughout the research process. Measures were implemented to protect participants' identities and sensitive information. Pseudonyms were used during data transcription and analysis to ensure anonymity (Bloch, 2008). Working with children requires additional precautions to avoid psychological or emotional distress. The interview process was designed to be sensitive, respectful, and child-friendly. Researchers ensured that questions were non-invasive and allowed children to express themselves freely. In cases where children appeared distressed, interviews were paused or terminated.

5.4 Results

This section presents findings from in-depth interviews conducted with children, selected community members, and key informants. The interviews focused on characterising climate change-induced migration in Chivi District. Diverse perspectives from the participants also provide an analysis of how parental migration, driven by climate-related factors, affects various aspects of children's lives and overall well-being.

5.4.1 *Characterisation of Climate Change-Induced Parental Migration*

In Chivi District, Ward 32, community members and local leaders described climate change as a persistent and overwhelming challenge that has significantly transformed local livelihoods and ways of life. Key informant interviews underscored that frequent droughts and poor harvests often force many adults, especially parents, to migrate to urban areas or cross the border into South Africa for employment opportunities. Some individuals sometimes migrate to countries such as Australia and the United Kingdom. Through established networks in destination areas, those who migrate find it relatively easy to find their footing. Migration has also become intergenerational, with some youths inheriting the practice from their parents as it is perceived to be the only viable strategy for survival. One community elder explained:

> Our fields used to sustain us, but now they barely produce anything. The rains have become so erratic, and our fields are no longer a reliable food source. Parents are forced to leave just to make ends meet. In most cases, migration occurs hastily, which indicates the urgency and desperation that drive migration as families face declining agricultural yields and dwindling income-generating opportunities due to erratic rainfall patterns.

Participants emphasised that failing crops, declining soil quality, and persistent water shortages create unbearable and unsustainable living conditions, necessitating migration in search of better opportunities. However, migration as an adaptation strategy often comes at a significant cost to family structures and children's welfare. Local leaders echoed these concerns, acknowledging the growing dependence on migration as a means of survival. A village head said:

> Parents have no choice but to leave for South Africa, Masvingo, or Harare. If our people stay here without jobs or food, they risk starvation. However, when they leave, the family breaks apart, and children suffer.

These accounts reveal the two-sided nature of climate-induced migration as a coping strategy for many families. While it provides livelihood opportunities, it comes with social costs, as it disrupts ideal family structures, with children being left without consistent parental guidance.

5.4.2 *Impacts of Climate Change-Induced Migration on the Welfare of Children*

5.4.2.1 Lack of Access to Developmental Support for Children Left Behind

A significant theme emerging from the interviews with children was the strain caused by prolonged separation from their parents. Many children expressed feelings of abandonment at critical stages of their lives, despite their understanding of the financial necessity of their parents' migration. One young boy said his mother left for South Africa 4 years ago and has not returned since then. Although she sends remittances back home, the boy indicated that her absence left a substantial void in his life. While remittances were acknowledged as important for meeting basic needs, participants highlighted that they cannot substitute the developmental support that parents provide. Key informants underscored that the absence of parents often disrupts a child's developmental support, as parents will no longer be present to oversee personal growth and all other key aspects of a child's development. Community members also observed that children who are left behind by migrating parents often lack the nurturing and support that only parents can provide. A relative who was taking care of the children left behind shared:

> We try our best but cannot deny that we are not their parents. These children need more than just food; they need their parents' love and advice. Local leaders or even schools should find community programmes to ensure children who are left behind find professional people who can help them navigate different stages of growth and development.

5.4.2.2 Impacts on Physical Health and Hygiene

The participants reported physical health challenges faced by children left behind as particularly severe. A key informant noted that these children are at a greater risk of illness because there is often no one to ensure that they receive regular medical check-ups or timely treatment. Participants underscored that, in the absence of their parents, many children were suffering from malnutrition due to poor diet and lack of medical attention. One of the children who is left behind shared a personal account of health-related challenges she is facing. She explained:

> Sometimes I feel sick, but my grandmother just tells me to wait until it passes. She does not have money for medication, not even for something as simple as a painkiller. Recently, I started my monthly period, but I do not have timely access to menstrual pads. Because of this, I end up missing school. My grandmother says my parents have not sent money to buy pads, and she cannot afford to buy them for me.

Community members also raised concerns over long-term health challenges for children who are left behind by their migrating parents at a tender age. One community member observed:

> We see many cases of kwashiorkor and stunted growth among the children who are left behind. Maybe these children are not eating balanced meals. The elderly who are left to take care of the young children may lack both the physical capacity and financial resources to provide nutritious food. This takes a toll on the elderly people, especially when the parents are not sending remittances.

5.4.2.3 Mental and Emotional Health of Children Left Behind

Children left behind by migrating parents experience notable emotional and mental strain. Participants widely reported feelings of loneliness, abandonment, and isolation. These emotions were said to have a profound impact on children's overall mental health. One key informant narrated that:

> There are noticeable behavioural changes among children who were left behind. Most of these children are withdrawn and do not participate in common activities among their peers. Some even go to the extreme extent of not going to school.

Children expressed these struggles, with some reporting a lack of interest in interacting or playing with others. They highlighted that they only want to stay home doing household chores or playing alone. Community members also observed the emotional burdens these children carry and pointed out that without mental health support, these emotional burdens could worsen, potentially leading to depression or risky behaviour.

5.4.2.4 Lack of Protection and Safety

Children who are left behind and without their parents are highly vulnerable to various safety risks, including abuse and exploitation. Local leaders expressed their concerns about the lack of adult supervision. A local leader remarked:

> There are cases of young girls who are being coerced into early marriages or transactional relationships, and boys are being exploited for labour. A young girl in our village, who is about 14 years old, eloped because her parents were not there to guide and protect her. Without their parents, some of these children are taken advantage of, and there is no one to protect them.

The above concerns were echoed by children who shared personal experiences of feeling unsafe. A young girl confided:

> We are always worried, and it is even worse at night. It is just the two of us here with my big sister, who is 15 years old. We lock all the doors at sunset, we are afraid of going out at night, and we just fear that anything bad can happen to us in the absence of our parents or any adult figure at home. We have no choice but to keep living in constant fear because our parents had to go and earn a living for us.

5.4.2.5 Poor Shelter and Living Conditions

The living conditions of children left behind often worsen after their parents migrate. Homes were reported by participants to be deteriorating due to the lack of maintenance, thus making children struggle with inadequate and unsafe housing. A community leader pointed out that some of these children are living in broken houses, with leaking roofs and no doors, and their parents are away and cannot fix these problems. Children themselves also spoke about the difficult conditions they face, with one child sharing:

> As you can see, our house no longer has window panes, and it is falling apart. It gets even worse when it rains; we have to find somewhere else to sleep or just find a corner to make sure that we stay dry. We have tried to tell our parents, who are in Harare, to fix the leaking roof, but they keep saying they do not have money. They insist that we should go to the fields to get thatching grass, but it is never enough. The growth of the grass is affected by the erratic rains, and the little that grows is destroyed by grazing animals.

This testimony illustrates the severe living conditions faced by children left behind. Participants also highlighted that the lack of proper shelter further exposes these children to physical health challenges, especially during rainy weather.

5.4.2.6 Educational Challenges for Children Left Behind

Due to climate-induced migration, education is one of the most disrupted aspects of children's lives in Chivi District. Key informants and community members noted that many children end up dropping out of school because they are needed for household labour. The absence of financial support from parents, especially those who fail to send sufficient remittances, leaves caregivers in difficult positions. Key informants and community members noted a common trend where children who once attended school regularly begin to miss classes, and some eventually drop out. They highlighted that in the absence of parents, there is no one to make sure that children who are left behind receive the necessary educational support and go to school regularly.

Children themselves voiced frustration over the barriers to their education. A 12-year-old boy said:

> In the absence of my parents, there is no one who values our education like they do. Some days, my grandfather makes me miss school because he insists that I should help him herd our cattle. Household responsibilities can weigh us down, and we end up missing school.

5.5 Discussion

In this discussion section, we critically engage with findings from the study to better understand the nexus between climate-induced migration and its effects on children's welfare. As we situate these findings within the frameworks of push-pull migration theory, the vulnerability and adaptation framework, and Bronfenbrenner's ecological systems theory, this section engages with the implications of climate change on migration patterns and the resultant impacts on children's lives. Premised on findings presented in the preceding section, this highlights the necessity for holistic approaches to address these complex challenges.

5.5.1 *Climate Change as a Driver of Migration*

From the findings, it has been noted that climate change emerges as a significant driver of migration, which transforms traditional livelihoods in rural Zimbabwe. The study further revealed that environmental degradation is a push factor, compelling families to reconsider their survival strategies. In Chivi District, erratic rainfall patterns and increasingly severe droughts have precipitated a sharp decline in agricultural productivity, forcing parents to seek alternative economic opportunities. The push-pull migration theory provides a comprehensive framework for understanding these migration dynamics. As Wesselbaum and Aburn (2019) have argued, environmental stressors push individuals away from their traditional homes, while potential economic opportunities in urban areas or abroad serve as compelling pull factors. This study confirms these dynamics and extends the narrative beyond simplistic environmental determinism to show the complex nexus of socio-economic factors that influence migration decisions in different ways. The environmental pressures are particularly acute in Zimbabwe's agricultural context. Kwanhi et al. (2024) have highlighted how climate change disproportionately impacts rain-fed agricultural systems. This in turn creates a cascade of economic vulnerabilities. In Chivi District, this was evident. What is clear and a significant takeaway from the above is that the migration process is not merely a response to immediate environmental stressors but is also influenced by broader socio-economic factors, which include poverty, unemployment, and lack of access to resources. This can be exemplified by the observation that families with limited access to farming equipment or financial resources tend to find themselves more vulnerable to the impacts of climate change. This increases their likelihood of migration. In addition, social networks are critical as they facilitate migration. Established connections in destination areas can be seen providing support and guidance, further reinforcing the patterns of movement observed in the Chivi community.

5.5.2 *Intergenerational Migration Patterns*

A significant and concerning trend emerging from the research is the intergenerational nature of migration. Migration is no longer viewed as a temporary survival strategy but has become a normalised way of life for many families. Young people are increasingly internalising migration as the primary pathway for economic survival, creating a cyclical pattern of displacement that threatens community stability. This trend raises serious questions about community resilience and long-term development. As noted earlier, Fambasayi and Addaney (2021) have argued that such continuous migration can erode local social structures and traditional livelihood strategies. This study reveals how children grow up in environments where migration is perceived as the default solution to economic hardship, potentially perpetuating a cycle of vulnerability that extends beyond individual family experiences. From the study, as we reflect on the responses of community leaders and parents, the reality is clear that while migration may provide essential remittances that support basic needs, it simultaneously disrupts family cohesion and emotional bonds. Thus, while the economic rationale behind migration is clear, with remittances providing essential financial support, this economic survival strategy comes at a significant social and emotional cost. Haagsman and Mazzucato (2020) have emphasised that parental absence's emotional and developmental impacts cannot be easily compensated for by financial support, creating long-term challenges for children and communities.

5.5.3 *Impacts on Child Welfare*

5.5.3.1 Developmental Support and Emotional Challenges

The absence of parents in most instances creates challenges for children's developmental trajectories. Bronfenbrenner's ecological systems theory has utility in providing a critical lens for understanding these impacts. It highlights how the family microsystem and immediate environment fundamentally shape child development. The study findings in Chivi confirm the efficacy of the arguments of this theory, and findings highlight emotional and psychological challenges as children experience significant feelings of abandonment and isolation. These findings align with research by Udrea and Guiu (2022) and Lu (2014), which demonstrates how parental migration disrupts children's developmental support systems. Consequently, children are often forced to assume adult responsibilities prematurely, which alters their childhood experiences and developmental pathways. In light of these findings, it becomes evident that community-based programmes providing mentorship and developmental support for left-behind children are essential. Local leaders and educators could be crucial in establishing initiatives that promote engagement, mentorship, and emotional well-being. This can help to fill the gaps left by absent parents. Such initiatives should be inclusive and tailored to address the specific needs of children in these vulnerable situations. This may ensure that they receive the social and emotional support necessary for healthy development.

5.5.3.2 Physical and Mental Health Implications

The physical health challenges faced by children left behind are alarming. Malnutrition, inadequate medical care, and limited access to healthcare emerge as critical issues. The absence of parental oversight often results in compromised nutritional intake and delayed medical interventions. This reflects broader socio-economic disparities, which are worsened by climate-induced migration. These dynamics highlight the necessity for health interventions that specifically target the needs of children in rural contexts such as Chivi. Mobile health clinics and community health education programmes that empower caregivers with knowledge and resources are critical interventions.

In addition, mental health impacts can be seen as being equally significant. It has been noted that children experience emotional burdens which manifest through withdrawal, anxiety, and potential long-term psychological challenges. The constant fear and uncertainty about parental well-being creates a persistent emotional stress that can have lasting developmental consequences. In light of these dynamics, mental health support services, including counselling and peer support groups, are of critical importance. They must be integrated into community initiatives to provide these children with safe spaces to express their feelings and develop coping strategies.

5.5.3.3 Safety, Vulnerability, and Educational Disruptions

The study reveals that the lack of adult supervision significantly heightens safety risks for children left behind, exposing them to various forms of exploitation and abuse. Young girls are particularly vulnerable, facing increased risks of forced early marriage, sexual exploitation, and transactional relationships. Economic desperation and the absence of protective adult figures worsen these threats. Boys are not immune to these vulnerabilities, as they encounter heightened risks of labour exploitation and premature economic responsibilities. Local leaders have emphasised the urgent need for community-based protective mechanisms, including awareness campaigns to educate families about these risks and provide resources for safeguarding children.

Educational continuity emerges as a critical casualty of climate-induced migration. Many children are compelled to drop out of school to assume household responsibilities or due to financial constraints resulting from their parents' absence. When parents are not present to advocate for their children's education, the perceived importance of schooling diminishes, jeopardising immediate learning opportunities and posing long-term threats to social mobility and economic prospects.

These findings highlight the dynamic ways in which climate change, migration, and child welfare are interconnected, creating a complex web of vulnerabilities that necessitate sophisticated, multidimensional responses. Educational programmes that provide scholarships, school supplies, and after-school support are essential to address these challenges. Such interventions can help mitigate the adverse effects of migration on children's education, ensuring that they remain engaged in learning and have the necessary resources to succeed. The study highlights the critical need for a holistic approach integrating protective measures with educational support to foster resilience among children left behind in climate-induced migration. As they address safety and educational disruptions, communities can better support vulnerable children and enhance their prospects for a healthier and more stable future.

5.6 Conclusion and Recommendations

This study provides critical insights into the relationship between climate change, migration, and child welfare in rural Zimbabwe. As it synthesised multiple theoretical perspectives, the study showed the dynamic challenges children and communities face during environmental and economic transformations. The study has revealed that this has implications for understanding how ecological shifts impact vulnerable populations. The study has shown that climate-induced migration significantly affects the welfare of children left behind, exposing them to increased safety risks, emotional distress, and educational disruptions. The absence of adult supervision creates vulnerabilities that can lead to exploitation and abuse, particularly for young girls, while boys also encounter pressures related to labour demands and economic responsibilities. Educational continuity suffers as children leave school to assume household roles, potentially compromising their future social and financial prospects. These findings reveal underlying systemic issues and challenges that point to urgent attention.

From the study, several policy recommendations emerged. These are mainly centred on developing targeted community support programmes. These initiatives should provide specialised developmental assistance for children who are left behind, with a strong focus on emotional and psychological support. Comprehensive mental health resources are critical for addressing the psychological impacts of family separation. Educational interventions are equally essential and can be used to mitigate migration's adverse effects on children's learning and academic engagement. Community-based protective measures are also very important for safeguarding children's well-being. This approach requires educating families about exploitation risks and providing resources to protect vulnerable children. Awareness campaigns and partnerships with local authorities can help monitor and prevent potential abuses. Creating sustainable economic alternatives represents a key strategy for reducing migration pressures, enabling families to remain together and thrive in their home communities.

Future research is essential on this issue. It should prioritise longitudinal studies that track the long-term developmental outcomes of children affected by climate-induced migration. Such research will provide important information that is useful for intervention effectiveness and community resilience strategies. Developing context-specific models that address the unique challenges of rural populations in Zimbabwe will be critical for meaningful progress. The study demonstrates that understanding the dynamic interactions between climate change, migration, and child welfare is essential for developing effective support strategies. By recognising the interconnected nature of these challenges, policymakers and community leaders can create more responsive and holistic approaches to supporting vulnerable children and families navigating complex environmental and economic transformations.

References

Almulhim, A. I., Alverio, G. N., Sharifi, A., Shaw, R., Huq, S., Mahmud, M. J., & Abubakar, I. R. (2024). Climate-induced migration in the Global South: An in-depth analysis. *Climate Action, 3*(1), 47. https://doi.org/10.1038/s41612-024-00115-4

Aswani, S., Howard, J. A. E., Gasalla, M. A., Jennings, S., Malherbe, W., Martins, I. M., & Watmough, G. R. (2018). An integrated framework for assessing coastal community vulnerability across cultures, oceans, and scales. *Climate and Development, 11*(4), 365–382. https://doi.org/10.1080/17565529.2018.1442795

Bakaki, Z. (2016). *Environmental refugees: The impact of climate change on emigration*. ETH Zürich. Retrieved from https://unige.ch/sciences-societe/speri/files/3014/5294/4496/Zorzeta_Bakaki_-_Environmental_refugees_ZBakaki.pdf

Bloch, M. (2008). Truth and sight: Generalising without universalising. *Journal of the Royal Anthropological Institute, 14*, S22–S32.

Boas, I., Farbotko, C., Adams, H., Sterly, H., Bush, S., Van der Geest, K., & Hulme, M. (2019). Climate migration myths. *Nature Climate Change, 9*(12), 901–903. https://doi.org/10.1038/s41558-019-0640-8

Bohra-Mishra, P., Oppenheimer, M., & Hsiang, S. M. (2014). Nonlinear permanent migration response to climatic variations, but minimal response to disasters. *Proceedings of the National Academy of Sciences, 111*(27), 9780–9785. https://doi.org/10.1073/pnas.1321795111

Bushu, N., & Kufakurinani, U. (2024, July 17). The Zimbabwean economic crisis. *Oxford Research Encyclopedia of African History*. Retrieved November 16, 2024, from https://oxfordre.com/africanhistory/view/10.1093/acrefore/9780190277734.001.0001/acrefore-9780190277734-e-1242

Chitongo, L., Dzvimbo, M. A., & Zhanda, K. (2021). Children's climate change activism and protests in Africa: Reflections and lessons from Greta Thunberg. *Bulletin of Science, Technology and Society, 41*(4), 87–98. https://doi.org/10.1177/02704676211036698

Clarke, B., Otto, F., Stuart-Smith, R., & Harrington, L. (2022). Extreme weather impacts of climate change: An attribution perspective. *Environmental Research: Climate, 1*(1), 012001. https://doi.org/10.1007/s44165-022-00001-1

Fambasayi, R., & Addaney, M. (2021). Cascading impacts of climate change and children's rights in Africa: A reflection on the principle of intergenerational equity. *African Human Rights Law Journal, 21*(1), 29–51. https://doi.org/10.17159/1996-2096/2021/v21n1a3

Feleky, G. A., & Gödrı, I. (2014). Why do they stay when they are not supposed to? Reconsidering the push-pull theory. In *European population conference 2014: Transitions: Opportunities and threats*. Hungarian Democratic Institute (HRDI).

Genienė, R., Šumskienė, E., Gevorgianienė, V., & Mataitytė-Diržienė, J. (2021). The deinstitutionalisation of persons with psychosocial disabilities from the perspective of ecological systems theory. *Socialinė Teorija, Empirija, Politika Ir Praktika, 22*, 28–43. https://doi.org/10.15388/STEPP.2021.27

Gonzales, M. (2020). The Bronfenbrenner micro- and meso-systems. In *Systems thinking for supporting students with special needs and disabilities* (pp. 81–92). https://doi.org/10.1007/978-981-33-4558-4_6

Haagsman, K., & Mazzucato, V. (2020). The well-being of stay-behind family members in migrant households. In T. Bastia & R. Skeldon (Eds.), *Routledge handbook of migration and development* (pp. 1–16). Routledge.

Hanna, R., & Oliva, P. (2016). Implications of climate change for children in developing countries. *Future of Children, 26*(1), 115–132.

Hoffmann, R. (2022). Contextualising climate change impacts on human mobility in African drylands. *Earth's Future, 10*, e2021EF002591. https://doi.org/10.1029/2021EF002591

Hung, C.-H., Hung, H.-C., & Hsu, M.-C. (2024). Linking the interplay of resilience, vulnerability, and adaptation to long-term changes in metropolitan spaces for climate-related disaster risk management. *Climate Risk Management, 44*, 100618. https://doi.org/10.1016/j.crm.2024.100618

Hutton, D. (2010). Vulnerability of children: More than a question of age. *Radiation Protection Dosimetry, 142*(1), 54–57.

IFRC. (2021). Displacement in a changing climate: Localised humanitarian action at the forefront of the climate crisis.. Retrieved from https://www.ifrc.org/sites/default/files/2021-10/IFRC-Displacement-Climate-Report-2021_1.pdf.

IPCC. (2023). *AR6 synthesis report: Climate change*. Intergovernmental Panel on Climate Change.

Kaczan, D. J., & Orgill-Meyer, J. (2020). The impact of climate change on migration: A synthesis of recent empirical insights. *Climatic Change, 158*(3), 281–300. https://doi.org/10.1007/s10584-019-02429-1

Källmark, L. (2018). *How does drought affect child health outcomes in Zimbabwe? An econometric analysis*. (Master's thesis). SLU, Dept. of Economics.

Kaushik, A., & Arokkiaraj, H. (2023). Migration and old age: Examining intersecting vulnerabilities and concerns. In *Handbook of aging, health and public policy: Perspectives from Asia* (pp. 1–25). Springer Nature.

Kwanhi, T., Modiba, F. S., Mago, S., Matindike, S., & Damiyano, D. (2024). Conceptualising climate-induced migration in Africa. *Environmental Development, 52*, 101049. https://doi.org/10.1016/j.envdev.2024.101049

Le Roux, N. (2009). *Seasonal maise yield simulations for South Africa using a multi-model ensemble system*. Doctoral dissertation, University of Pretoria.

Lu, Y. (2014). Parental migration and education of left-behind children: A comparison of two settings. *Journal of Marriage and Family, 76*(5), 1082–1098. https://doi.org/10.1111/jomf.12139

Lu, Y., Zhang, R., & Du, H. (2021). Family structure, family instability, and child psychological well-being in the context of migration: Evidence from sequence analysis in China. *Child Development, 92*, e416–e438. https://doi.org/10.1111/cdev.13496

Maganga, T., & Suso, C. C. (2022). Human mobility and climate change adaptation in small-scale farming areas in Eastern Zimbabwe. *Africa Review, 14*(1), 68–97.

Mayer, B. (2014). "Environmental migration" as advocacy: Is it going to work? *Refuge: Canada's Journal on Refugees, 29*(2), 27–41.

McLeman, R. (2017). Thresholds in climate migration. *Population and Environment, 39*, 319–338. https://doi.org/10.1007/s11111-017-0340-4

Milán-García, J., Caparrós-Martínez, J. L., Rueda-López, N., & de Pablo Valenciano, J. (2021). Climate change-induced migration: A bibliometric review. *Globalisation and Health, 17*(1), 74. https://doi.org/10.1186/s12992-021-00694-4

Ncube, T., Zualii, L., Murray, U., Nguyen, N., Liebig, T., Krendelsberger, A., & Spillane, C. (2024). Understanding the climate, migration, and social protection nexus from a youth mobility dimension: Can social protection address the drivers of climigration? *Climate and Development*, 1–22. https://doi.org/10.1080/17565529.2024.2380380

Ogunrinde, A. T., Oguntunde, P. G., Akinwumiju, A. S., & Fasinmirin, J. T. (2021). Evaluation of the impact of climate change on the characteristics of drought in the Sahel Region of Nigeria: 1971–2060. *African Geographical Review, 40*(2), 192–210.
Onafeso, O. D. (2020). Analysis of climate change-induced forced migration in sub-Saharan Africa. *Annals of the University of Bucharest. Geography Series, 20*, 71–83.
Serdeczny, O., Adams, S., Baarsch, F., et al. (2017). Climate change impacts in Sub-Saharan Africa: From physical changes to their social repercussions. *Regional Environmental Change, 17*, 1585–1600. https://doi.org/10.1007/s10113-015-0910-2
Shockley, K. (2017). Individual and contributory responsibility for environmental harm. In S. M. Gardiner & A. Thompson (Eds.), *Oxford handbook of environmental ethics*. Oxford University Press.
Shrestha, S., Shrestha, M., & Babel, M. S. (2017). Assessment of climate change impact on water diversion strategies of the Melamchi Water Supply Project in Nepal. *Theoretical and Applied Climatology, 128*, 311–323. https://doi.org/10.1007/s00704-016-1724-9
Stapleton, S. O., Nadin, R., Watson, C., & Kellett, J. (2017). *Climate change, migration and displacement: The need for a risk-informed and coherent approach*. Overseas Development Institute. Retrieved from https://www.undp.org/sites/g/files/zskgke326/files/publications/MIgration_Report.pdf
Stavi, I., Roque de Pinho, J., Paschalidou, A. K., Adamo, S. B., Galvin, K., de Sherbinin, A., & van der Geest, K. (2022). Food security among dryland pastoralists and agropastoralists: The climate, land-use change, and population dynamics nexus. *The Anthropocene Review, 9*(3), 299–323. https://doi.org/10.1177/20530196211069185
Stojanov, R., Rosengaertner, S., de Sherbinin, A., & Nawrotzki, R. (2021). Climate mobility and development cooperation. *Population and Environment, 43*(2), 209–231. https://doi.org/10.1007/s11111-021-00322-0
Tang, L., Xiang, X., & Liu, Y. (2024). Family migration and well-being of Chinese migrant workers' children. *Scientific Reports, 14*, 12862. https://doi.org/10.1038/s41598-024-63589-5
Thalheimer, L., Williams, D. S., Van der Geest, K., & Otto, F. E. (2021). Advancing the evidence base of future warming impacts on human mobility in African drylands. *Earth's Future, 9*(10), e2020EF001958. https://doi.org/10.1029/2020EF001958
Tom, T. (2024). Decades of land and agrarian reform in Zimbabwe: A review of transformative social policy lessons for other African countries. *The African Review*. Epub Ahead of Print. https://doi.org/10.1163/1821889x-bja10143
Udrea, G., & Guiu, G. (2022). The impact of parents' work migration on the social, communication, and educational experiences of left-behind adolescents. *Central and Eastern European Migration Review, 11*(2), 101–117. https://doi.org/10.54667/ceemr.2022.14
Wei, L., Yang, Y., Zhang, J., & Si, L. (2023). Rural–urban migration, family arrangement, and children's welfare: Evidence from China's rural areas. *Family Relations, 72*(4), 1586–1606. https://doi.org/10.1111/fare.12720
Wesselbaum, D., & Aburn, A. (2019). Gone with the wind: International migration. *Global and Planetary Change, 178*, 96–109. https://doi.org/10.1016/j.gloplacha.2019.03.008
Ziervogel, G., & Taylor, A. (2023). A co-produced national climate change risk and vulnerability assessment framework for South Africa. *Frontiers in Climate, 5*. https://doi.org/10.3389/fclim.2023.1197167

Chapter 6
Climate Change and Children's Rights in Zimbabwe: The Case of Mashonaland Central Province

Vincent Chenzi and Robson Pahuwa

6.1 Introduction

Climate change represents an existential threat to children's rights in Zimbabwe, a country positioned among the world's most climate-vulnerable nations and particularly susceptible to severe droughts, floods, and unpredictable weather patterns. The impacts of climate variability are especially pronounced in Mashonaland Central Province, an agriculturally dependent region where families rely predominantly on rain-fed farming for food security and livelihoods (Mateyisi et al. 2024). Since agriculture substantially contributes to Zimbabwe's economy and food security, disruptions in agricultural production from extended droughts, erratic rainfall, and extreme weather events create cascading crises affecting nutrition, health, education, and child protection across vulnerable communities. As established in the introductory framework for this volume (see Chap. 1), climate change poses an acute threat to children because they bear minimal responsibility for greenhouse gas emissions yet experience disproportionate consequences, representing a significant climate injustice.

While climate change research increasingly recognises broad human rights impacts, children remain significantly underrepresented in the scholarly literature on climate vulnerability in African contexts (UNDP, 2017b). Mashonaland Central Province exemplifies this gap, as the region experiences severe climate shocks, including intensifying droughts, flooding, and environmental degradation, that directly violate children's rights to survival, development, health, education, and protection from exploitation (OHCHR, 2018). Children in this province face

V. Chenzi (✉)
Department of Peace, Security, and Society, University of Zimbabwe, Harare, Zimbabwe

R. Pahuwa
Graduate Centre for the Study of Culture (GCSC), Justus Liebig University, Giessen, Hesse, Germany

E. Ndhlovu, C. Chipenda (eds.), *Climate Change and Children's Rights in Zimbabwe*, https://doi.org/10.1007/978-981-95-6005-9_6

heightened vulnerability due to compounding factors, including poverty, weak infrastructure, limited access to healthcare and education, and deepening food insecurity. Beyond immediate physical harm, climate-induced economic stress pushes children into survival strategies that compromise their rights, including child labour, early marriage, sexual exploitation, and school dropout. These interconnected vulnerabilities demand a comprehensive analysis beyond treating children as passive climate victims, instead positioning them as rights holders whose protection requires transformative policy responses addressing structural inequalities.

This chapter examines how climate variability in Mashonaland Central Province systematically undermines multiple dimensions of children's rights simultaneously, revealing the integrated nature of climate impacts on child welfare. The analysis is guided by three core questions: How has climate change affected Mashonaland Central Province? What are the specific effects of climate change on children and minors in this region? What evidence-based measures can effectively address climate change impacts on children's rights? By integrating documentary analysis with qualitative interviews and quantitative household data, the chapter reveals critical patterns whereby climate shocks create immediate threats to children's health and nutrition while simultaneously generating longer-term vulnerabilities through livelihood collapse, educational disruption, and erosion of child protection systems.

6.2 Materials and Methods

This research employed a mixed-methods approach combining qualitative and quantitative data collection between November 2022 and April 2024. Qualitative data included four in-depth face-to-face interviews with key informants and two focus group discussions (FGDs) held on 23 February 2024 at Tabex community hall in Tsakare and at Tsakare community church, each lasting approximately 1.5–2 h. FGD participants included African Initiated Church (AIC) members, medical personnel, law enforcement officers, and elderly community members. All ethical protocols were followed, with informed consent obtained from all participants; sensitive information was protected with pseudonyms. Quantitative data were collected from 250 households using structured questionnaires with closed-ended questions derived from the three main research questions. Data collection in the Tsakare case study occurred between March 15 and 30, 2024, while Musami village data collection occurred between February 1 and 15, 2024.

Tsakare resettlement was selected because it represents a commercial agricultural community established in 1982 specifically for agricultural resettlement, with major economic activities including cotton, tobacco, and livestock farming conducted primarily through rain-fed agriculture. Musami village, located 71 km from Harare, represents a different agricultural profile, focusing on market gardening of tomatoes, onions, cucumbers, butternuts, and peas using river water and underground water from wells and boreholes for irrigation. Both sites have experienced significant climate stress from erratic rainfall over the past decade (2013–2023), aligned with broader climate projections for northern Zimbabwe predicting higher temperatures and reduced rainfall. This methodological approach allowed for comparative analysis of how climate impacts manifest differently across distinct agricultural contexts within the province. Data analysis employed summative content analysis of interview transcripts and thematic presentation of quantitative findings in tabular format, with interpretations informed by the researchers' extensive experience in climate change and environmental research spanning more than 5 years. Clearance was obtained from the Rural District Council (RDC) offices before data collection commenced, and all participants were adults above 21 years of age who provided information on behalf of their families.

6.3 Literature Review and Conceptual Framework

6.3.1 Global Climate Change and Children's Rights: Establishing the Nexus

Climate change represents one of the most significant contemporary threats to the global realisation of children's rights, as environmental degradation systematically undermines access to survival, development, health, education, and protection. Under numerous regions of the world, people's rights to life, food, health, water, shelter, and education are under acute threat due to climate variability drastically reshaping environmental conditions. Rising temperatures expand the geographical range of tropical diseases, water scarcity creates severe infrastructure bottlenecks affecting consumption and sanitation, and extreme weather events destroy livelihoods and essential services upon which children depend (Schater, 2017). The 2018 IPCC Special Report "Global Warming of 1.5 Degrees" comprehensively documented how climate change affects multiple human rights, with scientific evidence demonstrating uneven geographical distribution of impacts whereby vulnerable populations, particularly in the Global South, experience disproportionate consequences despite minimal responsibility for emissions (Intergovernmental Panel on Climate Change, 2018).

Human rights experts, domestic, regional, and international judicial authorities, and development specialists increasingly recognise that climate change impacts extend beyond ecological dimensions to constitute human rights challenges requiring international responses sensitive to social vulnerabilities. For Humphreys (2010), the human rights implications of climate change demand integrated approaches addressing both environmental degradation and social vulnerability. Knox (2016), in his report to the United Nations Human Rights Council, argues that climate change not only threatens individual rights to life, health, and a clean environment but simultaneously generates international obligations for their protection (UNHCHR 2017). These findings emphasise that environmental degradation disproportionately impacts marginalised populations, with children facing difficulty due to their developmental needs and dependence on adult caregivers. Climate-specific impacts on children include disproportionate disruptions to essential services such as healthcare and education, heightened exposure to disease vectors, nutritional deficiencies from agricultural collapse, and increased vulnerability to exploitation during household economic crises (UNDP, 2017a).

6.3.2 Climate Change, Children's Rights, and the Rights to Health, Education, and Protection

Climate change affects children's physical, psychological, and social well-being through multiple pathways, with health impacts representing an immediate and severe threat to child survival and development (ACERWC, 2018). Exposure to prolonged droughts creates conditions facilitating malnutrition, dehydration, and waterborne diseases. At the same time, flooding generates contaminated water supplies and disease outbreaks, particularly affecting children whose developing immune systems render them more susceptible than adults to infection (UNICEF, 2016). When families lose agricultural income due to climate shocks, reduced household food consumption directly impairs children's nutritional status, undermining cognitive development, physical growth, and academic achievement during critical developmental windows. Destruction of health infrastructure by climate-related disasters prevents treatment of injuries and illnesses while simultaneously increasing disease burden, creating healthcare access crises where treatment becomes unavailable precisely when disease incidence escalates. Unclean conditions and inadequate sanitation during and after disasters facilitate rapid transmission of infectious diseases, especially diarrhoeal diseases and cholera among children and infants, conditions causing dehydration and malnutrition that can prove fatal without timely medical intervention (UNICEF, 2016).

Climate-induced education disruptions occur directly through physical destruction of schools and indirectly through household economic stress, compelling school withdrawal. As documented in complementary chapters examining sectoral impacts (Mando et al., Chaora et al., in this volume), extreme weather events damage educational infrastructure, disrupt transportation, and reduce school attendance through weather-related illness, malnutrition-induced cognitive impairment, and household labour demands. Schools in flood-prone areas face physical destruction and may be repurposed as emergency shelters. At the same time, drought-affected regions experience school closures due to water shortages and the inability to feed learners. When agricultural livelihoods collapse, parents withdraw children from school to engage them in income-generating activities or domestic labour, perpetuating cycles of poverty and limiting future socio-economic mobility (Chenzi et al. 2024). The Ministry of Primary and Secondary Education in Zimbabwe documented that primary school dropout rates reached 4.5% in 2014 due primarily to illness. Meanwhile, erratic weather increasingly drives school closures that deny continuous academic progress and disproportionately affect girls facing compounded vulnerabilities. Higher rates of climate-related school disruption and dropout accumulate to diminish children's educational attainment, reducing their capacity for informed participation in climate decision-making and limiting their future adaptive capacity.

6.3.3 Climate-Induced Vulnerabilities: Child Labour, Early Marriage, and Sexual Exploitation

Climate change exacerbates pre-existing vulnerabilities and creates new pathways through which children's rights are violated, primarily through economic survival strategies that compromise protection. When agricultural production fails and household incomes collapse, families facing immediate subsistence crises turn to deploying children's labour as a survival mechanism, directly violating rights to education, health, protection from exploitation, and childhood development. In Zimbabwe, families in rural areas, including Mashonaland Central, are experiencing climate-related income loss and sending children as young as 12 years old into hazardous work, including informal mining, agricultural labour, or migration to distant regions in search of income-generating opportunities. This pattern represents economic necessity driven by climate shocks, whereby immediate family survival supersedes educational investment, disrupting children's schooling and exposing them to workplace hazards that impair health and development.

Beyond child labour, climate-induced food insecurity and economic desperation drive increased rates of early marriage, primarily affecting girls in agricultural communities dependent on rain-fed farming (Chenzi et al, 2024a). When harvests fail and families face severe poverty, young daughters become economic liabilities, prompting parents to arrange marriages with bride price payments, providing immediate material resources while reducing household food burdens, in communities where members of African Initiated Churches (AICs) predominate, cultural practices combining bride price systems with church doctrines create conditions facilitating child marriage and sexual exploitation masked by religious justification. These compounding vulnerabilities, economic desperation, cultural acceptance of early marriage, weak law enforcement, and political protection of perpetrators create systematic violations of children's rights to safety, health, education, and freedom from sexual exploitation, with girls bearing disproportionate burdens.

6.3.4 A Human Rights-Based Approach to Understanding Climate Vulnerabilities

This chapter adopts a multidimensional human rights-based approach (HRBA) to unpack the complex relationships between climate change and children's rights, recognising that child protection in climate contexts demands consideration of interconnected vulnerabilities across multiple dimensions of rights. The Universal Declaration of Human Rights and HRBA principles establish that every child has the right to life, shelter, healthcare, food, water, and protection from violence. However, human rights experts stress that adequate child protection extends beyond emergency humanitarian response to long-term initiatives addressing structural inequalities and strengthening community resilience. Economic inequality amplifies children's susceptibility to climate hazards, especially in underdeveloped areas like Mashonaland Central, where poverty intersects with environmental vulnerability to create compounded exposure.

HRBA centres on participation, empowerment, and accountability principles, providing a theoretical foundation for ensuring active engagement of children and communities in climate resilience activities while advancing advocacy for child rights and inclusivity. This approach simultaneously empowers children and creates stakeholder accountability for protecting children's rights through child-sensitive budgeting and resource allocation prioritised in disaster-prone areas. Adopting HRBA in climate policy may catalyse comprehensive reforms, placing children's rights at the centre of climate action strategies, advancing justice for marginalised child populations, and addressing structural inequalities that determine differential climate vulnerability. As advanced in the introductory chapter (Chipenda & Ndhlovu, Introduction in this volume), integration of climate justice frameworks with human rights principles reveals how distributive, procedural, and recognition justice must inform climate adaptation, ensuring that vulnerable children benefit from adaptation resources and participate meaningfully in decisions affecting their futures.

6.4 Findings and Discussion

6.4.1 Climate Change Impacts: Environmental Degradation and Livelihood Disruption

The study findings are organised around the three research questions guiding the investigation, with each question forming a thematic focus through which climate impacts manifest in Mashonaland Central Province. Research findings reveal that climate change impacts Mashonaland Central through interconnected environmental and livelihood disruptions that create cascading vulnerabilities for dependent populations, particularly children.

Participant observations document widespread recognition of climate variability across the study sites, with 78.5% of respondents in Tsakare observing gradual climate changes compared to 18.8% reporting no observed changes and 2.7% unaware of changes. Specific climate manifestations identified by participants include delayed rainfall (72.9%), insufficient rainfall and droughts (32.5%), destructive heavy rains (12.0%), shorter rain seasons (24.0%), and extreme temperatures (53.0%). These observed patterns align with national climate data, demonstrating that Zimbabwe's average annual rainfall has declined by approximately 5% since 1901, with further decline projected to reach 10–25% by 2080, particularly affecting south-western and south-eastern regions, including Mashonaland Central (Mateyisi et al. 2024; GoZ, 2024).

Environmental consequences of climate variability were observed by 87% of study participants in Tsakare, with identified changes including extensive deforestation (94%), artisanal mining activities (61%), increased soil erosion (30%), reduced ground cover (18%), and drying of rivers and wells (14%). These environmental changes reflect both climate-driven drought stress reducing vegetation and water availability and human livelihood adaptations whereby climate-induced agricultural failure drives a shift from farming to artisanal mining, a process termed deagrarianisation that significantly restructures rural economies and creates new hazards for children. The convergence of declining rainfall, rising temperatures, soil degradation, and water scarcity creates increasingly inhospitable environmental conditions to rain-fed agriculture, the primary livelihood strategy sustaining most families in the region.

6.4.2 Climate Change Effects on Children's Health, Nutrition, and Food Security

Climate change effects have directly impacted child health through multiple pathways, with poor nutrition and increased disease burden representing immediate threats to survival and development. Food insecurity resulting from agricultural collapse due to erratic rainfall directly undermines children's nutritional status while simultaneously creating economic desperation that pushes women and girls into transactional sex arrangements, exchanging sexual access for food and money (Zondo, 2022). This survival strategy generates cascading harms, including high prevalence of sexually transmitted infections, gender-based violence, domestic violence, and rape, violations of bodily autonomy and protection rights compounded by climate-induced poverty (Mutumbame, 2023).

Study findings revealed that 91% of respondent families in Tsakare were forced to change dietary patterns due to climate-induced low food production. The majority responded by reducing meal frequency from three meals daily to two meals (47.4%), and others reduced portion sizes to extend food supplies (23.2%). In contrast, others shifted to cheaper, nutritionally inferior food alternatives (29.4%).

These dietary reductions directly compromise children's nutritional intake during critical developmental periods, impairing physical growth, cognitive development, immune function, and academic achievement. Seasonal food scarcity, common in Zimbabwe, drives acute malnutrition (wasting), particularly affecting young children, whose developmental vulnerabilities render them most susceptible to nutritional deficiencies. As complementary research on climate-induced nutrition impacts documents (Ndhlovu & Chipenda, Chap. 8, in this volume), climate-related food insecurity affects approximately 580,000 young children living in severe food poverty in Zimbabwe, creating cascading health consequences, including stunting, micronutrient deficiencies, and impaired immune function.

Climate-driven disease burden additionally threatens child health through increased exposure to vector-borne illnesses, including malaria, whose transmission is facilitated by warmer temperatures and altered rainfall patterns, creating breeding conditions for disease vectors. Hot and humid conditions favour malaria reproduction, with increased cases documented following rainy seasons in central Zimbabwe regions. Young children are particularly susceptible due to developing immune systems and reduced malaria-acquired immunity compared to older populations, translating into higher morbidity and mortality rates. Waterborne diseases, including cholera, typhoid, and diarrhoeal illnesses, proliferate when water infrastructure is damaged during floods and contaminated water becomes the primary supply during droughts, disproportionately affecting children whose hygiene practices and immune systems render them more vulnerable than adults. Heat-related illnesses, including heat strokes, heat exhaustion, and skin infections, escalate with rising temperatures, while healthcare access limitations in rural areas prevent timely treatment and prevention. These health impacts accumulate to undermine children's right to the highest attainable standard of health, directly violating UNCRC provisions while simultaneously compromising educational attendance, cognitive development, and long-term life prospects.

6.4.3 Climate Change, Educational Disruption, and Child Protection Crises

Climate change undermines children's right to education through direct infrastructure destruction, indirect household economic stress, livelihood disruptions, and compelling school withdrawal, each pathway creating educational inequities that disproportionately affect vulnerable children. Findings from the study indicate that climate-induced agricultural failure and resulting food insecurity have triggered livelihood transformations whereby families shift from agricultural production to alternative income strategies, with implications for child education and protection. In Tsakare, the discovery of gold in 2016 accelerated deagrarianisation, with artisanal mining emerging as the primary livelihood strategy as rainfall patterns became increasingly unreliable. This is where young boys aged 9–17 have been reportedly recruited into mining gangs to explore unsafe underground mine shafts after being offered substantial daily remuneration (US$100 per day) (Jeremiah, 2024), far exceeding potential agricultural income during drought periods. Junior learners increasingly dropped out of school to join artisanal mining as unskilled labourers, driven by either peer pressure from other mining participants or parental pressure to supplement household income when agricultural output failed. This school dropout pattern directly violates children's rights to education while exposing them to severe occupational hazards, including shaft collapse, toxic exposure, and traumatic injury, hazards rural children would not otherwise encounter (Chimanikire, 2023). Furthermore, access to mining income enabled teenage marriage through the ability to pay bride price, facilitating early sexual activity, sexually transmitted infection transmission, and HIV/AIDS transmission among minors unprepared for sexual relationships and lacking comprehensive sexual health education (Zondo, 2022).

Beyond occupational displacement from education, climate-induced food insecurity and economic desperation have driven increased rates of child marriage, primarily affecting girls in agricultural communities. Families facing severe poverty due to crop failure from drought and erratic rainfall make strategic decisions to reduce household food burdens by arranging marriages for young daughters in exchange for bride price payments, providing immediate material resources. In Mashonaland Central Province, where African Initiated Churches (AICs) maintain a strong community presence, child marriage practices intersect with religious doctrines and cultural acceptance of early marriage, creating systematic vulnerability whereby girls are forced into sexual relationships with older men before reaching legal maturity (Zondo, 2022). Under Zimbabwean law (Statutory Instrument 2 January 2024), sexual intercourse with persons below 18 years constitutes statutory rape, carrying maximum sentences of 10 years imprisonment (The Herald, 2024). However, enforcement remains severely compromised by weak institutional commitment, political protection of perpetrators, and community complicity, whereby law enforcement officials and courts remain unwilling to pursue cases due to strong political ties between AIC leaders and the ruling ZANU PF party (Bwanya, 2023). Rural areas housing both AIC strongholds and ZANU PF political control create environments where government leaders maintain membership in these churches to secure political support during elections, in exchange for tolerating or protecting criminal practices within church communities.

Interview data from Mashonaland Central Province revealed that ZANU PF officials frequently threaten police, medical personnel, and NGO staff attempting to prosecute AIC members for statutory rape, with consequences including dismissal from employment, death threats, and physical assault. Parents and community members whose daughters experience rape remain unwilling to cooperate with law enforcement and courts, compounding impunity through community protection of perpetrators (Zondo, 2022). Consequently, thousands of children, particularly girls, fall victim to statutory rape while receiving no justice, with some succumbing to death during childbirth in church shrines after being denied hospital access by church leaders forbidding modern medical care. These religious prohibitions against medical treatment ostensibly prevent "Western influence" but effectively conceal criminal sexual abuse while denying girls specialised medical attention their immature reproductive systems require. Some AICs justify sexual intercourse with minors as necessary for acquiring healing and deliverance from family challenges, directly incentivising rape within religious frameworks and creating religious sanction for child sexual abuse. Even when perpetrators are arrested and convicted, presidential pardons result in early release, communicating that such crimes receive governmental protection rather than accountability. This systematic failure of child protection institutions, whereby climate-induced poverty enables child marriage, religious institutions sanction sexual abuse, political actors shield perpetrators, and communities silence victims, represents a comprehensive violation of children's rights to life, health, protection from sexual exploitation, education, and bodily autonomy.

6.4.4 Addressing Climate Change Impacts on Children's Rights: Evidence-Based Adaptation and Protection Strategies

Effective responses to climate change impacts on children's rights require integrated approaches simultaneously addressing immediate humanitarian needs, educational access, health security, and structural factors enabling child protection violations. In nations like Zimbabwe, where economic shocks from climate-related disasters compel families towards coping mechanisms violating children's rights, climate change adaptation must prioritise child protection objectives alongside livelihood resilience. Research demonstrates that cash transfer programmes provided to drought-affected families, such as initiatives implemented in Ethiopia, enable families to maintain children in school while responding to economic adversity, reducing pressures to deploy child labour or arrange early marriages. Similar financial assistance programmes adapted for Mashonaland Central could substantially improve school attendance rates, currently declining during drought periods when children are withdrawn for labour.

Community-based resilience strategies, including drought early-warning systems, allow families to prepare for climate shocks by maintaining livelihood diversity and reducing sudden income loss that triggers child protection crises. Early warning systems implemented in Kenya have enabled families to maintain children's school attendance and avoid pushing them into labour markets during drought. Implementation of comparable community-based resilience programmes in Mashonaland Central could stabilise children's lives and education while reducing incidences of child labour, school dropout, early marriage, and sexual exploitation that accelerate during severe climate shocks. Long-term adaptation strategies must be grounded in sustainable development, addressing poverty and restricted educational capacity through mechanisms empowering children and communities. School feeding programmes already demonstrating effectiveness during droughts in Zimbabwe could be extended to Mashonaland Central, ensuring children obtain adequate nutrition from school meals while reducing household food burdens that otherwise compel parental decisions to marry daughters or deploy children's labour.

Environmental education programmes that build children's climate literacy and adaptation skills create the dual benefits of developing a long-term understanding of climate hazards while building children's agency and resilience through participation in community environmental management. Tree planting, soil conservation, and water harvesting initiatives engaging children and local stakeholders in Mashonaland Central would foster ecological restoration and child empowerment, enabling children to contribute meaningfully to community climate adaptation while developing adaptive skills for their futures. Integrating climate adaptation into national child protection policies creates protective frameworks where children benefit from adaptation resources while participating meaningfully in climate decisions affecting their lives. Government systematic integration of child protection into climate policies ensures that children's rights to health, education, and protection from natural hazards remain central rather than peripheral to climate action, addressing the critical implementation gap between Zimbabwe's comprehensive policy frameworks and inadequate ground-level child protection currently documented.

6.5 Conclusion

Climate change poses unprecedented threats to children's rights in Mashonaland Central Province and throughout Zimbabwe, manifesting through cascading impacts on health, nutrition, education, economic opportunity, and protection from exploitation. Evidence presented in this chapter demonstrates that these are not abstract future concerns but present realities affecting millions of children whose rights are violated daily through climate-induced food insecurity, disease exposure, educational disruption, child labour deployment, early marriage, and sexual abuse. The province's extreme vulnerability stems from economic dependence on rain-fed agriculture increasingly disrupted by erratic rainfall patterns, rising temperatures, and extreme weather events that compress livelihood options and push families towards survival strategies compromising child protection.

Future climate projections indicate that Zimbabwe's vulnerability will intensify, with projected temperature increases and rainfall declines threatening nutrition, health, education, and water security, services essential for child survival and development. These projections necessitate well-coordinated policy responses integrating climate mitigation and adaptation with child protection frameworks, ensuring that climate action prioritises children's rights rather than exacerbating existing inequalities. Robust measures addressing children's rights violations must incorporate climate change dimensions to develop effective solutions, recognising that child welfare cannot be secured through child protection mechanisms alone when climate shocks continue driving families towards rights-violating survival strategies. The path forward requires policy reforms prioritising climate-informed child protection, evidence-based adaptation safeguarding educational access and nutritional security, institutional accountability for enforcing child protection laws regardless of perpetrator status or political position, and meaningful participation of children and communities in adaptation decision-making. Until climate adaptation explicitly centres children's rights and addresses the structural factors enabling violations of those rights, poverty, weak institutions, political impunity, and gender inequality, climate change will continue eroding developmental gains while perpetuating intergenerational cycles of vulnerability and injustice.

References

Interviews

Elder Jeremiah, Local pentecostal church elder from Tsakare, 26 April 2024.
Mr Chimanikire, Tsakare community local village headman, 19 April, 2023.
Mr Zondo, community Pentecostal pastor, 21 November, 2022.
Rtd. Colonel Mutumbame, local villager from Tsakare resettlement, 19 April, 2023.

Text Books, Reports and Journal Articles

ACERWC. (2018). *General comment no 5 on "State party obligations under the African charter on the rights and welfare of the child (article 1) and systems strengthening for child protection"*. African Union Commission.

Bwanya, M. (2023, August 8). Prison authorities defend 'Mnangagwa huchi' rape convict's premature release. *Zimlive*. Retrieved November 19, 2024, from https://www.zimlive.com/prison-authorities-defend-mnangagwa-huchi-rape-convicts-premature-release/

Chenzi, V., Chivasa, N., & Murau, N. T. (2024). Climate change, religion, health and structural violence in post-colonial Zimbabwe. In E. Chitando & S. M. Kilonzo (Eds.), *The Palgrave handbook of religion, health and development in Africa*. Palgrave Macmillan.

Chenzi, V., Mateyisi, M., Nangombe, S., & Maoela, M. A. (2024a). Emerging adaptation constraints in Mount Darwin District, Zimbabwe. In M. Matsa, L. Chapungu, & G. Nhamo (Eds.), *Climate change resilience in Rural Southern Africa: The dynamics, prospects & challenges*. Springer Nature.

Government of Zimbabwe. (2024). *Zimbabwe national climate change adaptation plan*. Ministry of Environment, Climate and Wildlife.

Humphreys, S. (Ed.). (2010). *Human rights and climate change*. Cambridge University Press.

Intergovernmental Panel on Climate Change (IPCC). (2018). *Special report on global warming of 1.5 degrees*. Retrieved June 30, 2024, from https://www.ipcc.ch/sr15/chapter/spm/

Knox, J. H. (2016). Human rights principles and climate change. *The Oxford handbook of international climate change law*, 213.

Mateyisi, M., Nangombe, S., Maoela, M. A., & Chenzi, V. (2024). The climate change landscape for rural Southern Africa. In M. Matsa, L. Chapungu, & G. Nhamo (Eds.), *Climate change resilience in Rural Southern Africa: The dynamics, prospects & challenges*. Springer Nature.

OHCHR. (2018). *The slow onset effects of climate change and human rights protection for cross-border migrants*. UN Doc. A/HRC/37/CRP.4.

Pedzisai, E., Charamba, S., & Mukurazhizha, R. (2023). Nexus between climate change and environmental social work in Africa. *African Journal of Social Work, 13*(2), 87–99.

Schater, B. (2017). *Climate change and the full enjoyment of children's rights*. United Nations Office of the High Commissioner.

Statutory Instrument 2 of 2024, Presidential Temporary Powers (Temporary Measures) (Criminal Laws) (Protection of Children and young Persons) Regulations 2024.

The Herald. (2024, January 13). Age of Consent Gazetted, offenders face a maximum sentence of 10 years. *The Herald*. Retrieved November 19, 2024, from https://www.herald.co.zw/age-of-consent-law-gazetted-offenders-face-maximum-of-10-years-jail/

UNDP. (2017a). *Zimbabwe human development report 2017: Climate change and human development: Towards building a climate resilient nation*. United Nations Development Programme.

UNDP. (2017b). *Zimbabwe human development report 2017: Towards building a climate resilient nation*. United Nations Development Programme.

UNHCHR. (2017). *Human Rights Council 34th session*. United Nations.

UNICEF. (2016). *Briefing note: Overview of El Niño response in Central and Southern Africa*. UNICEF.

Chapter 7
The Resilience of Children in Rural Zimbabwe in the Face of Climate Change: A Case of Ward 39, Gutu District, Masvingo Province

Witness Chikoko and Philemon Chihiya

7.1 Introduction and Background

Climate change represents one of the most pressing threats to children's rights in contemporary Zimbabwe, with rural children facing disproportionate vulnerabilities due to their dependence on climate-sensitive livelihoods and limited access to adaptive resources. The United Nations Convention on the Rights of the Child (UNCRC) (UN, 1989) and the African Charter on the Rights and Welfare of the Child (ACRWC) (OAU, 1990) provide comprehensive frameworks protecting children's rights to survival, development, protection, and participation, yet climate change systematically undermines these rights across multiple dimensions. As Chingwanda (2016) argues, climate change encompasses changes in standard weather patterns over extended periods, characterised by excessive weather events such as the intensity of heatwaves, heavy rainfall, floods, and droughts. Like many African nations, Zimbabwe experiences serious climate change challenges that directly impact food security, income generation, and nutritional outcomes, particularly for children in rural areas. Building on the national vulnerability context established by Chipenda and Ndhlovu and Chipenda and Chawanda (in this volume), which positions Zimbabwe as the 15th most vulnerable country to climate change globally, this chapter examines how these macro-level vulnerabilities translate into specific survival strategies and resilience mechanisms among rural children in Gutu District.

The agricultural foundation of Zimbabwe's economy intensifies children's vulnerability to climate variability. Zimbabwe's agro-based economy renders agriculture extremely vulnerable to climate change, with significant implications for children who depend on agricultural productivity for their survival and development. Manyeruke et al. (2013) point out that Africa has experienced unpredictable

W. Chikoko (✉) · P. Chihiya
Department of Social Work, University of Zimbabwe, Harare, Zimbabwe

E. Ndhlovu, C. Chipenda (eds.), *Climate Change and Children's Rights in Zimbabwe*, https://doi.org/10.1007/978-981-95-6005-9_7

floods and erratic rainfall for the past three decades, significantly affecting the agricultural sector. Crop production and animal domestication have failed to adapt adequately to changing climate conditions, and many people, especially children in rural Zimbabwe, depend on agriculture for food and income. The impacts of climate change manifest directly and indirectly across multiple dimensions of children's well-being, including health, employment, livelihoods, education, and housing (Bhatasara, 2018; Mpambela & Mabvurira, 2017).

The agricultural sector's centrality to Zimbabwe's economy highlights the severity of climate impacts on children's rights and well-being. The Zimbabwe United Nations Development Assistance Framework (ZUNDAF, 2011, p. 9) notes that the agricultural sector is the central economic pillar of Zimbabwe, contributing 15–20% to GDP, 40% to exports, and 60% of raw materials used in the industrial sector. Nelson et al. (2009) articulate that increasing global temperatures will reduce crop production, leading to absolute poverty among rural populations. Statistically, approximately 2 billion people worldwide depend on crop production and animal husbandry as essential industries sustaining their livelihoods (Feyissa, 2007, p. 103). Nelson et al. (2009) further argue that about 75% of the world's population lives in rural areas where agriculture serves as their primary income source, and it is in these rural areas that climate change effects have been most drastic due to a lack of proper infrastructure, such as irrigation systems.

Climate-induced disasters create cascading violations of children's rights, as evidenced by recent catastrophic events in Zimbabwe and neighbouring countries. These changes have impacted children severely, as demonstrated during Cyclone Idai of 2019, when approximately 270,000 people, including 90,800 children, were affected, 139 schools were destroyed in Manicaland, causing massive school dropout among rural children, while 340 people, including children, died due to cyclone-related floods (Chatiza, 2019). Many children lost parents and relatives, their environments were degraded, and food reserves and lands were destroyed, creating multiple simultaneous rights violations. The United International Children's Emergency Fund (UNICEF, 2019) discovered similar patterns in Kenya, where severe drought occurs every 4 years, impacting crop production and increasing prices of basic needs. UNICEF (2013) also discovered that children residing in agro-ecological regions four and five in Zimbabwe are seriously affected by climate change impacts such as food shortages, malnutrition, and hunger. Similarly, Gutu District falls under three agro-ecological regions: three, four, and five. It has been severely affected by droughts for extended periods, resulting in increased school dropout, child labour, child marriage, child prostitution, child abuse, gold panning, and drug selling and abuse among children.

The vulnerability of children to climate change is amplified by their developmental stage and dependence on adult protection systems that are themselves compromised by climate impacts. Chingwanda (2016) notes that climate change-related difficulties make communities more exposed to disasters, particularly affecting children due to their age and developmental vulnerabilities. Climate change brings physical, human, and economic casualties while inhibiting poverty eradication strategies globally and nationally. The manifestations of climate change include food insecurity, environmental degradation, biodiversity loss, livelihood destruction, and worsening socio-economic conditions in many countries. Climate change has been linked to increased food insecurity, malnutrition, high mortality rates, and climate-related diseases such as cholera, malaria, yellow fever, dengue fever, measles, and meningitis, all of which disproportionately affect children (Mordecai et al., 2020). UNICEF (2013) points out that during climate change events, children's major concerns include food and water scarcity, health problems, and educational disruptions. In Zimbabwe, climate-related challenges such as flooding occur frequently during prolonged heavy rains and storms, resulting in overflowing rivers, particularly in low-lying areas (UNICEF, 2013).

The educational rights of children in rural areas face severe threats from climate-induced disruptions to household economies and school infrastructure, directly compromising Article 28 of the United Nations Convention on the Rights of the Child (UNCRC) (UN, 1989) and Article 11 of the African Charter on the Rights and Welfare of the Child (ACRWC) (OAU, 1990), which guarantee children's right to education. UNICEF (2013) observes that children in rural areas are affected academically during droughts and floods because parents fail to pay school fees and provide adequate food, leaving many children hungry during lessons and unable to concentrate, thereby contributing to massive school dropouts. This educational vulnerability documented in Gutu District mirrors patterns identified by Chaora et al. (in this volume) in rural Lupane, where extreme weather and water scarcity create social, academic, and psychological effects on learners, and by Mando et al. (in this volume) in Bikita District, where climate change extends children's rights inequalities and exacerbates violations among rural school learners.

Despite these multifaceted challenges, children in rural Zimbabwe demonstrate remarkable resilience through various adaptive strategies, although many of these strategies simultaneously constitute violations of their rights. Their surviving strategies and the mechanisms supporting their adaptation remain insufficiently documented and theorised within the climate change and children's rights nexus. Therefore, this study seeks to critically examine the resilience of children in rural Zimbabwe in the face of climate change, using Ward 39 of Gutu District as a case study. The chapter employs a qualitative case study research design to generate empirical evidence. It adopts resilience theory to understand and interpret how children in Ward 39 of Gutu District adapt to climate change impacts. Research findings suggest that rural children resort to numerous strategies during calamities precipitated by climate change, including employment (child labour), prostitution, and securing help from community members, relatives, government programmes, and religious organisations, among others. By examining the adaptive strategies children employ and the rights violations these strategies may entail, this chapter contributes to understanding the dynamic relationship between climate resilience and children's rights protection in rural African contexts.

7.2 Theoretical Framework

This research is guided by resilience theory developed by Norman Garmezy, which provides a framework for identifying and establishing factors that contribute to the adaptation of children in rural Zimbabwe in the face of climate change. Resilience theory is especially relevant to understanding children's responses to climate change. This is because it addresses both individual capacities and systemic supports that enable positive adaptation despite significant adversity, thereby illuminating the intersection between environmental challenges and children's rights to development and protection. Davidson et al. (2005) defines resilience as one's ability to bounce back or recover from adversity. Wright and Masten (2004) describe resilience as one's ability to recover and display positive adaptation in the face of significant risk or harsh conditions. The theory addresses people and social systems' strengths when facing disasters, crises, or problems (Van Breda, 2018).

Resilience theory conceptualises human adaptation as a dynamic process shaped by interactions between individual characteristics and environmental supports. It is suited to analysing children's responses to climate change within their socio-ecological contexts. The theory can also be defined as the successful development and adaptation of human beings despite external risks (Sikorska, 2014). Humans may be considered resilient only if they face challenges or external threats such as climate change-related problems, economic challenges, and violence, yet they can bounce back and develop properly (Luthar, 1991; Masten et al., 2007). The theory emphasises how people survive adversity and succeed later in life (Prince-Embury & Saklofske, 2003). The theory stresses that when people encounter challenges, they develop strategies or tactics to overcome that adversity. However, examining whether these strategies uphold or compromise fundamental rights, particularly for children, is critical.

O'Leary (1998) puts forward four models that facilitate resilience theory: the challenge model, vulnerability model, protective factor model, and compensatory model. These four models provide complementary lenses for understanding how children navigate climate-induced adversities while maintaining or compromising their protection, development, and participation rights. The challenge model posits that risk factors motivate individuals, groups, or communities to overcome adversities, improving their resilience (Ungar, 2012). This model suggests that risk factors that are not too extreme can help people adapt and prepare them for subsequent challenges (O'Leary, 1998). The protective factor model helps formulate helpful outcomes and healthy personality characteristics that shield people from life shocks or stressors (Ungar, 2012). These protective factors include planning skills, life skills, problem-solving skills, emotional management skills, academic and job skills, interpersonal skills, and the ability to restore self-esteem (Ungar, 2012).

The compensatory model of resilience recognises that individual capacities can offset environmental risks. However, in the context of children's rights, it is essential to ensure that compensatory strategies do not constitute rights violations. The compensatory model stresses the idea of individuals' intrapersonal abilities as contributing factors to resilience. As argued by O'Leary (1998), the compensatory model of resilience perceives resilience as a factor that dilutes exposure to associated risks. Factors such as intellectual competence, self-esteem, direction or mission, insights, optimism, empathy, determination, and perseverance are characteristics of the compensatory model of resilience (Kumfer & Hopkins, 1993, cited in Ungar, 2012). Resilience theory also encompasses facets of complete change, development, improvement, and adaptation from hard times, aiming at improving life conditions affecting an individual, group, or community (de Bruijne, 2010; Manyena, 2011).

Resilience theory's multilevel perspective, from individual psychological resources to family and community systems, aligns well with a rights-based approach to understanding children's climate adaptation. Ay Masten (1990) argued, resilience theory excels at explaining and addressing life stressors among different populations and improving people's resilience and coping capacities through establishing robust protective factors. It brings about change in policy formulation, thereby improving the adaptation of children in rural Zimbabwe. The theory was chosen because it stipulates how human development and adaptation are shaped and modified by interactions ranging from molecular levels to social and ecological systems). Davidson et al. (2005) argue that resilience can be found within a person through self-efficacy and self-esteem. Masten argues that different pathways contribute to resilience within an individual, including cognitive, genetic, neural, and immunological pathways, as well as the interaction between a person and their environment. Ungar (2012) identifies intrapersonal traits, qualities, and behaviours of people as chief contributors to resilience.

This theoretical framing helps identify pathways such as interpersonal relationships, family systems, community interventions, and institutional supports that facilitate resilience among children in rural areas while also revealing when these pathways may compromise children's rights. This theory helps researchers identify pathways such as interpersonal relationships, family systems, community interventions, and institutions that facilitate the resilience of children living in rural areas. Resilience is dynamic, varying from one individual to another depending on their contexts and the resources available to support adaptation. By applying resilience theory to the climate-children's rights nexus in rural Zimbabwe, this chapter illuminates the strengths children demonstrate and the systemic inadequacies that force them into adaptive strategies that violate their rights to protection, education, and development.

7.3 Research Methodology

7.3.1 Research Design and Approach

This study utilises a qualitative research approach, which Weathington et al. (2010) define as a research method with neither numerical nor quantitative findings. The qualitative approach was selected because it enables in-depth exploration of children's lived experiences with climate change and the meanings they attach to their adaptive strategies, essential for understanding how climate impacts intersect with children's rights in rural contexts. A qualitative research approach was utilised in this study because it provides detailed data for topics or behaviours based on primary evidence, explores local knowledge, and gives a better understanding of children in rural areas' experiences, meanings, societal, and cultural relationships in the face of climate change (Creswell, 2009).

An exploratory case study design was utilised to understand children's resilience in rural Zimbabwe due to climate change. Creswell (2009) stresses the usefulness of exploratory case studies, particularly for helping researchers develop an in-depth examination of a case, event, programme, process, and activity for one or more individuals. The case study approach was considered appropriate for this research because it allowed for a detailed examination of how climate change impacts manifest in specific local contexts and how children's adaptive strategies reflect and reshape their rights.

7.3.2 Sampling and Study Participants

A sample of 12 children aged between 15 and 17 from child-headed families, single-parent families, grandparent families, and those who dropped out of school while residing in Ward 39 of Gutu District for the past 3 years were purposively selected for the study. The sample size of 12 was chosen because it allowed the researcher to obtain sufficient data saturation without participant repetition. At the same time, in-depth interviews would become tiresome with a larger sample size. Six participants were male, while the remaining six were female, ensuring gender balance to promote gender equality and generate valid results for the study. In addition, four key informants, two women and two men, were conveniently selected to participate in the study, including the ward councillor, chief, probation officer, and headman, who possessed appropriate knowledge regarding children's adaptation strategies in the community.

7.3.3 Data Collection Methods

In-depth interviews, key informant interviews, and 4 focus group discussions with 8–10 participants each were utilised as data collection tools, providing triangulation of perspectives on children's resilience strategies and their implications for children's rights. The in-depth interviews are appropriate when studies aim at exploring beliefs, values, experiences, opinions, and attitudes of specific groups of people. In-depth interviews proved helpful in this study as they provided detailed information on how children in rural Zimbabwe adapted to climate change. The key informant interviews as one-on-one qualitative research methods where researchers gather information from people with appropriate knowledge regarding the group under study. Focus group discussions are qualitative data collection methods where researchers gather information from groups of people by discussing the research topic (Babbie & Mouton, 2004). Focus group discussions allowed the researcher to collect insights and assess validity through evaluating responses across participants within groups (Babbie & Mouton, 2004). Data collection tools, including in-depth interview guides, key informant interview guides, and focus group guides, were therefore developed and utilised to explore the adaptive strategies children employ and the rights implications of these strategies.

7.3.4 Data Analysis

The thematic analysis technique was used to analyse data obtained from in-depth interviews, key informant interviews, and focus group discussions. As argued by McKenna and Denver (2013), thematic analysis is a method for identifying, analysing, and reporting patterns within data. The research findings were analysed using the five-step process of thematic analysis proposed by Creswell and Poth (2018:187), which includes managing and organising research data, reading and memorising emergent ideas, describing and classifying codes into themes, developing and accessing interpretations, and finally presenting the data. This systematic approach ensured rigorous analysis while allowing themes related to both resilience strategies and rights implications to emerge from the data.

7.3.5 Ethical Considerations

The study received clearance from the University of Zimbabwe's Ethics Committee and the Government of Zimbabwe's Department of Social Development under the Ministry of Public Service, Labour, and Social Welfare. Informed consent was obtained from parents, guardians, and children to ensure that all participants understood the research purpose and their rights. Participation in the study was entirely voluntary, with participants informed of their right to withdraw without consequences. Pseudonyms and confidentiality measures were utilised to protect the identity of participants, which was very important given the sensitive nature of some adaptive strategies that involved rights violations such as child labour and prostitution.

7.4 Research Findings

Research findings reveal that children in Ward 39 of Gutu District employed multiple adaptive strategies in response to climate change impacts. The data presentation and analysis are centred on the following themes: child labour, child prostitution, drug use and abuse, support from relatives, support from government, support from non-governmental organisations, and support from religious groups, among others. Pseudonyms were used throughout the study to protect participants' identities and maintain confidentiality.

7.4.1 Employment (Child Labour)

The study discovered that some children in rural areas of Zimbabwe engaged in employment at an early age due to climate change impacts. This represented a direct violation of Article 32 of the UNCRC (UN, 1989), which protects children from economic exploitation, and Article 15 of the ACRWC (OAU, 1990), which safeguards children from hazardous employment that interferes with their education or development. It was established that children in rural Zimbabwe developed different and multiple survival strategies in the face of climate change impacts. During in-depth interviews, one participant named Tinotenda, aged 15 years, explained:

> I used to go to school without eating anything because we produced nothing this season, so I ended up dropping out of school, and I am now working as a herd boy in order to provide food for my siblings and my grandparents (17-11-2022).

This testimony highlights how climate-induced food insecurity directly undermines children's right to education, forcing them into labour roles that compromise their development. In focus group discussions, participants mutually agreed that some children in rural Zimbabwe were practising vending and domestic chores, such as housemaids and herd boys, chrome, and gold panning to earn a living. One group participant stated:

> I am a fruit and airtime vendor at Basera Shopping Centre. I got my stock from Birchenough Bridge. I generate income for a living through vending. Sometimes, customer turnout is very low, but I will keep on hustling because I do not have any other option since I am an orphan (18-11-2022).

Another group member named Faith said:

> I dropped out of school in grade 5 due to a shortage of school fees. From there, I worked as a housemaid at Chin'ombe Rural Clinic. I got some money to survive and to help my parents (18-11-2022).

These narratives demonstrate how climate change forces children into survival-oriented labour that, while demonstrating resilience, simultaneously violates their rights to education and protection from exploitation. This echoes patterns documented by Ndhlovu and Chipenda (in this volume) in examining child labour in Zimbabwe's agricultural sector. Supporting findings from in-depth interviews and focus groups, one key informant noted:

> Many children who dropped out of school in this community migrated to nearby towns such as Masvingo, Gutu, and Chiredzi, looking for greener pastures. Others went to Bikita Minerals for chrome panning, while the rest worked as herd boys and housemaids. Even those still in school also have to practice vending at our local shopping centre during weekends and after school hours (17-11-2022).

This key informant testimony reveals the systemic nature of child labour as a climate adaptation strategy, indicating that even children who remain in school must supplement family income through work. This, however, compromises their time for study, rest, and play, which are fundamental rights enshrined in the UNCRC.

7.4.2 *Child Prostitution*

The study also discovered that several children, especially girl children, engaged in child prostitution as a result of hunger and starvation caused by excessive droughts in rural Zimbabwe, representing an extreme violation of Article 34 of the UNCRC (UN, 1989). This Article protects children from all forms of sexual exploitation and abuse, together with Article 27 of the ACRWC (OAU, 1990), which protects children from sexual exploitation and harmful practices. From in-depth interviews, Praise, a girl child in Ward 39, stated:

> Many of us are severely affected by the consequences of climate change in this area. As a result, we were left with no option except that of selling our bodies and getting something to eat and drink (17-11-2022).

Precious also explained:

> We do not care about our health. All we need is money for food and clothes in these difficult times of climate change. We hang out with sugar daddies and young men as long as they give us money to buy food (17-11-2022).

These testimonies reveal how extreme climate-induced poverty drives some girls into sexual exploitation, prioritising immediate survival over long-term health and safety, and illustrating the gendered dimensions of climate vulnerability. From focus group discussions, it was overwhelmingly evident that child prostitution had become a survival option for some children. The consensus emerged that:

> Child prostitution is now common in Ward 39. Children are now practising prostitution for a living. They walk semi-naked to attract customers, some were dancing in beer halls and nightclubs at our local shopping centre (19-11-2022).

In clear support of these findings, one key informant stated:

> It is very sad and culturally unacceptable for people to practice sex work as a source of living. Our girl children are selling their bodies for just a single meal due to hunger and starvation caused by climate change. We urge immediate intervention from the government and private organisations on ways that can ameliorate child prostitution (19-11-2022).

The emergence of child prostitution as a climate adaptation strategy demonstrates the most severe intersection between climate vulnerability and children's rights violations, indicating systemic failures in child protection mechanisms during climate crises.

7.4.3 Community Support Systems

Empirical evidence demonstrates that rural social systems played a crucial role in facilitating children's resilience in the face of climate change, partially fulfilling the spirit of Article 18 of the UNCRC (UN, 1989). The Article recognises parental responsibilities and the need for community support. Article 25 of the ACRWC (OAU, 1990) emphasises that children deprived of family care shall be provided with alternative care that respects their cultural values. During in-depth interviews, one participant, Fatso, from a child-headed family, explained:

> In 2019, during Cyclone Idai, our hut was destroyed, and we moved to stay in the custody of our headman. I did this together with my little brother until the end of the cyclone. The community then built us two huts and gave us food at no cost. Until now, we have been a happy family, although we still encounter climate-related challenges (17-11-2022).

This testimony is important in highlighting how community social protection mechanisms can uphold children's rights during climate disasters, although the sustainability and adequacy of such informal support systems remain questionable. It was mutually agreed in focus group discussions that the community played a crucial role in promoting children's resiliency in the face of climate change. One group member named Tererai stated:

> Community members considered children from vulnerable families to benefit from any developmental issues within the community. They put them upfront, for example, in BEAM, Drought Relief Programme, and Harmonised Social Cash Transfer Programme, among others. This helps them to bounce back in the face of climate change (19-11-2022).

During key informant interviews, the headman explained:

> Our culture as Africans taught us to be our brother's keeper. For as long as he or she is among us, a human being, those with many resources will help those with nothing. We were socialised in such a way that we share, care for each other, and we believe in the African proverb that says, '*Chekudya hachinyimwi munhu*', meaning that we have to share food with those without (19-11-2022).

These findings demonstrate how African communitarian values and *Ubuntu* philosophy provide important social protection for vulnerable children during climate crises. However, such informal mechanisms cannot substitute for systematic rights-based child protection systems.

7.4.4 Government Interventions

The research noted that some families and children in rural Zimbabwe managed to remain resilient in the face of climate change due to governmental interventions. However, the residual nature of these approaches limits their effectiveness in comprehensively protecting children's rights during climate crises. It is important to note that although much of the government's interventions are residual in approach, they heavily contributed to the adaptation of some children in rural Zimbabwe. During in-depth interviews, Tafadzwa, aged 17, stated:

> My siblings and I got help from the government through BEAM ever since the death of our father. Now I am in Form Three. I thank God for that because if it were not for the government's intervention, I could have dropped out of school many years ago. Yes, we sometimes face food and income challenges due to climate change, but academically, we are covered (17-11-2022).

This testimony demonstrated how targeted government programmes can protect children's right to education during climate-induced economic stress. However, the selective nature of such programmes leaves many vulnerable children without support. From focus groups, rural children agreed that the government played a pivotal role in their academic adaptation to climate change. They stated:

> The government is trying to help us remain academically resilient in the face of climate change. Nowadays, the government is paying school fees, providing stationery and paying exam fees for vulnerable children through the BEAM programme (19-11-2022).

One key informant confirmed:

> Since the introduction of BEAM by the government, most of our children managed to complete their ordinary level regardless of the effects of climate change. However, the only problem is that BEAM is selective in nature in that it only accommodates the most vulnerable children, thereby leaving other needy populations at risk (19-11-2022).

These findings reveal both the strengths and limitations of current government interventions. While programmes like BEAM protect some children's educational rights during climate stress, their selective targeting leaves significant gaps in rights protection for many vulnerable children.

7.4.5 *Drought Relief Programme*

The study revealed that the government's Drought Relief Programme (DRP) through the Department of Social Development contributed to the resilience of some children in rural Zimbabwe. However, its temporary and reactive nature limits its capacity to build long-term climate resilience while protecting children's rights. During in-depth interviews, one participant, named Sharon, aged 15, explained:

> I appreciate the efforts from our government through the Social Development Department. They give us maize grain on a monthly basis from August to March or April the following year. Agricultural inputs such as maize seed and fertilisers were also distributed towards the rainy season. This greatly helped us since hunger and starvation impacted this area (18-11-2022).

From focus group discussions, all participants credited the role of the Zimbabwean government in promoting the resilience of numerous children in rural areas in the face of climate change. They also endorsed the role of government in encouraging people to grow fast-growing and drought-resistant crops through providing agricultural inputs such as maize and sorghum seeds and fertilisers and the introduction of zero-tillage farming that requires no livestock labour. Supporting these observations, the ward councillor stated:

> We receive monthly help from the government through the drought relief programme, where people are given maize grain and agricultural inputs for smoother preparation during the rainy season. This minimises hunger and starvation while contributing to the coping capacities of many children in our community (18-11-2022).

While drought relief programmes provide critical short-term support for children's right to adequate nutrition during climate crises, their reactive rather than proactive nature highlights the need for more comprehensive, rights-based climate adaptation strategies that address the structural causes of vulnerability rather than merely responding to crises as they emerge.

7.4.6 *The Role of Non-governmental Organisations (NGOs)*

The study found that apart from governmental interventions, NGOs in rural Zimbabwe contributed to children's resilience through complementary programmes, although coordination challenges and limited coverage constrain their effectiveness in comprehensively protecting children's rights during climate change. In complementing government efforts, NGOs provide assistance with food and school fees and empower rural populations to remain self-reliant. From in-depth interviews, Trust, a boy aged 16, stated:

> NGOs such as WFP, Children Tariro, and Care help us a lot with nutritious food to boost our health. They also pay school fees and provide stationery to some children in rural areas (18-11-2022).

From focus group discussions, it was agreed that NGOs complemented government efforts in many ways. It was noted that NGOs campaign for children's rights through various efforts, denouncing issues of child marriage and child labour that are common due to climate-related challenges. NGOs also provided food handouts and fee payment for children in some rural areas of Zimbabwe. One key informant supported this by stating:

> NGOs played an important role in empowering community members to attain sustainable development. They improved community members' self-reliance by introducing income-generating projects, for example, the gardening project initiated by Care International along the Dewure River with the village here, residents were empowered to utilise available community resources to fend for their families (19-11-2022).

These findings reveal that NGOs contribute to immediate relief and long-term empowerment, addressing survival needs and developmental rights. The challenge is that the sustainability and scale of such interventions remain limited in the face of escalating climate impacts.

7.4.7 *The Role of Religious Groups*

The study discovered that religious groups in rural Zimbabwe contributed to children's resilience in the face of climate change through both material support and psychosocial care. This represents an important community asset that partially fills gaps in formal child protection systems. These religious groups include both Pentecostal and Apostolic sects. From in-depth interviews, Mercy, one of the respondents, stated:

> Our family church played a pivotal role in imparting faith and hope to us. Church members visited us at home, giving us food and clothes handouts while helping us with domestic chores (17-11-2022).

From focus groups, it was also agreed that religious groups contributed to children's resilience in rural areas as they act as charity organisations. One participant explained:

> Our church pastor helped us with food whenever things got tough for us. He visited us several times, checking on us, giving pastoral counselling and encouraging us to pray for a better future (19-11-2022).

In supporting findings from in-depth interviews and focus groups, one key informant shed light on religious groups' contribution to the resilience of some children in rural Zimbabwe, stating:

> Religious groups are important in this community as they preach the word of God and encourage people to love and help each other to enter the kingdom of heaven. They preach biblical verses, for example, 'love your neighbour as you love yourself', which gives people the spirit of sharing with vulnerable children in the face of climate change. Religious sects such as the Roman Catholic Church also donated food hand-outs to child-headed families and single-parent families in our community (19-11-2022).

These findings demonstrate how religious organisations provide material support and emotional/spiritual care that address children's psychosocial needs during climate crises, contributing to holistic well-being beyond mere survival. However, such support remains informal and inconsistent.

7.4.8 Extended Family System

The study discovered that the extended family system in Zimbabwe played a central role in the resilience of some children in rural areas in the face of climate change, upholding Article 20 of the UNCRC (UN, 1989). This Article provides for alternative care within the family environment and strongly aligns with Article 25 of the ACRWC (OAU, 1990), which emphasises that children's care should occur within the extended family network in keeping with African cultural values. This is because the rural family system is structured so that all relatives of the same clan live in the same area or village. During in-depth interviews, one participant explained:

> My parents died some time ago, and we are now under the custody of my father's brother, together with my nieces. He treated us just like his biological children; he sent us to school and provided everything we wanted. We call him 'baba', and only a few know he is not our biological father (18-11-2022).

From focus groups, many children revealed how their relatives helped them remain resilient in the face of climate change. Participants mutually agreed on the role played by relatives, stating:

> Our relatives played an important role in supporting and providing basic needs and academic items like stationery to us children in rural Zimbabwe in the face of climate change (19-11-2022).

One key informant supported this by stating:

> In our culture, there are no orphans; this is because all children with deceased parents are looked after under the custody of immediate family members. We believe in the merits of the extended family system rather than the Eurocentric nuclear family set-up. It is a taboo to neglect orphans in this community. Neglecting them calls for the whole family to be cursed by the Gods or even fined by the chief (19-11-2022).

These findings demonstrate how African extended family systems function as resilience mechanisms that uphold children's rights to family care and protection as articulated in Article 20 of the UNCRC and Article 25 of the ACRWC. The goal is to facilitate the provision of alternative care arrangements that maintain children's connections to family, culture, and community during climate-induced adversities.

7.5 Discussion

Research findings suggest that children in Gutu District engaged in various survival strategies in the face of climate change, some of which enhanced their resilience while simultaneously compromising their rights as enshrined in international and regional instruments. These strategies include child labour, child prostitution, drug use and abuse, support from religious sects, and support from extended family members, among others. A critical analysis of these findings through the lens of children's rights frameworks reveals complex tensions between survival imperatives and rights protection. It highlights the inadequacy of current climate adaptation mechanisms in safeguarding children's comprehensive rights to survival, development, protection, and participation.

The study discovered that some children in rural Zimbabwe engaged in child employment as a way of surviving in the face of climate change, with children migrating to nearby towns such as Masvingo, Gutu, Mpandawana, and Chiredzi in search of better living conditions. In contrast, others were employed as herd boys and housemaids in their local areas. These findings parallel those discovered in Pakistan during the 2010 flood disaster, where children were sexually abused for food, became street beggars, and worked as street vendors for survival. While child labour demonstrates children's agency and resilience, it directly violates Article 32 of the UNCRC, which protects children from economic exploitation and work that interferes with their education or is harmful to their health or development, and Article 15 of the ACRWC, which protects children from economic exploitation and hazardous employment. Although child labour and child employment are regarded as violations of children's rights, the study documented them as resilient strategies employed by some children in rural Zimbabwe in the face of climate change, revealing the tension between survival needs and rights protection.

These findings illuminate the paradox at the heart of climate-induced resilience strategies. Children's adaptive responses may ensure immediate survival while simultaneously undermining their long-term developmental rights and perpetuating intergenerational cycles of vulnerability. The findings bring into focus the main thrust of resilience theory that addresses the strengths that people and social systems possess in the face of disasters, crises, or problems (Van Breda, 2018). Jobs and life skills are protective factors of resilience that improve adaptation among some children in rural Zimbabwe (Ungar, 2012). Resilience theory helps establish that some children in rural Zimbabwe managed to recover and demonstrate positive adaptation through different life skills, such as employment. However, from a children's rights perspective, the necessity of child labour as a survival strategy represents a failure of state obligations under Article 27 of the UNCRC to ensure children's right to an adequate standard of living and Article 20 of the ACRWC regarding parental responsibilities and state assistance. The findings align with the resilience theory perspective that sustainable resilience requires robust approaches and plans to promote the well-being and coping capacities of individuals, groups, and communities at large. However, these findings also demonstrate that when climate change severely impacts rural Zimbabwe, children's resilience through employment comes at the cost of their educational rights (Article 28 of UNCRC and Article 11 of ACRWC) and their right to rest, leisure, and play (Article 31 of UNCRC), revealing how climate adaptation strategies may perpetuate rather than address structural inequalities affecting children.

Empirical evidence demonstrates that community members and social systems contributed to children's resilience in rural Zimbabwe in the face of climate change. They partially fulfil the spirit of Articles 18 and 20 of the UNCRC and Article 25 of the ACRWC, which emphasise community responsibility in supporting children's care and protection. It was revealed that community leaders care for vulnerable children during catastrophes precipitated by climate change, with community leaders exercising social responsibility by organising community members to support each other during calamities. This reflects African communities mobilised around *the Ubuntu* philosophy and basic tenets of African moral philosophy, such as brotherhood, collective unity, goodwill, collective identity, generosity, and protection of community welfare and interests (Tutu, 2000). Each community member contributes something to improve other people's lives, thereby enhancing the resilience of some children in rural Zimbabwe in the face of climate change.

Utilising resilience theory alongside children's rights frameworks reveals that community support systems function as protective factors that partially compensate for inadequate state provision. However, as argued earlier, they cannot substitute for systematic rights-based child protection mechanisms required under international law. The resilience theory approach depends on various systems collectively contributing to individuals' or groups' development and coping capacities. In this case, communities comprising individuals, groups, local institutions, and social systems contributed to the resilience of numerous rural children in Zimbabwe in the face of climate change. Samkange and Samkange (1980) argue that African communities are structured and socialised to care for each other regardless of social status. However, while these community-based mechanisms align with the ACRWC's emphasis on African values and communal responsibility (as reflected in the Preamble), they remain vulnerable to the same climate stresses affecting individual families, highlighting the need for state parties to fulfil their obligations under Article 4 of the UNCRC and Article 1 of the ACRWC to undertake legislative, administrative, and resource allocation measures to realise children's rights progressively and sustainably, even during climate crises.

The study discovered that religious organisations played important roles in facilitating children's resilience in rural Zimbabwe in the face of climate change. This contributed to children's rights to spiritual development (Article 14 of UNCRC and Article 9 of ACRWC) while providing material support that addresses rights to adequate living standards. Religious organisations pray on behalf of children, preach the word of God, citing biblical verses that impart faith and hope, and provide spiritual answers for better outcomes. These religious groups are paramount in promoting resilience among some children in rural Zimbabwe. They foster mutual understanding among community residents while encouraging them to love and help the needy during troubled times. Even the social work profession originated from religious grounds where people helped the needy religiously. Local Pentecostal and Apostolic sects help children from child-headed families, single-parent families, and grandparent families with pastoral counselling, food handouts, and clothing.

Religious organisations function as community assets and institutions contributing to rural children's resilience in the face of climate change. The challenge is that their informal and voluntary nature means they cannot guarantee consistent fulfilment of children's rights as required under Articles 4 and 6 of the UNCRC, which establish state obligations to ensure children's survival and development. These findings parallel those by Chikoko and Mwapaura (2022), where people with disabilities received religious help during the 2019 pandemic, which contributed to their adaptation. However, from a children's rights analytical perspective, while religious support provides valuable psychosocial care, it also addresses Article 24 of the UNCRC (right to health, including mental health) and Article 14 of the ACRWC (right to health and health services). However, reliance on voluntary religious charity as a primary climate adaptation mechanism reflects systemic failures in state provision of social protection and essential services required under Articles 26 and 27 of the UNCRC and Article 20 of the ACRWC, particularly during climate-induced emergencies that disproportionately affect vulnerable children.

Closely related to this child protection concern is the observation that government interventions through BEAM facilitated the academic resilience of some children in rural Zimbabwe in the face of climate change. This partially fulfilled state obligations under Article 28 of the UNCRC and Article 11 of the ACRWC to ensure children's right to education based on equal opportunity. Although the approach is selective, focusing on the most vulnerable children, the intervention is important. Government programmes such as drought relief positively impacted the lives of many children in rural areas, thereby temporarily promoting food security among rural populations by providing grain and agricultural inputs to reduce hunger and starvation. Some families received cash handouts through the Harmonised Social Cash Transfer programme. At the same time, the government pays school fees for vulnerable children through BEAM, reducing hunger, starvation, and early school dropouts caused by climate change among some rural children.

These findings align with the protective factor model of resilience, which articulates connections between adversity and protective measures that help reduce the bearing of shocks on children (O'Leary, 1998). In this case, government intervention is a protective measure, ameliorating hunger, starvation, and massive school dropout among some children in rural Zimbabwe in the face of climate change. The findings parallel those of the World Food Programme (2020) in its study on people affected by Cyclone Idai of 2019, where affected populations received food, temporary shelters, and clothing handouts from the government. However, critical analysis through the lens of Articles 4 and 27 of the UNCRC and Article 20 of the ACRWC reveals significant limitations. While government programmes demonstrate efforts towards progressive realisation of children's rights, their residual and selective nature falls short of comprehensive, rights-based social protection systems necessary to ensure all children's rights during climate crises, particularly those enshrined in Article 26 of the UNCRC regarding children's right to benefit from social security.

It is crucial to note that although the government attempted to facilitate resilience among some children in rural Zimbabwe, the approach is unsustainable and problematic within African contexts. African problems require robust, multisectoral, social developmental approaches that empower people through income-generating projects to achieve self-sufficiency soon. From a children's rights perspective, temporary relief measures, while necessary for immediate survival (Article 6 UNCRC, proper to survival), do not adequately address children's rights to development (Article 6 UNCRC), which require sustained investments in education, health, and social protection systems resilient to climate shocks. Furthermore, the selective nature of programmes like BEAM raises concerns about non-discrimination principles enshrined in Article 2 of the UNCRC and Article 3 of the ACRWC, as many vulnerable children remain excluded from support despite facing similar climate-induced hardships. The findings thus reveal a critical gap between state obligations to ensure children's rights under international law and actual implementation of climate-responsive child protection mechanisms. They echo Moyo et al.'s (in this volume) concerns regarding implementation gaps between Zimbabwe's comprehensive policy frameworks and actual child protection.

The emergence of child prostitution as a climate adaptation strategy represents the most severe intersection between climate vulnerability and children's rights violations, constituting breaches of multiple rights, including protection from sexual exploitation (Article 34 UNCRC and Article 27 ACRWC), protection from harmful practices (Article 21 ACRWC), and rights to health and dignity. The findings revealed that hunger and starvation caused by excessive droughts drove some girl children into prostitution, demonstrating how climate-induced poverty can lead to extreme protection failures. This phenomenon illustrates the gendered dimensions of climate vulnerability, where girls experience disproportionate impacts through climate-induced time poverty and compromised safety, with prostitution representing an extreme manifestation of how climate change amplifies pre-existing gender inequalities and protection risks.

From a children's rights analytical perspective, the resort to child prostitution as a survival mechanism indicates catastrophic failures across multiple state obligations. There is failure to ensure adequate standards of living (Article 27 UNCRC), failure to protect children from all forms of violence and exploitation (Articles 19 and 34 UNCRC, Article 16 ACRWC), and failure to ensure children's rights to survival and development (Article 6 UNCRC, Article 5 ACRWC). The testimonies from girls who stated they 'don't care about our health' and are 'left with no option except that of selling our bodies' reveal how extreme climate-induced poverty creates conditions where children's immediate survival needs override all other rights considerations, including their rights to health, education, and future development. This represents a failure of the 'best interests of the child' principle enshrined in Article 3 of the UNCRC and Article 4 of the ACRWC, which requires that children's best interests be the primary consideration in all actions, including climate adaptation and disaster response strategies.

The key informant's statement that 'our girl children are selling their bodies for just a single meal due to hunger and starvation caused by climate change' highlights the urgent need for immediate intervention, as such practices violate not only protection rights but also children's inherent dignity and rights to optimal development. Article 16 of the ACRWC explicitly protects children from sexual abuse and exploitation, while Article 27 of the ACRWC addresses harmful social and cultural practices that affect children's welfare, health, and development. The documentation of child prostitution as a climate adaptation strategy thus reveals how climate change acts as a threat multiplier that exacerbates pre-existing protection vulnerabilities. It creates conditions where even the most fundamental rights protections collapse, demonstrating the necessity of integrating child protection mechanisms into all climate adaptation and disaster risk reduction strategies. This is advocated by Chipenda and Chawanda (in this volume) in their analysis of climate justice imperatives for children's rights in Zimbabwe.

The other aspect worth discussing is the extended family system. In Zimbabwe, it has functioned as a central resilience mechanism upholding children's rights to family care as articulated in Article 20 of the UNCRC, which provides that children deprived of their family environment are entitled to special protection and alternative care, and Article 25 of the ACRWC, which emphasises that children's care should occur within the family and extended family network in keeping with African values. The findings demonstrated how children orphaned or otherwise separated from parents found care within extended family structures, with relatives treating them 'just like biological children' and ensuring their continued access to education and basic needs. The key informant's statement that 'in our culture there is no orphan' reflects African communitarian values that provide protective frameworks for vulnerable children during climate crises and other adversities.

From a children's rights analytical perspective, the extended family system represents an important protective factor that aligns with the ACRWC's emphasis on African values and community-based childcare approaches, as reflected in the Charter's Preamble, which notes that 'the child occupies a unique and privileged position in the African society'. The extended family's functioning during climate crises demonstrates resilience at the family system level, maintaining children's connections to their cultural heritage, identity, and support networks as protected under Article 8 of the UNCRC (right to identity) and Article 9 of the ACRWC (freedom of thought, conscience, and religion within cultural contexts). However, it is critical to recognise that extended family systems, while valuable, face their own climate-related stresses that may limit their capacity to provide adequate care and that informal kinship care cannot substitute for comprehensive state obligations under Article 4 of the UNCRC to undertake measures for the implementation of children's rights, including through resource allocation and policy development that addresses explicitly climate impacts on family care systems.

The findings suggest that while extended family systems provide crucial support upholding children's rights to family care during climate adversities, these systems require complementary support from state and non-state actors to ensure sustainable fulfilment of all children's rights, especially rights to adequate standards of living

(Article 27 UNCRC), education (Article 28 UNCRC), and health (Article 24 UNCRC), which extended families alone may struggle to provide during prolonged climate stress. The resilience demonstrated by extended family systems thus highlights the strengths of African communitarian approaches to childcare and the need for integrated, rights-based climate adaptation strategies that support rather than undermine these traditional protective mechanisms.

7.6 Conclusion and Recommendations

This chapter has interrogated the resilience of children in rural Zimbabwe in the face of climate change, revealing complex intersections between adaptive strategies and children's rights as enshrined in the UNCRC and ACRWC. The findings demonstrate that children in Ward 39, Gutu District, employ multiple survival strategies, including child labour, prostitution, and mobilising support from community networks, relatives, government programmes, and religious organisations. While these strategies demonstrate remarkable resilience and agency, many simultaneously constitute violations of children's rights. They highlight the inadequacy of current climate adaptation mechanisms in safeguarding children's comprehensive rights during environmental crises.

The study reveals several critical patterns at the intersection of climate change and children's rights in rural Zimbabwe. First, climate-induced economic stress forces children into survival-oriented labour and, in extreme cases, sexual exploitation, directly violating their rights to protection from economic and sexual exploitation. Second, while community support systems, extended families, and religious organisations provide crucial protective factors that partially uphold children's rights to care and holistic development, these informal mechanisms face climate-related stresses and cannot substitute for systematic state obligations to ensure children's rights progressively and sustainably. Third, government interventions such as BEAM and drought relief programmes provide important but insufficient protection of children's educational and nutritional rights, with their residual and selective nature falling short of comprehensive, rights-based social protection systems necessary to ensure all children's rights during climate crises.

The findings highlight tensions between immediate survival imperatives and long-term rights protection in climate-vulnerable contexts. Children's adaptive responses ensure short-term survival while potentially undermining developmental rights and perpetuating intergenerational vulnerability cycles. This paradox reflects systemic failures in climate adaptation frameworks that inadequately integrate child-specific vulnerabilities and rights protections. The documentation of child prostitution as an extreme adaptation strategy reveals how climate change functions as a threat multiplier that exacerbates pre-existing protection vulnerabilities. It creates conditions where even the most fundamental rights protections collapse, demonstrating catastrophic failures across multiple state obligations.

From a children's rights analytical perspective grounded in the UNCRC and ACRWC, the research findings reveal critical gaps between state obligations and implementing climate-responsive child protection mechanisms. While the UNCRC and ACRWC establish comprehensive frameworks protecting children's rights to survival, development, protection, and participation, current climate adaptation responses in rural Zimbabwe inadequately address how climate impacts systematically undermine these rights. Articles 4 of the UNCRC and 1 of the ACRWC require states to undertake progressive legislative, administrative, and resource allocation measures to implement children's rights. However, the reliance on residual government programmes, voluntary community support, and children's survival strategies indicates insufficient systematic approaches to climate-responsive child protection. The 'best interests of the child' principle requires that children's best interests be the primary consideration in all actions. However, climate adaptation and disaster response strategies often fail to prioritise child-specific needs and rights protections. The gendered dimensions of climate vulnerability documented in this chapter and interconnected patterns across different districts demonstrate that climate-induced rights violations are not isolated incidents but systemic challenges requiring comprehensive policy responses. The educational disruptions documented in Gutu District reveal consistent patterns of how climate change extends children's rights inequalities across diverse rural contexts in Zimbabwe.

While illuminating children's adaptive capacities and protective factors supporting their coping during climate adversities, resilience theory must be complemented by rights-based frameworks that ensure adaptation strategies uphold rather than compromise children's rights. The challenge model, protective factor model, and compensatory model of resilience help explain how children navigate climate-induced adversities. Yet, from a rights perspective, resilience-building interventions must address structural determinants of vulnerability rather than merely supporting individual or family-level coping that may perpetuate rights violations. Sustainable resilience requires robust, multisectoral approaches that empower children and families through systematic social protection, economic empowerment, and rights-based climate adaptation strategies rather than temporary relief measures or survival strategies that compromise children's long-term development.

Building on this chapter's empirical evidence and analytical insights, several integrated recommendations emerge for strengthening child-centred, rights-based climate adaptation in rural Zimbabwe. Social workers and child protection professionals should conduct comprehensive climate change risk assessments among rural children to identify specific vulnerabilities and develop targeted intervention strategies that uphold rather than compromise children's rights. There is an urgent need to empower rural children through life skills development, educational support, and economic opportunities that enable adaptation without resorting to rights-violating survival strategies such as hazardous labour or sexual exploitation. Traditional social protection mechanisms such as the *Zunde raMambo* system should be revisited, strengthened, and integrated with contemporary social protection frameworks to create comprehensive safety nets supporting children's rights during climate crises. Social workers must link vulnerable children with resources through systematic case management approaches while mobilising community resources and raising awareness regarding children's rights and climate vulnerabilities, ensuring communities understand that survival strategies violating children's rights require alternative interventions rather than acceptance as inevitable adaptations.

Policymakers must urgently establish comprehensive climate change adaptation strategies specifically addressing children's rights and vulnerabilities, moving beyond residual approaches to transformative social protection systems that ensure all children's rights during environmental crises. Climate change resilience policies and legislation should be adopted and implemented with provisions protecting children's rights to survival, development, protection, and participation as enshrined in the UNCRC and ACRWC. There is a critical need to develop alternative climate policies integrating child-centred perspectives and ensuring that climate adaptation and disaster risk reduction strategies prioritise children's best interests across all sectors, including agriculture, education, health, and social protection. Policy frameworks must address the selective nature of current interventions and ensure comprehensive coverage of vulnerable children while strengthening coordination between government programmes, NGO initiatives, and community-based support systems to create coherent, rights-based protection mechanisms during climate adversities.

Private organisations, NGOs, and faith-based groups should network resources for children in rural Zimbabwe facing climate change, channelling reliable supporting services that address immediate survival needs and long-term developmental rights. These actors should provide family and community support services that strengthen rather than substitute for family care systems, recognising the value of extended family networks while providing complementary resources ensuring children's adequate living standards, education, and health rights. There is an urgent need for advocacy advancing children's rights in climate contexts, challenging the acceptance of rights-violating survival strategies, and promoting comprehensive, rights-based alternatives that address structural vulnerabilities. Civil society organisations must hold the government accountable for fulfilling state obligations under the UNCRC and ACRWC, particularly regarding progressive implementation of children's rights and non-discrimination in access to climate adaptation support.

Researchers should conduct further scientific investigation regarding climate change effects in rural Zimbabwe with a specific focus on children's rights implications, employing interdisciplinary approaches integrating environmental science, social science, and human rights frameworks. Qualitative research should explore strategies for improving children's livelihoods in rural areas facing climate change while ensuring these strategies uphold rather than compromise rights to protection, education, and development. There is a particular need for longitudinal studies examining long-term developmental outcomes for children employing different adaptive strategies, assessing whether survival mechanisms such as child labour create lasting impediments to educational and economic opportunities. Research should also investigate effective models for integrating traditional African protective mechanisms, such as extended family care and *Ubuntu* philosophy, with contemporary rights-based child protection systems, identifying how these complementary approaches can create resilient, culturally appropriate frameworks for safeguarding children's rights during climate crises.

In conclusion, addressing climate change impacts on children's rights in rural Zimbabwe requires paradigm shifts from residual relief approaches to comprehensive, transformative policies that tackle structural inequalities while building systematic resilience. The resilience demonstrated by children in Ward 39, Gutu District, while remarkable, should not obscure the reality that children forced into labour, sexual exploitation, or dependence on informal charity as climate adaptation strategies are experiencing violations of their fundamental rights that demand urgent, comprehensive intervention. Climate adaptation frameworks must prioritise children's rights as defined in the UNCRC and ACRWC, ensuring that survival, development, protection, and participation rights remain inviolable even during environmental crises, while building long-term resilience through systematic social protection, economic empowerment, and child-centred development strategies that address the root causes of vulnerability rather than merely managing their symptoms.

Acknowledgements This research was part of Philemon Chihiya's Master of Social Work Dissertation in the Department of Social Work, University of Zimbabwe.

Declaration We declare that the study on the resilienceof children in rural Zimbabwe, a case of ward 39 of Gutu District, is our own work. This study has no known conflict of interest or external funding. All the sources used have been acknowledged by means of complete references.

References

Babbie, E., & Mouton, J. (2004). *The practice of social research*. Oxford.

Bhatasara, S. (2018). *Understanding adaptation to climate variability in smallholder farming systems in eastern Zimbabwe: A sociological perspective*. University of Zimbabwe.

Chatiza, K. (2019). *Cyclone Idai in Zimbabwe: An analysis of policy implications for post-disaster institutional development to strengthen disaster risk management*. Oxfam.

Chikoko, W., & Mwapaura, K. (2022). Resilience of persons with road accident disabilities in the face of the COVID-19 pandemic in Budiriro High Density residential suburb, Harare, Zimbabwe. *Journal of Urban Systems and Innovations for Resilience in Zimbabwe, 4*(1), 283–300.

Chingwanda, E. (2016). *A framework for building resilience to climate change through girls' education programming*. Centre for Universal Education.

Creswell, J. W. (2009). *Research design: Qualitative, quantitative, and mixed methods approaches* (4th ed.). Sage Publications.

Creswell, J. W., & Poth, C. N. (2018). *Qualitative inquiry and research design: Choosing among five approaches*. Sage Publications.

Davidson, C., Karen, A., Dominguez-Francisca, L., Carola, E., & Patrick, A. P. (2005). Psychometric properties of the Connor-Davidson Resilience Scale for South America (CD-RISC-25SA) in Peruvian adolescents. https://www.mdpi.com/journal/children

De Bruijne, M. B. E. M. (2010). Resilience: Exploring the concept and its meanings. In *Designing resilience: Preparing for extreme events*. University of Pittsburgh Press.

Feyissa, R. (2007). The sub-Saharan African agriculture: Potential, challenges and opportunities.

Luthar, S. S. (1991). Vulnerability and resilience: A study of high-risk adolescents. *Child Development, 62*, 600–616.
Manyena, S. B. K. R. (2011). Disaster resilience: A bounce back or bounce forward ability. *Local Environment, 5*(16), 417–424.
Manyeruke, C., Hamauswa, S., & Mhandar, L. (2013). The effects of climate change and variability on food security in Zimbabwe: A socio-economic and political analysis. *International Journal of Humanities and Social Science, 3*.
Masten, A. (1990). *Resilience in individual development: Successful adaptation despite risk and adversity* (pp. 3–25). Routledge.
Masten, A. S., Cutuli, J. J., Herbers, J. E., & Reed, J. M. (2007). Resilience in development. In S. J. Lopez & C. R. Snyder (Eds.), *The Oxford handbook of positive psychology*. Oxford University Press.
McKenna, S. A., & Denver, D. S. (2013). *The role and influence of key informants in community-engagement research: A critical perspective*. Sage Publications.
Mordecai, E. A., Ryan, S. J., Caldwell, J. M., Shah, M. M., & LaBeaud, A. D. (2020). Climate change could shift disease burden from malaria to arboviruses in Africa. *The Lancet Planetary Health, 4*, 416–423.
Mpambela, M., & Mabvurira, V. (2017). Effects of climate change and their indelible impact on social work profession in Zimbabwe. *African Journal of Social Work, 7*(2), 30–35.
Nelson, G. C., Rosegrant, M., Koo, J., Robertson, R., Sulser, T., Zhu, T., Msangi, S., Ringler, C., Palazzo, A., Batka, M., Magalhaes, M., & Lee, D. (2009). *Climate change: Impact on agriculture and costs of adaptation*. International Food Policy Research Institute.
OAU. (1990). *African Charter on the Rights and Welfare of the Child (ACRWC)* (OAU Doc. CAB/LEG/24.9/49). Organization of African Unity.
O'Leary, V. (1998). Strength in the face of adversity: Individual and social thriving. *Journal of Social Issues, 54*, 425–446.
Prince-Embury, S., & Saklofske, D. H. (2003). *Resilience in children, adolescents, and adults: Translating research into practice*. Springer.
Samkange, S., & Samkange, T. M. (1980). *Hunhuism or Ubuntuism: A Zimbabwe indigenous political philosophy*. Graham Publishing.
Sikorska, I. (2014). *Theoretical models of resilience and resilience measurement tools in children and young people*. The National Science Centre.
Tutu, D. (2000). *No future without forgiveness: A personal overview of South Africa's Truth and Reconciliation Commission*. Rider Random House.
UNDAF. (2011). *Policy framework document (with signatures)*. Retrieved October 25, 2012, from www.unfpa.org/zimbabwe/drive/2012-2015ZUNDAF_FINAL_withsignatures(1).pdf
Ungar, M. (2012). *Social ecologies and their contribution to resilience: A handbook of theory and practice*. Springer.
UNICEF. (2013). *Children and climate change in Zimbabwe*. Institute of Environmental Studies, University of Zimbabwe.
UNICEF. (2019). *Exploring the impact of climate change on children in South Africa: Summary of findings*. UNICEF South Africa.
United Nations. (1989). *United Nations convention on the rights of the child (UNCRC)*. United Nations.
Van Breda, A. D. (2018). A critical review of resilience theory and its relevance for social work. *Social Work, 54*(1), 1–18.
Weathington, B. L., Cunningham, C. J., & Pittenger, D. J. (2010). *Research methods for the behavioral and social sciences*. Wiley.
Wright, M. D., & Masten, A. S. (2004). Resilience processes in development: Fostering positive adaptation in the context of adversity. In *Handbook of resilience in children*. Kluwer.

Part III
Climate Change Impact on Children's Health, Education, and Welfare Through a Climate Justice Lens

Chapter 8
Climate Change Impact on Children's Nutrition: Harnessing AI for Safe Food and Healthy Diets in Zimbabwe

Emmanuel Ndhlovu and Clement Chipenda

8.1 Introduction

Climate change is one of the contemporary disasters facing humanity (Intergovernmental Panel on Climate Change (IPCC), 2014). Climate change is defined by the IPCC (2022) as "a change in the state of the climate that can be identified … by changes in the mean and/or the variability of its properties, and that persists for an extended period, typically decades or longer". It causes snowballed temperatures, altered rainfall patterns, and amplified occurrence of extreme weather events. These factors result in floods, droughts, storms with strong winds, wildfires, and erosion-inducing landslides, which have costly impacts, particularly for financially developing countries. Climate change undermines development by drawing back gains in global health, poverty reduction, and food security, excessively impacting vulnerable communities and worsening prevailing inequalities through amplified hunger, disease, displacement, and economic hardship due to extreme weather events (Farah et al., 2025; Wakweya, 2025). This crisis threatens livelihoods, biodiversity, and access to essential resources like water and arable land, leading to increased competition and instability. Climate change also poses a significant and intensifying threat to child nutrition, forming a complex network of challenges that affect food systems, health, and livelihoods. Children, particularly those in vulnerable regions, are excessively impacted, and without substantial urgent action, climate change could reverse years of progress in combating

E. Ndhlovu (✉)
College of Business and Economics, University of Johannesburg, Auckland Park, South Africa

C. Chipenda
South African Research Chair in Social Policy, College of Graduate Studies, University of South Africa, Pretoria, South Africa

E. Ndhlovu, C. Chipenda (eds.), *Climate Change and Children's Rights in Zimbabwe*, https://doi.org/10.1007/978-981-95-6005-9_8

malnutrition. Zimbabwe, a country in Southern Africa, is in one of the regions where climate change is significantly slowing progress.

In recent years, climate change has had disastrous impacts in Southern Africa, where Zimbabwe is located. It has been increasing the regularity and concentration of extreme weather events in the sub-region, leading to more severe droughts, floods, heatwaves, and fires, all threatening human lives, infrastructure, and economic stability. Significant events in Zimbabwe include Cyclone Eline in 2000, Cyclone Idai in 2019, and the Durban floods of 2022. These events highlight the overwhelming impact of climate change, which is excessively affecting vulnerable communities. Several recommendations have been made to deal with the challenges. These include developing robust early warning systems, implementing climate-resilient infrastructure, and accelerating global efforts to lessen climate change (IPCC, 2022; Zhao et al., 2025). However, one of the aspects lacking in the climate change literature is the exploration of how it aggravates the conditions of population groups that are already vulnerable, such as children. This is particularly concerning in countries such as Zimbabwe, where children's rights rarely attract academic attention or take centre stage in development discourses. This is a gap with substantial policy and practical implications. This chapter contributes towards closing this knowledge gap. This chapter sits at the intersection of two strands of literature: the literature on climate change and the literature on children's rights. Traditionally, these strands do not sufficiently engage each other. However, bringing them together can highlight how children's rights are easily ignored even during major crises such as climate change.

This chapter (1) explores how climate change impacts the possibilities for safe food and child nutrition in Zimbabwe and then (2) proposes how artificial intelligence can be leveraged to ensure safe food and healthy child nutrition in the country. A study on the impact of climate change on children's nutrition is critical. Children are not just small adults; they have unique physiological, cognitive, and developmental vulnerabilities that make them disproportionately vulnerable to climate impacts. Their developing bodies and minds are more sensitive to environmental hazards, and the long-term consequences of climate-related events can affect them for the rest of their lives. Studying the impact of climate change on children's nutrition is crucial because it can inform policy and action. It provides the evidence to create child-responsive climate policies, adaptation strategies, and disaster risk reduction plans that address children's needs. It also sheds light on the crucial ethical issue that children, who have contributed the least to climate change, will bear the brunt of its impacts. The study also helps identify the most vulnerable populations of children and the most effective interventions to protect them, such as strengthening healthcare systems, ensuring food and water security, and providing mental health support. Understanding and addressing the effects on children can help ensure a healthier, more stable, and more equitable future for the next generation. A child-centred approach to climate action is a moral imperative and a strategic investment in the long-term resilience of communities and societies. Policymakers, non-governmental organisations (NGOs), students, academics, and other stakeholders interested in the welfare of children can find the chapter interesting and informative.

This chapter is organised as follows: The following section reviews related literature. An outline of the adopted research methods follows this. After, the findings of the review are presented in two subsections. The challenges to AI adoption in Zimbabwe are then discussed, leading to the conclusion and recommendations.

8.2 Literature Review: Climate Change in Zimbabwe

Literature on child malnutrition abounds globally (Blackie & Luckett, 2025; Nwachukwu & Affen, 2023), and it is defined as a "lack of proper nutrition or bad nutrition", which includes both stunting and obesity (Raimi & Phiri, 2024, p. 3). It is a consequence of hunger and poverty. It is caused by deficient dietary consumption, insufficient access to clean water, poor sanitation, and insufficient income to ensure quality food (Siddiqui et al., 2020). Malnutrition is also exacerbated by limited access to basic facilities such as shelter, health, and education facilities, which can improve the quality of life in impoverished environments (UNICEF, 2023). The World Health Organisation (WHO) (2020a) opines that malnutrition is a monetary and social issue, affecting almost all countries to different degrees. Malnutrition affects both adults and children, but it is more common in children, particularly those below the age of five (UNICEF, 2023). The WHO (2020b) reports that out of the 1.9 billion people battling overweight, 41 million of them are children less than 5 years old. Another 159 million people are stunted, while 462 million are underweight.

Despite the support from the UNICEF, WHO, and WB towards nutrition, the world is still far from eliminating malnutrition. The March 2020 WHO report revealed inadequate progress towards the set targets for 2025 and the SDGs set for 2030 (WHO, 2020b). The report revealed that about 144 million children under 5 years had stunted growth, 47 million children were wasted, and 14.3 million were severely wasted, while 38.3 million were overweight or obese. The UNICEF (2023), however, reveals that while stunting has decreased from 33% to 22.3% in 2022, globally, malnutrition remains high in Africa, where over 1.4 million children live with stunting in Eastern and Southern Africa alone, while another 6.5 million are recorded in West and Central Africa (Rasaq, 2022; UNICEF, 2023). Figure 8.1 illustrates the trend of malnutrition in Sub-Saharan Africa (SSA), showing an increase over the past 20 years, followed by a slowdown after 2010.

According to Rasaq (2022), malnutrition is more common in African children due to the consumption of poor-quality, cheap foods often preferred by households due to affordability issues. Even in South Africa, which is the second biggest economy on the continent, malnutrition was found to be high. The 2016 South Africa Demographic and Health Survey placed wasting at 2.5% and underweight at 6%, while stunting was high at 27.0% among children under 5 years (May et al., 2020).

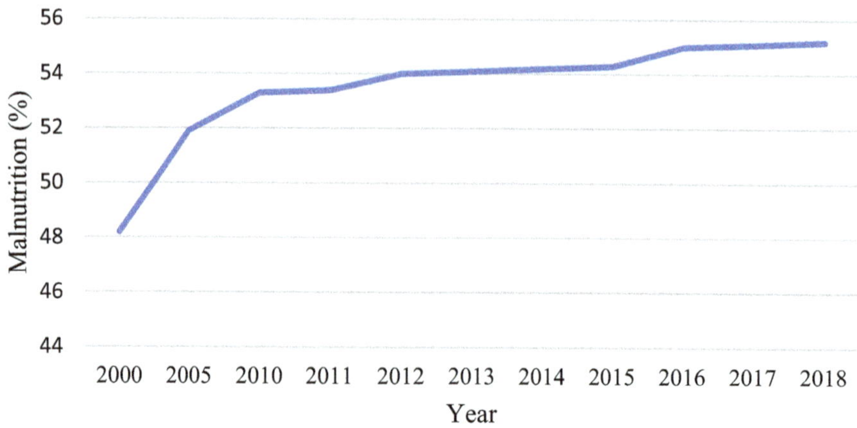

Fig. 8.1 Trend of malnutrition in SSA. Source: Based on UNICEF data

About 45% of deaths reported among children under the age of 5 years were linked to undernutrition (Vollmer et al., 2017).

The reviewed literature primarily categorises the causes of child malnutrition into three categories, namely, individual, household, and community-level factors. At the individual level, the risk factors for malnutrition include age, gender, birthweight, breastfeeding, and childhood comorbidities (Govender et al., 2021). Teenage pregnancy, lower parental education, low birthweight, insufficient breastfeeding, and personal food preference were also identified as individual causes of child malnutrition (Ahmed et al., 2025; Ancira-Moreno & Hernandez-Cordero, 2025). Even though low birthweight is regarded as a personal factor, it is also determined by parental health and nutritional status, particularly the mother's, and food security within the household and the broader community.

With the household setup, gender, age, religion, geographical area, household income and size, level of education by parents' maternal education, and healthcare access were critical factors that had a significant link to child malnutrition (Warssamo et al., 2025). The problem causing malnutrition at the household level is the poor financial status. This problem is usually accompanied by poverty, a disjointed family structure, and obliviousness of health issues (Sukulao et al., 2025; Watkins et al., 2024). Govender et al. (2021) found that inadequate knowledge about food nutrition and cultural, religious, and community beliefs lead to malnutrition among children under the age of 5 (Govender et al., 2021). The kind of upbringing children receive early in their lives also plays a crucial role in ensuring their health in adulthood (Ahmed et al., 2025).

At the community level, childhood malnutrition is partly influenced by the location of residence, household shelter, income, and ethnicity (Kasanzu et al., 2025). The area of residence can help determine children's nutritional status regarding withstanding environmental risks. Children's nutrition can also be influenced by the availability of and access to health services (Abate & Belachew, 2019). These communal factors have a significant influence on children's health.

The reviewed literature, however, disregards environmental factors which are equally important. Environmental factors significantly influence child malnutrition through poor water, sanitation, and hygiene, polluted food, insufficient waste disposal, and the presence of poisonous substances like mycotoxins and lead. These aspects increase exposure to infections, leading to poor nutrient absorption and chronic malnutrition. Additionally, climate change contributes to food shortages and illness, while factors such as dirt floors and indoor air pollution from solid fuel burning also increase the risk of stunting. This chapter closes this gap by focusing on how environmental factors, particularly climate change, contribute to child malnutrition, focusing on Zimbabwe.

8.3 Materials and Methods

This chapter draws from a review of primary and secondary literature on climate change and children's nutrition in farming in Zimbabwe. The terms "climate change", "child nutrition", "paediatric nutrition", "infant and young child nutrition", "child sustenance", "dietary needs of children", "feeding of children", "nourishment for kids", "food for children", and "Zimbabwe" were used as key search terms. Each text identified for analysis needed at least one of the key terms in the title, abstract, or keywords. Texts published between 2015 and 2025 were selected to ensure recency. There was no specific database used to ensure that all relevant texts stood an equal chance of being selected for review. All articles needed to be in the English language and freely accessible in order to be selected. Articles that did not meet this inclusion criterion were excluded from the review.

Document analysis was then used to examine the identified texts. Document analysis entails iterative superficial scanning of a document, thorough studying, and interpretation so that the message being communicated by the text can be used in a specific context of research. Document analysis falls under the qualitative research design.

Latent coding was used to organise the findings. Data collected from the selected documents were arranged into codes to solicit their meaning whilst linking them to the study's research objectives. In using latent coding, the author could probe the texts deeper than surface-level observations to unearth the texts' underlying meanings, interpretations, and implicit messages. The method was flexible, allowing the author to move back and forth from a review of research policy documents and academic texts. It generated a rich in-depth analysis and allowed the author to handle many texts. The method was also cost-effective and unobtrusive, with no possibility of replication.

A total of 31 texts were identified for review. These included 21 academic texts (journal articles and book chapters) and reports by government and non-government organisations, including the WB, UNICEF, WHO, ReliefWeb, and the

CIMMYT. These texts provided the basis for the conclusions made in this chapter. The findings were categorised thematically. A total of five themes emerged from the review.

The methodological approach used in this chapter, however, has several limitations. It is mainly subjective and depends on the author's analytical ability. Biases and omissions may have been made. In addition, replication is not guaranteed. As a result, it is hoped that future studies will adopt more case study-specific and empirical methodologies to either confirm or problematise the conclusions made in this study.

8.4 Findings and Discussion

The findings are presented under two sections. First, the conduits through which climate change impacts children's nutrition are outlined. Second, the chapter explores how AI can improve the situation.

8.4.1 Climate Change Impact on Children's Nutrition in Zimbabwe

The review shows that Zimbabwe is on a trajectory of snowballing temperatures, reduced rainfall, and more recurrent extreme weather events like droughts and floods, which negatively impact water resources, agriculture, and infrastructure (Chanza & Gundu-Jakarasi, 2020; Chikoko & Chihiya, 2023; Muoni et al., 2025). The country's susceptibility to climate change impacts is high (Chipato, 2025), requiring urgent adaptation strategies. Previous IPCC valuations show Zimbabwe and its sub-regional counterparts as hotspots for climate variability. On the Notre Dame Global Adaptation Index, which ranks susceptibility to, and capability to adapt to, climate impacts, Zimbabwe ranked 174 out of 182 countries. Extreme weather events, particularly drought, have significantly impacted the country's population and the broader economy (Chikoko & Chihiya, 2023; Ndhlovu & Dube, 2024). The drought that hit the country between 1991 and 1992 is known in the country's history as the worst in living memory. The drought resulted in a 25% plunge in manufacturing output and a 6% reduction in foreign exchange earnings (World Bank (WB), 2024). The 2007 drought also affected six million people, while the 2013 drought affected over four million people, with an estimated economic damage of up to US$500 million (EM-DAT, 2015). The country is also susceptible to riverine floods and storms (Samu & Akıntuğ, 2020); Cyclone Idai affected over 270,000 people (Chabata, 2025), with damage costs approximated at US$622 million (WB, 2024).

The climate change literature on Zimbabwe shows that yearly mean surface temperatures have increased while rainfall has decreased since 1900 (Tirivangasi & Nyahunda, 2025). According to the Government of Zimbabwe (GoZ) (2022), the yearly mean surface temperature increased by around 0.9 °C from 1900 to 2018, while average annual rainfall has plunged by around 5%. The WB (2024) posits that although the impact of reduced rainfall has not gained centre stage in policy and academic discussions, the occurrence of mid-season dry spells has been high. Rainy seasons have also narrowed, particularly since 1960. The exception is the mid-Zambezi region, which has experienced a suppression of dry spells by about 10 days, especially between 1980 and 2016, while the rest of the country has experienced an up to 20-day increase in the length of dry spells (GoZ, 2022). When the temperature increases, evapotranspiration rates worsen, and soil moisture lowers. This aggravates the brutality of droughts and mid-season dry spells, especially in areas such as Chiredzi, Malipati, and Beitbridge (Ndhlovu, 2022; Ndhlovu, 2023).

According to the WB (2024), drought is particularly a high risk in Zimbabwe because many people in the country engage in agricultural activities for income and livelihood. Ndhlovu and Dube (2024) also found that most people in the country engage in agricultural activities for livelihood and income. However, agriculture in Zimbabwe is mainly rainfed (Sharma et al., 2022). Therefore, poor rains and high temperatures have an immediate bearing on many people, rural dwellers. The rain's late onset and early cessation have been observed for all five central agroecological regions. These observed climate changes show the country is moving towards more arid conditions.

The agricultural sector has always been a backbone of the economy of Zimbabwe, alongside other sectors such as mining and manufacturing, contributing around 12% of GDP and 40% of export earnings. It also provides approximately 68% of raw materials to the manufacturing sector (WB, 2024). In 2021, agricultural exports were valued at US$1.2 billion, a fall by around 30% since 1995. Agricultural productivity has fallen particularly since the land reforms of the 2000s, which acquired farms from white farmers who owned much of the land and redistributed it to landless peasants and aspiring small-scale farmers. The 2000s land reform created about 146,000 family farms on around 5.8 million hectares and about 16,000 commercial farms (A2 farms) on three million hectares. Together with farms on communal land, the land reforms transformed Zimbabwe's agriculture and made it principally smallholder driven, exposing it to dry shocks (Chisadza et al., 2025). Less than 1% of these farmers have access to irrigation.

Due to climate change, Zimbabwe's agricultural sector has been the most affected, with output on a declining trajectory (see Fig. 8.2).

Maise, the country's staple crop, accounts for over 50% of the average calorie consumption for more than 85% of Zimbabwe's population. Therefore, the disruption of maise production by climate impacts easily translates into a food security issue. Reviewed literature shows that since 2000, Zimbabwe has been battling food insecurity, with production now way below the 2.2 million tonnes required to meet the needs of humans and livestock. Climate impacts on maise yields are projected to be minus 20% by the 2040s (WB, 2024).

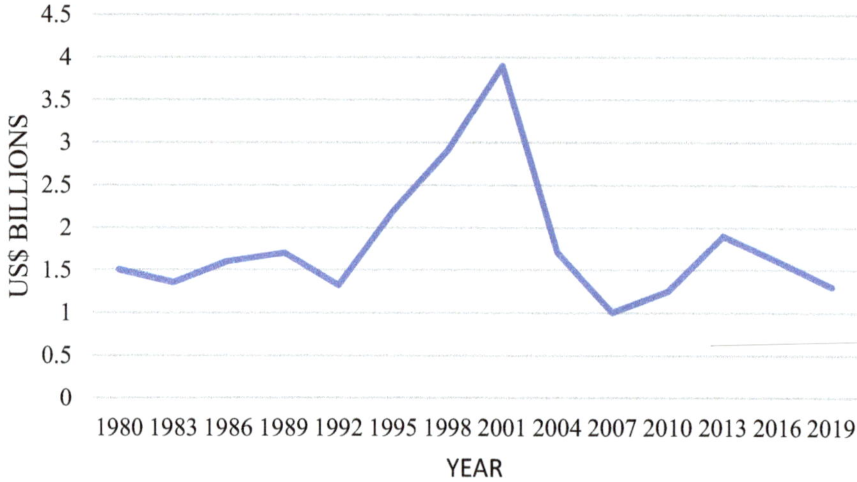

Fig. 8.2 Agricultural output in Zimbabwe (1980–2019). Source: World Bank (2024)

These climate impacts have resulted in food insecurity, including among children. Child food insecurity is reported as a significant problem in Zimbabwe, driven by factors like poor diet diversity, economic hardship, and climate-related issues like droughts (Sukulao et al., 2025). Many children are reported as lacking access to nutrient-rich foods, impacting their health and development, with children in severe food poverty being more susceptible to malnutrition (Mukwedeya & Mudhara, 2023). Less than 10% of children in Zimbabwe consume five or more food groups daily, which is essential for proper growth (Chidarikire & Saruchera, 2024). Child malnutrition has become a crisis in the country, with about 3.5 million children requiring urgent humanitarian assistance due to an El Niño-induced drought in 2025 (Lukwa et al., 2024).

Malnutrition has been surging since the late 1980s in Zimbabwe. For instance, the literature shows that from 1988 to 2014, the number of children presenting severe wasting increased from 0.4% to 0.7%. The percentage of underweight children also soared from 8% to 11.2% in that period (United Nations Children's Fund (UNICEF), 2025). By 2016, the country faced malnutrition figures, with approximately 33,000 children requiring urgent medication for severe malnutrition (CIMMYT, 2024).

With El Niño-induced drought on the rampage, the number of food-insecure households in the country quickly doubled by the end of 2016. According to the UNICEF (2025), about 2.1% of children below the age experienced severe acute malnutrition in 2016. The number of food-insecure families also soared from 16% in May 2015 to 37% in January 2016. UNICEF (2025) also reports that on average, 35% of families had insufficient water supplies for domestic use in the same period. With water scarcity, children, particularly girls, were forced to walk longer distances to fetch water. Inadequate water also exposed children to higher risks of diarrhoea, typhoid, and other waterborne diseases, including cholera (Chikoko & Chihiya, 2023).

The rates of both severe and moderate acute malnutrition continued to rise, with figures for 2024 showing an even greater increase in cases (Reliefweb, 2024). In 2024, the country faced an increase in malnutrition, with over 1.1 million children at risk of severe acute malnutrition due to the El Niño-induced drought (Kasanzu et al., 2025). Child wasting surged to 4.9% in rural areas by 2024, and 31.4% of rural children under five were reported as stunted (Pencil et al., 2024). A national disaster was declared in response to the drought, which significantly impacted agriculture and food security, leading to a significant deficit in maise production and increased food needs. Notwithstanding efforts, only 7% of the target population received life-saving interventions by October 2024. By early 2025, the number of children under five facing acute malnutrition reached 2.3 million, with an additional 714,439 children at risk of severe acute malnutrition (CIMMYT, 2024).

Child malnutrition in Zimbabwe has severe social and economic implications, perpetuating poverty and impeding national development. The effects are long term, impacting individuals throughout their lives and creating a significant burden on the country's healthcare system and economy. The social consequences of child malnutrition are far-reaching, affecting health, education, and overall well-being. On the child health and development front, malnutrition, particularly stunting (low height for age) and wasting (low weight for height), leads to impaired physical and cognitive development. Stunted children are at a higher risk of lifelong health issues and have reduced mental capacity. Malnutrition is also an underlying factor in a significant portion of child deaths in the country.

Regarding education, malnourished children are less likely to attend school, and, even if they do, they tend to have a reduced ability to concentrate and learn (Lukwa et al., 2024). Poor nutrition is linked to lower school enrolment, higher dropout rates, and poor academic performance (Watkins et al., 2024). This limits a child's educational attainment and prospects, leading to a less skilled workforce. In addition, child malnutrition excessively affects susceptible populations, including those in rural areas and low-income households. This creates and broadens social and economic inequalities, as children from poorer backgrounds are more likely to be malnourished and, therefore, have fewer opportunities to break the cycle of poverty.

The economic costs of child malnutrition in Zimbabwe are substantial, affecting both individuals and the national economy. The long-term effects of malnutrition, including impaired cognitive and physical development, result in lower productivity in adulthood. This reduces individual earning potential and eventually results in significant losses to the national GDP. Malnutrition also increases the burden on the public healthcare system. The costs associated with treating illnesses and conditions related to malnutrition, such as infections and chronic diseases, place a significant financial strain on an already limited health infrastructure. In addition, malnutrition is both a consequence and a cause of poverty. Families struggling with poverty often cannot afford nutritious food, which leads to malnutrition. In turn, the reduced earning capacity and increased health expenses resulting from malnutrition trap families in a continuous cycle of poverty. For instance, childhood anaemia alone is associated with a 2.5% drop in adult wages (Alaba et al., 2023).

In recent years, AI has been identified as having the potential to revolutionise lives and livelihoods. Therefore, AI can also be leveraged to improve child nutrition, including in countries like Zimbabwe.

8.4.2 Harnessing AI for Safe Food and Healthy Diets in Zimbabwe

AI can improve child nutrition in Zimbabwe by improving food systems, from production to consumption. In addition, AI can also achieve this by offering personalised dietary plans, early detection of malnutrition, and enhancing nutrition education. By analysing vast amounts of data, AI technologies can shift the approach to child nutrition from a one-size-fits-all model to a more precise, data-driven system.

8.4.2.1 Improving Food Systems

The review shows that Zimbabwe is an agrarian country, with over 70% of the population depending on farming for livelihood and income (Ndhlovu, 2024). Therefore, improving child nutrition can start by improving the entire system, particularly food production. AI can improve food production by optimising every stage of the food supply chain, from farming to processing and distribution. This increases efficiency, higher yields, enhanced food safety, and reduced waste.

AI technologies, such as computer vision, machine learning, and drones, enable a highly targeted approach to farming, known as precision agriculture. Instead of applying resources uniformly across a field, AI-powered systems analyse data to treat crops and soil with pinpoint accuracy. Drones and ground-based sensors furnished with AI cameras can analyse data on soil quality, moisture levels, and plant health in real time. This will allow farmers to identify nutrient shortages or water stress early on and apply the precise amount of water, fertiliser, or pesticides only where needed, significantly reducing environmental impact and waste. AI algorithms can analyse images of crops to detect early signs of disease or pest infestations, often before they are visible to the human eye. This enables targeted intervention, preventing the spread of diseases and reducing the need for widespread chemical spraying. In addition, AI models can analyse historical data, weather patterns, and current crop health to predict crop yields accurately. This can help farmers make better decisions regarding planting calendars, resource distribution, and market-ready quantities. This will ensure adequate food availability, which can contribute towards the achievement of child nutrition.

In food processing plants, AI-powered systems are used to automate and optimise tasks to ensure product consistency, quality, and safety in Zimbabwe. Robots with advanced vision systems can sort food products based on size, shape, colour, and quality. They can also detect and remove defective, contaminated, or foreign objects from the production line with high precision, which is much more effective than manual inspection. This can ensure that food is processed in environments that ensure food safety. AI algorithms can also monitor the performance of machinery on the production line, analysing sensor data to predict when equipment might fail. This enables proactive upkeep, preventing unexpected breakdowns that can affect the level of production required to meet food demands.

AI can help to streamline the entire food chain in the country, from the farm to the consumer, leading to greater efficiency and less food waste. By analysing historical sales data, facilitating weather forecasts, and consumer trends, AI can precisely forecast demand for specific products. This can help producers and retailers optimise inventory levels, minimising the risk of overproduction, stockouts, and spoilage. AI algorithms can optimise delivery routes to reduce fuel consumption and ensure products are transported efficiently. In addition, AI can track and trace food items from their origin, providing transparency and allowing for quicker, more accurate recalls in the event of a safety issue.

8.4.2.2 Personalised Nutrition

AI can help create personalised dietary plans for children by analysing various factors, such as age, gender, weight, height, activity level, dietary preferences, and any pre-existing health conditions. Unlike traditional methods, AI can continuously adapt these plans in real time, making them more effective. For instance, AI-powered apps can suggest recipes based on available ingredients, catering to picky eaters while ensuring they meet their nutritional needs. Chatbots or virtual assistants can also guide parents on healthy eating habits and suitable meal regularity.

8.4.2.3 Early Detection and Monitoring

AI can help with the early detection and prevention of malnutrition, including undernutrition and overweight. AI-powered mobile apps can analyse photos of a child to assess signs of undernutrition or obesity by measuring physical indicators. This is particularly useful considering the challenges faced in Zimbabwe's health sector. For example, the Method for Extremely Rapid Observation of Nutritional Status (MERON) system uses facial photographs to predict a child's nutritional status. By analysing health records, growth charts, and socio-economic data, AI algorithms can identify children at high risk of malnutrition before a crisis occurs, allowing for timely interventions. AI can also be used to process data from schools, health clinics, and mobile health units to track nutritional trends in communities or on a national level. This can help public health organisations detect emerging patterns of food insecurity or nutrient deficiencies.

8.4.2.4 Improving School Feeding Programmes

AI can be used to optimise school feeding programmes, ensuring children receive balanced, nutritious meals. AI algorithms can plan diverse and balanced menus that meet the nutritional requirements of children while staying within a budget and using locally available foods. AI can also monitor food consumption and waste levels to adjust menus and portion sizes, reducing food waste and improving the efficiency of these programmes.

8.4.2.5 Education and Accessibility

AI-based tools can make nutrition education more accessible and engaging for children and parents. Interactive apps and games can teach children about healthy eating in a fun, engaging way. AI can create culturally relevant educational content that is easy for parents and children to understand, promoting long-term behavioural changes in the country. With much of Zimbabwe's population living in rural areas, AI-enabled telehealth services can connect children and their families with nutritionists and paediatricians for virtual consultations, ensuring access to professional advice regardless of location.

8.5 Challenges of AI Adoption to Improve Child Nutrition in Zimbabwe

The challenges to adopting AI for child nutrition in Zimbabwe are primarily related to infrastructural, economic, and human capital limitations. While AI is promising to improve public health outcomes, these systemic barriers hinder its effective implementation and scaling. Zimbabwe currently faces enormous socio-economic challenges that make adopting AI a mammoth task. Economic instability, characterised by high informality (85.5% of employment), broadening inequality, and frequent issues with inflation and liquidity, alongside infrastructure and social service deficits, persists (Tshuma et al., 2025). Climate-related factors, particularly droughts, also worsen the challenges this African country faces, which heavily relies on farming. A significant impediment to AI adoption is the country's underdeveloped digital infrastructure. Many rural areas, where most of the population resides, lack reliable access to electricity and internet connectivity (Kurebwa et al., 2025). AI solutions require a stable network and power supply, particularly those involving mobile applications and data transmission. This foundational infrastructure makes deploying and maintaining AI-powered tools at scale impossible. In addition, effective AI depends on large, high-quality datasets. Zimbabwe faces a shortage of a structured data ecosystem and comprehensive, high-quality health data, especially in rural areas (Xiao et al., 2017). Available data may be incomplete, fragmented, or of poor quality. Moreover, there is a lack of financial and technical resources to invest in developing, deploying, and maintaining complex AI systems (Kurebwa et al., 2025).

Zimbabwe also has a significant gap in the technical skills needed to develop, implement, and manage AI solutions (Marima et al., 2025). The country faces a shortage of AI experts, data scientists, and technicians. Furthermore, a lack of digital literacy among healthcare workers and the general public can hinder the adoption and effective use of AI tools. Training and capacity building are essential but are often underfunded and hard to access.

The use of AI in healthcare, particularly for vulnerable populations like children, raises significant ethical concerns. These include data privacy, security, and the potential for algorithmic bias. If AI models are trained on biased or incomplete data, they may perpetuate or worsen health disparities. There is a need for clear regulations and government policies to govern the ethical and responsible use of AI in healthcare. However, such frameworks are currently in their nascent stages in Zimbabwe.

8.6 Conclusion

This chapter explored how climate change impacts the possibility of safe food and healthy diets for children in Zimbabwe. The chapter showed that climate change impacts child nutrition by disrupting food production, processing, storage, and consumption. It also damages water systems, increasing illness and clogging the absorption of nutrients. These factors lead to higher rates of child malnutrition, including stunting and wasting, with long-term consequences for children's health and development. Zimbabwe is an agrarian country, and any slight impact of climate change has enormous implications for its social and economic activities. Due to climate-related events, the review showed that food production, particularly the staple maise, has been significantly affected, leading to increased nutrition challenges, particularly for children. The chapter proposed the adoption of AI to deal with these challenges.

While AI holds much potential to help improve child nutrition in Zimbabwe, the chapter showed that many social, economic, and cultural factors inhibit adoption. Zimbabwe is undergoing an economic crisis due to intense political stand-offs, corruption, maladministration, climate change, and other factors. Therefore, while AI can help with the challenges, it is not a one-size-fits-all solution. Therefore, the chapter concludes that tackling child malnutrition in Zimbabwe requires a multifaceted and integrated approach addressing the root causes, often food insecurity, poverty, climate change, and limited health services. The government, in partnership with international organisations and nonprofit actors, needs to work to combat this issue.

References

Abate, K. H., & Belachew, T. (2019). Chronic malnutrition among under five children of Ethiopia may not be economic. A systematic review and metaanalysis. *Ethiopian Journal of Health Sciences, 29*(2), 265–277. https://doi.org/10.4314/ejhs.v29i2.14

Ahmed, M., Alsherawi, A., & Doi, S. (2025). Commentary on "Comparison of complications in isolated aesthetic liposuction procedures across different techniques: A systematic review and meta-analysis". *European Journal of Plastic Surgery, 48*, 45. https://doi.org/10.1007/s00238-025-02303-8

Alaba, O. A., Chiwire, P., Siya, A., et al. (2023). Socio-economic inequalities in the double burden of malnutrition among under-five children: Evidence from 10 selected sub-Saharan African countries. *International Journal of Environmental Research and Public Health, 20*, 5489. https://doi.org/10.3390/IJERPH20085489

Ancira-Moreno, M., & Hernandez-Cordero, S. (2025). Editorial: Challenges, opportunities, and actions for improved maternal and child nutrition. *Frontiers in Nutrition, 12*, 1580113. https://doi.org/10.3389/fnut.2025.1580113

Blackie, M., & Luckett, K. (2025). Embodiment matters in knowledge building. *Science & Education, 34*, 717–730. https://doi.org/10.1007/s11191-024-00506-2

Chabata, L. (2025). Cyclone Idai Disaster in Zimbabwe: A new testament ethical analysis of Matthew 24: 37-39. *HTS Theological Studies, 81*(1), a9952. https://doi.org/10.4102/hts.v81i1.9952

Chanza, N., & Gundu-Jakarasi, V. (2020). Deciphering the climate change conundrum in Zimbabwe: An exposition. In J. P. Tiefenbacher (Ed.), *Global warming and climate change*. https://doi.org/10.5772/intechopen.84443

Chidarikire, M., & Saruchera, M. (2024). Exploring multifaceted impacts of El Niño-driven drought on child-headed rural learners' well-being in drought-prone Chivi, Zimbabwe. *Interdisciplinary Journal of Rural and Community Studies, 6*, 1–13. https://doi.org/10.38140/ijrcs-2024.vol6.17

Chikoko, W., & Chihiya, P. (2023). Climate change and vulnerabilities of children in rural Zimbabwe: The case of ward 14 of Bikita District, Zimbabwe. *African Journal of Social Work, 13*(2), 78–86. https://doi.org/10.4314/ajsw.v13i2.4

Chipato, F. (2025). Rural livelihood, accumulation and class formation in post-development-induced displacements in Zimbabwe. *Cogent Social Sciences, 11*(1). https://doi.org/10.1080/23311886.2025.2461258

Chisadza, B., Gwate, O., Musinguzi, S. P., et al. (2025). Resilient agriculture in semi-arid Zimbabwe: Adaptation strategies and influencers among smallholder farmers. *Discover Agriculture, 3*, 76. https://doi.org/10.1007/s44279-025-00234-3

CIMMYT and GOAL team up to help farmers in Zimbabwe fight fall armyworm: Identifying best practices to fight the invasive pest. Retrieved December 12, 2024., from https://www.cimmyt.org/news/cimmyt-and-goal-team-up-to-help-farmers-in-zimbabwe-fight-fall-armyworm/

EM-DAT. (2015). *Natural disaster data book 2015: An analytical overview*. Asian Disaster Reduction Centre. https://www.adrc.asia/publications/databook/ORG/databook_2015/pdf/DataBook2015_e.pdf

Farah, A. A., Mohamed, M. A., Musse, O. S. H., et al. (2025). The multifaceted impact of climate change on agricultural productivity: A systematic literature review of SCOPUS-indexed studies (2015–2024). *Discover Sustainability, 6*, 397. https://doi.org/10.1007/s43621-025-01229-2

Govender, I., Rangiah, S., Kaswa, R., et al. (2021). Malnutrition in children under the age of 5 years in a primary health care setting. *South African Family Practice, 63*(1), e1–e6. https://doi.org/10.4102/safp.v63i1.5337

Government of Zimbabwe. (2022). *Zimbabwe national climate policy*. Government of Zimbabwe. https://afsafrica.org/wp-content/uploads/2021/10/ncps-cli.-report-zimbabwe.pdf

IPCC. (2014). *Climate change 2014 mitigation of climate change: Working Group III Contribution to the Fifth Assessment Report of the Intergovernmental Panel on Climate Change*. Cambridge University Press. https://www.ipcc.ch/site/assets/uploads/2018/02/ipcc_wg3_ar5_full.pdf

IPCC. (2022). Climate Change 2022: Impacts, adaptation and vulnerability. https://www.ipcc.ch/report/ar6/wg2/downloads/report/IPCC_AR6_WGII_SummaryVolume.pdf.

Kasanzu, S., Chirenda, J., & Marume, A. (2025). Diet and sociodemographic predictors of the double burden of malnutrition in urban Zimbabwe. *African Journal of Primary Health & Family Medicine, 17*(1), e1–e7. https://doi.org/10.4102/phcfm.v17i1.4834

Kurebwa, M., Moyo, A., & Lumbe, A. (2025). Analysing the digital divide in Zimbabwe: Exploring the obstacles and consequences for access to quality education in open and distance e-learning at Zimbabwe Open University. *Journal of Research Innovation and Implications in Education, 9*(2), 567–576. https://doi.org/10.59765/vhr9y64

Lukwa, A. T., Wayas, F. A., & Lambert, E. V. (2024). Stakeholder mapping to explore social and economic capital of Rotating Savings and Credit Associations (ROSCAs) to increase demand for and access to healthy food. *Frontiers in Sustainable Food Systems, 8*, 1301578. https://doi.org/10.3389/fsufs.2024.1301578

Marima, I. J., Chekera, F., & Mukute, S. (2025). Evaluating the adoption of AI systems and technologies in Zimbabwean businesses: Case of Masvingo Town. *African Journal of Education, Science and Technology, 8*(2), 180–185. https://ajest.org/index.php/ajest/article/view/727

May, J., Witten, C., & Lake, L. (2020). *Food and nutrition security. Children's Institute*. https://www.researchgate.net/publication/349647969_South_African_Child_Gauge_2020_Food_and_Nutrition_Security

Mukwedeya, B., & Mudhara, M. (2023). Factors influencing livelihood strategy choice and food security among youths in Mashonaland East Province, Zimbabwe. *Heliyon, 9*, e14735. https://doi.org/10.1016/j.heliyon.2023.e14735

Muoni, T., Kihara, J., Madamombe, S. M., et al. (2025). Climate change vulnerability and drivers of low maize yields under smallholder farming systems in semi-arid area of Marange in Zimbabwe. *Discover Sustainability, 6*, 394. https://doi.org/10.1007/s43621-025-01189-7

Ndhlovu, E. (2022). Political economy of Chisa livelihoods in rural Zimbabwe. In K. Helliker, J. Matanzima, & P. Chadambuka (Eds.), *Livelihoods of ethnic minorities in rural Zimbabwe* (pp. 123–139). Springer International Publishing.

Ndhlovu, E. (2023). Resuscitation of neoliberalism in Zimbabwe: Exploring implications for agriculture policy development. In B. Nyagadza & T. Rukasha (Eds.), *Sustainable agricultural marketing and agribusiness development: An African perspective*. CAB International.

Ndhlovu, E. (2024). Building farming resilience to climate change through social assistance in South-Eastern Zimbabwe. *International Journal of Research in Business and Social Science, 13*(10), 105–117.

Ndhlovu, E., & Dube, K. (2024). Contract farming and climate change adaptation in rural Zimbabwe. *Mankind Quarterly, 64*(3), 579–594.

Nwachukwu, D., & Affen, M. P. (2023). Artificial intelligence marketing practices: The way forward to better customer experience management in Africa (systematic literature review). *International Academy Journal of Management, Marketing and Entrepreneurial Studies, 9*(2), 44–62.

Pencil, A., Matsungo, T. M., Chuchu, T. M., et al. (2024). The Double Burden of Malnutrition among Adolescents from Zimbabwe: A Cross-Sectional Study. *Obesities, 4*, 9–23. https://doi.org/10.3390/obesities4010002

Raimi, R., & Phiri, A. (2024). More landless, more problems: Investigating the relationship between land and income inequality in Africa. *South African Journal of Economic and Management Sciences, 27*(1), a5774. https://doi.org/10.4102/sajems.v27i1.5774

Rasaq, R. (2022). *Different dimensions of inequality and sustainable economic growth in Africa*. PhD thesis, Dept. of Economics, Nelson Mandela University. Retrieved October 15, 2024, from http://vital.seals.ac.za:8080/vital/access/manager/Repository/vital:62483?site_

name=GlobalView&view=list&f0=sm_creator%3A%22Raimi%2C+Rasaq+Being%22&sort=sort_ss_sm_creator+asc

Reliefweb. (2024). *Zimbabwe: Cholera outbreak—December 2024*. Reliefweb. Retrieved March 12, 2024, from https://reliefweb.int/disaster/ep-2024-000233-zwe#:~:text=The%20outbreak%20has%20been%20reported%20in%20the,areas%20that%20had%20not%20previously%20reported%20cases

Samu, R., & Akıntuğ, B. (2020). Pre-disaster planning and preparedness: Drought and flood forecasting and analysis in Zimbabwe. *Water SA, 46*(3), 8655. https://doi.org/10.17159/wsa/2020.v46.i3.8655

Sharma, D., Alwang, J. R., & Chingozha, T., Hoy, C. A., Marvellous, F., & Rodas, P. A. (2022). *Reversing the tide: Reducing poverty and boosting resilience in Zimbabwe - overview*. World Bank. https://documentos.bancomundial.org/es/publication/documentsreports/documentdetail/099925110032237739/p1767360af8e5705a089bd086ffbfec43ab

Siddiqui, G. K., Taj, S., & Maqsood, F. (2020). Metacognitive awareness, procrastination and its impact on students' academic performance. *Sir Syed Journal of Education & Social Research, 3*(4), 400–406.

Sukulao, T., Kurevakwesu, W., & Tshugulu, A. N. (2025). Perceived causes and consequences of food insecurity in rural Zimbabwe: Using a decolonised methodology. *Journal of Social Development in Africa, 40*(1), 27–61. https://doi.org/10.4314/jsda.v40i1.3

Tirivangasi, H. M., & Nyahunda, L. (2025). Determinants of transformative climate change adaptation in rural Zimbabwe: An afrocentric analysis. *Climate Policy*, 1–15. https://doi.org/10.1080/14693062.2025.2521486

Tshuma, D., Makwara, E., & Puputla, N. (2025). Aligning the geography curriculum with sustainable development goal 5: A case study of a University in Zimbabwe: An examination of mourning rituals and practices among the Vatsonga and the Tachoni people: A comparative study. In M. N. Amutabi (Ed.), *New frontiers of development in Africa* (pp. 205–223). CEDRED Publications.

UNICEF. (2025). *The state of the world's children 2025: Ending child poverty: Our shared imperative*. UNICEF. Retrieved November 14, 2024, from https://www.unicef.org/reports/state-of-worlds-children/2025

UNICEF Zimbabwe. (2023). Annual report 2023. https://www.unicef.org/zimbabwe/media/9961/file/UNICEF%20Zimbabwe%20Annual%20Report%202023.pdf.

Vollmer, S., Harttgen, K., Kupka, R., et al. (2017). Levels and trends of childhood undernutrition by wealth and education according to a composite index of Anthropometric Failure: Evidence from 146 Demographic and Health Surveys from 39 countries. *BMJ Global Health, 2*, e000206. https://doi.org/10.1136/bmjgh-2016-000206

Wakweya, R. B. (2025). Impacts of climate change on crop production and food security in Ethiopia. *Discover Sustainability, 6*, 158. https://doi.org/10.1007/s43621-025-00830-9

Warssamo, B. B., Belay, D. B., & Chen, D. G. (2025). Determinants of child malnutrition and morbidity in Ethiopia: A structural equation modeling approach. *Frontiers in Pediatrics, 13*, 1535957. https://doi.org/10.3389/fped.2025.1535957

Watkins, A. E., El Zerbi, C., McGovern, R., et al. (2024). Exploration of fathers' mental health and well-being concerns during the transition to fatherhood, and paternal perinatal support: Scoping review. *BMJ Open, 14*, e078386. https://doi.org/10.1136/bmjopen-2023-078386

WHO. (2020a). Health 2020 policy framework and strategy. Retrieved December 17, 2024, from https://iris.who.int/server/api/core/bitstreams/15751957-6d3c-4e65-a290-48379b844524/content

WHO. (2020b). *Monitoring health for the SDGs, sustainable development goals*. World Health Organization. Licence: CC BY-NC-SA 3.0 IGO.

World Bank. (2024). Zimbabwe economic update: Improving resilience to weather shocks and climate change. Retrieved October 12, 2024, from https://www.worldbank.org/en/country/zimbabwe/publication/zimbabwe-economic-update-improving-resilience-to-afe-weather-shocks-and-climate-change#:~:text=Recent%20observations%20indicate%20that%20climate,to%20the%20five%2Dyear%20average

Xiao, W., Wang, M., Zhen, W., et al. (2017). Corpus-based research on English word recognition rates in primary school and word selection strategy. *Frontiers of Information Technology & Electronic Engineering, 18*(3), 362–372. https://doi.org/10.1631/FITEE.1601118

Zhao, L., Zhou, G., & Li, C. (2025). Research on the impact of tourism cooperation on urban public health. *Frontiers in Public Health, 13*, 1556789. https://doi.org/10.3389/fpubh.2025.1556789

Chapter 9
Child-Centred Approaches to Climate Change and Food Insecurity: Evaluating Vulnerabilities and Interventions in Mbire, Zimbabwe

Iggy Gamuchirai Saviere, Gladman Nyasha Makwenya, and Yasin Adam

9.1 Introduction

Food insecurity remains a critical challenge in sub-Saharan Africa. Still, its manifestation in rural communities such as Mbire District, Zimbabwe, cannot be understood outside the framework of climate injustice and children's rights violations. While climate change poses an existential threat to all vulnerable populations, children bear disproportionate consequences despite contributing minimally to the problem. According to the Food and Agriculture Organization (FAO, 2020), over 25% of Zimbabwean children suffer from chronic malnutrition, a condition directly exacerbated by climate-induced agricultural disruptions and resource scarcity. In Mbire, where frequent droughts and erratic rainfall patterns have eroded agrarian productivity by up to 50% over the past 5 years, food shortages undermine children's fundamental rights to health, development, and education. These challenges, compounded by limited access to adaptive resources and inadequate policy implementation, represent systematic violations of children's rights to an adequate standard of living, as enshrined in the United Nations Convention on the Rights of the Child (UNCRC).

The intersection of climate change and food insecurity in Mbire cannot be addressed as merely a technical or development problem but is fundamentally a children's rights crisis. Climate-induced food shortages create cascading vulnerabilities that extend beyond immediate malnutrition. Children in food-insecure households experience developmental delays, cognitive impairments, and

I. G. Saviere (✉)
Department of Environmental Sustainability and Climate Action, Elevate Trust, Harare, Zimbabwe

G. N. Makwenya · Y. Adam
Department of Social Work, Reformed Church University, Harare, Zimbabwe

E. Ndhlovu, C. Chipenda (eds.), *Climate Change and Children's Rights in Zimbabwe*, https://doi.org/10.1007/978-981-95-6005-9_9

educational disruptions. They are at a heightened risk of school dropout, exploitation, and child labour. The long-term implications are severe: stunted growth, neurological impairments, reduced earning potential, and perpetuation of intergenerational poverty and inequality. These outcomes directly violate children's rights to survival, development, health, education, and protection from economic exploitation. As Chipenda and Ndhlovu (in this volume) argue, addressing climate vulnerabilities demands a transformative policy that tackles structural inequalities rather than merely managing symptoms, positioning children not as passive victims but as rights holders with agency in adaptation processes.

To address these pressing issues, this chapter evaluates three child-centred interventions—the Integrated Management of Acute Malnutrition (IMAM), the Utariri Project, and the Integrated School Feeding Program—through an explicitly rights-based lens. Each intervention approaches food insecurity from a distinct perspective, yet each operates within the current policy architecture that inadequately connects climate adaptation to children's rights protection. The study explores not only the immediate effectiveness of these programmes but also whether they adequately advance children's rights in the context of climate change. By grounding the analysis in the climate justice imperatives established in this volume, the research asks three fundamental questions: How do current interventions address the structural drivers of child vulnerability to climate-induced food insecurity? To what extent do existing programmes recognise and protect children's rights? What barriers prevent comprehensive, rights-based responses to climate-induced food insecurity?

This analysis is underpinned by two complementary frameworks providing a comprehensive lens for understanding children's experiences and designing equitable solutions. Ecological systems theory (EST)_illuminates how climate impacts cascade across interconnected systems, from immediate family dynamics to community resources to national policies, with each level influencing children's vulnerability and resilience. The child rights approach (CRA), grounded in international instruments, including the United Nations Convention on the Rights of the Child, ensures that the analysis focuses explicitly on children's fundamental rights and the state's obligations to protect them. Together, these frameworks emphasise that food insecurity among children in Mbire is not simply a matter of meeting physical needs but a systemic failure to protect children's legally binding rights to nutrition, health, education, and protection from harm.

9.2 Theoretical Framework

9.2.1 Ecological Systems Theory and Child Rights Approach

Ecological systems theory (Bronfenbrenner, 1979) provides a comprehensive lens for examining the multiple layers of environmental, societal, and institutional factors that influence children's well-being and vulnerability to climate impacts. The theory posits that human development is influenced by interactions within five interconnected systems: the microsystem (immediate environments such as family and school), the mesosystem (interconnections between these environments), the exosystem (broader influences such as community resources and institutional services), the macrosystem (societal, cultural, and economic conditions), and the chronosystem (historical context and temporal dimensions). In the context of climate-induced food insecurity in Mbire, this framework reveals how climate variability at the macrosystem level (regional rainfall patterns, agricultural collapse) directly shapes conditions at the microsystem level (household hunger, child malnutrition, parental stress), with cascading effects on children's health, education, and protection. A child's nutritional status, school attendance, and vulnerability to exploitation are determined not by individual or family circumstances alone but by the dynamic interplay of climate shocks, agricultural systems, health services, education infrastructure, and social protection mechanisms operating at multiple ecological levels.

The child rights approach, grounded in the United Nations Convention on the Rights of the Child (UNCRC), provides a critical complementary lens that ensures analysis focuses on children's entitlements rather than treating food security as a development or humanitarian issue. The UNCRC establishes that children have rights to survival, protection, development, and participation, with particular emphasis on the child's best interests. Critically, the convention establishes the right to adequate food (Article 27) and to the highest attainable standard of health (Article 24), making food security and nutrition a matter of legal obligation for states rather than charity or discretionary programming. When climate change undermines children's access to food, it violates their rights. Similarly, when school closures due to drought prevent children from attending school or when malnutrition impairs cognitive development, these violate children's rights to education and development.

Integrating ecological systems theory with the child rights approach is essential for this analysis because it bridges individual and systemic understanding while emphasising justice and accountability. While EST maps the layers of influence on children's lives, the CRA contextualises how climate change and food insecurity violate children's rights at each ecological level. This intersection allows for a nuanced analysis of systemic failures, inadequate irrigation infrastructure, weak early warning systems, insufficient social protection mechanisms, and policy gaps, constituting rights violations for which states and stakeholders bear accountability. The framework directs attention to immediate interventions addressing hunger and underlying structural inequalities and policy failures that perpetuate children's vulnerability to climate impacts.

9.2.2 *Child-Sensitive Approaches to Climate-Induced Food Insecurity*

A child-sensitive approach prioritises children's unique needs and rights within broader climate adaptation and food security interventions, recognising children as vulnerable yet resourceful individuals whose environmental and social contexts shape their development. This approach, grounded in international frameworks, including the UNCRC, operates from the premise that children are not simply smaller versions of adults but also have distinct developmental vulnerabilities and capacities that must be central to intervention design and implementation. Child-sensitive approaches must integrate traditional knowledge systems with international rights standards while remaining vigilant against perpetuating harmful practices in the name of cultural relevance. In rural Zimbabwe, indigenous practices such as intergenerational knowledge transmission and community-led child rearing contain valuable insights for building resilience. However, these systems often require alignment with global standards to ensure they uphold children's rights, particularly in patriarchal societies where children's voices may be marginalised. A child-sensitive approach thus demands careful negotiation between respect for local contexts and the protection of children's rights.

Globally, initiatives such as Kenya's Home-Grown School Feeding Program demonstrate how child-sensitive approaches to climate-induced food insecurity can simultaneously address immediate nutritional needs, strengthen local food systems, and create income opportunities for smallholder farmers. Similarly, Ethiopia's Productive Safety Net Programme integrates child-focused cash transfers to alleviate immediate food shortages while building long-term resilience. Comparing these regional benchmarks with Zimbabwe's policy frameworks, including the Food and Nutrition Security Policy and the National Climate Policy, reveals significant implementation gaps and inadequate integration of child-specific vulnerabilities into climate adaptation strategies. The challenge is thus not the absence of policy rhetoric around child protection but the systemic failure to translate these commitments into adequate funding, institutional coordination, and ground-level accountability mechanisms.

9.3 Research Design and Methods

This study employed a pragmatic mixed-method approach, integrating qualitative and quantitative data to address how climate change undermines children's rights to food security and how existing interventions advance or hinder these rights. The research focused on Mbire District, specifically Wards 8 Karai, 10 Chitsungo, and 15 Mahuhwe, which were selected due to their high vulnerability to climate-induced food insecurity and the presence of child-focused interventions. These communities are heavily dependent on rain-fed agriculture, increasingly threatened by climate variability, providing a critical context for understanding the intersection of climate vulnerability, food insecurity, and children's rights.

9.3.1 Data Collection and Participant Engagement

The study combined semi-structured interviews with key stakeholders, including local community leaders, programme managers, health workers, teachers, and organisational staff, with focus group discussions among parents, community members, and local educators. Key informant interviews provided institutional perspectives on climate adaptation frameworks and practical implementation realities. At the same time, focus groups fostered the dynamic discussion of community-specific vulnerabilities, coping strategies, and barriers to child protection. Critically, the study incorporated child-centred participatory tools, particularly storytelling, allowing children to express their experiences and perspectives on food insecurity in non-threatening, creative formats. Storytelling proved especially valuable for capturing nuanced lived experiences of children who might find formal interview settings intimidating, ensuring that children's voices, not merely adult perspectives on children, were central to understanding vulnerabilities and designing solutions.

Participant sampling was purposive, involving 23 individuals selected across the three wards: ten children aged 8–17, five parents or caregivers, three local leaders, and five professionals from relevant ministries (Health and Child Care, Primary and Secondary Education, and Lands and Agriculture) and organisations (African Wildlife Foundation, DanChurchAid, FAO, and Agritex). This purposive selection ensured that participants had direct experience with climate impacts, food insecurity, and child-centred interventions, allowing for a rich, contextually grounded understanding. Quantitative data complemented qualitative findings by collecting nutritional metrics, including child malnutrition rates, growth indicators, and programme performance data from existing reports, community health assessments, and official nutrition statistics.

9.3.2 Data Analysis and Analytical Approach

Thematic analysis was employed for qualitative data, identifying key themes and response patterns from interviews, focus groups, and storytelling narratives. This process involved systematically coding responses around themes, including climate impacts on household food production, child vulnerability mechanisms, interventions' effectiveness, and community-proposed solutions. For quantitative data, descriptive statistics and comparative analysis assessed trends in nutritional outcomes and programme performance metrics. Critically, the triangulation of qualitative and quantitative findings provided complementary perspectives: quantitative data offered objective measurements of intervention impact and validated the frequency of qualitative insights, while qualitative data revealed underlying mechanisms, contextual factors, and community perspectives that numeric data alone cannot capture. This integration enhanced the credibility and comprehensiveness of findings, providing a holistic understanding of how climate change violates children's rights and how existing interventions either advance or undermine rights protection.

9.3.3 *Ethical Considerations and Participatory Commitment*

The study adhered to ethical guidelines, ensuring informed consent, confidentiality, and respect for participants' rights, with special attention to children's consent through age-appropriate methods and parental or guardian involvement. Recognising that research with vulnerable populations carries the risk of exploitation, the study prioritised participatory approaches that positioned participants not as research subjects but as knowledge holders contributing to solutions. Children's participation in data analysis and feedback processes ensured their voices shaped the findings, interpretation, and communication. Ethical approval was sought from relevant local and institutional review boards, and all protocols prioritised the protection of children's dignity and rights throughout the research process.

9.4 Literature Review: Climate Change, Food Insecurity, and Children's Rights in Zimbabwe

9.4.1 *Climate Change and Food Insecurity in Southern Africa and Zimbabwe*

The African continent faces unprecedented climate vulnerability, with Southern Africa experiencing some of the most severe impacts globally. Zimbabwe ranks as the 15th most vulnerable country to climate change globally and is positioned in the top three most vulnerable within Southern Africa, according to the 2021 Global Climate Risk Index. The country's climate trajectory presents alarming trends that directly threaten children's futures: the national average temperature has warmed at approximately 0.1 degrees Celsius per decade, with projections of a 1.0–1.5 °C increase by 2040 and 1.3–3.5 °C by 2080 (GoZ, 2024). Compounding these temperature increases, average annual rainfall has declined by approximately 5% since 1901, with projections suggesting a further decline of up to 10% nationally, and 25% in southwestern regions by 2080. These gradual but persistent changes intersect with escalating extreme weather events: drought frequency has increased from 10% between 1902 and 1979 to 25% from 1980 to 2018, with notable episodes in 1991–1992, 2002–2003, 2015–2016, 2018–2019, and 2023–2024 (Gwitira et al.,

2024). The convergence of rising temperatures, declining rainfall, and intensifying extreme events creates a compounding climate crisis, particularly devastating in rain-fed agricultural systems like those in Mbire.

In Mbire, these climate trends manifest as severe agricultural collapse and food insecurity. A 2018 study documented that climate variability led to severe crop failures, dramatically diminishing food availability for rural households. The district is heavily dependent on rain-fed agriculture, which is increasingly unreliable, leaving households vulnerable to the cascading effects of climate shocks. These agricultural disruptions directly threaten children's nutrition and health. Research indicates that prolonged food insecurity in rural areas has led to chronic malnutrition, stunting, and increased child mortality. According to UNICEF (2025), the sub-Saharan African region remains the only region where the number of stunted children continues to increase in both East and Southern Africa and West and Central Africa. The most significant numbers of stunted children were reported in South Asia (56 million) and sub-Saharan Africa (62 million). In this context, children in climate-vulnerable regions like Mbire face the greatest risks. Stunted children face not only immediate health complications but also long-term cognitive impairments, reduced educational opportunities, and decreased earning potential in adulthood, perpetuating cycles of poverty and vulnerability across generations.

9.4.2 *Child Vulnerability and Rights Violations in Climate-Induced Food Insecurity*

Children in rural Zimbabwe are especially vulnerable to climate-induced food insecurity due to their physiological dependence on caregivers for nutrition, healthcare, and education, combined with their heightened developmental sensitivity to malnutrition and stress. Food insecurity threatens children's survival, development, nutrition, health, education, and access to basic social services, recognised as children's rights under the UNCRC and the African Charter on the Rights and Welfare of the Child (ACRWC). When droughts destroy crops and reduce household income, children do not simply experience hunger; they experience systematic violations of their rights.

The mechanisms through which climate-induced food insecurity violates children's rights are multifaceted and interconnected. Food scarcity reduces children's access to nutritious meals, directly violating the right to an adequate standard of living. Malnutrition impairs physical growth and cognitive development, violating the right to health and development. School absenteeism, driven by hunger and children's need to fetch water or engage in agricultural labour, violates the right to education. As households face economic desperation, food insecurity increases the risks of child labour, early marriage, and sexual exploitation, violating children's rights to protection from economic and sexual exploitation. These are not separate challenges but interconnected manifestations of how climate change systemically undermines children's rights across multiple dimensions of their lives. As documented in different chapters in this volume, climate-induced displacement and migration create additional vulnerabilities, with children left behind facing emotional distress and heightened risks of exploitation and abuse.

9.4.3 *Existing Interventions and Policy Frameworks in Zimbabwe*

Zimbabwe has developed a substantial policy architecture addressing climate change and food security, including the National Climate Policy (NCP), the Child Friendly Climate Policy (CFCP), the National Climate Change Response Strategy (NCPRS), and the Food and Nutrition Security Policy. Agricultural policies include the Draft National Agriculture Policy Framework (2018–2030), the Comprehensive Agriculture Policy Framework (2012–2032), and the Zimbabwe Climate Smart Agriculture Framework (2018–2028), all promoting climate-smart practices and food security. Water resource management is addressed through the National Water Policy (2013) and the Water Act, while the Draft Disaster Risk Management Policy and the Civil Protection Act govern disaster management. Environmental protection is covered under the Environmental Management Act (2002) and the Zimbabwe Drought Risk Management Strategy and Action Plan (2017–2025).

Despite this comprehensive policy framework, critical implementation gaps persist between policy rhetoric and ground-level child protection. Three child-centred interventions have been implemented to address food insecurity: the Integrated Management of Acute Malnutrition (IMAM), launched in 2017 to treat severe malnutrition through community-based therapeutic care; the Utariri Project, initiated in 2019 to build climate resilience through sustainable agricultural practices; and the Integrated School Feeding Program (ISFP), which provides school-based nutrition support and educational incentives.

The IMAM programme succeeds in reducing child mortality from severe malnutrition, with over 70% of treated children showing significant recovery within 6 weeks. However, its focus on treatment rather than prevention, combined with resource limitations and inadequate integration with climate adaptation frameworks, limits its ability to address systemic causes of food insecurity. The Utariri Project promotes drought-resistant crops and conservation farming practices, and 60% of participating households report increased food availability. Yet many participants note that benefits are undermined by limited irrigation infrastructure, revealing how agricultural interventions divorced from water security infrastructure cannot fully address climate-induced vulnerabilities. The ISFP emerges as widely praised, with participating schools reporting 45% improvement in attendance rates and teachers observing better health and energy among participating children. However, seasonal food shortages disrupt programme continuity, and resource constraints limit reach and consistency.

Across these interventions, critical gaps persist. Programmes often fail to explicitly centre children's rights, treating food insecurity as a technical or humanitarian problem rather than a systemic violation of children's legal entitlements. Interventions operate at different ecological levels without sufficient coordination: IMAM addresses individual treatment, the Utariri Project targets household-level agricultural systems, and ISFP focuses on institutional-school-level provision. Few mechanisms ensure multi-level integration that addresses how macro-level climate impacts cascade into microsystems. Additionally, while Zimbabwe has clear policies and legislation addressing climate change and food security, there is a lack of policies explicitly referring to children's concerns, as documented in this volume's examination of implementation gaps between policy frameworks and child protection on the ground.

9.4.4 Critical Gaps in Knowledge and Practice

Despite the existing body of research on climate change, food insecurity, and child welfare, critical gaps persist in understanding the specific intersection of these issues in Zimbabwe's rural communities. Most studies focus on the macro-level impacts of climate change on agriculture, with a limited exploration of the direct effects on children's rights and long-term development. While numerous interventions have been implemented, rigorous evaluations assessing their effectiveness in meeting children's unique needs remain scarce. There is a particular need for research integrating the child rights approach with climate change adaptation policies, ensuring that interventions are explicitly designed to protect and advance children's rights rather than simply managing humanitarian crises. This study addresses these gaps by critically analysing existing interventions through an integrated lens of ecological systems theory and child rights approach, exploring how climate impacts violate children's rights and how programmes can be redesigned to advance children's rights protection in the context of climate change.

9.5 Findings: Climate Impacts, Intervention Effectiveness, and Children's Rights

9.5.1 Climate Change and Food Insecurity: Impact on Children's Rights

The study revealed that climate change has significantly undermined children's rights to food security and nutrition in Mbire, as evidenced by declining agricultural productivity, prolonged droughts, and erratic rainfall patterns that directly violate

Table 9.1 Effects of food insecurity in Mbire

Effect	Percentage of respondents reporting
Chronic hunger	92%
Growth stunting	65%
School absenteeism	56%
Increased illness	48%

children's right to an adequate standard of living. A local community leader from Ward 8 described the scale of agricultural collapse:

> Our maize harvests have dropped by over 50% in the last five years. Children go to bed hungry more often now, and some drop out of school because they are too weak to attend.

This statement encapsulates how climate impacts cascade across multiple rights violations: malnutrition threatens health and development, while school dropout violates the right to education. Focus group discussions with parents highlighted the pervasive nature of hunger, with most agreeing that food scarcity has become normalised. Quantitative data supported these qualitative insights: 78% of households in the study area face food shortages lasting more than 6 months annually. In addition, 65% of parents reported that their children had experienced growth stunting or weight loss attributed to poor diets.

Table 9.1 summarises the reported effects of food insecurity on children in Mbire.

These quantitative findings translate into concrete rights violations. Chronic hunger undermines survival and development. Growth stunting impairs physical and cognitive development. School absenteeism violates the right to education and increases vulnerability to exploitation. Increased illness reflects failures to protect the right to health. Beyond these direct effects, climate-induced food insecurity creates secondary vulnerabilities: children's participation in water fetching and agricultural labour reduces school attendance; desperation may drive families towards child labour, early marriage, or sexual exploitation; and emotional stress from prolonged hunger and family vulnerability affects children's psychosocial well-being. The study thus documented not isolated hunger but systematic violation of children's rights across multiple dimensions of their lives.

9.5.2 Evaluating Intervention Effectiveness Through a Rights Lens

The evaluation of the three interventions revealed that while each addresses important gaps, none fully operationalises a comprehensive rights-based approach to climate-induced food insecurity. IMAM was noted for its success in reducing child mortality from acute malnutrition, with health workers reporting that over 70% of treated children showed significant recovery within 6 weeks. However, resource limitations, including inadequate therapeutic supplies and insufficient staffing, undermined effectiveness. One health worker remarked: '…we save lives, but the demand is overwhelming. We sometimes run out of therapeutic food, leaving some children without immediate help.' This statement reveals not merely a resource constraint but a systemic failure to adequately resource interventions protecting children's rights to survival and health. The programme's focus on treating severe malnutrition rather than addressing systemic causes or preventing malnutrition illustrates how interventions can be effective at the microsystem level yet inadequate at addressing macrosystem-level climate vulnerabilities.

The Utariri Project demonstrated mixed outcomes, reflecting the gap between agricultural resilience and food security for children. Focus group discussions revealed that while 60% of participating households reported increased food availability, many noted that limited irrigation facilities undermined benefits. A parent from Ward 15 expressed the barrier: '…the new seeds grow well, but without water, they cannot thrive. More boreholes would make a big difference'. This illustrates how agricultural interventions, while important, cannot fully protect children's rights to food without complementary infrastructure investment. Climate-smart agriculture addresses part of the vulnerability but not the full scope of what children require: water security, diverse income sources, and resilient food systems.

The Integrated School Feeding Program emerged as the most universally praised intervention, with teachers reporting 45% improvement in school attendance and parents observing better health and energy among participating children. This finding reflects the programme's strength in addressing multiple rights simultaneously: it improves nutrition (right to food and health), increases education access (right to education), and potentially reduces child labour through improved attendance. However, seasonal food shortages disrupted some schools' programmes, revealing how interventions vulnerable to supply-side disruptions cannot ensure consistent rights protection in climate variability. In addition, programmes functioning at the institutional level require sustained commitment and funding; without linkages to agricultural production and water security, they remain dependent on external resource flows rather than building community-based resilience.

9.5.3 Community-Proposed Solutions and Rights-Based Priorities

Participants offered several practical solutions reflecting their understanding of what would advance children's rights to food security in the context of climate vulnerability. When asked about priorities, participants identified the following: expanding access to water (85% of respondents), scaling up feeding programmes (70%), community-based agriculture (65%), and enhancing agricultural inputs (50%).

Table 9.2 Summary of the identified solutions

Proposed solution	Percentage of respondents
Expanding access to water	85%
Scaling up feeding programmes	70%
Community-based agriculture	65%
Enhancing agricultural inputs	50%

The quantitative analysis revealed the prioritisation of solutions as shown in Table 9.2.

The prioritisation of water expansion reveals community understanding that water security is foundational to food security. Without water, agricultural improvements cannot translate into production. Children cannot attend school if they must spend hours fetching water. Communities cannot build long-term climate resilience without addressing water scarcity. A child participant shared during storytelling: '… If we had water, my family could grow more vegetables, and I could help sell them at the market to buy food for my siblings.' This child articulated the interconnection between water access, agricultural productivity, income generation, and improved nutrition, demonstrating that children understand the systemic nature of their vulnerabilities. The proposal to scale feeding programmes reflects the recognition that school-based interventions work, while community-based agriculture proposals indicate a commitment to local solutions and sustainability.

9.6 Discussion

The findings reveal that climate change in Mbire significantly exacerbates food insecurity among children through the well-documented mechanisms of erratic rainfall, prolonged droughts, and soil degradation. These climatic changes translate into malnutrition, school dropout, reduced cognitive development, and heightened vulnerability to exploitation. These outcomes are not natural consequences of climate variability but systematic violations of children's rights, violations for which states and stakeholders bear legal and moral accountability under international children's rights frameworks.

Applying ecological systems theory, the study demonstrates how macrosystem-level climate impacts cascade into microsystems, with each level of impact representing both an opportunity for intervention and a barrier to rights protection if left unaddressed. Climate change at the macrosystem level (regional rainfall patterns, agricultural policy frameworks) directly shapes conditions at the exosystem level (agricultural infrastructure, health and education services), which in turn determines opportunities and constraints at the mesosystem level (family-school-community connections), ultimately affecting microsystem dynamics (household hunger, parental stress, child vulnerability). Effective rights-based responses must address vulnerabilities at each level, not treating interventions as isolated programmes but as components of integrated systems change. However, current interventions often function in isolation, addressing single ecological levels without sufficient coordination.

While valuable, the child rights approach framework reveals that existing interventions fail to operationalise a comprehensive commitment to children's rights. IMAM saves lives but operates at the crisis response level rather than addressing prevention and systemic causes. The Utariri Project builds agricultural resilience but does not ensure food access for children. ISFP improves educational continuity and nutrition but depends on external resource flows. Critically, none of these programmes explicitly frames their work as rights protection, nor do they establish accountability mechanisms ensuring that children's rights are advanced. Without this explicit rights framework, programmes risk perpetuating the notion that child welfare is a charitable endeavour rather than a state obligation rooted in international legal commitments.

The community-proposed solutions reveal a sophisticated understanding of interconnected vulnerabilities and highlight what transformation towards rights-based climate adaptation would require. The emphasis on water expansion addresses the foundational infrastructure gap, limiting both agricultural production and school attendance. Scaling feeding programmes acknowledges what works at the local level. Community-based agriculture proposals prioritise local ownership and sustainability. Together, these proposals suggest pathways for integration: water infrastructure investment enables agricultural productivity, which supports both household food production and school feeding programme sustainability, which supports school attendance and child protection, which enables children to thrive and develop.

This analysis also reveals the governance and policy gap identified across this volume: Zimbabwe has developed comprehensive policies addressing climate change and food security, yet implementation remains inadequate and inadequately resourced and fails to centre on children's rights explicitly. Coordination between sectors remains weak; climate adaptation is often treated separately from child welfare and education policy. Transforming this situation requires additional resources and a fundamental reorientation towards rights-based climate adaptation that treats child protection as non-negotiable rather than supplementary.

9.7 Conclusion

This study highlights the significant impact of climate change on children's food security and nutrition in Mbire, Zimbabwe, demonstrating that climate vulnerability constitutes a systematic violation of children's rights to survival, development, health, education, and protection. The evaluation of three existing interventions—the IMAM, the Utariri Project, and ISFP—reveals that while these programmes make important contributions, they fail to comprehensively address the complex, multi-sectoral nature of climate-induced food insecurity and its rights dimensions.

Critically, current interventions operate largely outside explicit rights frameworks, limiting their ability to establish accountability, ensure systemic change, or address root causes of child vulnerability. Advancing children's rights in climate-induced food insecurity requires transformative policies integrating climate adaptation, child protection, education, and health systems under an explicit children's rights framework.

The following recommendations emerge from the research findings and participatory engagement with communities: first, child-centred climate adaptation must be elevated from a peripheral concern to a central priority in national climate policy and resource allocation. The Government of Zimbabwe should establish explicit commitments to protecting children's rights through climate action, integrating child-specific vulnerabilities into the National Climate Change Adaptation Plan and ensuring adequate budgetary allocation for child-centred interventions. Second, existing interventions should be strengthened and integrated into a comprehensive framework addressing vulnerabilities at multiple ecological levels. IMAM should be expanded with consistent funding and integrated with prevention programmes and school-based nutrition. The Utariri Project should be linked with water infrastructure investment and school feeding programmes to ensure that agricultural productivity translates into improved nutrition for children. ISFP should be scaled up and sustained by integrating local agricultural production systems. Third, multi-stakeholder collaboration must move from rhetorical commitment to concrete institutional mechanisms ensuring coordination across sectors and governance levels. Water, agriculture, health, education, and child welfare ministries should establish joint planning and budgeting processes. Community leaders, teachers, health workers, parents, and children should participate in decision-making, ensuring that interventions reflect local knowledge and priorities. Fourth, international frameworks and commitments should be operationalised nationally through explicit policy integration. The UNCRC and ACRWC mandate that protecting children's rights to food, health, and education should translate into legally binding obligations with accountability mechanisms and resource commitments.

Based on these recommendations, this chapter proposes an Integrated Child-Centred Climate Resilience Program (ICCCRP) designed to systematically address the interconnected challenges of climate change, food insecurity, and children's rights violations in communities like Mbire. The ICCCRP operates through three integrated components: climate-resilient agriculture and nutrition, combining sustainable farming practices with school feeding programmes using locally grown, climate-resilient foods; child-focused climate education, establishing programmes in schools addressing climate awareness, sustainable practices, and environmental stewardship; and multi-stakeholder collaboration, fostering partnerships between the government, non-governmental organisations (NGOs), schools, and communities to enhance service delivery, mobilise resources, and ensure culturally appropriate, context-specific interventions. This model addresses climate-induced food insecurity not as an isolated humanitarian problem but as a systemic challenge requiring integrated, rights-based, multi-level responses.

Ultimately, protecting children's food security in the context of climate change demands that societies fundamentally reorient their commitments from managing crises to preventing violations of children's rights. As climate impacts intensify, the window for adequate adaptation narrows. Zimbabwe's children deserve nothing less than comprehensive, well-resourced, integrated responses that recognise their agency, honour their rights, and ensure they can survive, develop, and thrive in a rapidly changing world. This requires policy reform and resource allocation and transformation in how climate adaptation is conceptualised and implemented, moving from technical solutions to justice-centred approaches that ensure climate action protects and advances the rights of Africa's most vulnerable citizens.

References

Bronfenbrenner, U. (1979). *The ecology of human development: Experiments by nature and design*. Harvard University Press.

FAO. (2020). *The state of food security and nutrition in the world 2020: Transforming food systems for affordable healthy diets*. Food and Agriculture Organisation of the United Nations. https://www.fao.org/publications/sofi/2020/en/

Government of Zimbabwe. (2024). *Zimbabwe national climate change adaptation plan*. Ministry of Environment, Climate and Wildlife.

Gwitira, I., Shekede, M. D., & Bhatasara, S. (2024). *Child-centred climate impact. Vulnerability and risk assessment for Zimbabwe*. UNICEF.

UNICEF. (2025). *Child malnutrition*. https://data.unicef.org/topic/nutrition/malnutrition/

Chapter 10
Climate Change and Access to Safety, Health, and Environmental Rights for Schoolchildren in Rural Zimbabwe

Ernest Kudakwashe Mando, Joshua Chibvuma, and Sydwell Zhou

10.1 Introduction

Extreme weather events associated with climate change have become more frequent and intense in recent years, disrupting communities, displacing populations and exacerbating inequalities in many parts of the world (Terre des hommes Lausanne, 2023). The impacts from extreme weather associated with climate change affect children the most (UNICEF, 2023). Climate-change-related shock affects different societies differently (Fruttero et al., 2024). Zimbabwe ranks at number 51 with a score of 6.1 on the Children's Climate Risk Index (UNICEF, 2023), indicating that Zimbabwe still has a lot to do in addressing child vulnerability to climate change. As Chipenda and Ndhlovu (Introduction, in this volume) demonstrate, Zimbabwe is ranked globally as the 15th most vulnerable country to climate change and is positioned very high (in the top three) in Southern Africa, according to the 2021 Global Climate Risk Index. The 6.5 million children (0–18 years old) in Zimbabwe, representing 47% of the population, face significant risks from climate-induced emergencies, with up to two-thirds of preventable illness and death from environmental

E. K. Mando (✉)
College of Agriculture and Environmental Sciences, University of South Africa (UNISA), Pretoria, South Africa
e-mail: 66328942@mylife.unisa.ac.za

J. Chibvuma
Department of Geography Geo-Information Sciences, Lupane State University, Lupane, Zimbabwe
e-mail: jchibvuma@lsu.ac.zw

S. Zhou
Department of Geography and Environmental Science, Gwanda State University, Filabusi, Zimbabwe
e-mail: sydwell.zhou@gsu.ac.zw

E. Ndhlovu, C. Chipenda (eds.), *Climate Change and Children's Rights in Zimbabwe*, https://doi.org/10.1007/978-981-95-6005-9_10

hazards occurring among them, predominantly those under 5 years of age. Due to the severity of the impacts of climate change, Goal 13 of the 2030 Agenda for Sustainable Development calls all United Nations member states to take urgent action to combat climate change and its impacts. Thus, this research aims to establish how climate change relates to child safety, health and environmental rights, using Bikita District as a case study.

Children are more vulnerable to climate change because they depend on adults to realise most of their rights (Akpambang & Ajidasile, 2020). Climate change severely threatens the enjoyment of various human rights (Bekink, 2024). Children, like adults, have the right to basic needs, like life, health, water, food and shelter, and to specific needs, like care from parents, education, rest, play and leisure (Sanz-Caballero, 2013). Unfortunately, climate change has posed a serious threat to these rights, such that there are growing calls for all stakeholders worldwide to tackle climate change impacts on children. The efforts to address climate-change-related effects with specific reference to children are enshrined in the United Nations Convention on the Rights of the Child (1989) and other international treaties (Akpambang & Ajidasile, 2020). Climate shocks disrupt children's education directly and indirectly by destroying schools, triggering illness, affecting attendance, causing school dropouts and reducing children's schooling time (UNICEF, 2023). Children are also particularly vulnerable to post-traumatic stress after extreme weather events (Thiery et al., 2021). Children are among the most vulnerable groups to the effects of climate change, including death or injury during natural disasters related to climate change. Such disasters affect children's safety, health and environmental rights in many parts of the world, including Zimbabwe. Climate change disasters threaten the rights of children to food, life, clean water, adequate food, health, adequate housing, education and recreational activities (Akpambang & Ajidasile, 2020).

This study has been prompted by the realisation that there is scant research on climate change vis-à-vis children's safety, health and environmental rights, particularly among those living in rural areas in Zimbabwe. Hence, it seeks to establish the nexus between climate change and schoolchildren's rights to safety, health and the environment in rural Zimbabwe, using Bikita District in Masvingo Province as a case study. The choice of Bikita District is significant, given that Masvingo Province has been identified as one of the regions where temperature increases are projected to be the most significant, alongside Matabeleland North and Matabeleland South provinces (Chipenda & Ndhlovu, Introduction, in this volume). In addition, the region experiences significant rainfall decline and has been affected by climate-change-related disasters like cyclones and droughts. Bikita District is one of the eight rural districts in Masvingo Province, Zimbabwe, that borders the Manicaland districts of Chipinge and Buhera. The district borders Gutu to the north, Zaka to the west, and Chiredzi to the south (Fig. 10.1).

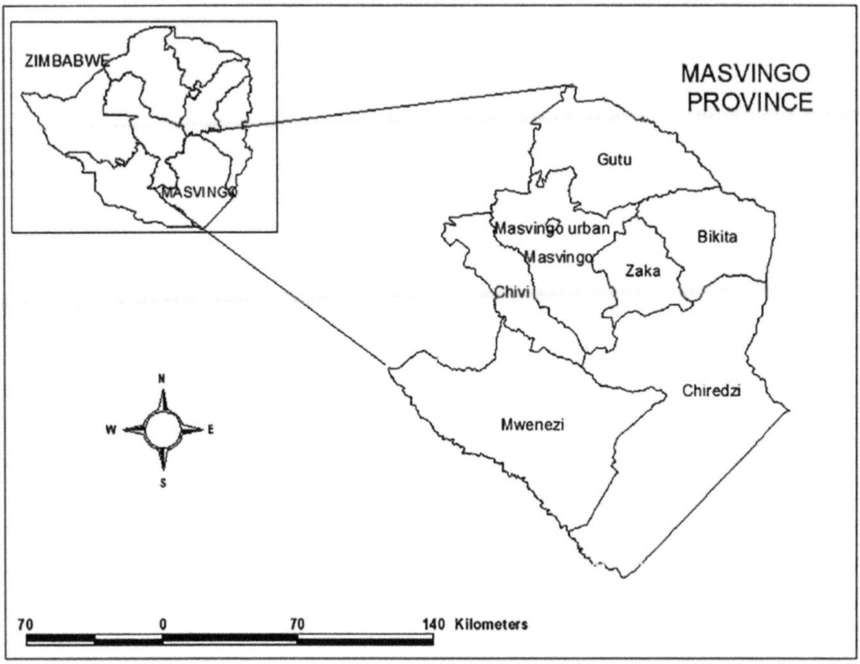

Fig. 10.1 Map of Bikita District (Source: Research Survey, 2024)

10.2 Methodology

Informed by an interpretivism philosophy, a qualitative approach was employed to understand the ways in which access to and enjoyment of safety, health and environmental rights were undermined among schoolchildren in rural Zimbabwe. The study population included school heads, teachers, parents and learners from ten purposively selected secondary schools within Bikita District in Masvingo Province. Both schools and participants constituted 30% of the study subjects. School heads were purposively chosen according to their leadership roles, while parents, teachers and learners were conveniently selected based on their availability on the day of data collection. This was because it was challenging to engage specific participants due to variations in field visit days and work timetables across schools. All participants were contacted at schools and during working days, with school heads facilitating meetings with parents from the local communities. Five teachers, the school head and five parents from each school participated in the study.

Following ethical clearance from relevant authorities and the informed consent of participating individuals, data were collected through face-to-face interviews with the aforesaid participants. In addition, qualitative data were collected through focus group discussions (FGDs) with learners at each school—one for girls and another for boys—to allow flexible expressions of gender-related-rights experiences in the context of climate change. Both interviews and FGDs consisted of structured and non-structured questions informed by three key themes: health, safety and environmental rights. Data collection was conducted over a period of 30 days, with each session taking roughly 30 minutes. The researchers integrated ethics into their study, including informed consent from participants, observation of autonomy and confidentiality and the right to withdraw at any time. The purpose of the study was also clearly explained to all the participants. Both interviews and FGDs were documented with the use of an audio recorder. Data were analysed thematically and informed by the United Nations Convention on the Rights of the Child (UNCRC).

10.3 Literature Review

School-going children's rights to safety and to a healthy and secure environment are under increasing and severe threat these days due to climate-change-related disasters, which lead to stress, mental health, illness, diarrhoeal diseases, vector-borne diseases and increased malnutrition (Proulx et al., 2024). Climate change is one of the greatest public health threats of the twenty-first century, affecting rural areas that are geographically isolated and suffer from greater health inequalities (Smith et al., 2023). Along this line, the United Nations Children's Climate Risk Index has brought attention to children's heightened exposure to climate and environmental hazards (UNICEF, 2024). The Children's Climate Risk Index analyses climate risk from a child-centred perspective, ranking countries based on children's exposure to climatic and environmental shocks (Smith et al., 2023). Approximately 47% of Zimbabwe's population is under the age of 18 years, and in 2023 the country ranked 51st globally with an aggregate score of 6.1, comprising 5.7 for climate and environmental risk and 6.5 for child vulnerability (UNICEF, 2023). Thus, there is a need to establish the link between climate change and children's safety, health and environmental rights in the face of climate change. Nearly half a billion children globally live in countries at extremely high risk due to climate change (UNICEF, 2024). This means there are many children whose safety, health and environmental rights are violated as a result of climate change. Climate-related illness, premature deaths and malnutrition in all its forms are increasing, exposing children to unsafe and unhealthy environments (Cissé et al., 2022).

Most extreme weather events linked to climate change affecting children's health and safety were reported in developing countries between 1970 and 2019 (Fruttero et al., 2024). In sub-Saharan Africa, the frequency of droughts tripled, the incidence of storms quadrupled, and the occurrence of floods increased tenfold between 2010 and 2019 (Zeufack et al., 2021). Children's safety and health are threatened by climate change through shifts in temperature and precipitation, extreme weather events and ecological and community disruptions (Ahdoot et al., 2024). Such disruptions have profound and far-reaching implications for children's welfare. Hence, the desire to carry out this research is shaped by various climate-related extreme events that cause much harm to Southern Africa and Zimbabwe. Undoubtedly, children's rights in rural areas are not an exception.

A study on the gendered impacts of climate change highlights varying effects in Brazil, Madagascar, Kenya and India (Fruttero et al., 2024). Indigenous peoples who live in geographically isolated, resource-deprived and impoverished communities are often at higher risk of climate-change-related health impacts due to the lack of safety nets (Ford et al., 2020). In such environments, children are more exposed than adults to the vagaries of climate. In Madagascar, children experienced adverse effects in school attendance due to droughts and cyclones (Fruttero et al., 2024). In Brazil, droughts have been recorded to impact the school performance of more girls than boys, though all children are affected (Fruttero et al., 2024). There remains limited evidence on how climate change is forcing children into labour, in violation of their rights to health and a safe environment (International Labour Organisation, 2023). In Zimbabwe alone, approximately 7.5 million children—constituting 47% of the population—are below 18 years of age and face increased risks of climate-change-induced challenges, such as food insecurity, water scarcity and disruption of basic services (UNICEF, 2024). Thus, it is necessary to continuously investigate how climate change affects children today and model its future impact on child safety, health and environmental rights. At present, little is known about countermeasures to protect children from climate-change-related threats, such as cold extremes, poor air quality, extreme rainfall, drought and heat extremes (Weeda et al., 2023). This means the right to life, adequate food, and safe and clean water, among other rights, are at stake since little research has illuminated how communities can safeguard rights to safety, to health and to a secure environment in the face of climate change. This forms part of the research gap that this study seeks to address.

10.4 Findings

The findings demonstrate that climate change–related impacts, including extreme heat, water scarcity, and deteriorating school infrastructure, have led to serious violations of the safety, health, and environmental rights of children in rural schools in Zimbabwe. This section discusses various forms of climate-related violations of schoolchildren's safety, health and environmental rights in rural Zimbabwe. The right to health shall include access to healthcare, clean water and nutritious food; the right to safety shall include protection from violence and exploitation, as well as access to a safe and secure learning environment; and environmental rights shall include access to environmental information, participation and protection from environmental hazards.

10.4.1 Climate Change and Safety Rights

10.4.1.1 Right to Protection and a Safe Learning Environment

The study also examined the climate change impacts of the right to protection from violence, including physical and psychological abuse, among rural schoolchildren. Findings revealed that climate change has compromised the right to safety and security of rural learners in Zimbabwe. The findings indicate that recurrent extreme weather conditions, especially drought-induced water shortages and heat waves, have exacerbated infringements of children's rights to protection and safe learning environments in rural schools, compounding existing vulnerabilities linked to resource constraints, school location, and inadequate emergency preparedness. For instance, most participants indicated that the long distances learners had to travel to and from school cause emotional stress in the face of extreme weather conditions such as heat waves. These findings resonate with patterns documented by Chaora et al. (Chap. 11, in this volume), who, drawing on evidence from Lupane District in rural Zimbabwe, describe how rising temperatures have transformed classrooms into "ovens," creating conditions that hinder effective learning and child development and illustrate the direct educational impacts of heat exposure on rural children. However, schools do not have enough facilities, such as food, clean and adequate water and electricity for cooling systems, to ensure that the welfare of such vulnerable children is met. The absence of adequate interventions to provide physical protection and psychosocial support for children in the context of climate change has contributed to heightened stress, reduced concentration, increased absenteeism, and other mental health challenges. Through FGDs, most children expressed concern over limited physical and psycho-social support systems in the face of climate change:

> As a student, I feel so stressed to learn at a school without adequate water, sanitation facilities and safety systems. Whenever I hear thunderstorms, I begin to think of how safe it is to go back home, crossing rivers will. The school dismisses us home in the assumption that we arrive home safely (Student 5, FGD 4).

> Our classes are not safe at all. Our roofs are old, and our walls are cracking. I am personally afraid to remain inside when heavy rain or strong winds come. I remember when I was in Form 1, we almost got injured when one of the window panes broke due to strong winds during the lesson. Our safety is under threat.

Further to the above findings, researchers also observed weak structures in most schools, including poor roofing and old drainage systems, suggesting that the buildings are non-resilient to extreme weather events such as cyclones. In emergency cases, rural children are at most risk, as most schools are located in isolated areas where there are no nearby alternative rescue or assembly points. Clearly, all these conditions demonstrate how climate change has compromised rural children's right to safety within and outside school environments.

10.4.1.2 Right to Protection from Exploitation

Children have the right to be protected from economic exploitation, including child labour. The study showed that climate-induced droughts have placed more household burden on rural children as they needed to engage in child labour to assist their parents and guardians in raising school fees. Participants raised concerns over deteriorating standards of living, which have triggered a rise in child labour activities, such as gardening, buying and selling. Most learners indicated that they engage in laborious activities before and after school, exposing them to continuous fatigue and exhaustion, ultimately affecting their enjoyment of their rights to protection and education:

> We are worried as parents; today, our children are more vulnerable to various forms of exploitation due to deteriorating standards of living, due to hunger and starvation resulting from climate change. Because we are not providing enough for their school needs, including fees and uniforms, even minors are engaged in casual part-time employment to raise money. The level of abuse is worrying to us because a child can work the entire weekend only to earn US $5, which cannot sustain her needs. This only started when we began to experience serious droughts in our local communities due to climate change. Before, there was nothing like this (Parent 9).

> Our local communities are no longer making reasonable harvests. As a result, parents no longer support children with adequate needs. Today, we have a serious challenge, especially with girl children, with most now engaged in early marriages, perceiving better lives. In contrast, others now engage in promiscuous relations to get money. Families are impoverished; children are being abused out there (School head 4).

Based on the study, it is clear that with standards of living deteriorating in most rural communities due to climate change, there is a rising rate of child exploitation. The alternative forms of livelihoods adopted by children have exposed them to various forms of abuse and human rights violations.

10.4.2 Climate Change and Health Rights

10.4.2.1 Access to Healthcare

The study noted that climate change has added to the problem of poor access to healthcare for learners in rural Zimbabwe. Along with the difficulty in accessing healthcare in rural areas over the years, extreme weather conditions, such as heat waves, have increased the frequency of health ailments among children. The research revealed that the frequency of health ailments and health-related absenteeism among rural children was relatively higher in the last quarter of 2024 due to heat waves. Children were severely affected by heat stress disorders, severe dehydration and fatigue. However, most schools do not have first aid resources, and government health facilities, such as clinics, are located far from school sites. All participants highlighted that access to healthcare has been a long-standing problem, with climate change further compounding the violation of children's health rights as the rising demand for healthcare remains unmet. One of the teachers expressed the following concern:

> Our nearest clinic is nearly 8 km from here. Our children cannot easily access it. Because of too much heat exposure, our children often suffer heat stress, and some even collapse. In such cases, we find it challenging to ensure that the child is immediately sent to the clinic because of the distance. We had about five heat stress collapse cases at this school in 2023 due to the heatwave. Traditionally, children could be released and go to the clinic, but with that magnitude, they cannot be allowed to go alone. So, accessibility to clinics has been seriously constrained by climate change.

Supporting the above narrative, a child who participated in the FGD indicated:

> Last year [2023], I felt very weak when it was very hot, and I could not even walk for 500 meters. I reported to my class teacher, who organised a scorch cart from our local community to take me to the clinic about 7km away from our school. I arrived after more than 2 hours because of the bad roads and the nature of transport.

Clearly, these narratives point to the increasingly constrained access to healthcare for rural children in the face of climate change. The increasing frequency and rate of climate-related ailments among children occur under restrictive healthcare conditions, putting children's health at risk and violating their healthcare rights.

10.4.2.2 Access to Clean Water and Nutritious Food

While some schools have successfully implemented water and sanitation programmes to cater for the health and welfare of their students, access to clean water and nutritious food remains a problem for most schoolchildren in rural Zimbabwe. The findings indicate that climate change, particularly recurrent droughts, has led to severe water shortages for both domestic and productive uses in schools. Limited access to groundwater has compelled many schools to abandon water-intensive agricultural projects, including those that previously supported school feeding programmes, especially at the primary school level. Most children revealed they have resorted to running water when borehole water is unavailable under extreme heat conditions. Although many learners appreciated traditional water purification methods such as boiling, results indicated that this was not practised. The non-operation of school agriculture projects, including orchards and fresh farm gardening, has deprived children of their access to nutritious food. This is a serious violation of the health rights of children, who walk long distances to school only to be denied access to basic needs like clean water and healthy food. The following excerpts from participants underscore a clear violation of children's right to clean water and nutritious food due to the impacts of climate change:

> We used to have a perennial borehole just by the school's main gate, for the community where our children could easily access water for drinking and cleaning their fruits. Due to

> persistent droughts in this region, the borehole has run out of water. Efforts to extend the depth and reach the water level have been fruitless. Today, our children carry water from home or resort to other open water sources, such as rivers, to wash their food or even drink (Parent 1).

> Due to perennial water shortages, we have since stopped some agricultural activities, such as market gardening. Even our orchard has suffered; it is no longer productive. We used to give our children some fruits periodically for their well-being, but now it is a thing of the past. This means the school can no longer provide any supplementary food for children. Imagine a learner can have his or her last meal in the morning around 5 am when departing for school, spends the whole day in school, and has no more food till he/she returns home around 5 pm. It is a health concern (Teacher 5).

The above empirical evidence clearly indicates that rural children are heavily affected by climate change in terms of access to clean water and nutritious food. The starvation experienced by rural children during learning times violates their right to both health and education.

10.4.3 Climate Change and Environmental Rights

10.4.3.1 Right to Participation and Access to Information

Children can access environmental information and participate in environmental programmes/initiatives. This study noted that while information dissemination occurs in class and as part of the school curriculum, most rural children are unaware of climate mitigation and resilience strategies. Many of the children come from impoverished family backgrounds, lacking adequate resources for early warning and real-time disaster communication systems. Furthermore, their participation in out-of-class climate action is minimal. Decision-making on environmental matters related to climate change is non-inclusive and often marginalises rural children. These issues emerged in most FGDs with children, as indicated in the following narratives:

> We only learn about climate change in class, for example, geography. When cyclones come, we are unaware, especially at home, because we do not have radios and cell phones that keep us updated (Student 14, FGD 3).

> Our school doesn't have climate programs, which we do every year. The last time we had a district competition on climate change was in 2021, when I was in form 1. We went for competitions at the district level, and it ended there (Student 3, FGD 4)

The above responses from FGDs reveal a concerning lack of adequate participation, capacity building and access to information for rural children with regard to climate change. Such exclusion violates their environmental rights.

10.4.3.2 Right to Protection from Environmental Hazards

Children have the right to be protected from environmental hazards, including pollution, toxic substances, and climate change. While the study noted limited climate change impacts, such as air pollution and exposure to hazardous chemicals in rural areas, the lack of adequate disaster preparedness and school resilience makes rural children more vulnerable. The study observed that most schools did not have assembly points, trained emergency response teams, or environmental hazards monitoring systems. In addition, rural learners spend relatively more time outdoors, either walking to school or participating in sports. Thus, extreme weather conditions make them easily exposed to environmental hazards such as heat waves or severe storms. Most school heads and teachers confirmed the foregoing, with others expressing the following sentiments:

> Our disaster risk reduction system is weak for now. We once had a teacher who was trained at the district level in first aid and emergency response, but he transferred. He was trying to implement some policies and procedures, but since then, no one has been able to do that. So, it is true that our children are vulnerable to climate risks such as extreme heat. We do not have adequate preventive mechanisms and facilities in place (School head 4).

> We do not have adequate emergency response systems. During Cyclone Idai, one of our learners drowned just close to our school at a nearby river. We never anticipated such risks. Today, we have developed a strict policy of children's movement within and outside the school environment during learning hours (School Head 1).

> Unfortunately, our school does not have adequate facilities to protect children from extreme weather conditions such as heat waves. Some children conduct lessons outdoors because of a shortage of classrooms, and during their practicals. These environmental hazards severely affected their well-being (Teacher 6).

The above narratives confirm that rural learners are relatively more exposed to various forms of environment due to limited emergency response facilities and resilience.

10.5 Discussion

The study aimed to examine how climate change has influenced schoolchildren's access to and enjoyment of safety, health and environmental rights in rural Zimbabwe. Based on this goal and informed by an interpretivism philosophy, we qualitatively gathered data through key informant interviews with school heads and teachers, as well as focus group discussions with children in rural schools. Key findings presented climate change implications in three key areas: the right to health, safety, and the right to the environment. Overall, results indicate that climate change has deprived children of their right to safety, health and the environment. Specifically, common violations relate to the right to protection from physical and psycho-social hazards, the right to a safe learning environment, protection from exploitation, access to environmental information, participation in environmental programmes, the right to healthcare and access to clean and nutritious food.

Regarding children's right to protection, results show that climate change impacts, especially droughts and subsequent decline in living standards, have exposed rural schoolchildren to various forms of exploitation, including child labour and early-marriage-related abuses. This directly violates Article 27 of the UNCRC (Bekink, 2024). The UNCRC states that all children have the right to a decent standard of living, which includes adequate food, housing and water (UNICEF, 2023). The persistent droughts experienced by rural communities have incapacitated parents from adequately providing for their children's school needs, exposing their children to exploitation and abuse as they attempt to supplement their expenses through part-time jobs. These patterns mirror the findings of Ndhlovu and Chipenda (Chap. 12, in this volume), who demonstrate how climate change, through unpredictable weather patterns, substantially worsens poverty, leaving peasant households exploring survival strategies, including resorting to child labour.

Furthermore, extreme weather conditions, such as heat waves, have severely affected rural schoolchildren during their outdoor education lessons and activities. Results showed that most rural schools do not have adequate resources to protect children against extreme weather conditions; hence, children are at a high risk of climate-induced ailments, such as heat stress, exhaustion, fatigue and other health illnesses. While some schools have electricity and water facilities, most schools in rural Zimbabwe do not. Thus, they are unable to mitigate extreme weather conditions, such as heat waves, for learners' safety, health and welfare through measures such as electrically powered ventilation and cooling systems. These findings align closely with Akpambang and Ajidasile (2020), who demonstrate that climate change disproportionately intensifies rural–urban inequalities by compounding existing infrastructural and service deficits in rural areas. In this context, climate-related heat stress not only magnifies educational disparities between rural and urban schools but also reinforces structural inequities in children's access to safe and enabling learning environments. Indeed, rural children are relatively more vulnerable to climate risks due to underlying institutional and environmental constraints that weaken climate resilience (Thiery et al., 2021).

The study also noted that most rural learners do not enjoy their right to a safe learning environment. Most learners walk long distances to school and experience environmental hazards such as floods, which expose them to risks of drowning. However, out-of-school disaster risk reduction measures are minimal in most schools. Studies show that children are at a high risk of climate hazards outside of school environments (Dapi et al., 2010). The lack of capacity-building systems for strengthening children's climate resilience in and outside school environments suggests that children cannot respond safely in case of climate-change-induced disasters, such as floods and lightning. Disaster risk reduction systems in rural schools are very weak, as evidenced by their lack of policies, procedures and resources for disaster management. Previous studies show that the lack of adequate disaster management measures for children is a clear violation of their right to protection, considering that children are mentally and physically young and more dependent (Fruttero et al., 2024; Ahdoot et al., 2024). For rural children, climate resilience therefore becomes critical, given the unfavourable conditions inherent in rural schools and homes.

Access to and enjoyment of environmental rights in the face of climate change were also very limited for rural schoolchildren. This is largely because access to environmental information remains limited to conventional, classroom based curriculum delivery, which prioritises academic achievement over equipping learners with the knowledge and skills necessary for climate resilience and adaptive capacity. Generally, there is a lack of tailor-made theoretical and practical educational activities that address that gap and promote children's full participation in environmental programmes and access to environmental information. There is minimal school-based and external stakeholder support towards the environmental rights of rural children. Article 12 of the UNCRC states that governments must seek children's views on matters affecting them and take them seriously. This contrasts with study findings that noted a deficit in children's access to information on climate change outside the curriculum context. Article 13 of the UNCRC specifically indicates children's right to seek and receive information UNICEF, 2023; Bekink, 2024). However, this study observed a serious violation of such an important right due to climate change. This is worsened by a lack of communication systems, such as radios, televisions and Internet access, for most children in rural areas. Communication is critical to disaster risk management (Diakakis et al., 2015; Chowdhury et al., 2022). Rural schoolchildren are marginalised when it comes to access to information and participation in environmental programmes. Yet, Article 29 of the CRC requires all children to learn about nature and participate in environmental issues affecting them locally and globally.

The study also noted that climate change is seriously affecting the health rights of schoolchildren in rural areas. Particularly, the rise in climate-related health problems among children due to extreme weather conditions, such as heat waves, is not met with adequate health systems. Healthcare centres are not easily accessible to children due to geographical location, proximity and road conditions. This is made worse by the fact that most schools do not have basic first aid facilities on site. Children in rural areas, therefore, suffer and do not get timely health assistance. Their right to a clean environment and health is further constrained by the lack of adequate water and sanitation facilities due to perennial water shortages caused by climate-induced droughts. Previous findings show that the lack of clean water presents risks of water-borne diseases (Achebak et al., 2019). This suggests that rural schoolchildren are becoming increasingly exposed to climate health risks. However, every child has the right to a healthy and sustainable environment, including access to clean water, sanitation and hygiene (WASH) facilities, according to Article 24 of the CRC. When a child finds good-quality healthcare and a clean environment, he or she achieves a high mental health score (Dapi et al., 2010). This suggests that the lack of enjoyment of health rights among rural children therefore compromises their right to education. The lack of water for school agricultural projects not only increases hunger and malnutrition but also amplifies physical and psychosocial stress, thereby hindering rural children's learning outcomes and overall educational achievement.

10.6 Conclusion

It is clear that disaster risk reduction is very weak in rural schools, leaving children relatively more vulnerable to climate risks. Their rights to safety, health and the environment have not been fully realised due to the impacts of climate change. In fact, climate change continues to widen the rural-urban divide at the expense of rural children. These findings highlight the urgent need articulated by Chipenda and Ndhlovu (Chap. 15, in this volume) for transformative policy frameworks that address deep-rooted inequities rather than symptomatic responses, positioning children as active agents in climate adaptation processes rather than passive victims. Therefore, these findings present the need to develop and implement disaster risk reduction models that address the contextual needs of schools through a human rights approach to safety, health and the environment. However, the study focused primarily on drought-prone regions which suggests that other important children's rights potentially affected by different climatic conditions may not have been fully captured. Subsequent studies should expand the scope to include multiple climatic zones, different rural school environments, and intersecting social vulnerabilities thereby offering more comprehensive insights to inform policies and interventions aimed at protecting the rights of school children in the face of climate change.

References

Achebak, H., Devolder, D., & Ballester, J. (2019). Trends in temperature-related age-specific and sex-specific mortality from cardiovascular diseases in Spain: A national time-series analysis from 1982 to 2018. *The Lancet Planetary Health, 3*(7), e297–e306.

Ahdoot, S., Baum, C.R., Cataletto, M.B., et al. (2024). Climate change and children's health: Building a healthy future for every child. *Pediatrics, 153*(3), e2023065505.

Akpambang, E. M., & Ajidasile, O.O. (2020, April 4). *International Journal of Economics, Commerce and Management.* Retrieved from International Journal of Economics, Commerce and Management website: https://ijecm.co.uk/wp-content/uploads/2020/04/8423.pdf

Bekink, M. (2024). The Fundamental Right of Children to Participate in Climate Change Decision-Making Processes: A South African Perspective. *Potchefstroom Electronic Law Journal (PELJ), 27*(1), 1–40.

Chowdhury, J. R., Parida, Y., & Agarwal, P. (2022). How flood affects rural employment in India: A gender analysis. *International Journal of Disaster Risk Reduction, 73*, 102881.

Cissé, G., McLeman, R., Adams, H., Aldunce, P., Bowen, K., Campbell-Lendrum, D., ... & Tirado, M. C. (2022). Health, wellbeing, and the changing structure of communities. *Climate change*, 1041–1170.

Dapi, L. N., Rocklöv, J., Nguefack-Tsague, G., Tetanye, E., & Kjellstrom, T. (2010). Heat impact on schoolchildren in Cameroon, Africa: potential health threat from climate change. *Global Health Action, 3*(1), 5610. https://pmc.ncbi.nlm.nih.gov/articles/PMC2998052/

Diakakis, M., Deligiannakis, G., Katsetsiadou, K., & Lekkas, E. (2015). Hurricane Sandy mortality in the Caribbean and continental North America. *Disaster Prevention and Management, 24*(1), 132–148.

Ford, J. D., King, N., Galappaththi, E. K., Pearce, T., McDowell, G., & Harper, S. L. (2020). The resilience of indigenous peoples to environmental change. *One Earth, 2*(6), 532–543.

Fruttero, A., Halim, D., Broccolini, C., Coelho, B., Gninafon, H., & Muller, N. (2024). Gendered impacts of climate change: evidence from weather shocks. *Environmental Research: Climate, 3*(4), 045018.

International Labour Organization. (2023). Issue paper on child labour and climate change. International Labour Organization. https://www.ilo.org/sites/default/files/wcmsp5/groups/public/@ed_norm/@ipec/documents/publication/wcms_894326.pdf

Proulx, K., Daelmans, B., Baltag, V., & Banati, P. (2024). Climate change impacts on child and adolescent health and well-being: A narrative review. *Journal of global health, 14*, 04061.

Sanz-Caballero, S. (2013). Children's rights in a changing climate: a perspective from the United Nations Convention on the Rights of the Child. *Ethics in science and environmental politics, 13*(1), 1–14.

Smith, D. J., Mizelle, E., Leslie, S. L., Li, G. X., Stone, S., Stauffer, P., ... & Thompson, L. M. (2023). Intervention studies to reduce the impact of climate change on health in rural communities in the United States: a systematic review. *Environmental Research: Health, 1*(3), 032001.

Terre des hommes Foundation Lausanne. (2023). Climate in-justice for children: How the climate crisis affects access to justice and children's rights (Advocacy brief). Terre des hommes Foundation Lausanne. https://tdh.rokka.io/dynamic/noop/57524e85ea82404bdbc62ba249986e6355bf8663/climate-in-justice-children-2023-enfinal-version.pdf

Thiery, W., Lange, S., Rogelj, J., et al. (2021). Intergenerational inequities in exposure to climate extremes. *Science*, 158–160.

UNICEF. (2023, November). Climate Insecurity Impacts on Children and Armed Conflict. New York, New York, United State of America.

United Nations Children's Emergence Fund. (2024, January). *United Nations Convention on the Rights of the Child.* Retrieved from UNICEF Web site: https://www.unicef.org/child-rights-convention

Weeda, L. J. Z., Bradshaw, C. J. A., Judge, M. A., Saraswati, C. M., & Le Souëf, P. N. (2023). First systematic review and meta-analysis of the risk magnitude of climate-change effects on child health. *Research Square, 10*, 57–75.

Zeufack, A. G., Calderon, C., Kubota, M., Kabundi, A. N., Korman, V., & Canales, C. C. (2021). Africa's Pulse, No. 23, October 2021. World Bank Publications.

Chapter 11
Learning in a Warming World: Impact of Climate Change on Child Education in Rural Schools in Lupane, Zimbabwe

Chipo Chaora, Joshua Chibvuma, and Tsitsi Prudence Humanikwa

11.1 Introduction

This chapter aims to synthesise the impact of climate change on child education in rural schools due to global warming. By examining the educational experiences of children in Lupane District, this chapter contributes to Theme 3 of this volume, which explores the impacts of climate change on children's health, education, and welfare through a climate justice lens (see Chipenda & Ndhlovu, Introduction, in this volume). Primary schools in Lupane District were sampled for the study. Lupane District was selected because it is one of the districts found in the semi-arid parts of Zimbabwe. The area receives very little rainfall (about 450 to 650 mm) annually and experiences high-average temperatures (over 35 °C). Over the years, climate change has been progressively recognised as a serious global issue affecting all aspects of human lives, including education systems. Children's right to education is increasingly becoming threatened due to global warming. Climate change violates child rights to education enshrined in both the United Nations Convention on the Rights of the Child (UNCRC) and the African Charter on the Rights and Welfare of the Child (ACRWC) (Pichhili, 2021). Children are among the most vulnerable groups to climate-related shocks due to their physical and socio-emotional fragility, making stable educational environments critical for their well-being and development (IPCC, 2023). Oppenheimer and Anttila-Hughes (2016) note that many children worldwide will face hotter and extreme temperatures more

C. Chaora (✉)
Department of Urban and Regional Planning, Lupane State University, Lupane, Zimbabwe
e-mail: cchaora@lsu.ac.zw

J. Chibvuma · T. P. Humanikwa
Department of Geography and Geo-Information Sciences, Lupane State University, Lupane, Zimbabwe
e-mail: jchibvuma@lsu.ac.zw; thumanikwa@lsu.ac.zw

E. Ndhlovu, C. Chipenda (eds.), *Climate Change and Children's Rights in Zimbabwe*, https://doi.org/10.1007/978-981-95-6005-9_11

frequently, with increased heatwaves threatening their health and making it harder for them to learn, exercise, and play outdoors. About 85% of the world's youth live in developing countries (Currie & Deschenes, 2016), and over 87.4% of children in Zimbabwe live in rural areas (ZIMSTAT, 2024). This demographic concentration in rural areas amplifies climate vulnerabilities as these communities lack the adaptive capacity and the resources available in urban centres, thereby creating what Chipenda and Chawanda (Chap. 2, in this volume) identify as critical climate justice concerns, where distributive inequities compound children's exposure to environmental hazards.

Children in less economically developed countries, especially students in hot and arid zones, are most affected by heat stress because of the limited resources to mitigate high temperatures in a harsh natural environment (UNICEF, 2021a). Some rural schools in sub-Saharan Africa lack proper ventilation and cooling systems, resulting in unbearably high classroom temperatures during heatwaves (Ministry of Primary and Secondary Education, 2020). Rising temperatures and other severe weather events have led to injuries, fatalities, and mental impacts among children, to the detriment of their education (Smith et al., 2023). Globally, the Intergovernmental Panel on Climate Change (IPCC) 6th Assessment Report has indicated with a high confidence level that temperatures have increased in all sub-regions, including Africa (da Cunha Bustamante, 2024). The increased frequency of extreme weather events has resulted in higher temperatures experienced in schools (Stott, 2016). Over a third of learners across the globe are exposed to extreme temperatures, and there is evidence that it has led to thermal distress among teachers and learners (UNICEF, 2021a). These patterns align with the broader climate trajectory, where it is documented that Zimbabwe's national average temperature has warmed at a rate of about 0.1 °C per decade, with projections indicating that temperatures will continue to increase throughout 2020–2040 for most districts (UNICEF, 2025), creating 'ovens in schools' where learners face new challenges that hinder effective learning and development.

The learning environment of schools includes the indoor environment, where students spend most of their time during school hours. Rising temperatures beyond tolerable limits have been associated with decreased concentration and have impaired students' and facilitators' cognitive function. The apparent result is ineffective learning, culminating in poor academic performance (Hsiang et al., 2017). Besides the indoor learning environment, most learners in developing countries engage in outdoor sporting activities. There are weaker infrastructures that can reduce the effects of temperature in poor developing countries (Rema & Paulina, 2016). These educational disruptions represent systematic violations of Article 28 of the UNCRC, which guarantees children's right to education, and Article 11 of the ACRWC, which obligates States Parties to ensure the child's best interests in all actions. When climate-induced heat stress forces school closures or diminishes learning quality, States fail in their obligations to protect and fulfil children's educational rights.

Another negative impact of climate change is food insecurity and water scarcity, especially in rural communities located in arid and semi-arid regions that are dependent on climate-sensitive livelihoods, specifically rain-fed agriculture (Mengistu et al., 2020). The discomfort caused by high temperatures, food insecurity, and water scarcity only makes it difficult for children to learn in a warming environment. Little is known about the generation of countermeasures that were successful in protecting children and the impact of increasing temperatures across different geographical scales around the globe (Weeda et al., 2024). This, therefore, calls for locally focused research studies to identify how temperature and other weather extremes affect children's education. Hence, this study seeks to contribute to understanding the impacts of increasing temperatures on children's education at the primary level using Lupane District as a case study. By providing empirical evidence from Lupane's rural primary schools, this chapter addresses the critical knowledge gap identified by Chipenda and Ndhlovu (Introduction, in this volume) regarding the need for context-specific research that documents how climate impacts cascade across multiple dimensions of children's well-being—from nutrition to education to protection against exploitation.

There exist knowledge gaps on the impacts of rising temperatures, especially from children's perspectives. The United Nations Children's Fund (UNICEF) (2023a) argues that children have been ignored despite being more vulnerable, and only 2.4% of key global climate funds can be classified as supporting child-responsive activities. This is a challenge for most developing countries since they have limited social safety nets, weak governmental institutions, fragile healthcare systems, and widespread poverty (Rema & Paulina, 2016). These financing gaps represent a significant climate injustice, wherein children—bearing minimal responsibility for greenhouse gas emissions—experience disproportionate consequences, a pattern extensively documented across Zimbabwe's diverse districts, as discussed in this volume (see Mando et al., Chap. 10; Chenzi & Pahuwa, Chap. 6, in this volume). There is a need to understand how the impacts of climate change, particularly heat stress, affect learning outcomes. The study aimed to investigate children's learning environment in the face of increasing temperatures as a result of climate change. Specifically, this chapter advances a rights-based analytical framework that positions education disruptions not merely as developmental challenges but as violations of children's rights as well, thereby contributing to the volume's overarching objective of integrating children's rights perspectives into climate vulnerability assessments and adaptation strategies. In light of this, the study's objectives were to assess the impacts of high temperatures in Lupane District, investigate how school children are affected by increasing temperatures, and identify strategies to cope with rising temperatures at the school level.

11.2 Methodology

11.2.1 Study Area

The study was conducted in Lupane District, a semi-arid region in Matabeleland North Province of Zimbabwe. The district experiences significant climate variability characterised by extreme temperatures and low rainfall (Manatsa et al., 2020). Lupane District exemplifies the climate vulnerability hotspots identified in the Introduction (Chipenda & Ndhlovu, in this volume), where southwestern Zimbabwe is projected to experience the greatest warming and precipitation decline, with future rainfall projections indicating a reduction of up to 10% of the mean national annual precipitation, particularly affecting Matabeleland North province. All administrative boundary data for Zimbabwean territories were downloaded from the Humanitarian Data Exchange Website (OCHA, 2018). The map was created using QGIS 3.34 'Prizren' (QGIS Development Team, 2024). All the data used to create the map were projected to Universal Transverse Mercator (UTM) Zone 35S (Fig. 11.1).

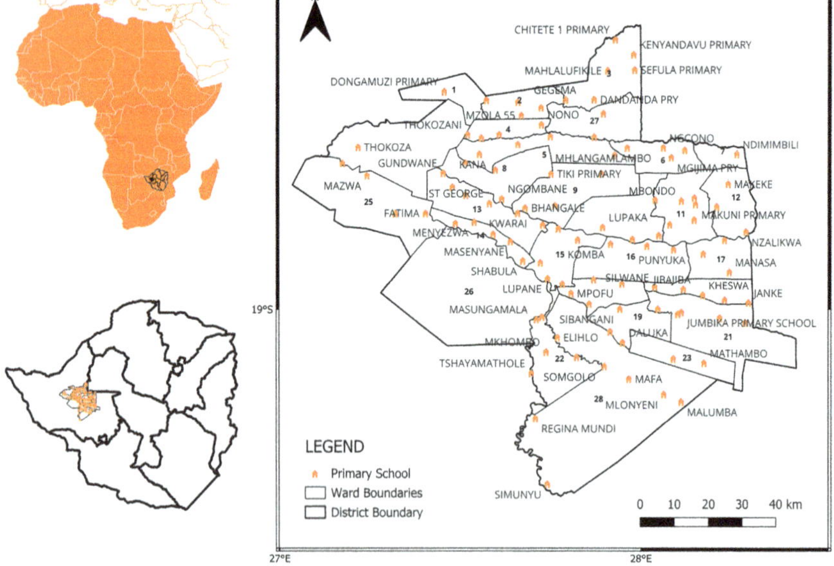

Fig. 11.1 Study map showing primary schools in Lupane District (Source: Research survey)

11.2.2 Methods and Tools

The study adopted a mixed approach whereby primary data were collected using questionnaires, observations, and interviews. Questionnaire surveys and five key informant interviews were used to collect primary data from the district. A sample of six rural primary schools was randomly selected to obtain data that were pertinent to the study. Since the study area was too big and complex to include all schools in the survey, sampling was done and observations and interviews were conducted at a few schools and with key informants to complement quantitative data from questionnaires. This mixed-method approach enabled the research to capture the quantitative extent of climate impacts on education and the qualitative dimensions of children's lived experiences, thereby addressing the methodological imperative that positions children as rights holders with agency rather than passive recipients of climate impacts. The collected data are presented in themes, guided by research objectives. Graphs and pie charts were used to analyse and present quantitative results since they give a visual picture for a quick comparison.

11.3 Literature Review

11.3.1 Global Perspectives on Climate Change and Children's Education

Climate change is a global problem affecting almost all countries across the world. Sanson and Burke (2020) highlight that since climate change is a worldwide problem, global cooperation is needed to come up with solutions to reduce its negative impacts. International organisations such as the World Bank Group have funded several studies on climate change, child education, and welfare. Marin et al. (2024) underscored the increased frequency and intensity of extreme events associated with climate change, such as cyclones, droughts (leading to famines), floods, heatwaves, tropical cyclones, and wildfires, in different parts of the globe. These natural disasters continue to have far-reaching consequences on children's education, such as dropouts and learning losses, despite climate mitigation efforts by different governing bodies. These global patterns of educational disruption represent systematic violations of children's educational rights as guaranteed under Article 28 of the UNCRC. This obligates States Parties to make primary education compulsory and freely available to all. Article 29 states that education shall be directed to developing the child's personality, talents, and mental and physical abilities to their fullest potential. These objectives are compromised when climate hazards disrupt learning environments and processes.

Heat-related adverse impacts on learning outcomes have not received much attention since they usually do not have direct effects. It may appear insignificant when looking at changes in average temperatures over time. However, those small, cumulative educational losses could have far-reaching social and economic impacts, especially for tropical areas such as Brazil. Therefore, they advocated for the inclusion of education in the climate policy agenda. Wang et al. (2020) argue that countries like Canada, the United States, France, England, and Germany, among others, have focused on improving all areas of the classroom climate as part of educational reform initiatives aimed at promoting quality education and the academic and psychological well-being of children. This disparity in climate adaptation investments between Global North and Global South countries exemplifies climate injustice, wherein distributive inequities in resources and infrastructure compound children's differential exposure to climate hazards, with children in the least responsible countries bearing the most significant burdens.

A report by the International Data Alliance for Children on the Move (IDAC, 2024) revealed that the latest statistics record about 4.4 million children were internally displaced due to disasters which include climate related disasters. Common disasters mentioned include record-breaking heatwaves, wildfires, drought, and flooding. The quality of education of these child migrants is severely affected as higher out-of-school rates usually extend for several months. On the other hand, some children are immobile and may be unable to migrate from the climate-high-risk areas in which they are settled. They will have to deal with absenteeism due to injuries sustained by teachers, parents, or themselves. Either way, different climate-related natural disasters negatively affect the education of both immobile and displaced children, creating cascading vulnerabilities that affect children's rights to education, protection, and family unity.

At the 28th Conference of the Parties to the United Nations Framework Convention on Climate Change (COP28), UNICEF made a clarion call to include children in the Global Stocktake (GST) and the Global Goal for Adaptation (GGA), particularly when talking about climate change (UNICEF, 2023a). Similarly, COP29 emphasised the importance of prioritising children in finding solutions to climate change, and immediate action must be taken (Chibvuma, 2024). However, voluntary carbon reduction commitments made after the Paris Agreement remain relatively weak and insufficient in avoiding climate change (Sanson & Burke, 2020). This leaves children vulnerable to the negative impacts of climate change, affecting their learning outcomes. Rousell and Cutter-Mackenzie-Knowles (2019) argue that many studies have indicated that children's understanding of climate change is generally limited, erroneous, and influenced by mass media. The UNCRC states that children have the right to participate in decision-making processes relevant to their lives (UN General Assembly, 1989), a principle enshrined in Articles 12 and 13 of the UNCRC, which guarantee children's right to express their views freely in all matters affecting them and to seek, receive, and impart information. Hence, there is a need to bring children on board regarding the impacts of climate change on their lives.

11.3.2 Regional Perspectives on Climate and Education in Africa

In 2022, CARE International investigated the relationship between education and climate change, focusing on Malawi, Mali, Somalia, and Zimbabwe. Their findings made them realise that the term 'climate change' does not fully capture the severity of the issues at hand but that 'climate crisis' and 'climate emergency' are rather more suitable. They highlighted education as a key factor, making some groups more vulnerable than others. CARE has been involved in capacity building for the less privileged to help them adapt to the changing climate through training, sustainable energy solutions, grant programmes, and many more initiatives. The progress is constantly reviewed through their monitoring and evaluation frameworks, which involve data collection for evidence-based decision-making (CARE, 2022). This recognition of climate change as a 'crisis' and 'emergency' reflects the urgency with which children's rights violations through climate impacts must be addressed, especially given that the Intergovernmental Panel on Climate Change (IPCC) indicates that the world has less than 10 years to make necessary transformations.

UNICEF (2023a) examined children's vulnerability to climate and environmental hazards and presented case studies of African responses. Common hazards include heatwaves, riverine floods, coastal floods, vector-borne diseases, water scarcity, tropical cyclones, and air, soil, and water pollution. UNICEF developed the landmark Children's Climate Risk Index (CCRI) in 2021 and extended it in 2023 to include water scarcity (UNICEF, 2023a), during which it popularised the term 'The Climate-Changed Child'. The CCRI was adopted from the Intergovernmental Panel on Climate Change's Framework for Climate Change Risk of 2014. The major dimensions include sensitivity ('immediate impact of hazard'), adaptive capacity ('ability to respond in the longer term'), and exposure to climate hazards. The major components of adaptive capacity to climate change for children are access to water, sanitation and hygiene (WASH); education; health and nutrition; and social protection. It also looked at different case studies for climate change across Africa. For example, in Zimbabwe, sustainable energy solutions, like solar energy, have been implemented by UNICEF and the Ministry of Health and Child Care in different health facilities in rural areas. This review shows that international and regional studies are funded by international organisations such as UNICEF and often incorporate a mixed-method approach. However, more localised research is required.

11.3.3 Local Context: Climate Change Impacts on Education in Zimbabwe

Rema and Paulina (2016) claim that developing countries will experience a disproportional rise in warm days, that is, days above 30 °C, and this is projected to increase in the tropics. Temperature records for Zimbabwe have been increasing by

0.1 °C each decade and are also predicted to increase by 2.5 °C by 2050 (Manjengwa et al., 2014). In Zimbabwe, rural areas, particularly those in semi-arid regions such as Lupane District, are more vulnerable to climate-related events such as droughts, floods, and heatwaves (Mugabe et al., 2018). These natural, inevitable distractions affecting learners in rural settings exacerbate the already-present inequalities and inequities in accessing quality education, a fundamental human right guaranteed under Article 28 of the UNCRC and Article 11 of the ACRWC (Ministry of Primary and Secondary Education, 2020). This pattern of compounded vulnerabilities demonstrates how climate impacts systematically undermine children's rights through multiple pathways, with rural location, poverty, and inadequate infrastructure creating overlapping disadvantages that disproportionately affect the most vulnerable children.

Most recently, Chikoko and Chihiya (2023) have investigated climate-change-induced vulnerabilities among rural children. They applied a qualitative research approach, with Ward 14 of Bikita District of Masvingo Province in Zimbabwe as the case study. The major climate-related disasters include droughts, floods, and heatwaves. Beyond diminished academic performance and school attendance, there have been reported cases of climate-change-related diseases (e.g., malaria), child labour and abuse, gold panning, food insecurity and hunger, early or forced marriages, child prostitution and sexual exploitation, and drug abuse, among others. The study by Chigumira et al. (2022) investigated the impact of climate change on education in Zimbabwe. Droughts, floods, and heatwaves are disrupting the education sector in Zimbabwe. Ndlovu and Chigumira (2023) took a gendered approach when they explored how climate-change-related events such as droughts, heatwaves, and floods disproportionately affect rural education in Zimbabwe, especially for girls. Both studies recommended climate-resilient infrastructure and climate-sensitive curricula in Zimbabwean schools, with Ndlovu and Chigumira (2023) emphasising more targeted support for girls, especially those from rural areas.

Climate change is a well-known phenomenon affecting all life sectors, including education. However, more can be said about heatwaves, which have become more frequent and intense in recent years. There is a need to investigate how rising temperatures affect education in more localised settings, especially in already vulnerable rural areas in semi-arid regions, preferably incorporating a mixed-method approach. Noticing the adverse impacts of climate change in Zimbabwe, the Government of Zimbabwe (2017) introduced the National Climate Policy. It included plans of climate-related adaptive and mitigation measures, such as building climate-resilient schools. Climate education has also been integrated into all educational curricula. However, funding shortages and limited technical capacity remain major drawbacks to implementing climate-resilient strategies (Chisadza et al., 2024). These implementation gaps between comprehensive policy frameworks and actual child protection on the ground reveal critical disconnections between Zimbabwe's legal commitments to children's rights and the lived realities of climate-vulnerable children, especially in rural and indigenous communities (see Moyo et al., Chap. 4, in this volume).

11.3.4 The Role of Stakeholders in Climate-Change Mitigation and Adaptation

Governments and non-governmental organisations (NGOs) must take the lead in addressing issues associated with climate change, primarily through capacity building. Some countries in sub-Saharan Africa have already engaged in low-cost interventions, such as tree planting to increase shade, creating vents for air flow in schools, painting roofs white, and using bamboo for insulation. All these efforts aim to improve children's learning environment to ensure a conducive space for effective learning. One notable example is the United Nations Children's Emergency Fund's (UNICEF's) Safe Schools Initiative, which shows that international collaboration is key to fostering climate resilience in educational systems (UNICEF, 2021b). Governing bodies should also consider social safety nets such as school feeding programmes and conditional cash transfers for disadvantaged children. These interventions position comprehensive social protection as essential for addressing structural inequalities that compound children's climate vulnerabilities.

On the other hand, school administrators and teachers should coordinate tree planting for shade and stagger their learning schedules and timetables during peak hours when it is hottest. These simple interventions go a long way in improving students' learning environment and well-being. Community engagement is pertinent in developing sustainable, culture-sensitive programmes, giving the natives a sense of ownership of the projects. Successful community-based programmes include community-managed school gardens, alternative livelihood training, and rainwater harvesting (Kibuka & Svodziwa, 2020). These community-based adaptation strategies emphasise the importance of acknowledging local knowledge systems, respecting community autonomy in adaptation decisions, and ensuring that marginalised voices, including children's, meaningfully shape climate responses. While numerous studies across the globe have dabbed a bit on the impacts of climate change on education, remote areas such as Lupane have been neglected. Furthermore, the intersection of climate change, children's rights, and education remains a grey area in Zimbabwe's academic literature. Henceforth, the purpose of this study is to fill these gaps.

11.4 Findings

Results are presented in this section based on data analysis from questionnaires, observations, and interviews. They are organised thematically to demonstrate how climate-induced temperature increases systematically violate children's rights to education, health, and development as guaranteed under international and regional children's rights frameworks.

11.4.1 Impacts of High Temperatures in Lupane District

Six schools participated in this study. Figure 11.2 shows the results of the participation from each of these schools.

Figure 11.2 shows schools that participated in the study. The results show that Mpofu Primary School had the highest % response rate of 30%, followed by Nono and Lupaka Primary Schools, which had 20% each. Somgolo, Makeke, and Punyaka Primary Schools had 10% each. Figure 11.3, which follows, shows the temperature changes noted over the past years.

Figure 11.3 shows that the majority (80%) agree that notable temperature changes have been observed in classrooms in the district. Only 20% disagree that notable temperature changes have been noted in the district. This overwhelming recognition of temperature changes by school community members confirms the climate trajectory wherein Zimbabwe's national mean surface temperature has increased by about 0.90°C from 1900 to 2018, with the greatest warming occurring in western and southern sections of the country, including Matabeleland North Province, where Lupane is located (Chipenda and Ndhlovu, Introduction in this volume). Figure 11.4 shows how often learners felt discomfort due to heat or cold during their school lessons.

Figure 11.4 shows how respondents feel discomfort during lessons while at school. The figure reveals that most of the respondents (90%) experience discomfort from temperature changes. Ten per cent sometimes experience temperature discomfort during lessons. This pervasive thermal discomfort represents a violation of Article 3 of the UNCRC, which requires that institutions, services, and facilities responsible for the care or protection of children conform with standards established by competent authorities regarding safety, health, and the suitability of their staff. When 90% of learners experience thermal discomfort during lessons, schools

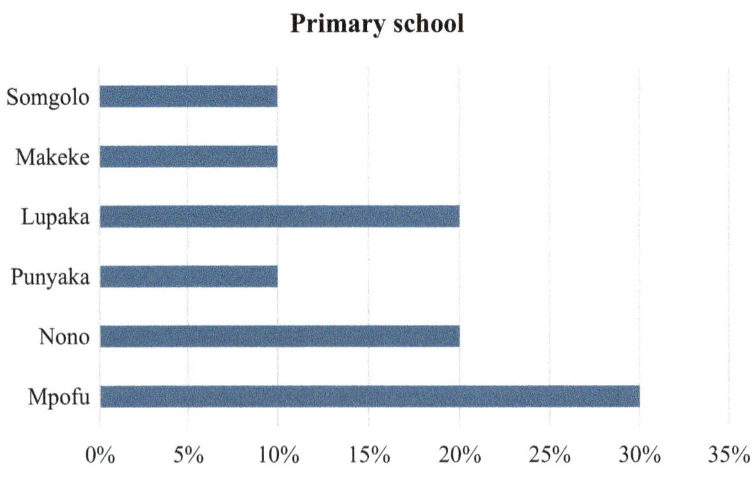

Fig. 11.2 Schools sampled during the study (Source: Research survey)

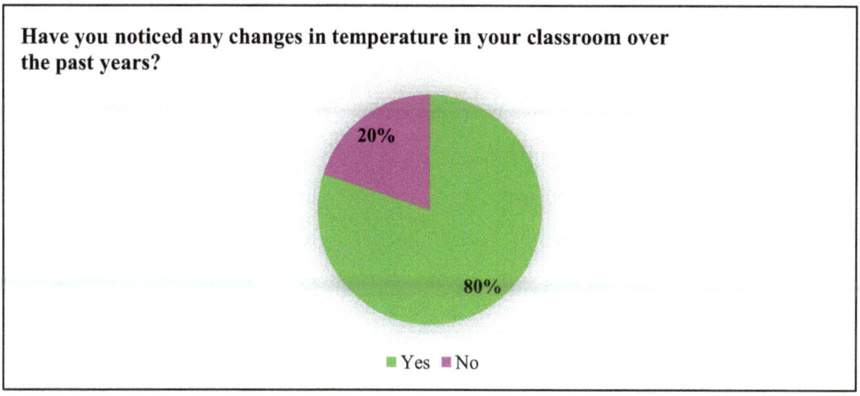

Fig. 11.3 Temperature changes noticed over the past years

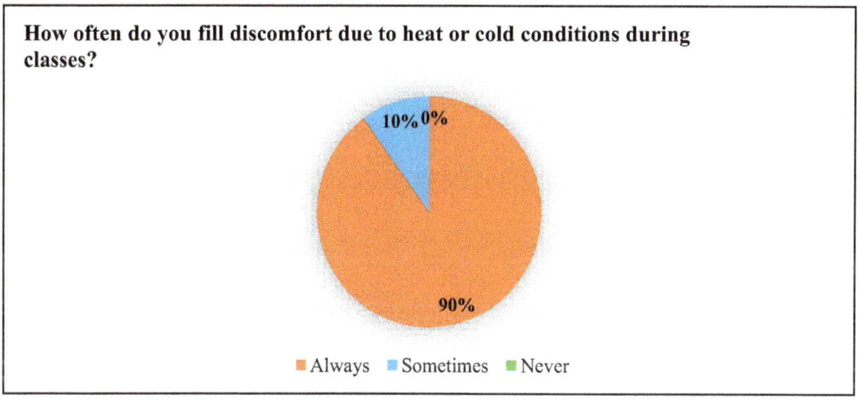

Fig. 11.4 Discomfort during lessons as perceived by respondents (Source: Research survey)

fail to meet the safety and health standards necessary to protect children's well-being and enable effective learning. Figure 11.5 shows the results on how respondents view heatwave episodes in their respective places. Respondents gave their views on duration of heat waves in their respective places.

The results in Fig. 11.5 show that most of the respondents (60%) agree that heatwaves last for more than 4 weeks. Twenty per cent (20%) of the respondents say heatwaves have been noted to last for 3–4 weeks and 1–2 weeks in a row. The extended duration of heatwaves, with 60% of reporting periods exceeding 4 weeks, aligns with projections that Zimbabwe will experience increased frequency and intensity of extreme weather events, including heatwaves. Future projections point towards an increase in heatwaves with dire consequences for human health, especially among children and the elderly. Figure 11.6 below shows whether school buildings were designed to cope with extreme weather events, especially heat.

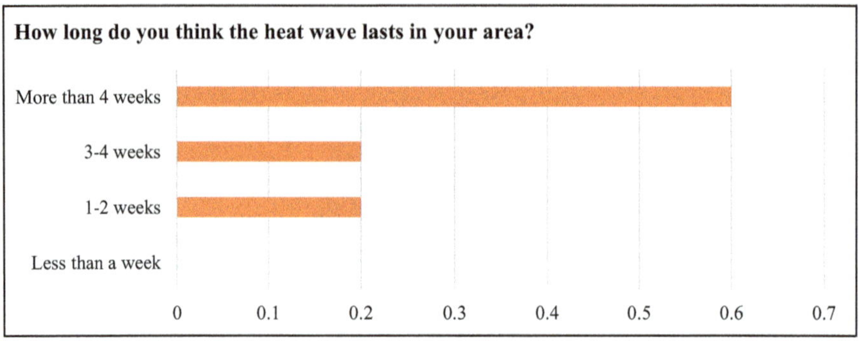

Fig. 11.5 Duration of heatwaves in the study area (Source: Research survey)

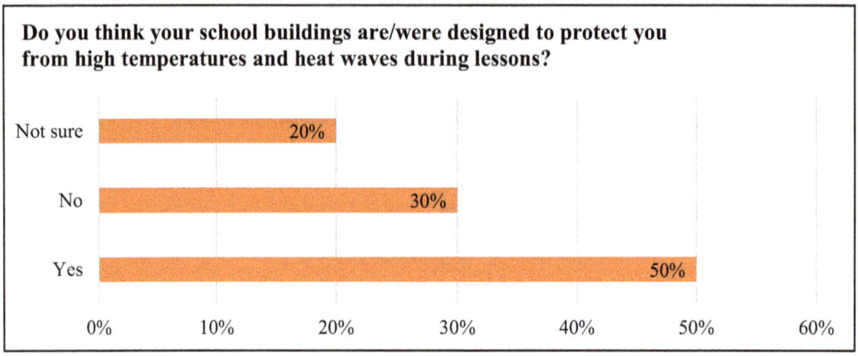

Fig. 11.6 Building structures designed to cope with high temperatures (Source: Research survey)

Most respondents (50%) in Fig. 11.6 reported that buildings were designed to cope with extreme weather events. Thirty per cent of the respondents said the buildings were not designed to deal with extreme weather. Only 20% were not sure of the significance of the building design in mitigating extreme weather events. The fact that only 50% perceive the buildings as adequately designed for extreme temperatures, with 30% explicitly stating an inadequate design, reveals infrastructural deficits. This violates Article 24 of the UNCRC, which recognises children's right to the highest attainable standard of health and requires States to take appropriate measures to combat disease and malnutrition, taking into consideration the dangers and risks of environmental pollution, which by extension must include climate-induced heat stress, which affects children's health and learning capacity.

11.4.2 Observed Temperature Effects and Infrastructure Designs in the Study Area

The state of school buildings in the selected schools was also observed and captured. Several observations were made during fieldwork. The fieldwork did not cover the whole district. Only selected parts were examined to provide a snapshot of the effects of extreme heatwaves on learners. One observation was that most learners travel long distances to and from school. This negatively affects their concentration during lessons since some of them were observed to arrive at school way after the official start of the day. During a visit to one school, it was observed that some learners felt sleepy or tired due to high temperatures. It was also noted that, in most cases, learners needed to endure temperatures above 40°C on most days. This was an observation made from smartphone temperature recordings. These findings document how climate-induced heat stress creates barriers to accessing quality education, violating Article 28(1)(a) of the UNCRC, which guarantees the right to primary education based on equal opportunity. When excessive heat forces late arrivals, induces fatigue, and impairs concentration, children from climate-vulnerable rural areas experience systematic disadvantage compared to peers in better-resourced settings with climate-controlled learning environments.

Plate 11.1 shows the type of school classrooms common in Lupane District.

Observations made during a school visit at a rural primary school reveal that all the classrooms were constructed using bricks, with asbestos roofing and concrete floors. All the classrooms had no air-conditioning but relied on ventilation through windows and doors. Plate 11.2 shows two different classrooms with different types of windows, as observed during the field visit.

Plate 11.1 Primary school classroom (Source: Research observation)

Plate 11.2 Two classrooms at the same school with different types of windows (Source: Field observation)

Another observation is that the classrooms have different types of windows, indicating that school buildings might have been built without following a specific standard requirement. This implies that these classes receive different lighting from the sun and have different ventilation capacities. According to the Model-Building By-laws of 1977 of Zimbabwe, public buildings such as classrooms must have adequate natural lighting and ventilation through windows. Natural or mechanical ventilation should be in place to allow free air circulation in these classrooms, especially to remove the excess heat being absorbed by brick walls and asbestos roofing. The absence of standardised building designs that account for climate considerations reflects implementation gaps between Zimbabwe's comprehensive policy frameworks and actual child protection on the ground in some schools in Lupane. Despite some clear policies and legislation that deal with climate change issues, there is a lack of policies which refer specifically to children's concerns and translate policy commitments into tangible protections.

The researchers also observed that some classrooms at some schools have asbestos or metal sheets for roofing material (Plate 11.3).

Plate 11.3 Asbestos and Metal sheet roofing materials on classrooms

These photos show that the roofing material used in school buildings at rural primary schools is asbestos and metal sheets (IBR), which are perfect heat absorbers. This creates an 'oven' condition within these classrooms, rendering them unconducive to effective learning. In addition, these classrooms lack a ceiling, which can help insulate the building from direct heat from the sun. This is why most survey respondents mentioned feeling uncomfortable in class due to high temperatures. These 'oven conditions' documented in Lupane schools exemplify the educational impacts of rising temperatures, wherein temperature increases in western and southern sections of Zimbabwe, including Matabeleland North Province, create environments where learners face new challenges that hinder effective learning and development. It was also observed that almost all the schools visited did not have air-conditioning facilities.

The last observation was that access to adequate water was a big challenge in most parts of the district. Water is vital, yet some learners travel long distances to and from school without water points. Water scarcity compounds climate vulnerabilities and violates Article 24(2)(c) of the UNCRC, which requires States to combat disease and malnutrition by providing adequate nutritious food and clean drinking water. In the climate change context, this must encompass heat-induced dehydration risks that threaten children's health and learning capacity.

11.4.3 How Children Are Affected by Increasing Temperatures at School

Figure 11.7 shows how temperature affects learners' ability to concentrate during lessons.

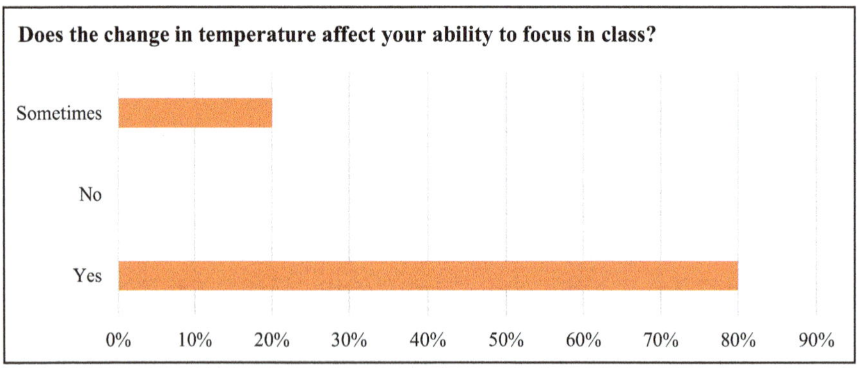

Fig. 11.7 How temperature change affects learners' ability to concentrate during lessons (Source: Research survey)

Most respondents (80%) agree that high temperatures affect learners' participation and concentration during lessons. Only 20% of the respondents say that, sometimes, the high temperatures affect learners' concentration during learning. This concentration impairment directly violates Article 29(1) of the UNCRC, which states that education shall develop the child's personality, talents, and mental and physical abilities to their fullest potential. When climate-induced heat stress systematically impairs children's cognitive functioning and concentration, it becomes impossible for education to fulfil its mandate of developing children's abilities to their fullest potential, thereby denying children their right to quality education. Figure 11.8 shows results on notable changes in the attendance of learners due to climate-change-induced temperatures.

Most respondents (80%) say attendance has been affected negatively by climate-change-induced excessive heat, while 20% have not noted changes in school attendance and participation due to high temperatures. This negative impact on school attendance violates Article 28(1)(e) of the UNCRC, which requires States Parties to encourage regular school attendance and reduce dropout rates. When climate-induced heat systematically undermines attendance, States fail to meet their obligations to ensure children's regular access to education.

Figure 11.9 shows how high temperatures are linked to participation in sporting activities and other outdoor school activities in the district.

Most respondents (70%) said heat affects sporting and other outdoor activities at school, while 30% say heat stress sometimes affects the district's sporting and outdoor activities. This was also confirmed by interview responses, which stated:

> Our schools do not have indoor sporting facilities to accommodate learners and encourage them to participate in year-round sporting activities. We rely on the school grounds and a few trees around the grounds. During the first term, we carry out athletics activities, and in the second term, we play ball games in these grounds, but training time is reduced due to the scorching heat. This place is hot, and the temperatures continue to increase. We try to avoid exposing our children to the sun for a long time by shortening practice time and frequency (Interviewee 1).

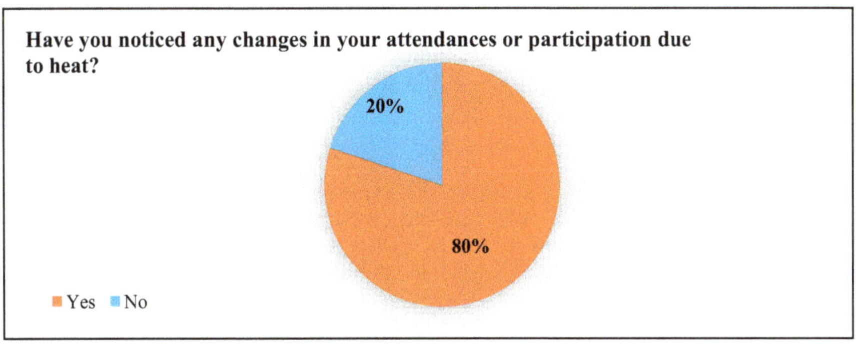

Fig. 11.8 Impact of excessive heat on school attendance (Source: Research survey)

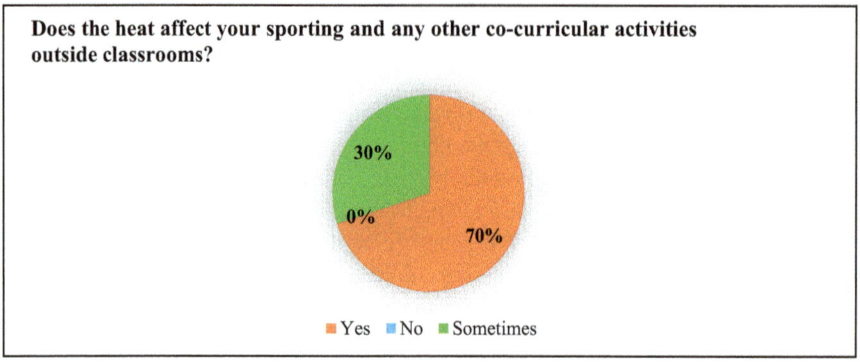

Fig. 11.9 Impact of heat on sporting and outdoor activities in Lupane District (Source: Research survey)

The comment from the key informant reveals that sporting activities are affected by high temperatures. Therefore, performance in sporting tournaments is usually poor. This was confirmed by another interviewee, who commented:

> We usually face challenges when we compete in sporting activities with schools from areas with better facilities, which are conducive to more training and practice for different sporting disciplines. We are also worried that some learners who are more gifted in sports than academics are affected negatively by the absence of a conducive sporting environment. The lack of conducive sporting facilities for all weathers makes them lag or miss out on their career opportunities. (Interviewee 2)

These testimonies reveal how climate impacts create systematic disadvantages for rural children, violating Article 31 of the UNCRC, which recognises the right of the child to rest and leisure and to engage in play and recreational activities appropriate to the child's age. When excessive heat restricts outdoor activities and sporting opportunities, children in climate-vulnerable areas are denied their right to physical development and recreation, compounding educational inequalities.

Plate 11.4, taken during field observation, shows that agricultural fields where learners do practicals rely on shading from trees.

It was also observed that most of these gardens are dry and seem abandoned due to increasing temperature and water scarcity, which is affecting children's learning, especially for practical subjects that require hands-on experience. The scorching sun and the lack of shade contribute to the adverse impacts of climate change on learning outcomes. An interviewee also confirmed the lack of a conducive learning environment for practical subjects, stating:

> Most schools in rural areas do not have proper shade for practical subjects such as agriculture and building. Learners and their facilitators must use three shades, which may be impossible, especially in agricultural activities where they must dig and prepare gardens during practical sessions according to the timetable slots. The Zimbabwean curriculum states that Agriculture is a compulsory subject in primary schools, so learners need to have the necessary theory and practical skills to pass. One of the challenges they face is that the heat waves and sometimes heavy storms disrupt learning processes, affecting their performance (Interviewee 4).

Plate 11.4 Agriculture field at a rural primary school

These observations demonstrate how climate-induced heat stress compromises theoretical learning and practical skill development essential for rural children's livelihoods. This undermines Article 28(1) of the UNCRC, which mandates the development of different forms of secondary education, including vocational education, and Article 29(1)(a), which requires education to be directed to the development of the child's personality, talents, and mental and physical abilities to their fullest potential. These objectives are systematically compromised when climate conditions render practical learning impossible.

11.4.4 Strategies to Reduce the Impacts of Increasing Temperatures on Primary School Learners at School

Respondents of the open-ended questions were given strategies to mitigate high heat and adapt to the ever-increasing temperatures in the district. These were also linked to the interview questions and observations made during fieldwork. These results are shown in Table 11.1, which follows.

Table 11.1 indicates that the most common response is encouraging learners to drink lots of water during the day or on their way to or from school. The least popular strategy highlighted was using an air-conditioning system in classrooms to cool the environment. These coping strategies, while demonstrating community agency and adaptation, remain inadequate responses to systematic violations of children's rights. The reliance on individual behavioural adjustments rather than structural infrastructural interventions reflects the broader pattern wherein climate adaptation burdens fall disproportionately on the most vulnerable populations. States can be seen failing to fulfil their obligations under Articles 3 and 24 of the UNCRC in ensuring that child-serving institutions meet adequate safety and health standards.

Table 11.1 Strategies to deal with high school temperatures to promote learning

Rank	Response
1	Encouraging learners to drink lots of water
2	Opening windows for ventilation
3	Encouraging learners to walk when temperatures are low
4	Sitting under trees in the shed when it is very hot
5	Minimising exposure to sunlight when it is very hot
6	Air conditioning

(Source: Research survey)

11.5 Discussion

The results of the study confirm that many more people live in contexts that are highly vulnerable to climate-change-related extreme events, such as heatwaves and associated high temperatures (IPCC, 2023). This is supported by responses from the majority (80%), who agreed that notable temperature changes have been observed in classrooms in Lupane District. Along this line of observation, Chisadza, et al. (2024) noted that severe droughts have been recorded in Lupane District in 1991, 1992, 1994, 1995, 2005, 2016, and 2017. The 2024–2025 season has also recorded one of the worst drought periods for the district and the country over the years. Thus, all drought indices indicated the dominance of extreme temperature conditions in Lupane and other parts of Western Zimbabwe (Mupepi, 2022). These drought conditions are associated with high temperatures, which affect the learning process in schools for primary school learners.

Most respondents (90%) from this study revealed that learners experience discomfort from high temperatures in Lupane District. This means that the child's best interests are lost when education cannot be received in comfort (Bekink, 2024). In this case, children are vulnerable to the effects of climate change, like heatwaves, which affect access to education, representing systematic failures to uphold the best interest principle enshrined in Article 3 of the UNCRC, which requires that in all actions concerning children, their best interests shall be the primary consideration. More respondents (60%) agree that heatwaves last for more than 4 weeks in a row. This is confirmed by several studies that show that global warming has become a reality in our lifetime (UNICEF, 2023b; Cuevas-Parra, 2020; Sanz-Caballero, 2013). Thus, we conclude that heatwaves negatively affect children's education since high temperatures reduce students' concentration during school activities.

Only 50% of the respondents in Fig. 11.6 said buildings were designed to cope with extreme weather events. This lack of proper school infrastructure, such as unequal investment in school air conditioning, which may reduce high temperature exposure during lessons, threatens children's physical and mental health (Ahdoot et al., 2024). Thus, it can be said that building designs in rural areas, such as the greater parts of Lupane, have not been designed with extreme and changing temperatures in view. This infrastructural deficit reflects broader climate injustice patterns wherein rural children in semi-arid regions, despite contributing minimally to greenhouse gas emissions, bear disproportionate climate burdens. The disparity between climate-controlled urban schools and inadequately ventilated rural classrooms creates systematic educational disadvantages that violate the equal opportunity principle embedded in Article 28 of the UNCRC.

Many respondents (80%) agree that high temperatures affect learners' participation and concentration during lessons. This is also confirmed by Ahdoot et al. (2024), who said that children's physical and mental health are threatened by climate change because of the increase in temperatures. So one can strongly argue that children in Lupane District are vulnerable to worsening temperature changes due to climate change. Their concentration and performance in school are thus affected negatively. Results reveal that most respondents (80%) agreed that attendance has been affected negatively due to climate-change-induced excessive heat. Such a conclusion is supported by varying evidence and literature on the effects of climate change on children (Proulx et al., 2024; UNICEF, 2024; da Cunha Bustamante, 2024). Children will not attend school due to several effects of high temperatures on other aspects of their lives, such as increased risk of diseases, food insecurity, and family disturbances (Smith et al., 2023). These cascading impacts demonstrate how climate change creates interconnected vulnerabilities that simultaneously affect multiple dimensions of children's rights. These include the right to health (Article 24 UNCRC), the right to education (Article 28 UNCRC), the right to an adequate standard of living (Article 27 UNCRC), and the right to development (Article 6 UNCRC), revealing the systemic nature of climate-induced violations of rights.

Coming up with climate change adaptation strategies is the current cry for most policymakers. However, in most countries in the Global South, severe restrictions and challenges impede proper adaptation and mitigation strategies. Engaging and empowering children has been noted to be a solution for reducing risks, ensuring safety, and promoting an environment for children to learn sustainably (Plan International, 2019). Thus, we conclude that it is vital to empower children in Lupane with knowledge on climate change, especially on severe warming. Hence, strategies such as encouraging children to stay hydrated, opening windows for ventilation, and minimising exposure to the sun have been realised. However, while considered valuable as immediate coping mechanisms, these strategies fail to address the structural dimensions of climate injustice. The proper fulfilment of children's rights requires not merely individual behavioural adaptations but systemic transformations in infrastructure, resource allocation, and policy implementation that position children's rights at the centre of climate action (see Chipenda & Ndhlovu, Chap. 15, in this volume).

One observation noted during the study was that most learners travel long distances to and from school. This negatively affects their concentration during lessons since some were noted arriving at school late. This means children are more vulnerable since they have to go to school daily during the school term, yet little is known about the effects of the distance they walk to school and the heat exposure associated with such educational needs (Weeda et al., 2024). Learners were observed to be feeling sleepy or tired due to high temperatures. This means their health is affected as a result of the temperature rise. Hence, the strongest effect of climate change on children has been pointed out to be temperatures becoming higher due to global warming (Weeda et al., 2024). These observations highlight how rural settlement patterns and inadequate school distribution compound climate vulnerabilities, creating multiple layers of disadvantages for rural children. The combination of long walking distances under extreme heat, inadequate water access along routes, and late arrivals affecting learning represents intersecting violations of children's rights to health, education, and development, demonstrating the need for integrated, multi-sectoral responses that address both climate adaptation and spatial inequalities in access to education.

11.6 Conclusion

Climate change has multidimensional impacts, ranging from physical to social to psychological. This chapter has demonstrated that rising temperatures in Lupane District systematically violate multiple children's rights as enshrined in the UNCRC and ACRWC. Therefore, a countering multi-stakeholder approach, including relevant policies, climate-resilient infrastructure, and community engagement, is pertinent. The findings from this study are foundational in the broader understanding of how climate change disrupts child education, particularly in rural arid settings. Empirical evidence from Lupane's six primary schools reveals that climate-induced educational disruptions constitute not merely developmental challenges but also systematic violations of children's rights, demanding urgent policy responses that recognise children as rights holders rather than passive beneficiaries of climate action. There is an urgent need for further research and for adaptive and mitigation interventions to ensure that our children learn in a safe and conducive environment. Understanding the context-specific challenges child learners face in these extreme climate events can build a more climate-smart and equitable education system for a sustainable future. Addressing climate impacts on children's education in Lupane and similar semi-arid regions requires transformative approaches that tackle structural inequalities, ensure adequate resource allocation to vulnerable communities, and position children's rights and voices at the centre of climate adaptation strategies. These are principles that align with the broader climate justice framework.

11.7 Recommendations

Based on the findings documenting systematic violations of children's educational rights due to climate-induced heat stress, the following recommendations are proposed to advance climate adaptation and the fulfilment of children's rights in Lupane District and similar contexts.

New infrastructure designs for primary school students must be high-temperature proofing. In this regard, air-conditioning facilities must be constructed for any new classroom blocks to ensure students learn in conducive environments with controlled temperatures. Alternative low-cost cooling technologies, such as improved natural ventilation systems, thermal insulation, reflective roofing materials, and strategic building orientations, should be prioritised when air conditioning is economically unfeasible. This will ensure that all children, regardless of geographic location or economic status, have access to thermally comfortable learning environments as required under Article 3 of the UNCRC.

Next, policymakers must ensure that timetables for learners in arid areas take note of very high temperatures. In this regard, some learners may be given more time to walk to school and back home. School schedules should be restructured to avoid peak heat hours—with early morning classes and afternoon breaks during the hottest periods—while ensuring such adaptations do not reduce total learning time or compromise curriculum delivery, protecting children's immediate health needs and long-term right to quality education.

Rural planners must recognise the need to promote clustered settlements to ensure schools are built near learners, rather than maintaining scattered settlements, which may lead some children to travel over 5 kilometres to or from school daily. This spatial planning intervention addresses both climate vulnerability and educational access, recognising that reducing exposure to heat stress during long walks is essential for protecting children's rights to health and education. Such planning must incorporate children's participation in decision-making processes as guaranteed under Article 12 of the UNCRC, ensuring their voices shape community development initiatives that directly affect their lives.

Safe drinking water points must be available for learners along the way to school. This enables them to access water when temperatures are very high. The adage 'water is life' makes much sense in this warming environment, where learners must always have access to adequate, clean water. Beyond the provision of water points along routes, it must be ensured that schools themselves have continuous access to safe drinking water throughout the day, with adequate storage and distribution systems that account for increased water needs during heatwaves. This infrastructure development is essential for fulfilling Article 24(2)(c) of the UNCRC, which requires States to combat disease and malnutrition through the provision of clean drinking water, which is particularly critical in the climate change context, where heat stress increases children's hydration needs and vulnerability to waterborne diseases.

Finally, Zimbabwe's government must allocate adequate climate funding that specifically targets the protection of children's rights in climate-vulnerable districts like Lupane, addressing the current gap wherein only 2.4% of global climate finance supports projects that reduce the effects of climate change on children. This financing should support comprehensive interventions, including infrastructure upgrades, teacher training on climate-responsive pedagogy, climate-smart curriculum development, early warning systems for extreme heat events, and monitoring mechanisms to track climate impacts on educational outcomes. Such investments are essential to fulfilling State obligations under both the UNCRC and ACRWC, ensuring the protection of children's rights to education, health, and development in the face of accelerating climate change while advancing the climate justice imperative that children who bear minimal responsibility for greenhouse gas emissions should not bear the disproportionate burdens of climate impacts.

References

Ahdoot, S., Baum, C. R., Cataletto, M. B., Hogan, P., Wu, C. B., & Beinstein, A. (2024). Climate change and children's health: Building a healthy future for every child. *American Academy of Paediatrics, Council on Environmental Health and Climate change, Council on children and disasters, Paediatrics, 153*(3).

Bekink, M. (2024). *The fundamental right of children to participate in climate change decision-making processes: A South African perspective.* PER/PELJ (27).

CARE. (2022). *Education & climate change: Findings from Malawi.* CARE.

Chibvuma, P. (2024). *COP29: Young people in Zimbabwe call for climate action NOW.* UNICEF Zimbabwe Blog.

Chigumira, E., Ndlovu, M., & Svodziwa, M. (2022). Climate change and its impact on education in Zimbabwe. *Journal of African Environmental Studies, 15*(3), 45–60.

Chikoko, W., & Chihiya, P. (2023). Climate change and vulnerabilities of children in rural Zimbabwe: The case of Ward 14, Bikita District, Zimbabwe. *African Journal of Social Work, 13*(2), 787–786.

Chisadza, B., Gwate, T., & Musinguzi, M. (2024). Drought impacts in rural Zimbabwe: A case study of Lupane District. *African Journal of Climate Studies, 12*(1), 22–39.

Cuevas-Parra, P. (2020). *Talk less and act more; the world needs help.* World Vision International.

Currie, J., & Deschenes, O. (2016). Children and climate change: Introducing the issue. In *The future of children*. Princeton-Brookings.

Da Cunha Bustamante, M. M. (2024). Climate change and children's health: A resilience challenge for Brazil. *Journal of Pediatria.*

Government of Zimbabwe. (2017). *National Climate Policy*. Ministry of Environment, Water, and Climate.

Hsiang, S., Kopp, R., & Jina, A. (2017). Estimating economic and educational losses due to climate change. *Nature Climate Change, 7*(9), 620–626.

IDAC. (2024). Climate mobility and childhood: Examining the risks, closing the data and evidence gaps for children on the move, *September Issue*.

IPCC. (2023). Sixth Assessment Report: Working Group II: Impacts, Adaptation and Vulnerability, *Intergovernmental Panel on Climate Change.*

Kibuka, P., & Svodziwa, M. (2020). Water scarcity and its impact on rural schools. *Zimbabwe Journal of Development Studies, 10*(2), 34–48.

Manatsa, D. et al. (2020). *Revision of Zimbabwe's agro-ecological zones.* Harare.

Manjengwa, J., Matema, C., Mataruka, J., Tirivanhu, D., Tamanikwa, M., & Feresu, S. (2014). *Children and climate change in Zimbabwe.* Institute of Environmental Studies, University of Zimbabwe.

Marin, S.V., Schwarz, L., & Sabarwal, S. (2024). *The impact of climate change on education and what to do about it.*

Mengistu, T., Onyeneke, R., & Mupepi, M. (2020). Climate variability and its effects on education in arid and semi-arid regions. *Climate and Society, 6*(2), 100–113.

Ministry of Primary and Secondary Education. (2020). *Education Sector Plan 2020-2025.* Government of Zimbabwe.

Mugabe, F. T., Munodawafa, A., & Gumbo, B. (2018). Climate change and its impacts on education in Zimbabwe. *Journal of Sustainable Development, 11*(3), 1–12.

Mupepi, O. (2022). *Remote sensing drought indices and their application in mapping spatial and temporal variations of drought in Zimbabwe.* Journal of Remote Sensing and GIS.
Ndlovu, S., & Chigumira, M. (2023). The gendered impact of climate change on rural education. *Gender and Climate Journal, 5*(1), 12–25.
OCHA. (2018). *'Zimbabwe - Sub-national Administrative Boundaries Data'.* United Nations Office for the Coordination of Humanitarian Affairs. Available at: https://data.humdata.org/dataset/cod-ab-zwe?#. Accessed: 22 December 2022
Oppenheimer, M., & Anttila-Hughes, J.K. (2016). The science of climate change. In *The future of children.* Princeton-Brookings.
Pichhili, R. A. (2021). *Children's education rights in the face of climate change: Adequacy of the International Children's Rights Framework and the way forward* (Master of Laws). Leiden University.
Plan International. (2019). *Climate Change: Focus on Girls and Young Women.* Plan International.
Proulx, K. et al. (2024). *Climate change impacts child and adolescent health and well-being: A narrative review*, Journal of Global Health. 2024.
QGIS Development Team. (2024). *QGIS geographic information system (Version 3.34 'Prizren') [Software].* Open Source Geospatial Foundation. Retrieved from https://qgis.org
Rema, H., & Paulina, O. (2016). Implications for climate change for children in developing countries. *The Future of Children, 26*(1), 115–132.
Rousell, D., & Cutter-Mackenzie-Knowles, A. (2019). A systematic review of climate change education: Giving children and young people a 'choice' and a 'hand' in redressing climate change. *Children's Geographies, 18*(2), 191–208.
Sanson, A.V., & Burke, S.E. (2020). Climate change and children: An issue of intergenerational justice. *Children and peace: From research to action,* 342–362.
Sanz-Caballero, S. (2013). *Children's rights in a changing climate: A perspective from the United Nations Convention on the Rights of the Child.* 13 Ethics in Science and Environmental Politics.
Smith, D. J. et al. (2023). *Intervention studies to reduce the impact of climate change on health in rural communities in the United States: A systematic review.* Environmental Research Review.
Stott, P. (2016). How climate change affects extreme weather events. *Science, 352*(6293), 1517–1518.
UNICEF. (2021a). *The impact of climate change on children in Sub-Saharan Africa.* UNICEF. *352*(6293), 1517–1518.
UNICEF. (2021b). *One billion children are at 'extremely high risk' of the impacts of the climate crisis.*
UNICEF. (2023a). *The Climate Changed Child: A Children's Climate Risk Index supplement.* UNICEF.
UNICEF. (2023b). *Children displaced in a changing climate Preparing for a future that's already underway.* UNICEF.
UNICEF. (2024). *Climate change impact on child health: Perspectives from children and caregivers in Zimbabwe.* UNICEF.
UNICEF (2025) When the rains don't come: Climate change through the eyes of Zimbabwe's children. Available at: https://www.unicef.org/zimbabwe/stories/when-rains-dont-come-climate-change-through-eyes-zimbabwes-children
Wang, M., Degol, J. L., Amemiya, J., Parr, A., & Guo, J. (2020). Classroom climate and children's academic and psychological well-being: A systematic review and meta-analysis. *Developmental Review, 57*, 100912.
Weeda, J. Z. et al. (2024). *How climate change degrades child health: A systematic review and meta-analysis*, Science of the total environment, 920.
Zimbabwe National Statistical Agency (ZIMSTAT). (2024). *2022 Zimbabwe population and housing census: Gender thematic report.* ZIMSTAT.

Chapter 12
The Climate Change: Child Labour Nexus Among Peasant Households in Zimbabwe: Impact and Implications

Emmanuel Ndhlovu and Clement Chipenda

12.1 Introduction

Climate change has been observed to significantly influence child labour in agriculture, particularly in rural farming communities, such as Zimbabwe (International Labour Organization (ILO)-United Nations Children's Fund (UNICEF), 2025). The Intergovernmental Panel on Climate Change (IPCC, 2022) defines climate change as 'a change in the state of the climate that can be identified... by changes in the mean and/or the variability of its properties, and that persists for an extended period, typically decades or longer'. The IPCC warns of snowballing temperatures, altering rainfall patterns, and amplified occurrence of extreme weather events, such as floods and droughts, which have costly impacts, particularly for developing nations. It is projected that by 2050, climate impacts may displace about 216 million people worldwide, 85.7 million of whom will be in sub-Saharan Africa (SSA) (Ndhlovu, 2024a).

Extreme natural hazards, harsh weather conditions, crop failures, and rising food prices compel peasant households to turn to child labour as an additional means to cope with economic hardship and maintain livelihoods. This is particularly true in regions such as Zimbabwe, where agriculture is the primary source of livelihood for about 70% of the population (Ndhlovu, 2022). Peasants are 'small-scale family farmers who mainly depend on family labour and produce a significant share of their own food and may use their labour for off-farm activities and wage labour' (Moyo, 2016, p. 1).

E. Ndhlovu (✉)
College of Business and Economics, University of Johannesburg, Auckland Park, South Africa

C. Chipenda
South African Research Chair in Social Policy, College of Graduate Studies, University of South Africa, Pretoria, South Africa

E. Ndhlovu, C. Chipenda (eds.), *Climate Change and Children's Rights in Zimbabwe*, https://doi.org/10.1007/978-981-95-6005-9_12

The 2024 global estimates show that there are still 138 million children engaged in child labour, with SSA continuing to bear the highest burden (ILO-UNICEF, 2025). Driven by poverty, conflict, and climate-change-related disruptions, SSA has experienced the most significant increase in child labour in recent years (Ibrahim et al., 2025). According to the ILO (2017), climate change can reverse decades of progress without immediate intervention, further entrenching vulnerability (Montgomery, 2025). Several studies have noted that climate shocks are felt more by vulnerable farming communities (Chamma, 2024; Ngongolo & Gayo, 2025). When households lose their crops, livestock, income, or homes, children are often withdrawn from school and co-opted into work. In Zimbabwe, drought, floods, storms, and unreliable rainfall continue to reduce crop yields and lead to the loss of livestock, forcing children into unsafe work, including mineral panning and vending, to complement family income. This often disrupts their education and exposes them to numerous risks. However, studies exploring the intersection of climate change and child labour in Zimbabwe remain limited. Considering the agrarian nature of this country, with over 70% of the population engaging in farming as the main or additional source of livelihood and income, a study of this nature is vital (Ndhlovu, 2022). Although child labour is common in the country, it rarely attracts academic interest. This has generated knowledge and policy gaps.

Studies on climate impacts in Zimbabwe rarely focus on children. The focus is mainly on impacts on agricultural productivity, livelihoods, and human welfare and how they can be mitigated. For instance, recent studies, such as the research by Sithole et al. (2023), have conceptualised how climate impacts can be mitigated to attain sustainable development in Zimbabwe, but they have rarely touched on the impact on children. Chanza and Gundu-Jakarasi (2020) explored climate impacts and identified mitigation strategies for farmers but ignored children who mostly provide free labour in the form of herding livestock and guarding fields from wildlife, such as birds. Ndlovu et al. (2020) analysed the impacts of climatic change on traditional farming systems in Gwanda, Mangwe and Matobo districts. They recommended climate education and capital investment to allow smallholder farmers to change their traditional practices. They also highlighted the need for increased climate responsiveness and blending traditional farming knowledge with modern practices. These scholars also ignored the presence of children in Zimbabwe's agricultural sector. Madamombe et al. (2024) also investigated awareness and climate change coping strategies among smallholder farmers in Zimbabwe. However, nowhere do the scholars mention child labour as part of the coping strategies. Ndhlovu and Dube (2024) explored the role of contract farming as an adaptation strategy to climate change in Zimbabwe. However, despite its dominance in livestock herding in the region, they did not mention child labour. This inadequacy in literature has generated theoretical, empirical and knowledge gaps with practical and policy implications. This chapter seeks to contribute to minimising these gaps.

This chapter (i) theorises child labour and (ii) explores the key conduits through which climate change impacts child labour in Zimbabwe. Zimbabwe is already reeling in poverty. The country's socio-economic landscape is characterised by substantial challenges, including poverty, high unemployment, and income inequality, despite the country's potential for growth. Therefore, understanding the connection between child labour and climate change in a country facing these challenges is vital because climate impacts aggravate the conditions that lead to child exploitation, creating a brutal cycle of poverty, environmental degradation, and human rights abuses. Accordingly, understanding the link between climatic shocks and child labour is critical for providing evidence-based policy recommendations to the government, civil society, and non-governmental organisations (NGOs) working with children in the country. Therefore, while this chapter is targeted at academics and students, Zimbabwean policymakers, politicians, and donors will find it informative.

This chapter proceeds as follows: after the introduction, the following section reviews the literature related to the study, focusing on the conceptualisation of child labour and its state globally. This is followed by an outline of the research methodology used in the review. Thereafter, the findings are presented and discussed concurrently. Lastly, interventions are evaluated, leading to recommendations and conclusions.

12.2 Literature Review: Perspectives and State of Child Labour

The literature related to the study is presented under two subsections. The first subsection focuses on how child labour is conceptualised globally. The second subsection provides a regional overview of the state of child labour.

12.2.1 Child Labour: A Conceptualisation

Child labour is a multifaceted and complex concept that often takes on diverse forms in legislation and literature. The term generally denotes any work that disrupts children and robs them of their potential, childhood, and dignity and is damaging to their development, physically and mentally (ILO, 2014; Visser, 2021). It incorporates mental, physical or morally unsafe work that interferes with a child's education by thwarting school attendance, causing premature school exit, or requiring a blend of school and unduly long or strenuous work (Ahad et al., 2020).

The negative consequences of child labour may have long-term effects. At the micro level, child labour undermines the welfare of children within households (Radfar et al., 2018). At the macro level, it affects overall sustainable growth, particularly in developing countries. This is because human resources are critical for attaining economic development (Weldeyesus & Alemu, 2024). Child labour also buttresses intergenerational cycles of untrained labour and persistent poverty (Zewdie et al., 2024).

Reviewed literature generally opines that child labour and other forms of child abuse can be prevented through the adoption, implementation, and protection of children's rights (Momen, 2020). This requires improving access to education and mobilising public support to protect children's rights (ILO-UNICEF, 2025). In 2025, approximately 138 million children were entangled in child labour worldwide, with 54 million of them participating in hazardous work that endangered their health and development (ILO-UNICEF, 2025). Although the world vowed to end child labour by 2025, the current trajectory of progress is not enough to meet this target. Both developed and developing global regions are still struggling to eliminate child labour. Approximately 71% of child workers are employed in agriculture (FAO, 2020). Most of this child labour takes place as part of household subsistence and on smallholder farms.

12.2.2 Child Labour: A Regional Comparative Overview

In the European Union (EU), although the number of children providing child labour has declined by 94 million since 2000, progress has slowed significantly since 2018 (ILO-UNICEF, 2025). In this region, child labour has a complex problem with deep roots in socio-economic factors and informal economies. The problem is not the same across the region. For instance, Eastern Europe has a significantly higher prevalence of child labour than Western and Southern Europe (Bekik, 2024). The EU and its members have adopted a comprehensive legal framework to combat child labour, including international conventions, such as the United Nations Convention on the Rights of the Child and the International Labour Organization (ILO) Conventions 138 (on minimum age) and 182 (on the worst forms of child labour). The EU Charter of Fundamental Rights was also adopted to prohibit child labour in the region. In addition, the EU has also executed regulations and directives to fight forced and child labour in supply chains, barring the import and sale of products made with such labour (Goulart et al., 2024). Most EU countries have national laws that set a minimum age for employment and regulate working conditions for young people (Bekik, 2024). However, the success of these laws depends on enforcement and monitoring. The EU and its members are also dedicated to providing social protection to vulnerable families to prevent them from resorting to child labour (Goulart et al., 2024). While substantial progress has been observed in Europe, child labour challenges remain because of the difficulty of data collection, the informal nature of the work, and the persistent issue of poverty and social exclusion.

Despite notable progress in reducing child labour in the Americas, the region faces challenges in meeting the 2025 elimination target. Although child labour has decreased since 2020, progress has stagnated, and the region still grapples with the issue, particularly in specific sectors and among vulnerable populations. According to a 2020 report from the ILO and UNICEF (2025), about 8.2 million children in Latin America and the Caribbean were engaged in child labour. The prevalence of child labour is highest in the Caribbean, where around 13% of children are affected, compared to 8% in Central America and 4% in South America (Abdullah et al., 2025). In the United States (US), while child labour is not as prevalent as in other parts of the Americas, there has been a significant increase in violations (US Department of Labour, 2025). Data from the Department of Labour indicates that between 2015 and 2022, the number of minors illegally employed soared by 283% (US Department of Labour, 2025). This includes a 94% increase in children working in risky jobs (Sukma & Ruslan, 2025). A substantial percentage of child labour in the Americas involves dangerous work that jeopardises the health, safety, and moral development of children (Türkelli, 2021). In Latin America and the Caribbean, two-thirds of child labourers are exposed to unsafe work environments (Abdullah et al., 2025).

Efforts to fight child labour in the Americas are multifaceted and involve international cooperation, national government policies, and the work of non-profit actors. These efforts aim to tackle the primary factors that drive children into work settings. Regarding international efforts, the ILO has been at the forefront in the fight against child labour through programmes and conventions across the Americas. ILO's Worst Forms of Child Labour Convention, 1999 (No. 182), which advocates for the immediate eradication of the worst forms of child labour, has been universally ratified in the Americas.

The Regional Initiative Latin America and the Caribbean Free of Child Labour also brings together governments, employers, and workers' organisations from 30 countries to share best practices and create policies to stop and eliminate child labour. The initiative has raised awareness and strengthened regional and national action plans (Weldeyesus & Alemu, 2024). Through the Summits of the Americas, countries in the Western Hemisphere have also made commitments to eliminate child labour, as seen in declarations from various summits. These commitments often focus on strengthening labour laws, increasing inspections, and improving access to education and social protection.

Regarding national policies, the American government is implementing various strategies to combat child labour. These often include strengthening legislation and enforcement. In this regard, many countries in the region have updated their national laws to align with international standards, although enforcement remains a key challenge. In the United States, the Department of Labour has focused on increasing investigations and imposing higher penalties on companies that violate child labour laws. Governments in Latin American countries are using conditional cash transfer programmes to encourage families to keep their children in school rather than sending them to work (Hoque, 2024). These programmes help reduce reliance on children's income by providing financial assistance. Another strategy being used is to promote the accessibility of quality education. Governments are investing in schools, particularly in remote areas where child labour is mostly occurring (Esteve et al., 2025). Educational programmes are also being used to raise awareness among children, parents, and communities about the dangers of child labour (Esteve et al., 2025; Hoque, 2024).

NGOs and civil society, like UNICEF, Save the Children, and Human Rights Watch, are also on the front lines, advocating for children's rights, conducting research, and providing direct services to affected children and their families. The Campaign to End US Child Labour is an example of a partnership of organisations working to close legal loopholes and strengthen protections for migrant and agricultural child workers. There is also a growing push to hold corporations responsible for child labour in their supply chains (Hoque, 2024). The UN Guiding Principles on Business and Human Rights and other international guidelines encourage businesses to conduct due diligence to ensure their operations and suppliers do not employ child labour. This includes verifying the age of workers and partnering with local organisations to address the issue.

The Asia-Pacific region has the largest number of children engaged in labour—78 million (5–17 years group)—with a frequency of 9% (second place after SSA, at 21%) (Association of Southeast Asian Nations (ASEAN), 2025). Over 50% of the child labourers in the region are involved in hazardous work (Das, 2022). While there is progress, the problem persists due to the combination of poverty, social factors, and inadequate enforcement of labour laws. According to the ILO-UNICEF (2025), Asia and the Pacific region are home to millions of child labourers. Southern Asia, in particular, remains a hotspot, with millions of children engaged in child labour. Countries like Afghanistan, Nepal, and Pakistan have historically had high rates of child labour (Caleo et al., 2025). Many children in the region are engaged in dangerous work (ILO, 2024). This includes work in brick kilns, carpet weaving, employment in garment factories, mining, and agriculture.

Governments, international organisations, and regional civil society groups work together to combat child labour through various strategies. For instance, many countries have enacted or strengthened laws prohibiting and punishing child labour (Hoque, 2024). This includes raising the minimum age of employability and increasing penalties for offenders. Governments are also implementing social safety nets, which provide financial support to families on the condition that their children attend school instead of work (Ahad et al., 2020). Efforts are also being made to ensure that education is more accessible, affordable, and relevant. This includes building schools in remote areas, providing scholarships, and ensuring the quality of teaching and curriculum (Kabir & Maitrot, 2017). Campaigns are also being conducted to change social norms and highlight the negative consequences of child labour on children. ILO's Asia Regional Child Labour (ARC) Project is an example of a multi-country initiative that brings together governments, employers, and workers' organisations to combat child labour in countries such as Afghanistan, Bangladesh, India, Nepal, and Pakistan. There is also a growing focus on holding companies responsible for child labour within their supply chains. This involves monitoring and auditing practices to ensure products are not made using child labour.

In SSA, the state of child labour is a critical and worsening human rights issue, with the region having the highest percentage of child labourers—globally. Despite decades of efforts to combat the problem, recent trends show a concerning increase, particularly in SSA. Approximately 92.2 million children were engaged in labour in 2025 (Ibrahim et al., 2025). Unlike other global regions that have seen a decline in child labour, SSA has experienced a significant rise. Between 2016 and 2020, child labourers increased by 20.1 million, a significant setback in the global fight to eliminate the practice (Chamma, 2024; Ngongolo & Gayo, 2025). A large portion of these children, approximately 41.4 million, are involved in risky jobs (Montgomery, 2025). This includes dangerous activities such as mining, working with toxic chemicals, and carrying heavy loads. Agriculture is the largest employer of child labourers in Africa, with over 85% of child labour occurring on family farms (Chamma, 2024). Child labour is also widespread in domestic work, street vending, and other informal sectors. In SSA, poverty is the most significant cause of child labour. Families in extreme poverty are often forced to rely on their children's income for survival.

African governments, often collaborating with international partners, such as the ILO and UNICEF, are trying to address the crisis. These actions include adopting legislation and policies designed to combat child labour. Many countries have ratified key international child labour conventions and developed national action plans to combat it. Some countries, like South Africa, have increased the number of labour inspectors and are taking steps to strengthen law enforcement against child labour violations. Tackling the root cause of poverty is a key part of the strategy, with initiatives like cash transfers and social protection programmes aiming to reduce the economic pressure on families (Ndhlovu, 2024b; Nzabamwita & Ndhlovu, 2024). There is also growing interest in using new technologies, such as blockchain, to create transparent supply chains and help companies and consumers verify that products, like cocoa and cobalt, were produced without child labour.

Despite these efforts, the challenge is immense. The current pace of progress is insufficient to meet the Sustainable Development Goal of eliminating all forms of child labour by 2025. A breakthrough in Africa is essential for achieving global goals.

Zimbabwe is one of the countries where child labour is a critical and worsening human rights issue, particularly due to the widespread participation of children in the agricultural sector.

12.3 Materials and Methods

This chapter draws from a review of primary and secondary literature on climate change and children's engagement in farming in Zimbabwe, focusing on peasant households. Peasant households were identified as households in communal areas, old resettlements, and A1 farmers who received land under the country's land reforms of the 2000s, using farming as their primary livelihood and income source. Literature in both grey and academic formats was targeted for analysis. The terms 'climate change', 'child labour', 'farming', and 'Zimbabwe' were used as key search terms. Each text selected for analysis needed to discuss how children are co-opted to participate in farming in response to climate change in Zimbabwe. Texts published between 2015 and 2025 were selected to ensure recency. There was no specific database used to ensure that all relevant texts stood an equal chance of being selected for review. All articles were required to be written in the English language and freely downloadable to be selected. Articles that did not meet this inclusion criterion were excluded from the review.

Document analysis, a methodical procedure for assessing and evaluating documents to make sense of their communication, was then used to examine the identified texts. Document analysis entails iterative surface glance at a document to grasp its overall message. It falls under the qualitative research design.

Latent coding was used to organise the findings. Data collected from the selected documents were arranged into codes to solicit their meaning while linking them to the study's research objectives. In using latent coding, the author could probe the texts deeper than surface-level observations to unearth the texts' underlying meanings, interpretations, and implicit messages. The method was flexible, allowing the author to move back and forth from a review of research policy documents and academic texts. It generated a rich in-depth analysis and allowed the author to handle many texts. The method was also cost-effective and unobtrusive, with no possibility of replication.

A total of 24 texts were identified for review. These included 17 academic texts (journal articles and book chapters), two dissertations, and five reports by government and non-government organisations, including the World Bank (WB), UNICEF, the US Department of Labour, and the International Maize and Wheat Improvement Center (CIMMYT). These texts provided the basis for the conclusions made in this chapter. The findings were categorised thematically. A total of five themes emerged from the review.

The research approach used in this chapter, however, has several limitations. The approach is mainly subjective and depends on the author's analytical ability. Biases and omissions may have been made. In addition, replication is not guaranteed. As a result, it is hoped that future studies will adopt more case-study-specific and empirical methodologies to either confirm or problematise the conclusions made in this study.

12.4 Findings and Discussion

The chapter first presents and discusses the climate change scenario in Zimbabwe. This is followed by a thematic outline and discussion of the conduits through which climate change leads to child labour. Table 12.1 summarises the themes that emerged from the review.

Table 12.1 Summary of themes

Theme	Description
Increased poverty	Climate change increases poverty, both at the national and household levels, resulting in the conscription of child labour.
Shifting livelihoods	Climate change shifts livelihoods away from farming activities, causing households to recruit children to assist in emergent livelihood strategies.
Changes in agricultural productivity	Climate change has produced labour-intensive new crops, forcing parents to tap into child labour.
Health issues	Climate change often creates health challenges for both humans and livestock. Where elders suffer ill health, children are often called to cover the gap.
Destruction of Basic Services and Infrastructure	When infrastructure such as schools is destroyed by extreme weather conditions, children are withdrawn from schools and often forced to provide labour.

12.4.1 Climate Change Scenario

The review showed that Zimbabwe is undergoing significant impacts from climate change, including more recurrent and intense droughts, floods, and heatwaves, which threaten the country's agriculture, water resources, and overall development. Extreme weather events are expected to deepen, potentially eroding about 12% of Zimbabwe's gross domestic product (GDP) yearly if mitigation and adaptation measures are not implemented (WB, 2025). Climate change is worsening droughts in the country, with the regularity of drought years increasing from 1 in 10 between 1902 and 1979 to 1 in 4 between 1980 and 2011 (World Bank (WB), 2025). The 2023/2024 season witnessed severe drought conditions linked to El Niño, causing a substantial drop in maize yield (WB, 2025). This is concerning, particularly because agriculture is central to Zimbabwe's livelihood and income. The sector contributes about 17% to GDP and employs 70% of the population (WB, 2024). However, Zimbabwe's dependence on rain-fed systems makes it highly exposed to increasingly severe climate events, such as El Niño. El Niño conditions often lead to above-average temperatures and below-average rainfall (Ndhlovu & Dube, 2024), resulting in droughts. In contrast, La Niña ignites above-average rainfall, which sometimes leads to floods.

The review further showed that lower rainfall, higher evaporation, and reduced groundwater infiltration decrease river flows and water shortages in Zimbabwe (Mwadzingeni et al., 2022). This also affects water quality due to more siltation and raises the cost of groundwater abstraction. Climate change also impacts crop production and livestock through reduced rainfall, increased soil degradation, and higher risks of pests and diseases for crops and livestock (Musasa et al., 2025). The shift in agroecological zones due to warming temperatures also affects agricultural suitability. Frequent and intense storms, floods, and heatwaves in Zimbabwe also lead to infrastructure damage, ecosystem disruption, and increased risk of wildfires (Parwada et al., 2025). Changes in temperature and precipitation patterns threaten plant and animal species, resulting in habitat destruction and biodiversity loss in the country (Madamombe et al., 2024). Collectively, these scenarios excessively affect vulnerable populations such as peasant households, particularly children, whose labour is sometimes called upon to intervene.

12.4.2 How Climate Change Exacerbates Child Labour

The review showed many conduits through which climate change worsens child labour. The following sub-sections show the five themes that emerged from the review.

12.4.2.1 Increased Poverty and Child Labour

The review indicated that climate-related disasters in Zimbabwe have often led to crop losses, reduced income, and increased food prices, pushing peasant households further into poverty and forcing them to revert to children's labour as an additional livelihood strategy. Climate change, poverty, and child labour are profoundly interrelated issues in Zimbabwe, creating a brutal cycle that excessively affects the country's most vulnerable populations. The primary link between them is the heavy reliance of the Zimbabwean economy and population on rain-fed agriculture (Kahomwe & Muzingili, 2025). Chikoko and Chihiya (2023) found that climate change in Zimbabwe was worsening poverty and child labour, particularly in rural areas, as households face increased economic hardship due to climate-related disasters. They also found that children were being withdrawn from school and engaged in dangerous work to support their families. Tirivangasi et al. (2023) posit that climate change worsens poverty in Zimbabwe through increased food insecurity, economic hardship, and displacement due to extreme weather events. Kahomwe and Muzingili (2025) observed that reduced agricultural yields, rising food prices, and damage to infrastructure from droughts, floods, and cyclones force vulnerable populations, such as peasant households, into deeper poverty. When households cannot meet their basic needs like food, water, healthcare, and education, they often force their children to work to get an extra income. In Zimbabwe, children are not just supplementing adult income but are often replacing it, as adult men often travel to neighbouring countries in the face of the collapsing national economy.

Children from impoverished households are more susceptible to exploitation. Ndhlovu (2023) found that in Mehenye, families often sent their children to work for more prosperous peasants as unpaid labour in exchange for accommodation, school fees, and food. The study also showed that children often became domestic workers, facing long hours, poor working conditions, and potential abuse. Some households send their children away to Mozambique to work as herd boys, making them vulnerable to labour exploitation by human traffickers.

12.4.2.2 Shifting Livelihoods and Child Labour

The review showed that climate change impacts also disrupt traditional farming practices in Zimbabwe, forcing peasant households to seek alternative, sometimes more dangerous, forms of income, including child labour. The issue of child labour in Zimbabwe is deeply intertwined with the country's economic challenges and the resulting shifts in livelihoods. Chipato (2025) observed that in the Chingwizi resettlement, as households faced increasing poverty and economic instability, they were often forced to adopt new survival strategies, such as children entering the workforce. High unemployment, economic crises, and a lack of resources for social welfare push households into a vicious cycle of poverty (Mhlanga & Ndhlovu, 2021). To meet basic needs like food, education, and healthcare, families resort to deploying all members, including children, into the labour force.

Due to economic collapse in Zimbabwe, the informal sector has become a significant source of income for many Zimbabweans. As farming activities fail under climate change, households deploy members, including children, to artisanal and small-scale mining, street vending, and domestic work (Nkomo & Mpofu, 2022). Children are often found in these sectors, which lack regulation and proper working conditions. Across Zimbabwe, children are employed in artisanal mining, such as gold in Shurungwi, lithium in Bikita, and scheelite in Mutandahwe, where they face hazardous conditions and exposure to dangerous chemicals like mercury and cyanide.

The review showed that most child labour in Zimbabwe (over 96%) occurs in the agricultural sector (WB, 2024). This often takes place on family farms, where children are involved in tasks like herding livestock, fishing, and farming (Kahomwe & Muzingili, 2025). They also work on large-scale commercial farms, producing crops like tobacco, tea, and sugarcane, where they may be exposed to unsafe conditions and chemicals (Tirivangasi et al., 2023). Therefore, the susceptibility of peasants to climate impacts and crop failures further pushes children into the workforce. The review posits that while the country has laws against child labour and has ratified international conventions, enforcement is often stalled by a lack of resources for law enforcement agencies (US Department of Labour, 2022). In addition, social and cultural beliefs view work as a positive way to build a child's character and provide them with skills.

To sum up, the livelihood shift towards informal and unregulated sectors in Zimbabwe has made child labour more prevalent and more complex to address. While some scholars argue that for some children work is a necessary survival strategy, it is clear that the lack of safer alternatives and the exploitative conditions under which they labour are detrimental to their health, development, and future.

12.4.2.3 Changes in Agricultural Productivity

Climate change severely impacts agricultural productivity, which in turn exacerbates child labour, especially in vulnerable communities. The relationship is complex, with climate change acting as a multiplier of existing socio-economic stressors that push families towards using their children for labour. The review showed that climate change has altered rainfall patterns in all five of Zimbabwe's agroecological regions, with temperature increases leading to soil degradation, negatively impacting crop yields and livestock production (Ndhlovu & Dube, 2024). As a result, agricultural productivity has significantly changed, with households shifting their focus to producing drought-resistant crops. For instance, in south-eastern Zimbabwe, Ndhlovu (2023) found that most households have shifted production to sorghum, cotton, and sesame—due to their drought-resistant characteristics—instead of the less resistant maize. However, cotton and sesame are labour-intensive crops, forcing families to intensify their labour efforts, including relying on children to work longer hours and in more dangerous conditions to ensure successful production. Additional measures include crop rotation on dry lands, which requires more labour as households move to clear new fields (Tavuyanago, 2016). This often sees children being called upon to provide such labour (US Department of Labour, 2022).

Additionally, climate impacts have led to reports of crop and livestock pests and diseases across the country (Muoni et al., 2025). Mwadzingeni et al. (2022) noted that climate change significantly affects the country by creating environments that favour the spread and increased severity of agricultural pests and diseases. This includes the emergence of new pests such as fall armyworm, tomato leaf miner, and cotton mealybug, as well as the worsening of existing pests like aphids, whiteflies, and stem borers. Warmer temperatures promote the expansion of pests and diseases into new regions, which devastate crops and livestock without natural resistance. Chanza and Gundu-Jakarasi (2020) likewise posit that climate change affects the distribution and severity of plant diseases, such as black shank, fusarium wilt and potato virus Y (PVY), leading to crop losses and impacting food security in the country.

12.4.2.4 Health Issues and Hazardous Child Labour

Climate change significantly impacts human health and child labour in Zimbabwe, particularly in rural, agriculture-dependent communities. The effects are interconnected, with climate-induced shocks aggravating poverty and leading to adverse health outcomes and an increase in child labour. Zimbabwe's economy and food supply rely heavily on rain-fed agriculture (WB, 2024). Climate-change-induced droughts and floods cause crop failures and livestock loss, leading to severe food shortages and malnutrition, especially among children (Kasanzu et al., 2025). UNICEF (2025) reports that in 2025, Zimbabwe experienced a severe food and nutrition disaster, with over 7.6 million people in need of urgent aid due to the effects of the 2024 El-Niño-induced drought. This has led to amplified child malnutrition. Although the government declared a national disaster in response to the 2024 drought, the impacts continue to worsen malnutrition, particularly among vulnerable populations (CMMYT, 2025).

Children from peasant households are often the most vulnerable and exposed to dangerous conditions like heavy machinery, harmful chemicals (pesticides), and extreme weather (Kabongo et al., 2025). Climate-change-related health issues, such as heat stress, respiratory problems, and infectious diseases, are often worsened by poor working conditions, further harming children's health and development. These health risks can lead to long-term disabilities and limit children's future opportunities (US Department of Labour, 2022).

12.4.2.5 Destruction of Basic Services and Infrastructure

The review showed that climate change damages or destroys essential infrastructure like schools, health centres, and water sources in Zimbabwe, making it harder for children to access education and healthcare (Sithole et al., 2023). This is leading to higher school dropout rates and increased vulnerability to child labour. In essence, climate change acts as a catalyst for child labour in agriculture by increasing poverty, reducing agricultural productivity, and creating a cycle of vulnerability and hardship for families and children. For instance, in 2019, Cyclone Idai caused significant damage to schools, forcing students to abandon their education in some cases in areas such as Chimaninimani and Chipinge (Ndhlovu & Dube, 2024). Poorly upheld infrastructure, such as derelict classrooms and a lack of sanitation facilities, also increases vulnerability to climate change impacts (Muzerengi et al., 2023). Cyclone Idai in 2019 caused catastrophic damage to the road network in eastern Zimbabwe, isolating entire districts, destroying schools, and displacing thousands of people from their homes. With basic infrastructure having been destroyed, children often participate in other labour activities to support the family during climate-related crises. The lack of social protection measures to help families deal with economic crises also means that when schools close, children are more likely to be forced into work (Ndhlovu, 2024b).

12.5 Interventions

Zimbabwe is grappling with a complex web of socio-economic challenges, many interconnected and with deep historical roots. These issues have led to widespread poverty, food insecurity, and a significant decline in social services. A defining feature of the country's economic crisis has been its periods of extreme hyperinflation since the late 1990s. The country experienced an inflation rate that rose from 32% in 1998 to 173% in 2004 to 605% in 2005 and approached 1600% in 2007 (Ndhlovu, 2017). In 2008, inflation peaked astronomically, effectively rendering the currency worthless. The country adopted a multi-currency system to cope, primarily using the US dollar. While this brought relative stability, a new local currency, the Zimbabwe Gold (ZiG), was introduced in 2024 to curb persistent inflation. However, its long-term stability remains a concern. The formal economy has shrunk dramatically, leading to a high unemployment rate. While some sources report a formal unemployment rate in the single digits, many working populations are engaged in the informal sector, where jobs are often precarious and low paying. Zimbabwe's capacity to intervene and reduce child labour under climate change has been constrained by its economic challenges.

In 2023, the country made some significant progress regarding the elimination of the worst forms of child labour. It approved revisions to the Labour Act to increase consequences for forced labour, from 2 years of incarceration to 10 years. It also renewed the National Steering Committee to Address the Worst Forms of Child Labour. Further, the Anti-Trafficking Inter-Ministerial Committee was appointed to facilitate public awareness regarding child labour and trafficking.

However, despite the various initiatives to fight child labour, Zimbabwe is evaluated as having made very little progress because of state-aligned actors threatening and intimidating trade unions and worker organisations, which are key stakeholders in the identification and prevention of child labour. The scope of current social programmes is insufficient to address child labour in all germane sectors, including agriculture. In addition, law enforcement agencies lack adequate personnel and operational resources to enforce child labour laws.

12.6 Conclusion and Recommendations

Climate change is widely recognised as one of Zimbabwe's main socio-economic challenges, worsening the current economic crisis since the late 1990s. Zimbabwe is primarily agrarian, with farming as a significant social and economic activity. Most of the country's rural dwellers rely on farming as their primary source of living. Urban dwellers also combine employment with farming in their rural communities. At retirement, those employed in urban areas often return to their rural communities, where they reintegrate into peasant life. However, climate change has presented significant challenges to the country's agricultural sector in recent decades. This chapter first examined Zimbabwe's current climate change trajectory and then explored the key conduits through which climate change impacts child labour in Zimbabwe. Drawing from a review of primary and secondary sources, the chapter showed that climate change has substantially worsened poverty through unpredictable weather patterns, which lead to crop failures, food insecurity, and increased vulnerability in Zimbabwe. It has induced changes in peasant livelihoods and agricultural productivity, destroyed basic services and infrastructure, and forced peasant households to explore a range of survival strategies, including tapping into children's labour for survival.

The review also showed that Zimbabwe does not have comprehensive policies for monitoring child labour, particularly in agriculture. As a result, child labour continues, largely unmonitored. This has enormous implications for the future of children and the possibilities of Zimbabwe attaining sustainable development. The chapter highlights the urgent need to address child labour in the agricultural sector as part of the human rights campaign in Zimbabwe.

References

Abdullah, A., Mensah, F., & Amponsah, E. B. (2025). Conceptualization of child labour: Contemporary understanding and gaps. *Child Abuse Review, 1-9*(34), e70025.

Ahad, M. A., Parry, Y. K., & Willis, E. (2020). Spillover trends of child labour during the coronavirus crisis- an unnoticed wake-up call. *Frontiers in Public Health, 8*, 488. https://doi.org/10.3389/fpubh.2020.00488

ASEAN. (2025). *ASEAN Roadmap on the Elimination of the Worst Forms of Child Labour by 2025*. ASEAN. https://asean.org/wp-content/uploads/ASEAN-Roadmap-on-the-Elimination-of-the-Worst-Forms-of-Child-Labour-by-2025-_Final_19Feb2021.pdf

Bekik, M. E. (2024). Child labour and the effectiveness of the ILO's program of ending child labour by 2025. *Sosyolojik Düşün, 9*(3), 298–325.

Caleo, G., Sadique, S., Yuce, D., et al. (2025). A Public health wound: Health and work among children engaged in the worst forms of child labour in the informal sector in Dhaka, Bangladesh: a retrospective analysis of Médecins Sans Frontières occupational health data from 2014 to 2023. *BMC Public Health, 25*, 1420. https://doi.org/10.1186/s12889-025-22483-z

Chamma, D. D. (2024). Climate change and economic growth in sub-Saharan Africa: An empirical analysis of aggregate- and sector-level growth. *Journal of Social and Economic Development*. https://doi.org/10.1007/s40847-024-00377-x

Chanza, N., & Gundu-Jakarasi, V. (2020). 'Deciphering the Climate Change Conundrum in Zimbabwe: An Exposition.' In: Tiefenbacher, J. (Ed.). (2020). *Global warming and climate change*. Intech Open. https://doi.org/10.5772/intechopen.84934.

Chikoko, W., & Chihiya, P. (2023). Climate change and vulnerabilities of children in rural Zimbabwe: The case of ward 14 of Bikita District, Zimbabwe. *African Journal of Social Work, 13*(2), 78–86. https://doi.org/10.4314/ajsw.v13i2.4

Chipato, F. (2025). Rural livelihood, accumulation and class formation in post-development-induced displacements in Zimbabwe. *Cogent Social Sciences, 1*(1), 2461258. https://doi.org/10.1080/23311886.2025.2461258

CMMYT. (2025). *Climate change and child malnutrition in Zimbabwe: Evidence to action*. CMMYT. https://www.cimmyt.org/projects/climate-change-and-child-malnutrition-in-zimbabwe-evidence-to-action/. Accessed 21 August 2025

Das, K. S. (2022). Child labour and its determinants in India. *Children and Youth Services Review, 138*, 106523. https://doi.org/10.1016/j.childyouth.2022.106523

Esteve, A., Torres, A. F. C., & Becca, F. (2025). Family change in Latin America: Schooling and labor market implications for children and women. *Oxford Open Economics, 4*(1), i292–i306. https://doi.org/10.1093/ooec/odae026

FAO. (2020). *FAO framework on ending child labour in agriculture*. Rome. https://doi.org/10.4060/ca9502en.

Goulart, P. V., Sobreira, N., Ferrittu, G., et al. (2024). What led to the decline of child labour in the European periphery? A cointegration approach with long historical data. *Social Indicators Research, 172*, 765–801. https://doi.org/10.1007/s11205-024-03315-w

Hoque, M. M. (2024). A critical review of Bangladesh's child labour regulations and policies. *World Development Sustainability, 5*, 100177. https://doi.org/10.1016/j.wds.2024.100177

Ibrahim, S., Golo, H. K., & Erinosho, B. T. (2025). Reconsidering child labour as a psycho-social dynamic and form of child rights violation: Insights from Ghanaian Marine small-scale fisheries. *The International Journal of Children's Rights, 33*, 81–106.

ILO. (2014). *Child labour "in a nutshell" - A resource for Pacific Island countries*. International Labour Office, International Programme on the Elimination of Child Labour (IPEC): ILO. file:///C:/Users/Manu/Downloads/wcms_304562.pdf

ILO. (2017). *Ending child labour by 2025: A review of policies and programmes*. ILO.

ILO. (2024). *Child labour in South Asia*. ILO. https://www.ilo.org/resource/child-labour-south-asia

ILO-UNICEF. (2025, 18 August). *Child labour: Global estimates 2024, trends and the road forward*. Joint Report. ILO-UNICEF. https://www.ilo.org/publications/major-publications/child-labour-global-estimates-2024-trends-and-road-forward

IPCC. (2022). *Climate Change 2022: Impacts, adaptation and vulnerability. Contribution of Working Group II to the Sixth Assessment Report of the Intergovernmental Panel on Climate Change*. Cambridge University Press. https://doi.org/10.1017/9781009325844.001

Kabir, A., & Maitrot, M. R. L. (2017). Factors influencing feeding practices of extreme poor infants and young children in families of working mothers in Dhaka slums: A qualitative study. *PLoS One, 12*(2).

Kabongo, J., Mudawarima, L., Majo, F. D., et al. (2025). Child play and caregiver support to promote convalescence following severe acute malnutrition in Zimbabwe: The Tamba-SAM pilot study. *Maternal & Child Nutrition, 21*(1), e13726. https://doi.org/10.1111/mcn.13726

Kahomwe, L., & Muzingili, T. (2025). Impact of climate change disasters on access to education and coping mechanisms for rural learners in Zimbabwe. *Cogent Education, 12*(1), 2517505. https://doi.org/10.1080/2331186X.2025.2517505

Kasanzu, S., Chirenda, J., & Marume, A. (2025). Diet and sociodemographic predictors of the double burden of malnutrition in urban Zimbabwe. *African Journal of Primary Health & Family Medicine, 17*(1), e1–e7. https://doi.org/10.4102/phcfm.v17i1.4834

Madamombe, S. M., Ng'ang'a, S. K., Öborn, I., et al. (2024). Climate change awareness and adaptation strategies by smallholder farmers in semi-arid areas of Zimbabwe. *International Journal of Agricultural Sustainability, 22*(1), 2293588. https://doi.org/10.1080/14735903.2023.2293588

Mhlanga, D., & Ndhlovu, E. (2021). Socio-economic and political challenges in Zimbabwe and the development implications for Southern Africa. *Journal of African Foreign Affairs, 8*(2), 77–100.

Momen, N. (2020). Child labor: History, process, and consequences. In W. Leal Filho et al. (Eds.), *No poverty*. Encyclopedia of the UN Sustainable Development Goals. https://doi.org/10.1007/978-3-319-69625-6_30-1

Montgomery, N. A. (2025). *Adverse health consequences of child labour in Sub-Saharan Africa: A research outline*. SSRN: https://doi.org/10.2139/ssrn.5332209

Moyo, S. (2016). *Family farming in sub-Saharan Africa: Its contribution to agriculture, food security and rural development* (Working paper number 150). Food and Agriculture Organisation of the United Nations and the United Nations Development Programme.

Muoni, T., Kihara, J., Madamombe, S. M., et al. (2025). Climate change vulnerability and drivers of low maize yields under smallholder farming systems in semi-arid area of Marange in Zimbabwe. *Discover Sustainability, 6*, 394. https://doi.org/10.1007/s43621-025-01189-7

Musasa, T., Shoko, C., Marambanyika, T., et al. (2025). Modelling soil erosion risk in rural subcatchments of Zimbabwe using RUSLE, remote sensing and machine learning. *Journal of Arid Environments, 229*, 105407. https://doi.org/10.1016/j.jaridenv.2025.105407

Muzerengi, F., Gandidzanwa, C. P., & Chirubvu, L. (2023). Impacts of climate change on household food security in Matande communal lands, Mwenezi district in Zimbabwe. *Jàmbá: Journal of Disaster Risk Studies, 15*(1), a1499. https://doi.org/10.4102/jamba.v15i1.1499

Mwadzingeni, L., Mugandani, R., & Mafongoya, P. (2022). Risks of climate change on future water supply in smallholder irrigation schemes in Zimbabwe. *Water, 14*, 1682. https://doi.org/10.3390/w14111682

Ndhlovu, E. (2017). *An analysis of household livelihoods under the fast-track land reform programme in Chiredzi, Zimbabwe* (MA dissertation) University of South Africa.

Ndhlovu, E. (2022). Changing Agrarian discourses and practices and the prospects for food sovereignty in Zimbabwe. In G. In Mkodzongi (Ed.), *The future of Zimbabwe's agrarian sector: Land issues in a time of political transition* (pp. 34–53). Routledge.

Ndhlovu, E. (2023). Accumulation and livelihoods strategies of the Hlengwe Peasantry in Mahenye, Along the Zimbabwe-Mozambique Border. In N. Pophiwa, J. Matanzima, & K. Helliker (Eds.), *Lived experiences of borderland communities in Zimbabwe: Livelihoods, conservation, war and covid-19*. Springer Cham.

Ndhlovu, E. (2024a). Extreme weather events and human displacement in sub-Saharan Africa: Toward social policy interventions. *Review of Socio-Economic Research and Development Studies, 8*(2), 70–100.

Ndhlovu, E. (2024b). Social protection instruments and strategies in Southern Africa. *International Journal of Innovation in Management Economics and Social Sciences, 4*(2), 44–59.

Ndhlovu, E., & Dube, K. (2024). Contract farming and climate change adaptation in rural Zimbabwe. *Mankind Quarterly, 64*(3), 579–594.

Ndlovu, E., Prinsloo, B., & Le Roux, T. (2020). Impact of climate change and variability on traditional farming systems: Farmers' perceptions from south-west, semi-arid Zimbabwe. *Jàmbá: Journal of Disaster Risk Studies, 12*(1), a742. https://doi.org/10.4102/jamba.v12i1.742

Ngongolo, K., & Gayo, L. (2025). Climate change impacts and mitigation strategies in Sub-Saharan Africa's livestock production sector. A brief review. *Pastoralism, 15*, 14225. https://doi.org/10.3389/past.2025.14225

Nkomo, S., & Mpofu, P. (2022). The impact of artisanal mining on career development of adolescents in Zimbabwe. *Interdisciplinary Journal of Rural and Community Studies, 4*, 36–47. https://doi.org/10.38140/ijrcs-2022.vol4.04

Nzabamwita, J., & Ndhlovu, E. (2024). Social grants impact on household livelihoods: Empirical evidence from international migrants in Cape Town, South Africa. *E-Journal of Humanities, Arts and Social Sciences, 5*(14), 2521–2537.

Parwada, C., Masere, T. P., Mandumbu, R., et al. (2025). Climate change and land degradation in semi-arid agricultural landscapes: A case study of Zimbabwean communal areas. *Trends in Environmental Sciences, 1*(2), 158–166. https://doi.org/10.17311/tes.2025.158.166

Radfar, A., Asgharzadeh, S., Quesada, F., et al. (2018). Challenges and perspectives of child labour. *Industrial Psychiatry Journal, 27*, 17–20. https://doi.org/10.4103/ipj.ipj10514

Sithole, D., Tagwireyi, C., Marowa, T., et al. (2023). Climate change mitigation in Zimbabwe and links to sustainable development. *Environmental Development, 47*, 100891. https://doi.org/10.1016/j.envdev.2023.100891

Sukma, W. L., & Ruslan, K. (2025). Digital economy challenge: Hidden exploitation of child labour through the use of digital devices. *Journal of Central Banking Law and Institutions, 4*(2), 259–290. https://doi.org/10.21098/jcli.v4i2.252

Tavuyanago B (2016). *Living on the fringes of a protected area: Gonarezhou National Park (GNP) and the indigenous communities of south-east Zimbabwe* (PhD thesis). University of Pretoria.

Tirivangasi, H. M., Dzvimbo, M. A., Chaminuka, N., & Mawonde, A. (2023). Assessing climate change and urban poverty in the context of the COVID-19 lockdowns: Rethinking personality and societal challenges in Zimbabwe. *Scientific African, 20*, e01710. https://doi.org/10.1016/j.sciaf.2023.e01710

Türkelli, G. (2021). Eradicating child labour: Ending economic exploitation of children as an objective of sustainable development. In W. Leal Filho, A. M. Azul, L. Brandli, et al. (Eds.), *Decent work and economic growth. Encyclopedia of the UN Sustainable Development Goals*. Springer. https://doi.org/10.1007/978-3-319-95867-5_3

UNICEF. (2025). *Zimbabwe*. UNICEF. https://www.unicef.org/media/166161/file/2025-HAC-Zimbabwe.pdf

US Department of Labour. (2022). *Findings on the worst forms of child labour: Zimbabwe*. US Department of Labour. https://www.dol.gov/sites/dolgov/files/ILAB/child_labor_reports/tda2022/Zimbabwe.pdf

US Department of Labour. (2025). *FY 2025 Department of Labor Budget in Brief*. Department of Labour. https://www.dol.gov/sites/dolgov/files/ETA/budget/pdfs/FY2025BIB_ETA.pdf

Visser, A. (2021). Child labour is a matter of national concern: What is the curriculum doing about it? *Journal of Education, 85*, 29–54. https://doi.org/10.17159/2520-9868/i85a02

WB. (2024). *Zimbabwe Country Climate and Development Report*. CCDR Series. World Bank. http://hdl.handle.net/10986/41137

WB. (2025). *Zimbabwe economic update: Improving resilience to weather shocks and climate change*. https://www.worldbank.org/en/country/zimbabwe/publication/zimbabwe-economic-update-improving-resilience-to-afe-weather-shocks-and-climate-change. Accessed 20 August 2025

Weldeyesus, M. A., & Alemu, B. A. (2024). Profiles of child labour: Prevalence, activities, contexts, and children's harm extent in Raya-Kobo and Angot Districts, Ethiopia. *ICEP, 18*, 4. https://doi.org/10.1186/s40723-024-00130-1

Zewdie, B. M., Berlie, A. B., & Mersha, L. A. (2024). Causes of child labor and working conditions in Ethiopia: Evidence from temporary inter-rural child labor migrants from *Sekela* district. *CMS, 12*, 28. https://doi.org/10.1186/s40878-024-00384-1

Part IV
Child-Centred Climate Adaptation and Resilience Strategies in the Green Economy and Just Transitions

Chapter 13
Gender-Transformative Climate Action for Children's Rights in Zimbabwe's Land Resettlement Areas

Clement Chipenda and Emmanuel Ndhlovu

13.1 Introduction

Climate change constitutes one of the most significant and urgent challenges of our time as it has altered environmental systems while simultaneously exposing and exacerbating deep-seated social inequalities across the globe. The climate emergency has revealed a stark asymmetry between those responsible for greenhouse gas emissions and those who suffer most severely from their consequences. The six largest greenhouse gas (GHG) emitters—namely China, the United States, India, the European Union, Russia, and Brazil—accounted for 63% of total global emissions in 2023, while the least developed countries (LDCs), comprising 46 nations that are vulnerable to economic and environmental shocks, contributed merely 3% of global GHG emissions (UNCTAD, 2023; Hausfather & Friedlingstein, 2024). This disparity has highlighted the inherent injustice of climate change, where those least equipped to adapt face the most severe consequences.

Within this global context of climate injustice, children emerge as among the most vulnerable populations, bearing disproportionate risks despite having no responsibility for the crisis. The global scale of children's climate vulnerability is staggering, with the United Nations Children's Fund's (UNICEF's) Children's Climate Risk Index (CCRI) revealing that nearly all children globally are already exposed to at least one major climate and environmental hazard, while almost half (1 billion children) live in countries at extremely high risk (UNICEF, 2021; Ud Din, 2025). Africa presents alarming statistics, with 39 out of 49 African countries

C. Chipenda (✉)
South African Research Chair in Social Policy, College of Graduate Studies, University of South Africa, Pretoria, South Africa

E. Ndhlovu
College of Business and Economics, University of Johannesburg, Auckland Park, South Africa

E. Ndhlovu, C. Chipenda (eds.), *Climate Change and Children's Rights in Zimbabwe*, https://doi.org/10.1007/978-981-95-6005-9_13

having overall CCRI scores in the 'extremely high' or 'high' risk class, affecting over 490 million children across the continent (UNICEF, 2021). The urgency of addressing children's climate vulnerability has gained international recognition through the Committee on the Rights of the Child's General Comment No. 26 (2023) on children's rights and the environment (CRC, 2023; Ud Din, 2025).

The implementation of such international frameworks, however, presents challenges, especially in Global South contexts where structural inequalities in knowledge production and agenda setting create significant implementation gaps. These challenges become evident when examining specific manifestations of climate vulnerability, such as displacement patterns demonstrating the acute risks facing African children. The scale of climate-induced displacement, for example, is an indication of the acute vulnerability of African children. Climate-induced displacement patterns reveal that 19.7 million child displacements occurred due to floods worldwide between 2016 and 2021, with African countries including Somalia, Ethiopia, South Sudan, Nigeria, and Sudan featuring among the top ten countries in absolute numbers (AECRW, 2025a, 2025b; Ud Din, 2025). Remarkably, six African countries appear among the top ten countries for child displacements relative to child population, highlighting the disproportionate burden borne by African children and the continent's vulnerability to climate-induced displacement.

Zimbabwe epitomises this global pattern of climate injustice, representing a case where minimal contribution to global emissions coincides with extreme vulnerability to climate impacts. The country is ranked as the 15th most vulnerable country to climate change globally and among the top three most vulnerable nations in Southern Africa. This is despite its minimal contribution to global emissions, according to the 2021 Global CCRI (UNICEF, 2025). Zimbabwe's climate trajectory presents deeply concerning trends that directly threaten children's futures. The national average temperature has warmed at approximately 0.1 degrees Celsius per decade, with the national mean surface temperature increasing by about 0.90 °C from 1900 to 2018 (GoZ, 2024). Future projections indicate with high confidence that mean daily minimum and maximum temperatures will continue to increase across most districts throughout 2020–2040. The national annual average temperature is likely to increase by 1.0–1.5 °C for this period and is projected to warm by 1.3–3.5 degrees by 2080 (GoZ, 2024).

With rising temperatures, Zimbabwe faces a concerning decline in precipitation that threatens agricultural productivity and water security. Average annual rainfall has declined by approximately 5% across Zimbabwe from 1901 to 2018, with future projections indicating a further decline by approximately 15% by 2060 and up to 25% by 2080, especially over the southwestern parts of the country (GoZ, 2024). The frequency of droughts has increased dramatically from 10% between 1902 and 1979 to 25% from 1980 to 2018, with notable drought episodes including 1991–1992, 1994–1995, 2002–2003, 2015–2016, 2018–2019, 2019–2020, and 2023–2024. These climatic changes pose acute threats to the nation's 6.5 million children, who comprise 47% of the population (Gwitira et al., 2024; UNICEF, 2025). Zimbabwe's acute vulnerability is compounded by limited adaptation funding and insufficient private sector financial flows (Madamombe et al., 2024; Mpala & Simatele, 2024). This has created conditions that threaten the rights of children across the country.

The intersection of climate vulnerability with Zimbabwe's complex post-colonial agrarian transformation adds additional layers of complexity to the realisation of children's rights. Zimbabwe's land reform process, undertaken to redress historical land injustices resulting from settler colonialism, evolved through multiple phases before culminating in the Fast Track Land Reform Programme (FTLRP), significantly transforming the country's agrarian structure. While the initial phases implemented from September 1980 to 1998 achieved limited success, acquiring only 3,498,444 hectares and resettling 71,000 families (Utete, 2003), the FTLRP succeeded in resettling approximately 180,000 families on 13 million hectares of land in just over a decade (Moyo, 2011). The FTLRP established two distinctive tenure models, the A1 (small-scale farming plots) and the A2 (medium-scale commercial farms). This created a trimodal agrarian structure that reshaped Zimbabwe's agricultural landscape alongside existing communal lands and remaining large-scale commercial farms. This transformation created the current agrarian structure, comprising 1.3 million small-scale farmers on 25.8 million hectares of land, medium-scale farmers on 4.4 million hectares, and 1618 large-scale commercial farms on 2.6 million hectares of land (Moyo, 2011). The land reform process has significantly impacted climate vulnerability and children's rights within resettled communities. Resettled communities have faced unique challenges in establishing productive agricultural systems while adapting to climate change, often with limited access to resources, technical support, and infrastructure. Remarkably, these communities that were resettled close to a quarter century ago continue to face persistent challenges in climate adaptation and child welfare, highlighting the long-term nature of these vulnerabilities. These challenges have been worsened by the disruption of traditional social networks and support systems, creating vulnerabilities for children and women in these communities. The persistence of these vulnerabilities across different resettlement phases demonstrates how factors specifically relevant from Global South perspectives are not adequately considered in climate change knowledge generation and mainstreaming, creating implementation-related challenges that are particularly significant and more pronounced in contexts like Zimbabwe's resettled farming communities.

This research addresses two critical questions emerging from the intersection of climate change, children's rights, and gender justice in rural Zimbabwe: How do climate change impacts affect the realisation of children's rights within resettled farming households in Goromonzi and Zvimba districts, with attention to differentiated experiences of girls and boys? What constitutes a gender-transformative just transition approach that effectively protects children's rights while addressing structural inequalities in rural communities? The research aims to analyse how climate change impacts violate children's rights within resettled farming households, with special attention to gendered differences in vulnerability and resilience. The aim is also to engage with a conceptual framework for a gender-transformative just transition that centres on children's rights and provides practical guidance for policy and programming in rural Zimbabwe.

Despite the growing recognition of the importance of addressing climate change impacts on children through gender-transformative approaches, significant gaps remain in understanding their intersection within Zimbabwe's resettled farming communities. Limited research examines how agricultural transitions affect children's rights or how gender-transformative approaches could enhance both agricultural outcomes and children's well-being in post-land reform contexts. Applying gender-transformative just transition frameworks to children's rights contexts remains theoretically underdeveloped, with insufficient guidance on operationalising approaches in rural African contexts. Children's role as agents of change in climate adaptation processes remains under-explored, with most research focusing on them as passive victims rather than active participants capable of contributing to gender-transformative climate responses.

13.2 Research Context and Methodology

This research was conducted in Goromonzi and Zvimba districts in Zimbabwe's agricultural heartland, representing exemplary cases of the country's land reform outcomes. Both districts are situated in the Mashonaland provinces within agro-ecological region II, characterised by optimal agricultural conditions. They experience a favourable climate with annual rainfall of 750–1000 mm and temperatures between 15 °C and 24 °C, providing ideal conditions for crop cultivation and livestock production. These agro-ecological advantages make both districts crucial to national food security while providing an optimal context for examining climate change impacts and children's rights in post-land reform settings. Substantial portions of former commercial farmland were redistributed to small and medium-scale farmers, creating dynamic settlement patterns, agricultural production systems, and social organisation. The diversity of farming systems, from subsistence-oriented smallholder plots to commercially oriented medium-scale farms, provides important variation for understanding how different post-land reform contexts shape children's climate change experiences.

This research employed a sequential explanatory mixed-method approach grounded in the pragmatic paradigm, conducted between 2022 and 2025. This methodological foundation enabled a comprehensive investigation of social transformation dynamics while bridging quantitative and qualitative methods. The pragmatic paradigm was selected for its compatibility with mixed-method research and emphasis on practical problem-solving. It is especially relevant for addressing complex intersections of climate change, land reform, and children's rights. The mixed-method approach captured both breadth and depth of experiences within resettled communities, with quantitative components systematically measuring climate impacts, household characteristics, and socio-economic conditions. In contrast, qualitative components enabled an in-depth exploration of lived experiences, decision-making processes, and social dynamics shaping children's vulnerability and resilience.

Data collection was conducted in two interconnected phases to capture comprehensive perspectives across different tenure regimes. Sample size determination utilised Cochran's formula, yielding a target of 384 respondents at a 95% confidence level. However, resource constraints necessitated an adjustment to 300 respondents while maintaining a 93% confidence level and a 5.6% margin of error. For comparative analysis, the quantitative phase employed random sampling to select 200 FTLRP beneficiary farmers across the A1 and A2 tenure regimes, plus 100 communal area farming households. The survey instrument captured approximately 1500 variables spanning multiple research dimensions. The qualitative phase built upon quantitative findings through purposive sampling, including interviews with 20 key informants representing government officials, resettled farmers, traditional authorities, and organisation representatives, followed by detailed household interviews with 30 households across three tenure regimes. Ethical approval was obtained from relevant institutional review boards, with informed consent secured from all participants, including special procedures for research involving children.

Data analysis employed an integrated framework combining quantitative and qualitative traditions. Quantitative survey data underwent statistical analysis through Statistical Package for the Social Sciences (SPSS), utilising descriptive statistics, correlation analysis, and comparative tests. Qualitative data underwent systematic thematic analysis using Atlas.ti software through a five-stage process, which included data familiarisation, code generation using inductive and deductive approaches, theme identification, iterative refinement, and final definition. Validity and reliability were strengthened through methodological triangulation combining quantitative and qualitative approaches, alongside data source triangulation incorporating primary and secondary sources.

13.3 Literature Review: Gender-Transformative Transition and Children's Rights in Climate-Vulnerable Communities

As the introductory section indicates, the intersection of climate change, gender inequality, and children's rights in post-land reform contexts represents one of the most complex challenges facing contemporary development scholarship and practice. This literature review examines how gender-transformative just transition approaches can address climate vulnerability among children in Zimbabwe's resettled farming communities, established through the FTLRP. To understand how these approaches can effectively address the multidimensional nature of climate vulnerability in these communities, it is essential first to establish the theoretical foundation upon which this analysis rests. The conceptual framework of gender transformation provides essential tools for understanding and addressing these challenges. Moving beyond gender-sensitive approaches that merely add women to existing processes, gender-transformative approaches challenge and reconstruct the social norms, power relations, and institutional structures that create and perpetuate inequality (Gero et al., 2018).

13.3.1 From Environmental Justice to Gender-Transformative Climate Justice

Gender-transformative climate justice emerged in the late twentieth and early twenty-first centuries through broader efforts to integrate gender lenses into environmental and climate policy, building on several foundational movements and theoretical frameworks. The concept has evolved significantly to encompass comprehensive frameworks for climate justice and social transformation. Contemporary understandings recognise that shifting to low-carbon economies must address historical injustices and structural inequalities, rather than reproducing or exacerbating them. This evolution represents a convergence of multiple social justice movements into a more inclusive framework for social transformation. Yet the full potential remains unrealised as long as gender inequality is treated as secondary rather than central to climate action (UNRISD, 2025).

The development of gender-transformative climate justice draws from environmental justice movements from the 1980s onwards, which highlighted how pollution and resource extraction negatively affect marginalised groups, including women of colour and low-income communities. Climate justice extends this framework to address global climate inequities, with gender as a core axis of analysis. Feminist and ecofeminist activism has been influential, emphasising how patriarchal structures exacerbate climate vulnerabilities and women's roles in resource management while advocating for systemic change beyond mere 'gender-sensitive' approaches. This advocacy has been amplified by groups like the Women and Gender Constituency at United Nations climate talks, which has pushed for gender-just solutions since the 2015 Paris Agreement.

Building on these activist foundations, the theoretical framework has been strengthened by intersectionality theory, drawing from scholars like Kimberlé Crenshaw (1989), to address overlapping oppressions, including gender, race, and class, in climate adaptation and policies. These diverse intellectual and activist roots have coalesced around principles prioritising recognition, resource redistribution, representation in decision-making, and reparations for historical harms, principles formalised in frameworks like UN Women's 'feminist climate justice' model (Turquet et al., 2023). Contemporary approaches emphasise creating equitable economic transitions that address how climate impacts exacerbate existing inequalities, especially women's over-representation in vulnerable sectors like agriculture.

The framework's expansion reflects a growing recognition that climate action cannot be separated from broader questions of social justice. Just transition approaches now encompass multiple dimensions of equity, including distributive justice (fair allocation of resources and burdens), procedural justice (meaningful participation in decision-making), and recognition justice (acknowledgement of diverse knowledge systems and experiences). However, just transition concepts are shaped by the recognition that climate change discourse and practice exist in dynamic tension, especially from Global South perspectives (Ud Din, 2025). The principle of common but differentiated responsibilities (CBDR) allocates environmental protection duties based on countries' historical contributions to environmental damage and their current capacity to address it (DGAP, 2025).

13.3.2 International Legal Frameworks and Children's Environmental Rights

The theoretical foundations of gender-transformative climate justice find practical expression in international legal frameworks that establish children's environmental rights. Applying a child-rights-based approach to the environment requires a full consideration of all children's rights under the United Nations Convention on the Rights of the Child (UNCRC) and the Optional Protocols (CRC, 2023). The landmark General Comment No. 26 (2023) recognises the right to a clean, healthy, and sustainable environment as part of the Convention through provisions concerning rights to life, health, adequate standard of living, and education. The Convention addresses environmental issues in Article 24(2)(c), which obliges States to combat disease and malnutrition while considering environmental pollution dangers, and in Article 29(1)(e), which requires them to direct children's education towards respect for the natural environment (CRC, 2023).

Regional frameworks strengthen this foundation through the African Charter on the Rights and Welfare of the Child (ACRWC), which provides instruments for protecting children's rights in Africa. Articles 11(2) and 14(2)(b) are especially relevant for addressing climate change impacts, although they require reinterpretation to fully address contemporary challenges in post-land reform contexts (Fokala & Muhumuza, 2024). African policy frameworks show progressive measures, including Sierra Leone's National Climate Change Policy 2021, Angola's National Strategy for Climate Change of 2017, the Gambia's 2050 Climate Vision, and legislative measures such as Nigeria's Climate Change Act (2021) and Uganda's National Climate Change Act (2021) (AECRW, 2025a, 2025b). The African Committee of Experts on the Rights and Welfare of the Child (ACERWC) has provided critical guidance through Resolution No. 18/2022, which outlines 12 key commitments for States Parties: incorporating child-specific risks into climate policies, upholding the best interests of the child in climate-related actions, and ensuring the meaningful participation of children in climate decision-making (AECRW Guidance Notes, 2025a, 2025b). Although not directly mentioned in the UNCRC or ACRWC, intergenerational equity promotes children's rights in climate contexts, ensuring that future generations are considered in current climate actions (Fambasayi & Addaney, 2021).

Despite these comprehensive legal and policy frameworks, their implementation faces significant practical challenges, especially in Global South contexts where the intersection of development needs and climate imperatives creates tensions. The tension between rapid decarbonisation demands and developmental needs is evident in debates over fossil fuel transitions and climate finance mechanisms. General Comment No. 26 emphasises the need to 'equitably phase out the use of coal, oil and natural gas' (CRC, 2023; Ud Din, 2025). This requirement poses challenges for Global South countries where coal remains a significant energy source. The challenge is compounded by structural biases in knowledge production, where considerations relevant to Global South contexts are often overlooked in climate change discourse (Ud Din, 2025). Ensuring equitable access to remedies for climate-affected children remains acute in Global South contexts, with questions about whether children can file cases relating to loss and damage in national and international judicial bodies.

13.4 Climate Change Impacts on Children: Global Context and Zimbabwe's Vulnerability

The practical implications of these legal frameworks become apparent when examining the lived realities of climate-vulnerable children globally and specifically in Zimbabwe's resettled farming communities. International recognition of the relationship between climate change and children's rights has grown substantially, with climate change and environmental degradation undermining children's rights, especially for the most disadvantaged. Children are the least responsible for climate change, yet they will bear its most significant impact. This climate injustice is illustrated by the asymmetry affecting marginalised populations in least developed countries (LDCs), which are most disproportionately impacted despite minimal contributions to global emissions (UNRISD, 2025). Every child on earth faces at least one climate and environmental hazard, with 850 million children (one in three) residing in regions where at least four climate and environmental shocks overlap and 330 million children (one in seven) living in areas affected by at least five major shocks (UNICEF-ESARO, 2025; UNICEF, 2025).

Gender disparities reflect structural inequalities that intersect with the vulnerabilities of children in, as in this case, resettled farming communities. Due to gender-based discrimination, women and gender-nonconforming persons have limited access to social protection systems and public services, exposing them to greater health risks from the climate emergency (UNRISD, 2025). These global patterns of climate vulnerability manifest with intensity in Zimbabwe, where children face mounting environmental pressures that threaten their rights and development, with specific implications for those in resettled farming communities established through land reform processes. This is where Zimbabwe's climate vulnerability is characterised by increasingly severe environmental changes that threaten children's well-being. The national average temperature has risen by 0.1 degrees Celsius per decade. It is projected to warm by 1.3–3.5 degrees by 2080, while average annual rainfall has declined 5% since 1901 and is projected to decline 15% by 2060 and 25% by

2080, especially in southwestern regions (GoZ, 2024). Drought frequency increased from 10% between 1902 and 1979 to 25% from 1980 to 2018, with notable episodes including 1991–1992, 1994–1995, 2002–2003, 2015–2016, 2018–2019, 2019-2020, and 2023–2024 (Gwitira et al., 2024). These deteriorating climate conditions create cascading effects across essential services for children's survival and development. Climate change negatively affects nutrition, health, education, and water, sanitation, and hygiene (WASH) systems, disproportionately impacting women, children, youth, people with disabilities, and the elderly (UNICEF, 2025; Gwitira et al., 2024).

The sectoral impacts of climate change demonstrate how environmental degradation systematically undermines the infrastructure and services upon which children's well-being depends. Climate vulnerabilities cascade across sectors critical to children's well-being, beginning with water resources where climate hazards cause increased evaporation, flooding and waterlogging, decreased water quality, and damage to water infrastructure (UNICEF ESARO, 2025; UNICEF, 2025). This can be especially severe in resettlement areas with less developed infrastructure. Agricultural systems providing food security and livelihoods face severe disruptions, including increased heat stress on crops and livestock, damage to agricultural infrastructure, increased evaporation and evapotranspiration, and changes in the distribution, incidence, and severity of insect pests, diseases, and weeds (Mirzabaev et al., 2023; Skendžić et al., 2021). For resettled farming communities, these challenges are worsened by limited access to credit, inputs, and technical support and ongoing adaptation to new farming environments (Chipenda, 2025).

Human settlements experience increasing vulnerabilities, including water pollution, heat stress and related diseases, exposure to pests and diseases, infrastructure and settlement flooding, and infrastructure safety risks. These converging sectoral impacts significantly threaten children's immediate safety and long-term development prospects across multiple domains (Gwitira et al., 2024). Climate change threatens children's lives and destroys schools, water supply and infrastructure, health care facilities, and children's play spaces, while reduced rainfall threatens crops critical to livelihoods and nutrition, potentially increasing poverty and children's protection risks (UNICEF, 2025). Among the most critical concerns is how climate change disrupts children's access to education, which is important for breaking cycles of poverty and vulnerability. Climate change critically disrupts children's education, with climate-exacerbated disasters hampering the education of nearly 40 million children globally, increasing yearly (UNICEF, 2021; Chipenda & Cochrane, 2024). In drought-affected areas, water insecurity reduces school attendance as children spend longer time fetching water, with 20% of girls and 5% of boys missing school time for water collection in normal circumstances in Ethiopia, increasing significantly during droughts (UNICEF, 2025).

Alongside educational disruption, the health consequences of climate change pose immediate and long-term risks to children's physical and mental well-being. Health impacts are multifaceted for women and children, with over 3.8 million people, primarily women and children, dying annually from indoor air pollution from unclean cooking, lighting, and heating systems (UNRISD, 2025). Children suffer more from air pollution than adults as they breathe faster and have vulnerable, developing organs, with household air pollution causing over 237,000 deaths of children under 5 per year globally (UNICEF, 2021, 2025). Mental health impacts are increasingly critical, with over 45% of children and young people ages 16–25 in ten countries reporting that climate change negatively affects their daily functioning. At the same time, extreme heat increases mental health problems, including post-traumatic stress disorder and depression, in children and adolescents (UNICEF, 2021, 2025).

13.5 Gender-Transformative Approaches in Rural Zimbabwe

Evidence from various districts across Zimbabwe illustrates the multifaceted nature of climate impacts on children, with attention to how these intersect with gender inequalities and structural marginalisation in ways that may be amplified in resettled farming contexts. In Bikita District, research has documented how climate change has had 'unprecedented' and 'debilitating' impacts on children's lives, resulting in school dropouts; child marriages; child labour, including illegal gold panning and vending; commercial sex work; food insecurities; and the spread of climate-induced diseases (Chikoko & Chihiya, 2023). Educational disruptions represent a significant dimension, with studies from Muzarabani District documenting how climate-induced disasters damage school infrastructure, leading to outdoor learning environments that negatively impact students' concentration and learning outcomes. Girls in particular are disproportionately affected as they face increased caregiving responsibilities and higher risks of permanent school dropout (Kahomwe & Muzingili, 2025).

Food security represents another critical pathway through which climate change affects children's rights in Zimbabwe. Research has demonstrated that climate change significantly influences child-feeding practices among rural households, with families often reducing the quantity and diversity of food provided to children as a coping mechanism during climate-stressed periods (Kembo et al., 2025). While necessary for household survival, this adaptation strategy directly undermines children's rights to adequate nutrition and can have lasting impacts on physical and cognitive development (Kembo et al., 2025). The gendered dimensions of food insecurity are significant, as women typically bear responsibility for household nutrition while having limited access to resources and decision-making power.

The literature reveals significant gender dimensions to climate vulnerability in Zimbabwe, with implications for children's rights that require gender-transformative approaches rather than merely gender-inclusive ones. Female-headed households consistently demonstrate lower levels of climate change knowledge and reduced access to adaptation resources, despite women's central roles in household food security and childcare (Bennie et al., 2025). This challenge has direct implications for children's well-being, as household adaptation strategies may inadvertently harm child nutrition and development when gender perspectives are not adequately considered.

Research has documented how climate stress exacerbates existing gender inequalities, with girls facing increased risks of child marriage, sexual exploitation, and educational exclusion during climate crises. The scarcity of resources and resulting increased poverty and stress pose a greater risk of violence against girls and women. This includes increased violence against children due to caregiver stress, sexual violence as girls are forced to fetch water from great distances, and the risk of transactional sex due to desperation for basic livelihood (UNICEF, 2025). A gender-transformative just transition approach recognises that incorporating a gender perspective into climate policy is not only just but also strategic (UNRISD, 2025). Such approaches must address the care economy, as women tend to be over-represented in informal and caring sectors, leaving them with fewer opportunities to participate in labour reskilling and retraining programmes while bearing primary responsibility for children's well-being during climate crises.

Emerging research in Zimbabwe has highlighted the importance of indigenous knowledge systems and community-based approaches to climate adaptation, with implications for gender-transformative just transition approaches in resettled farming communities. Studies employing Afrocentric methodologies have documented the value of traditional ecological knowledge in developing effective, culturally relevant adaptation strategies (Tickamyer, 2020). Integrating indigenous knowledge systems is especially appropriate for children's rights, as traditional child-rearing practices and community support systems may offer essential resources for protecting children during climate stress. However, the literature also reveals tensions between traditional practices and children's rights when harmful practices such as child marriage are used as climate adaptation strategies. Research in Chimanimani District has established that communities require disaster and climate-resilient infrastructure as a determinant for climate change adaptation, with gender-transformative approaches to infrastructure development considering how infrastructure design and access affect women, children, and marginalised groups differently (Tirivangasi & Nyahunda, 2025).

13.6 Policy Responses and Research Implications

Zimbabwe has developed an extensive climate policy architecture, yet significant gaps remain in addressing children's rights and gender equality. Key instruments include the National Climate Change Response Strategy (2014) and National Climate Policy (2017), which recognise children's and women's climate vulnerabilities (Gwitira et al., 2024). However, these policies have not adequately integrated gender-transformative approaches or addressed structural inequalities that shape children's climate experiences in post-land reform contexts. Thus, there exist critical research gaps in understanding how gender-transformative just transition approaches can be operationalised to protect children's rights in post-land reform settings. While theoretical frameworks exist, insufficient empirical research demonstrates their practical application where traditional social structures have been disrupted. In addition, children's agency in climate adaptation remains underexplored, with most research positioning them as passive victims rather than recognising their potential contributions to resilient communities.

This literature review establishes the importance of adopting gender-transformative just transition approaches to address climate change and children's rights in rural Zimbabwe's resettled farming communities. Informed by Global South perspectives and General Comment No. 26 (2023), the analysis reveals that climate impacts are gendered, with girls experiencing unique vulnerabilities amplified by structural inequalities and post-land reform circumstances. Children in Zimbabwe face unprecedented climate risks despite minimal contribution to global emissions, a significant climate injustice. In resettled farming communities, climate vulnerability manifests through disrupted agricultural livelihoods, educational disruption, health impacts, and infrastructure damage. Girls face additional risks, including increased caregiving responsibilities, higher dropout rates, and greater exposure to gender-based violence during climate crises.

The significance of this research thus extends beyond academic understanding to urgent policy needs. With less than 10 years to avoid the worst climate impacts, developing effective strategies to protect children's rights while addressing structural inequalities is both a moral and a strategic necessity. Gender-transformative just transition approaches offer a pathway for achieving these dual objectives but require careful adaptation to post-land reform contexts where traditional social structures have been disrupted. This research will thus fill critical knowledge gaps regarding gender-transformative approaches in post-land reform settings, offering perspectives to guide policy and programming for more resilient and equitable communities. The path forward requires recognising that climate justice and social justice are inextricably linked and that effective climate action must simultaneously address structural inequalities that create vulnerability while empowering children as agents of change in their communities.

13.7 Findings: Climate Vulnerability and Children's Rights in Zimbabwe's Resettlement Areas

Empirical evidence from Goromonzi and Zvimba districts reveals dynamic intersections between climate vulnerability and infrastructural challenges that shape children's rights realisation within FTLRP communities. Drawing on data from resettled farming households and key informants, this section examines how climate change compounds existing infrastructure deficits to create differentiated vulnerabilities for children, emphasising the gendered dimensions in which girls and boys experience these challenges differently.

13.7.1 Climate-Induced Water Insecurity and Gendered Educational Access

The intersection of water scarcity and educational access reveals how climate change systematically violates girls' rights to education while perpetuating gendered labour burdens in resettlement communities. This represents a critical manifestation of the climate-children's rights nexus, where environmental degradation directly translates into human rights violations. Field observations and interviews revealed significant gender-based disparities in water collection patterns that become critically acute during climate stress, with girls bearing disproportionate responsibility compared to their male counterparts. Infrastructural disparities between settlement types create unequal access to basic services. In Goromonzi A1 settlements, only 36% of households reported having water sources within 5 metres, compared to 86% of A2 households. This disparity creates significant inequities in children's time allocation and educational opportunities. Interview data consistently indicated that children participate in water collection, with distance directly affecting time investment. Crucially, this burden falls disproportionately on girls, who help mothers or female household members collect water before school, negatively impacting schedules and performance compared to boys, who are typically exempt. Climate variability intensifies these disparities dramatically as drought conditions force girls to travel longer and increasingly dangerous distances. An A1 farmer in Zvimba reported:

> In this area, we have faced water challenges for a long time; the major challenge has been access to safe drinking water. It is better now as there are a lot of boreholes that have been drilled by farmers and the government. When collecting water, the burden is usually on women and children. It is part of their daily tasks to ensure water is available for cooking, cleaning and other household tasks. Girls, even very young ones, participate in these tasks, and for poor households without wheelbarrows or scotch carts, it is hard work. It negatively affects children as it is a burden that they undertake, and it affects their schooling, play time, and engagement in other activities.

From a children's rights analytical framework, these water access patterns constitute systematic violations of multiple interconnected UNCRC rights. Article 28's guarantee of education becomes compromised when girls spend multiple hours daily collecting water, time that increases during dry seasons and when there are droughts, directly conflicting with school attendance and study. Boys typically maintain more consistent attendance as they are largely exempt from water collection. Article 24's provision for the highest attainable health standard is compromised when inadequate water access creates conditions for waterborne diseases and hygiene problems, disproportionately affecting girls. Article 19's protection from violence takes on critical dimensions when girls face increased risks of abuse and physical harm while travelling long distances to water sources during climate emergencies, risks that boys rarely encounter due to limited involvement.

Temporal analysis of water collection reveals the profoundly gendered nature of climate vulnerability. In Goromonzi A1 areas, 12% of households require up to an hour for water collection under normal conditions, while in Zvimba A1 settlements, 32% spend 31–60 minutes, and 2% spend over an hour daily. During dry seasons, these times reportedly double or triple, with women and girls primarily responsible for this labour-intensive task, directly conflicting with school attendance. This creates cumulative disadvantage as missed hours compound over time, generating educational gaps that are increasingly difficult to overcome. An A1 farmer and woman in Goromonzi stated:

> Access to clean water is essential for our daily lives. On this farm, we have many plots that make up A1 settlements. The boreholes that were on this farm were vandalised long ago, and we have to rely on the goodwill of those who drilled their boreholes, or we have to use wells. Many of us struggle because we have to walk far to get water suitable for drinking, and if it is from someone's borehole, we need to pay. Others are better off; they fill their tanks and buckets outside their homes or have taps inside their houses. The burden of collecting water falls on us, mothers and the girls. I have to admit, it is frustrating to see differences between households, as some of us have challenges getting basic drinking water while others have it right inside the house.

Through extensive interviews, a gendered assumption was observed, reportedly originating from communal areas, that assigns water collection responsibility exclusively to women and girls while exempting men and boys. This gender-based division reflects broader patriarchal structures that prioritise boys' education and development over girls. Addressing these challenges requires moving beyond infrastructure provision alone to simultaneously transforming climate adaptation and gender relations.

The climate-children's rights nexus becomes evident when examining escalating climate-related challenges. Climate change exacerbates disparities through increased drought frequency and intensity, rising from 10% between 1902 and 1979 to 25% from 1980 to 2018 in Zimbabwe. Gendered implications become clear in water transportation methods. In the study, it was noted that 49% of A1 households transport water by head, a physically demanding method performed primarily by girls and women, compared to 34% in A2 settlements, where 56% have tap access, versus only 23% in A1 areas. The physical demands of head-loading containers weighing up to 20 kilograms over distances exceeding 2 kilometres created long-term health implications, including neck, back, and spinal problems and delayed physical development by study participants. When men and boys participate, they are said to typically use more efficient methods such as bicycles, wheelbarrows or scotch carts, reducing both physical burden and time investment. In Zvimba, a respondent pointed out:

> When I was growing up, which is not so long ago, we collected water from different sources, but at times, if there was a prolonged dry spell, some of the water sources failed, and we had to go to alternatives which were far. It is a norm, an unwritten rule that women and girls collect water; this is changing gradually, but that is how it was then. We had to carry heavy loads over great distances. I think I was used to it because then I could cope; remember, it is something you would be doing every day. When I look back now, I think it created some form of cycle of physical exhaustion. If it was not collecting the water, it was collecting firewood or working on the farm. I am sure it influenced my schooling in a different way and affected my potential.

Daily water consumption patterns provide additional evidence of how climate vulnerability translates into immediate rights violations with differential impacts. In Goromonzi A1 settlements, 56% of households use only 51–80 litres daily, well below the World Health Organization's (WHO's) recommendation of 100–200 litres per household for adequate supply. This reflects constraint, not choice, as a rural district council official noted: '…water consumption patterns are not about choice or actual household needs. Many families, especially in A1 settlements, are forced to limit their daily water use due to access challenges. When households use only 50–80 litres per day, I believe it reflects infrastructure constraints rather than their actual requirements.' During prolonged dry spells, this inadequate consumption drops further. Respondents noted that women and girls, while primary collectors, are also responsible for minimising wastage, often restricting their own use. For girls, this impacts health, hygiene, and the ability to manage menstruation with dignity, challenges that boys do not face to the same extent. This gendered water scarcity creates compounded barriers to school attendance. It negatively impacts girls' welfare and well-being more severely than boys', who maintain greater daily flexibility and face fewer hygiene-related challenges.

These findings reveal a clear pattern where climate-induced water insecurity creates a cascade of rights violations that disproportionately affect girls by virtue of the intersection of environmental vulnerability, infrastructural inadequacy, and entrenched gender norms. This represents a serious challenge to achieving gender equality and children's rights realisation within climate-vulnerable communities.

13.7.2 Food Security and Climate Variability

Climate-induced changes to agricultural productivity create systematic patterns of educational disruption that disproportionately affect girls through culturally embedded gender hierarchies and household survival strategies. Research revealed how unpredictable rainfall patterns and increased drought frequency directly impact household food security, triggering gendered responses that compromise children's rights to education and adequate nutrition. Field observations and household interviews consistently demonstrated climate change's impact on crop yields across both districts, with the production of maize, the staple food crop, declining during drought years compared to regular seasons. This reduction directly translates into reduced household food and income, compromised nutrition, and increased food insecurity, forcing families to adopt survival strategies that disproportionately burden children.

Zimbabwe's declining precipitation creates conditions where families must make impossible choices between children's immediate survival and long-term development. Agricultural production data illustrate yield volatility and its direct impact on household income and food security. In Goromonzi, A1 households experienced significant variations between 2018–2019 and 2020–2021. While maize production increased 27.5% (from 6586 kg to 8396 kg per household), tobacco production declined drastically by 82.8% (from 3483 kg to 600 kg per household). Similarly, Zvimba A1 settlements showed modest maize growth of 5.9% per household, but the absolute production levels remained low (2204 kg to 2333 kg), indicating persistent food security challenges. A2 farmers demonstrated more resilient patterns, with Goromonzi A2 households achieving 52.3% maize production growth per household (from 51,180 kg to 77,958 kg), highlighting differential climate impact across settlement types. These volatilities translate directly into economic challenges that affect children differently. Interview data revealed that a dramatic decline in tobacco production, a critical cash crop, severely compromised household income for A1 farmers, forcing some families to reallocate children's time to income-generating activities and agricultural labour to compensate for reduced productivity and revenue.

Government initiatives have been implemented to promote climate-resilient farming practices in response to these climate-related agricultural challenges. The *Pfumvudza/Intwasa* programme, a government-sponsored conservation agriculture initiative, has been introduced to enhance household food security and build resilience against climate impacts. An agricultural extension officer in Goromonzi explained: '…we are actively promoting drought-resistant crop varieties including small grains like sorghum, pearl millet, and finger millet, which perform better under low rainfall conditions. The *Pfumvudza* programme which targets smallholder farmers is important because it helps farmers achieve food security using small plots through intensive farming methods. We encourage farmers to plant these climate-smart crops alongside traditional maise to diversify their production and reduce climate risks. However, adoption rates vary, with some farmers reluctant to shift from maise due to cultural preferences and market considerations.' Another agricultural extension officer in Zvimba noted: 'In the district, we also encourage the planting of small grains to supplement maise production for food security purposes in case of erratic rainfall patterns or input shortages. Some of the former communal area farmers who are beneficiaries of land reform of whom are many in this area have brought their experience and expertise in growing small grains.' While these government-led agricultural interventions aim to mitigate climate impacts on household food security, they inadvertently introduce new challenges for children as implementing climate adaptation strategies intensifies labour demands that fall disproportionately along gendered lines.

Labour demands of climate adaptation strategies create additional burdens for children, varying significantly by gender. Boys are increasingly required to engage in cattle grazing, often walking long distances to find adequate pasture during dry seasons, while girls face intensified domestic responsibilities, including fetching water over greater distances to water family gardens during droughts. These climate-induced labour demands directly compete with other activities, especially school attendance, creating systematic barriers to education access.

From a children's rights framework, climate-induced food insecurity violates CRC Article 27, which guarantees every child's right to an adequate standard of living sufficient for physical, mental, spiritual, moral, and social development. Empirical evidence demonstrates that reduced crop yields and household income force families into survival modes where children's immediate labour contributions take precedence over development. However, gendered dimensions of food distribution reveal how this right is systematically denied to girls through culturally embedded practices prioritising male household members during periods of scarcity. Article 2's non-discrimination principle is violated when, as indicated by a respondent, girls eat last and least in food-scarce households, creating nutritional deficiencies that compromise their cognitive development, educational performance, and long-term health outcomes, including future maternal mortality risks.

Climate-related income shocks, exemplified by the 82.8% decline in tobacco production per household in Goromonzi A1 areas, forced households to divert financial resources from some expenses to immediate recovery needs, including purchasing food during lean seasons, replacing damaged agricultural equipment, and seeking alternative livelihood strategies. The stark contrast between A1 and A2 production resilience—where A2 households in Goromonzi achieved 52.3% maize production growth, while A1 tobacco production declined—demonstrates how settlement type determines climate impact vulnerability. This financial reallocation affects women and girls more, exemplified by their education being considered less essential during economic hardship than that of boys. Female-headed households, comprising an important portion of resettlement communities, face heightened vulnerability to climate shocks due to limited access to agricultural inputs, credit, and climate information.

Agricultural support infrastructure access patterns demonstrate how climate adaptation capacity varies significantly across settlement types, directly impacting children's rights realisation. These disparities become critical during climate stress when households must maximise the utility of limited agricultural resources to maintain food security. For example, grinding mill access, essential for food processing during climate stress, showed marked disparities: 94% of Goromonzi A1 households and 90% of Zvimba A1 households have access compared to 72% and 46%, respectively, in A2 areas. During droughts, when families depend on stored grains and drought-resistant crops, access to processing facilities becomes critical for maintaining children's nutrition and preventing violations of their right to adequate food. An agricultural extension officer in Zvimba explained: 'Farmers in A1 areas rely more on local processing facilities due to their smaller landholdings, reasonable cost, accessibility and higher population density. When crop yields are low due to drought, having access to grinding mills becomes even more critical because families need to process whatever grain they have harvested efficiently to maximise its nutritional value and shelf life.'

The interconnection between infrastructure access and climate resilience extends beyond food processing to encompass the entire agricultural recovery cycle. Access to equipment repair facilities becomes crucial during post-drought recovery when functional agricultural tools determine whether families can rebuild livelihoods or face continued vulnerability. Data shows disparities: 94% in Goromonzi A1 versus 78% in A2, while 74% in Zvimba A1 versus 20% in A2. These patterns directly influence household recovery capacity and children's welfare during and after climate events. However, post-climate disaster recovery places additional financial strain on households, as families must allocate scarce resources to repairing or replacing damaged farming equipment, purchasing seeds for replanting, and covering increased food costs during lean periods, often at the direct expense of resources earmarked for children.

Financial constraints created by climate-induced agricultural losses translate directly into increased labour demands for children, creating a vicious cycle where climate impacts simultaneously reduce household income and increase children's workload. Research revealed that climate change has intensified children's involvement in agricultural labour, with tasks distributed along gender lines. Boys reported increased time herding livestock to distant grazing areas and constructing soil conservation structures. At the same time, girls described extended hours fetching water from increasingly distant sources to maintain household gardens during dry seasons. These labour-intensive tasks often require children to wake early and return home late, leaving little time for homework or rest. This increased labour burden represents a direct consequence of climate-induced agricultural stress, where children's time becomes a critical household resource mobilised for survival, directly competing with educational development.

The cascading effects of climate-induced agricultural disruption create a temporal pattern of vulnerability that extends far beyond immediate weather events, establishing prolonged periods of developmental disadvantage for children. Production data reveal that despite years of overall growth, such as the 27.5% increase in Goromonzi A1 maize production, a simultaneous decline of cash crops, like tobacco, creates mixed economic outcomes, compromising household stability. Households reported that recovery from severe production losses typically takes two to three agricultural seasons, during which children's development and well-being remain compromised due to ongoing economic constraints and increased labour demands. This extended timeline means a single climate event can disrupt children's development for multiple years, making cumulative effects increasingly difficult to reverse. This is especially pronounced for girls, whose lives can be permanently disrupted compared to boys.

For study participants, climate-induced agricultural disruptions create intergenerational cycles of vulnerability that perpertuate gender inequalities. For example, girls who miss extended schooling due to climate-related family survival needs enter adulthood with reduced adaptive capacity, limiting their ability to protect their children from future climate impacts, creating a reinforcing cycle where climate vulnerability begets educational disadvantage, increasing future climate vulnerability. Research documented cases where challenges, including climate-induced ones, led to permanent school dropout for girls as families prioritised immediate survival over long-term educational investment. An education officer in Zvimba described this phenomenon as creating '…a lost generation of girls whose education becomes secondary to family survival'. This pattern was reportedly observed in households where agricultural income had declined, forcing families to choose between paying school fees and purchasing food during extended droughts. Income decline represents a critical tipping point where households shift from temporary educational disruption to permanent educational abandonment, especially for girls, whose future earning potential is systematically sacrificed to address immediate climate-induced economic stress.

13.8 Energy Infrastructure, Climate Adaptation, and Gendered Time Poverty

Universal dependence on climate-vulnerable energy sources creates systematic violations of children's rights to education and development, primarily through intensified domestic labour burdens that expand during environmental stress. Research findings highlight near-complete reliance on firewood (100% in most settlements) across all household types, creating critical vulnerabilities during climate extremes when traditional fuel sources become scarce or inaccessible. Study participants indicated that climate change has significantly altered biomass fuel availability and accessibility, creating a cascading effect on children's rights through increased time poverty and physical exhaustion. This energy dependency intersects with gender roles to create climate-induced time poverty, disproportionately affecting girls who bear primary responsibility for fuel collection in the context of increasing environmental degradation.

The climate-children's rights nexus becomes evident when examining how environmental changes directly translate into increased labour burdens for children, creating systematic barriers to development. Electricity access disparities demonstrate how infrastructure inequities translate into differential climate adaptation capacity with significant negative implications for the realisation of children's rights. In Goromonzi, A2 settlements achieve 56% electricity connectivity compared to only 2% in A1 areas, while Zvimba shows 34% versus 6%, respectively. These disparities become critical during climate emergencies when electricity-connected households can access weather information, preserve food during power outages following storms, and maintain communication during disasters. Children in electrified households benefit from consistent lighting for evening study, reduced exposure to indoor air pollution from biomass burning, and relief from fuel collection responsibilities, allowing better school attendance. Households without electricity cannot adapt to changing climate patterns through technology, forcing continued dependence on traditional systems and creating intensified labour burdens for girls.

Field observations and focus group discussions revealed multifaceted ways in which climate change has intensified energy-related challenges for children. A focus group discussion revealed critical issues, including climate change negatively affecting firewood availability, increased heat and intense veld fires contributing to firewood scarcity, prolonged drought periods killing vegetation and reducing biomass regeneration rates, and extreme weather events damaging existing forest resources. These climate-induced changes directly translate into higher physical exhaustion for children involved in fuel collection, increased school absenteeism, and severely limited time for homework completion in households lacking alternative energy sources, which primarily affects girls more than boys, who are typically exempt from fuel collection responsibilities. From a children's rights perspective, this constitutes a violation of Article 2's non-discrimination principle as climate-vulnerable girls face systematically reduced opportunities for educational achievement and personal development. In addition, Article 28's education guarantee is compromised when girls are forced to sacrifice school attendance for an increasingly time-consuming fuel collection task. At the same time, Article 24's health provision is undermined by children's exposure to indoor air pollution and physical strain from carrying heavy fuel loads over extended distances.

The theoretical availability of alternative energy sources contrasts sharply with practical barriers, maintaining children's vulnerability to climate-induced energy scarcity. While showing high nominal access rates (96–98% in Goromonzi, 22–26% in Zvimba), gas usage patterns mask the reality that prohibitive costs prevent meaningful utilisation during climate stress. Interview data thus revealed that even when alternative fuels are theoretically accessible, economic constraints force households to reserve these resources for extreme emergencies, maintaining girls' primary responsibility for biomass fuel collection regardless of available alternatives. As women explained during interviews, when available, gas remains reserved for specific emergencies, while firewood remains the primary cooking fuel, sustaining girls' collection responsibilities. Gas distribution networks are absent in remote and difficult-to-access settlements, leaving households completely reliant on firewood. Unfortunately, this reliance is being increasingly challenged by climate change effects, including prolonged droughts, increased fire frequency, and reduced forest regeneration rates.

Key informant testimony provides concrete evidence of how climate change has systematically degraded the biomass fuel base upon which children depend. A lands officer in Goromonzi stated:

> Many households in this area rely on firewood, but it has become scarce. It has been used for a long time, and in many instances, it has not been replaced. The impact of climate change is also affecting vegetation here; trees, in particular, have been negatively affected. Firewood must be collected, but it is increasingly available from distant locations. The burden falls on women as well as girl children. A considerable amount of time must be invested in collecting firewood, which is hard work and not easy. Families with electricity and other sources of fuel, or those who planted gum trees over the years, are better off, even those who use trucks and scotch carts to collect or buy firewood.

This testimony illustrates how climate change creates a vicious cycle. Environmental degradation reduces fuel availability, forcing longer collection journeys that further compromise children's development and educational participation, exposing them to increased physical and safety risks. The intersection of climate vulnerability and energy poverty creates compounding violations of children's rights, requiring comprehensive interventions that address both infrastructure and social inequalities. Climate change has thus significantly altered the risk profile associated with fuel collection, creating new dimensions of vulnerability for children, especially girls. Climate implications of energy infrastructure become evident through deforestation, forcing girls to travel increasingly dangerous distances for household fuel needs. Respondents reported that nearby forests have been severely depleted due to both overuse and climate-induced vegetation loss, forcing women and girls to venture into unfamiliar areas where they face risks of physical harm, wildlife encounters, and sexual violence. These risks are compounded when desperation for fuel sources leads families to send children to increasingly remote and dangerous locations, directly violating Article 19's protection from violence and abuse.

Community responses to energy challenges demonstrate both the potential for collective action and the limitations of grassroots initiatives in addressing climate-induced infrastructure deficits. An A1 farmer in Zvimba district indicated that, in recognition of energy challenges over the past few years, some farming communities have spearheaded community initiatives to pool resources and electrify their farms. Over the years, several farming communities have been electrified through this initiative, but progress has been slow due to the lack of resources. However, these initiatives remain geographically limited and economically exclusive, often benefiting more prosperous households while leaving the most vulnerable families, especially those with limited financial resources, dependent on increasingly scarce biomass fuels. The overall study picture indicated that collective action for energy alternatives remains limited, leaving girls to bear individual responsibility for increasingly complex fuel collection tasks, significantly worsened by climate change impacts, including reduced forest cover, increased fire frequency, and prolonged drought periods that limit vegetation regeneration.

Findings reveal how climate change has transformed energy poverty from a development challenge into an urgent children's rights crisis, where environmental degradation directly translates into systematic violations of girls' rights to education, health, and protection from harm. The climate-energy-children's rights nexus demonstrates how environmental vulnerabilities compound existing inequalities to create new forms of disadvantage that disproportionately affect the most marginalised children in climate-vulnerable communities.

13.8.1 Health Infrastructure Deficits and Climate-Sensitive Disease Burden

Climate change has significantly transformed the health landscape in rural Zimbabwe's resettlement areas, creating new disease vulnerability patterns while undermining the infrastructure needed to respond to these challenges. Limited health infrastructure creates acute vulnerabilities to climate-sensitive diseases, disproportionately affecting women and girls through their roles as primary caregivers and their reduced mobility during health emergencies. The climate-children's rights nexus becomes evident in health outcomes, where environmental degradation directly translates into violations of Article 24's guarantee of the highest attainable health standard, with girls experiencing heightened vulnerabilities due to intersecting gender, age, and climate factors.

Spatial inequalities in health infrastructure are exacerbated by climate change impacts on transport networks and emergency access, creating life-threatening barriers to healthcare for children, especially girls. Research revealed disparities in healthcare access, becoming critical during climate-related health crises. In Goromonzi's A2 settlements, 0% of households have health centres within 5 kilometres due to their large land area, while 82% of A1 households have such access. However, climate-induced infrastructure damage frequently negates these proximity advantages, including roads rendered impassable by flooding, bridges destroyed by extreme weather events, and transport disrupted during seasonal rains. Focus group discussions revealed that these infrastructure challenges reflect underlying economic constraints and cultural norms, systematically disadvantaging women and girls in accessing healthcare, with climate change adding additional vulnerability layers.

Extreme weather events and health infrastructure deficits create cascading rights violations that affect children's access to essential healthcare services. An A1 farmer in Goromonzi explained:

> Having good health facilities nearby is important for us. It is frustrating that we often have to travel far to get even the most basic healthcare in our area. The situation is terrible when we have emergencies, and the most affected are women and children. During the rainy season, roads become impassable, and rivers flood, making it impossible to reach clinics even when we have health emergencies. Some women have had to deliver babies at home because they could not cross flooded rivers to reach the clinic. We see farmers in other areas getting the health services they need right at their doorstep, and many agree with me that this is unfair.

This reveals how climate-induced infrastructure damage compounds spatial inequalities in health access, creating emergencies where children and women face life-threatening delays in accessing healthcare. These disparities occur in a context where climate-sensitive disease patterns create specific vulnerabilities for women and adolescent girls, whose reproductive health needs intersect with climate-related health risks in ways that violate multiple dimensions of their rights. Climate change has thus created new health risks while simultaneously degrading the systems needed to address them, establishing vulnerability patterns that affect children and adolescents. Interview data revealed that extreme heat events, which increased in frequency and intensity, create health risks for children, including heat exhaustion, dehydration, and exacerbation of respiratory conditions. Water scarcity during dry seasons forces families to rely on unsafe water sources. This leads to increased incidence of waterborne diseases, including cholera, typhoid, and diarrheal diseases, affecting children due to lower immunity levels. Interviews indicated that when extreme weather events occur, they disrupt already limited reproductive health services, creating conditions where women and girls face increased risks of early pregnancy, unsafe deliveries, and maternal mortality. Research documented cases where flooded rivers and damaged roads prevented pregnant women and girls from accessing healthcare facilities, forcing home deliveries under unsafe conditions. Women, especially those in remote settlements, at times deliver babies at home due to distance challenges compounded by unreliable transport systems and severely damaged roads, illustrating how climate impacts create cascading health rights violations that affect young women.

Water scarcity creates specific health vulnerabilities for girls, intersecting with cultural practices to compound disadvantage during climate stress periods. Research found that prolonged droughts create acute challenges for menstrual hygiene management as water scarcity forces families to prioritise water use for drinking and cooking over hygiene needs. Girls reported being unable to maintain proper menstrual hygiene during water-scarce periods, leading to infections, school absences, and psychological distress. Cultural restrictions on girls' mobility during menstruation are compounded by water scarcity, creating situations where girls face health risks from inadequate hygiene while simultaneously being restricted from seeking healthcare due to cultural taboos.

Extreme weather events create immediate health risks, exposing children to life-threatening conditions while simultaneously disrupting the healthcare systems they depend on for treatment. Field observations documented how extreme heat events, increasingly common due to climate change, create vulnerabilities for children who spend extended hours outdoors for agricultural labour, water collection, and livestock herding. Children reportedly experience symptoms including headaches, dizziness, nausea, and heat exhaustion, with girls facing additional risks due to cultural expectations that they continue domestic duties even during extreme heat periods. Research found that healthcare facilities lack adequate infrastructure and heat-related treatment protocols, leaving children without appropriate care during extreme temperatures.

Mental health implications of climate stress reveal gendered patterns of psychological distress, receiving minimal attention in resettlement communities with limited psychosocial support infrastructure. Interview data revealed that girls report significantly higher levels of climate anxiety, environmental distress, and trauma related to extreme weather events compared to boys. Like women, they worry about drought impacts on family food security, fear flooding and extreme weather events, and experience anxiety about their future in the context of environmental degradation. However, cultural norms discouraging girls' emotional expression and restricting their mobility limit their access to mental health support, creating a pattern where those most psychologically affected by climate change have the least access to support services. The absence of mental health services that specifically address climate-related trauma means that children's psychological well-being needs remain unmet, violating Article 24's provision for mental health as part of overall health standards.

Infrastructure damage from extreme weather events creates long-term health system vulnerabilities that affect children's access to preventive healthcare and treatment of chronic conditions. Research documented how flooding, storms, and extreme weather damage health facilities and disrupt vaccination programmes, creating gaps in preventive healthcare for children. Health workers reported that extreme weather events frequently damage clinics and make roads impassable, disrupting health service provision and immunisation schedules. These disruptions create windows of vulnerability where children face increased risks of preventable diseases, with recovery periods extending for months after extreme weather events.

Findings demonstrate how climate change has transformed health challenges from isolated medical issues into systematic violations of children's rights, where environmental degradation creates cascading health vulnerabilities that intersect with gender, infrastructure, and cultural practices to disproportionately harm girls. The climate-health-children's rights nexus reveals how environmental changes directly translate into health inequalities, compounding existing disadvantages and creating new forms of vulnerability for the most marginalised children in climate-affected communities.

13.9 Conclusion

This research has revealed the significant and systematic ways in which climate change impacts intersect with post-colonial agrarian transformation to create unprecedented violations of children's rights in Zimbabwe's resettlement areas. The empirical evidence from Goromonzi and Zvimba districts demonstrates that climate vulnerability operates not as an isolated environmental challenge but as a dynamic web of intersecting inequalities that disproportionately affects girls by amplifying existing structural disadvantages. Through systematic analysis of household experiences across the two districts, this research shows how climate change impacts operate through four interconnected pathways that undermine children's rights within resettled farming communities. These include climate-induced water insecurity, which creates gendered educational barriers; food security disruptions, which compel survival-oriented labour mobilisation; energy infrastructure deficits, which intensify domestic work burdens; and health system vulnerabilities, which compound climate-sensitive disease risks. These pathways demonstrate how environmental degradation becomes embedded within existing social structures, amplifying gender inequalities while creating new forms of disadvantage for girls who navigate intensified household responsibilities during environmental stress.

The empirical evidence reveals the specific mechanisms through which climate impacts generate differentiated vulnerabilities for children across settlement types. The stark disparities between A1 and A2 settlements demonstrate how post-land reform settlement patterns intersect with climate vulnerability, creating systematic inequalities in children's development opportunities. The decline in tobacco production in Goromonzi A1 areas, contrasted with maize production growth in A2 settlements, illustrates how climate-induced agricultural shocks affect different communities unequally, with direct implications for children's welfare and educational participation.

The gender-transformative just transition framework from this analysis requires recognition that climate action cannot be separated from broader social justice imperatives. The evidence demonstrates that climate adaptation strategies that fail to address structural gender inequalities will inevitably reproduce and amplify existing patterns of disadvantage. When girls spend multiple hours daily collecting water from increasingly distant sources while boys maintain consistent school attendance, when girls eat last and least during climate-induced food scarcity, and when girls bear primary responsibility for fuel collection from depleted forests, these patterns represent not unfortunate side effects of climate impacts but systematic violations of human rights principles.

The theoretical significance of these findings extends beyond the specific context of Zimbabwe's resettlement areas to broader questions of climate justice and development. The research reveals how the intersection of environmental vulnerability, post-colonial agrarian transformation, and gender inequality creates new forms of structural violence that cannot be addressed through technical adaptation measures alone. The framework of climate-induced time poverty that emerges from the data, where environmental degradation directly translates into increased labour burdens for girls, provides a critical analytical tool for understanding how climate change operates as a mechanism of social reproduction that perpetuates intergenerational inequalities.

The policy implications are both urgent and far-reaching. The research demonstrates that interventions addressing climate adaptation, infrastructure development, and children's rights must be conceived as integrated responses rather than separate policy domains. The evidence that 490 million children across Africa face extremely high climate risks while Zimbabwe ranks as the 15th most vulnerable country globally despite its minimal contribution to emission highlights the moral imperative for transformative approaches that simultaneously address environmental challenges and structural inequalities. Theoretically, the research contributes to expanding the understanding of how gender-transformative approaches can be operationalised in post-land reform contexts where traditional social structures have been disrupted but gender hierarchies remain entrenched. The findings reveal that resettlement areas represent spaces of both opportunity and vulnerability, where new forms of social organisation can reproduce existing inequalities or create foundations for more equitable development patterns.

The temporal dimensions of climate vulnerability documented in this research, where drought events create development disruptions over the years, highlight the cumulative nature of climate-induced disadvantage. This temporal pattern is especially significant for girls, whose educational disruptions during climate stress often become permanent due to cultural priorities favouring boys' long-term development over immediate household survival needs. The research thus reveals how climate change creates not just immediate hardships but also systematic patterns of intergenerational inequality transmission. The urgency of the research findings cannot be overstated. With climate projections indicating that Zimbabwe's national average temperature will increase by 1.3–3.5 degrees by 2080 while precipitation declines by up to 25%, the violations of children's rights documented in this research will intensify dramatically without transformative interventions. The current generation of children in resettlement areas faces unprecedented environmental challenges that threaten not only their immediate welfare but also their capacity to protect future generations from accelerating climate impacts.

The path forward requires a recognition that climate justice and gender equality are inextricably linked imperatives that cannot be pursued through separate policy frameworks. Gender-transformative just transition approaches offer a pathway for addressing these interconnected challenges, but their implementation requires political commitment to confronting structural inequalities that extend far beyond environmental policy domains. The evidence presented in this research demonstrates that protecting children's rights in the climate crisis requires nothing less than transforming the social systems that create and perpetuate vulnerability. This research thus contributes to a growing body of scholarship that positions climate change not merely as an environmental challenge requiring technical solutions but also as a catalyst that exposes and amplifies existing injustices while creating new forms of structural violence. The children of Zimbabwe's resettlement areas, bearing no responsibility for the climate crisis yet facing its most severe consequences, represent both the moral urgency and transformative potential of gender-transformative climate action. Their experiences reveal that the climate crisis is ultimately a justice crisis, requiring responses that centre on equity, transformation, and the dignity of those most affected by environmental change.

References

ACERWC. (2025a). *ACERWC study on climate change & children's rights in Africa: A continental overview - 2024*. ACERWC Secretariat.

ACERWC. (2025b). *Guidance Note on Prioritising Child-Rights Based Climate Action at the Africa Climate Summit 2025*. Retrieved September 25, 2025, from https://www.acerwc.africa/en/key-documents/substantive-guidelines/guiding-note-prioritizing-child-rights-based-climate-action

Bennie, A., Hoveni, J., Madhi, Y., Farr, V., & Ngcukana, L. (2025). *A care approach to achieving gender justice in southern African food systems in the context of climate change*. Working paper for the Climate Ambition to Accountability Project. Retrieved September 27, 2025, from https://www.iej.org.za/wp-content/uploads/2025/04/Working-Paper_-Food-systems-and-care.pdf

Chikoko, W., & Chihiya, P. (2023). Climate change and vulnerabilities of children in rural Zimbabwe: The case of ward 14 of Bikita District, Zimbabwe. *African Journal of Social Work, 13*(2), 78–86. https://doi.org/10.4314/ajsw.v13i2.4

Chipenda, C. (2025). Transformative social policy through land reform, women's economic agency and rural social change in Zimbabwe, *Journal of Asian and African Studies*. https://doi.org/10.1177/00219096251313546

Chipenda, C., & Cochrane, L. (2024). Out of school children in the context of new policy trajectories and interlocking crises in Zimbabwe: A transformative social policy perspective. *SN Social Sciences, 4*, 131. https://doi.org/10.1007/s43545-024-00938-1

Committee on the Rights of the Child. (2023). General comment No. 26 (2023) on children's rights and the environment, with a special focus on climate change: Committee on the Rights of the Child. *International Human Rights Law Review, 12*(2), 322–355. https://doi.org/10.1163/22131035-12020006

Crenshaw, K. (1989). Mapping the margins: Intersectionality, identity politics, and violence against women of colour. *Stanford Law Review, 43*(6), 1241–1299. https://doi.org/10.2307/1229039

Fambasayi, R., & Addaney, M. (2021). Cascading impacts of climate change and the rights of children in Africa: A reflection on the principle of intergenerational equity. *African Human Rights Law Journal, 21*(1), 29–51. https://doi.org/10.17159/1996-2096/2021/V21N1A3

Fokala, E., & Muhumuza, N. (2024). Chapter 9 Eroding Children's Rights: An Analysis of the Utility of the African Charter on the Rights and Welfare of the Child to Climate Action in Africa. In *The Social, Economic and Cultural Rights of Children in Africa*. Brill | Nijhoff. Retrieved September 29, 2025, from https://doi.org/10.1163/9789004685604_010

German Council on Foreign Relations (DGAP). (2025). *Common But Differentiated Responsibilities (CBDR)*. Glossary, Climate Policy. Retrieved September 29, 2025, from https://dgap.org/en/research/glossary/climate-foreign-policy/common-differentiated-responsibilities-cbdr#:~:text=The%20principle%20of%20Common%20But,environmental%20destruction%20associated%20with%20it

Gero, A., Winterford, K., Megaw, T., Kauhue, E. & Tangi, T. (2018). *Beyond a token effort: Gender transformative climate change action in the Pacific*. Retrieved September 28, 2025, from https://wrd.unwomen.org/practice/resources/beyond-token-effort-gender-transformative-climate-change-action-pacific

Government of Zimbabwe. (2024). *Zimbabwe National Climate Change Adaptation Plan*. Ministry of Environment, Climate and Wildlife.

Gwitira, I., Shekede, M. D., & Bhatasara, S. (2024). *Child-centred climate impact, vulnerability, and risk assessment for Zimbabwe*. UNICEF.

Hausfather, Z., & Friedlingstein, P. (2024). Analysis: Global CO_2 emissions will reach new high in 2024 despite slower growth. *Carbon Brief*, 13 November. Retrieved September 26, 2025, from https://www.carbonbrief.org/analysis-global-co2-emissionswill-reach-new-high-in-2024despite-slower-growth/

Kahomwe, L., & Muzingili, T. (2025). Impact of climate change disasters on access to education and coping mechanisms for rural learners in Zimbabwe. *Cogent Education, 12*(1), 2517505. https://doi.org/10.1080/2331186X.2025.2517505

Kembo, G., Kairiza, T., Dembedza, M. P., Manditsera, F. A., & Macheka, L. (2025). Climate change knowledge and changes in child feeding practices in rural Zimbabwe. *Journal of Hunger & Environmental Nutrition*, 1–14. https://doi.org/10.1080/19320248.2025.2532132

Madamombe, S. M., Ng'ang'a, S. K., Öborn, I., et al. (2024). Climate change awareness and adaptation strategies by smallholder farmers in semi-arid areas of Zimbabwe. *International Journal of Agricultural Sustainability, 22*(1), 2293588.

Mirzabaev, A., Kerr, R. B., Hasegawa, T., Pradhan, P., Wreford, A., Pahlen, M. C. T. V. D., & Gurney-Smith, H. (2023). Severe climate change risks to food security and nutrition. *Climate Risk Management, 39*, Article 100473. https://doi.org/10.1016/j.crm.2022.100473

Moyo, S. (2011). Changing agrarian relations after redistributive land reform in Zimbabwe. *Journal of Peasant Studies, 38*(5), 939–966.

Mpala, T. A., & Simatele, M. D. (2024). Climate-smart agricultural practices among rural farmers in Masvingo district of Zimbabwe: Perspectives on the mitigation strategies to drought and water scarcity for improved crop production. *Frontiers in Sustainable Food Systems, 7*, 129890.

Skendžić, S., Zovko, M., Živković, I. P., Lešić, V., & Lemić, D. (2021). The impact of climate change on agricultural insect pests. *Insects, 12*(5), 440. https://doi.org/10.3390/insects12050440

Tickamyer, A. R. (2020). Parsing the concepts and practices of gender, development, disaster, and climate change: Visions of transformation. *Journal of Development Perspectives, 4*(1–2), 23–38. https://doi.org/10.5325/jdevepers.4.1-2.0023

Tirivangasi, H. M., & Nyahunda, L. (2025). Determinants of transformative climate change adaptation in rural Zimbabwe: an afrocentric analysis. *Climate Policy*, 1–15. https://doi.org/10.1080/14693062.2025.2521486

Turquet, L., Tabbush, C., Staab, S., Williams, L., & Howell, B. (2023). *Feminist Climate Justice: A Framework for Action. Conceptual framework prepared for Progress of the World's Women series*. UN-Women.

Ud Din, A. (2025). Protecting children's rights from climate change: analysing the CRC's general comment through global south perspectives. *Children's Geographies*, 1–14. https://doi.org/10.1080/14733285.2025.2556421

UNCTAD (UN Conference on Trade and Development). (2023). *The Least Developed Countries Report 2023*. UNCTAD. Retrieved September 27, 2025, from https://unctad.org/system/files/official-document/ldc2023_en.pdf

UNICEF. (2021). *The climate crisis is a child rights crisis: Introducing the Children's Climate Risk Index*. UNICEF.

UNICEF. (2025). *When the rains do not come: Climate change through the eyes of Zimbabwe's children*. Retrieved September 24, 2025, from https://www.unicef.org/zimbabwe/stories/when-rains-dont-come-climate-change-through-eyes-zimbabwes-children

UNICEF East Asia and Pacific Regional Office. (2025). *Climate-resilient child protection systems in East Asia and the Pacific: Technical brief*. UNICEF.

UNRISD (United Nations Research Institute for Social Development) and GI-ESCR (Global Initiative for Economic, Social and Cultural Rights). (2025). *Ensuring Justice in Transition: A Gender-Transformative Approach*. UNRISD.

Utete, C. M. B. (2003). *Presidential land review committee under the chairmanship of Dr C.M.B. Utete, Volume 1 main report and Volume 2 special studies*. Government Printers.

Chapter 14
Corporate Social Responsibility and Child-Centred Climate Resilience in Zimbabwe's Mining and Manufacturing Sectors

Funa Moyo, Mthuthukisi Ncube, and Clement Chipenda

14.1 Introduction

Climate change disproportionately threatens children, with nearly one billion children, almost half the world's 2.2 billion young lives, residing in countries at extremely high climate risk (UNICEF ESA, 2025). This crisis is especially acute in regions facing systemic vulnerabilities, where climate shocks amplify existing inequalities and developmental challenges. In Eastern and Southern Africa, 51 million children face overlapping crises intensified by climate-exacerbated weather patterns. Zimbabwe exemplifies this vulnerability, ranking 15th globally and among the top three in Southern Africa on the 2021 Global Climate Risk Index (UNICEF, 2021). The country's 6.5 million children confront escalating droughts, erratic rainfall, flooding, and rising temperatures, which threaten their rights to survival, development, health, and education (UNICEF ESA, 2025; UNICEF, 2025).

These climate vulnerabilities do not manifest as abstract statistics but rather translate into concrete threats that directly compromise children's daily lived realities and developmental trajectories. Zimbabwe's climate crisis manifests through interconnected pathways that compound children's vulnerabilities. Prolonged droughts have crippled food and water supplies; extreme weather events, like Cyclone Idai in 2019, destroyed schools and infrastructure; and changing disease

F. Moyo (✉) · M. Ncube
Institute of Development Sciences, National University of Science and Technology, Bulawayo, Zimbabwe
e-mail: funa.moyo@nust.ac.zw; mthuthukisi.ncube@nust.ac.zw

C. Chipenda
South African Research Chair in Social Policy, College of Graduate Studies, University of South Africa, Pretoria, South Africa

E. Ndhlovu, C. Chipenda (eds.), *Climate Change and Children's Rights in Zimbabwe*, https://doi.org/10.1007/978-981-95-6005-9_14

patterns increasingly affect child health (Gwitira et al., 2024). In Southern Africa alone, over 30 million people suffer from severe drought, with rural communities pushed to the brink of collapse as rain shortfalls critically affect crop growth, leading to widespread harvest failures and acute hunger (UNICEF ESA, 2025). These climate impacts directly undermine children's rights as articulated in the United Nations Convention on the Rights of the Child (UNCRC), especially Article 24, which mentions considering 'the dangers and risks of environmental pollution' in fulfilling children's rights (UN, 1989).

Zimbabwe's mining and manufacturing sectors, which contribute over 60% of national exports (Zimbabwe Chamber of Mines, 2022) and serve as economic pillars, are uniquely positioned yet underutilised in addressing this crisis. Despite possessing considerable financial resources and technical capacity, these industries have been slow to recalibrate their corporate social responsibility (CSR) approaches to respond to emerging climate imperatives. While some companies have initiated isolated environmental efforts—for example, Zimplats' environmental conservation initiatives and Delta Corporation's renewable energy exploration (Zimplats, 2020; Delta, 2020)—these remain largely peripheral activities disconnected from the urgent, intersectional challenge of climate-threatened children's rights. Traditional CSR investments have predominantly concentrated on conventional infrastructure provision, health programmes, and education initiatives, with funding allocations that neither prioritise the most climate-vulnerable populations nor integrate a child rights lens into their design and implementation.

This misalignment is concerning, given the compounding nature of climate impacts on children. Seasonal food scarcity, a driver of child wasting, is common in Zimbabwe, while climate-induced displacement increases children's vulnerability to violence and exploitation. The scarcity of resources and the resulting poverty pose greater risks of violence against girls and women, including sexual violence, as girls are forced to fetch water from greater distances (UNICEF, 2025). However, corporate responses remain inadequately targeted towards these compounding vulnerabilities, revealing a critical disconnect between CSR practice and the lived realities of climate-affected children.

This critical gap persists despite Zimbabwe's commitment to multiple frameworks, including the National Climate Policy (2017), Nationally Determined Contributions (2021), and the Children's Act (Chapter 5:06). The absence of adequately resourced, climate-responsive, child-centred CSR strategies represents a missed opportunity and a governance failure, limiting the sectors' potential contribution to climate resilience while undermining the progressive realisation of children's rights in a rapidly changing environment. These challenges necessitate examining how CSR initiatives in Zimbabwe's mining and manufacturing sectors can be strategically reoriented to protect and advance children's rights in the context of climate change and what governance frameworks and policy mechanisms are necessary to unlock private-sector resources for child-centred climate resilience. To address these questions, this chapter pursues two interconnected objectives: first, examining the potential and dynamics of CSR in realising children's rights within Zimbabwe's climate-vulnerable context by identifying barriers, opportunities, and existing practices in the mining and manufacturing sectors and, second, developing actionable frameworks and policy recommendations that incentivise and guide private-sector investment in climate-responsive CSR that prioritises children's rights, survival, and development.

This analysis is grounded in stakeholder theory, which recognises that businesses hold responsibilities extending beyond shareholders to diverse stakeholders, including children, employees, local communities, and the environment (Freeman, 1984). The theory emphasises the interdependence of various groups, including mining companies, local communities, government institutions, and non-governmental organisations (NGOs), in fostering effective CSR initiatives that address climate impacts on children. By examining stakeholder dynamics and governance, the chapter highlights the importance of collaboration in crafting sustainable child-centred climate-resilient initiatives.

The chapter's significance lies in integrating three critical domains: climate change adaptation, children's rights, and CSR within Zimbabwe's context. As climate vulnerabilities intensify and African nations seek innovative, multidisciplinary approaches for sustainability, understanding how to mobilise private-sector resources for child protection becomes a strategic imperative. This chapter seeks to position Zimbabwe's resource-endowed industries as meaningful contributors to an Africa-centric and sustainable response to the climate crisis that places children's rights at the centre of corporate climate action.

14.2 Methodology

The study adopted a pragmatic paradigm, integrating qualitative and quantitative methods through an explanatory-sequential mixed-method approach to examine climate-responsive, child-centred CSR in Zimbabwe's mining and manufacturing sectors. This design combined systematic literature review and document analysis to provide comprehensive insights into the realisation of mechanisms, challenges, and opportunities for CSR-driven children's rights.

A systematic literature review was conducted using the PRISMA (Preferred Reporting Items for Systematic Reviews and Meta-Analyses) framework to ensure structured and transparent analysis. During identification, academic databases (Scopus, Web of Science, Google Scholar) and grey literature (policy documents, NGO reports) were systematically searched using the following keywords: 'climate finance', 'corporate social responsibility', 'mining and manufacturing sector', 'children's rights', 'Zimbabwe', and 'Southern Africa'. The initial search yielded 65 records. Following duplicate removal and screening based on titles and abstracts against pre-defined inclusion criteria, 50 full-text articles were retrieved for detailed eligibility assessment. The final 50 articles provided substantive perspectives on climate-responsive CSR financing mechanisms and children's rights considerations.

Document analysis focused on publicly available corporate governance reports from mining and manufacturing sectors, government policies on climate change and child welfare, and industry standards. The authors analysed only publicly accessible documents without seeking proprietary information, employing fair, balanced, and evidence-based critique while acknowledging potential biases through mitigation strategies, including multiple sources, triangulation, and peer review. Thematic synthesis extracted key findings, focusing on existing frameworks, practices, and gaps through familiarisation with data, initial coding, theme identification, review and refinement, validation, and reporting. Integration involved cross-validating findings between the literature review and document analysis, identifying convergence and divergence patterns. Triangulation through the combination of multiple sources and methods strengthened validity and reliability. This approach enabled the development of a cohesive narrative highlighting key themes, patterns, and relationships relevant to unlocking private-sector resources for child-centred climate resilience in Zimbabwe.

14.3 Theoretical Framework: Stakeholder Theory and Child-Centred Climate Action

Stakeholder theory, introduced by Freeman (1984), posits that organisations have responsibilities extending beyond shareholders to all stakeholders, including employees, customers, suppliers, local communities, and the environment. The theory recognises that organisations operate within dynamic relationship webs where actions significantly impact various stakeholders (Freeman et al., 2010). This theory proves relevant in the context of CSR and climate resilience financing as organisations must consider their operational impacts on environments and local communities, taking steps to mitigate harm (Carroll & Shabana, 2010). This includes investing in climate resilience initiatives benefiting organisations and their stakeholders, especially vulnerable populations such as children (Linnenlucke et al., 2013). By adopting a stakeholder approach, organisations can better manage social and environmental impacts, reduce risks, and capitalise on climate-related opportunities (Sullivan et al., 2018).

Within Zimbabwe's mining and manufacturing contexts, Stakeholder theory gains heightened significance when children's vulnerabilities are centred. These businesses hold responsibilities extending to diverse stakeholder groups, namely employees, customers, suppliers, local communities, and, critically, children whose rights and developmental needs must be recognised rather than subsumed within broader community categories. This perspective is essential in addressing climate change resilience, as varied climate risk impacts demand inclusive decision-making that acknowledges children as stakeholders in their own right with unique physiological, psychological, and social developmental vulnerabilities.

In industries like mining and manufacturing, companies such as Zimplats and Delta Corporation face direct and indirect climate-related challenges that affect their stakeholders. Employees contend with altered working conditions and safety concerns, while local communities, especially children, face vulnerabilities from environmental degradation and climate-induced disruptions (Jenkins & Yakovleva, 2006). Children's physiological vulnerability during critical developmental periods amplifies these risks. Maternal under-nutrition, infection, pollution exposure, and illness during pregnancy can cause lifelong damage, including physical stunting, neurological impairments, and immune dysfunction (UNICEF, 2025). In addition, customers and investors increasingly favour businesses prioritising sustainability and exhibiting proactive climate risk management (Mitchell et al., 1997).

Aligning corporate strategies with stakeholder interests, especially children's rights, is essential for the legitimacy and effectiveness of resilience initiatives. However, current applications of stakeholder theory in corporate climate responses often relegate children to an undifferentiated category within 'community' rather than recognising them as primary stakeholders whose developmental trajectories are disproportionately shaped by climate impacts. Delta Corporation's exploration of renewable energy options and sustainable water management techniques, for example, demonstrates nascent alignment (Delta, 2020), yet these initiatives remain predominantly operational in focus rather than designed to advance children's rights to health, education, and development.

By collaborating with stakeholders, involving local communities in adaptive strategies, engaging investors to align financial goals with sustainability objectives, and prioritising children's needs as central rather than incidental considerations, companies can co-create environmentally sustainable and socially beneficial value. For mining and manufacturing companies, resilience efforts must address various stakeholder interests while recognising children as vulnerable stakeholders whose participation in decision-making processes (age-appropriately mediated) can enhance climate interventions' legitimacy and effectiveness. Climate risks directly affect employee safety and working conditions, while local communities face severe disruptions from environmental degradation and climate-induced challenges (Jenkins & Yakovleva, 2006).

Stakeholder theory thus provides a normative framework for integrating stakeholder concerns, especially children's rights, into resilience planning. This approach fosters trust, reduces disproportionate harm, and enhances companies' capacity to innovate and adapt to climate challenges, ensuring long-term success and societal alignment.

14.4 Zimbabwe's Mining and Manufacturing Sectors and CSR Climate Responses

14.4.1 Economic Significance and the Climate-Child Nexus

Zimbabwe's mining sector constitutes a critical economic component, contributing significantly to national gross domestic product (GDP), export earnings, and employment (Mutambanengwe, 2021). The country's vast mineral resources, including gold, platinum, coal, and diamonds, offer substantial investment and development opportunities. Mining drives the majority of national exports, positioning the sector as an economic pillar (Zimbabwe Chamber of Mines, 2022). However, this sector is associated with substantial environmental degradation, including deforestation, water pollution, and soil erosion, which are further exacerbated by the impacts of climate change (Houghton, 2018). Climate-related challenges, including droughts and changing precipitation patterns, threaten mining operations and the sustainability of local communities, making climate change resilience a priority for the sector and broader society. The manufacturing sector, encompassing food processing, textiles, and chemical industries, similarly contributes to industrialisation and employment while exacerbating climate change through fossil fuel dependence (Nhamo, 2018).

These environmental impacts disproportionately affect children through multiple, interconnected pathways that compound developmental vulnerabilities. Mining practices, including open-pit and artisanal mining, are linked to deforestation, land degradation, and water pollution, which directly threaten children's health, nutrition, and development. Climate change directly affects determinants for good child nutrition, influencing food consumption patterns, diet quality, and diversity by affecting local and global food availability. Seasonal food scarcity, common in Zimbabwe, drives child wasting. The increasing frequency and intensity of climate shocks negatively affect basic services, including health, education, water, sanitation and hygiene, nutrition, and protection, all of which are critical to the realisation of children's rights under the UNCRC. The adverse impacts of climate change erode development gains through education, health system disruption, and water insecurity, negatively impacting drinking water access and food production (UNICEF, 2025). Environmental risks, including poor solid waste management, indoor and outdoor air pollution, unsafe water, lack of sanitation, and inadequate hygiene, cause irreversible and lasting negative impacts on children, affecting their health, education, and future earnings, creating intergenerational inequality cycles.

While some Zimbabwean mining companies have engaged in CSR activities, these efforts often limit themselves to community development initiatives, including infrastructure provision and social welfare programmes (Moyo & Ncube, 2020). Although representing tangible investments, these efforts often remain disconnected from the challenges that climate change poses, including water scarcity, altered rainfall patterns, and ecosystem restoration needs, particularly in how these challenges uniquely affect children's developmental trajectories, health outcomes, and rights fulfilment. In addition, the absence of systematic monitoring frameworks that assess CSR outcomes, specifically against children's rights indicators, obscures whether such investments meaningfully advance child well-being or merely generate favourable corporate narratives.

Given the scale and resource endowments of Zimbabwe's mining sector, there is significant potential for mining companies to redirect CSR investments towards climate change resilience initiatives that prioritise children's rights, primarily through adaptive infrastructure projects, renewable energy initiatives, and community-based climate mitigation and adaptation efforts that address specific vulnerabilities (Nhamo & Nyikahadzoi, 2017). Realising this potential requires a reconceptualisation of CSR—from discretionary philanthropy to rights-based obligations that centre on children's developmental needs and constitutional entitlements.

14.4.2 CSR and Climate Change: Conceptual Foundations and Global Practice

CSR involves voluntarily integrating social, environmental, and ethical considerations into business operations to benefit society (Carroll, 1999). Regarding climate change, CSR encompasses reducing carbon footprints, improving energy efficiency, and supporting adaptation projects. In environmentally impactful sectors like mining and manufacturing, CSR can significantly address climate challenges, although adoption depends on factors such as regulations, corporate culture, market incentives, and stakeholder influence (Matten & Moon, 2008). Globally, CSR initiatives in these sectors have proven instrumental in fostering adaptive capacity, mitigating environmental impacts, and promoting sustainable development, especially in climate-vulnerable regions like sub-Saharan Africa (Hamann, 2003; Jenkins, 2004).

Regional examples demonstrate CSR's transformative potential when adequately resourced and strategically directed. Anglo American's Socio-Economic Development Programme in South Africa has invested over US$150 million in community development projects since 2005 (Anglo-American, 2020a, 2020b), while Rio Tinto's Community Development Programme in Madagascar invested in education, healthcare, and infrastructure development (Rio Tinto, 2019). Barrick Gold's Water Management Programme in Tanzania improved clean water access for local communities (Barrick Gold, 2020). Manufacturing companies show similar engagement. For example, Unilever's Sustainable Living Plan aims to reduce environmental impact and improve social outcomes in Africa (Unilever, 2020), while Coca-Cola's Replenish Africa Initiative (RAIN) improves access to clean water and sanitation (Coca-Cola, 2020). Within Zimbabwe, Zimplats implemented CSR initiatives focused on environmental conservation and community development (Zimplats, 2020), while in South Africa, Anglo-American-launched initiatives aimed at reducing greenhouse gas emissions and promoting renewable energy (Anglo-American, 2020a, 2020b). In Ghana, Gold Fields implemented CSR initiatives focused on community development and environmental sustainability (Gold Fields, 2020), demonstrating how regional companies address environmental and social concerns.

Despite these investments, significant analytical and practical gaps in linking CSR to children's rights within climate contexts persist. While companies increasingly recognise the theoretical need to adopt child-centred approaches in CSR strategies, implementation remains superficial, with children's vulnerabilities and capacities rarely mainstreamed into broader climate adaptation efforts beyond rhetorical commitments. Child-centred approaches should address immediate needs while building long-term community-level adaptive capacity (Mitchell & Borchard, 2014). Community-based adaptation projects demonstrate that when children's needs are prioritised, outcomes are more sustainable and impactful, enhancing overall community resilience (Mitchell & Borchard, 2014), yet such prioritisation remains exceptional rather than normative in corporate practice.

Businesses are increasingly urged to shift from 'business-as-usual' approaches to more strategic perspectives in CSR activities, fulfilling economic, legal, ethical, and philanthropic responsibilities to protect environments and support climate change mitigation (Liedong et al., 2022). However, the persistence of voluntary, discretionary CSR frameworks allows companies to determine which responsibilities warrant resource allocation, frequently resulting in the marginalisation of children's rights considerations in favour of more visible, politically expedient interventions. By integrating climate change as a core CSR issue, companies can contribute to reducing global warming while creating conditions that enhance profitability and competitive advantage (Liedong et al., 2022), although this business-case framing risks subordinating children's rights to economic imperatives rather than recognising them as intrinsic legal and moral obligations.

14.5 Barriers to Child-Centred Climate-Responsive CSR

Despite CSR's potential to foster child-centred climate resilience, several barriers limit mining and manufacturing sector engagement in climate-responsive CSR initiatives in Zimbabwe. Primary challenges include the lack of coherent and comprehensive regulatory frameworks that mandate or incentivise private-sector contributions to climate-change-resilience efforts that prioritise children's rights (Rugemalira, 2018). While Zimbabwe ratified international climate agreements, including the Paris Agreement, and committed to the UNCRC and the African Charter on the Rights and Welfare of the Child (ACRWC), national policies often lack enforceable mechanisms or incentives for companies to invest in climate-resilient initiatives that benefit children. The absence of clear guidelines and frameworks as well as weak enforcement mechanisms contribute to corporate reluctance to engage in climate change initiatives, especially when short-term financial returns remain uncertain and children's rights considerations appear peripheral to core business operations rather than central to the maintenance of a social licence.

14.5.1 Regulatory, Policy, and Traditional CSR Limitations

In Zimbabwe, inconsistent and weak regulatory frameworks complicate climate-responsive programme implementation. Although policies govern environmental protection, such as the Environmental Management Act (Chapter 20:27) and the Children's Act (Chapter 5:06), which establishes legal protections for children, enforcement suffers from limited resources and political challenges (Chikova, 2019). Mining companies, including Zimplats and Bindura Nickel Corporation, have made CSR commitments to mitigate environmental impact, yet without robust regulatory oversight, these commitments sometimes remain under-fulfilled with minimal accountability (Environmental Management Agency, 2021). Zimplats faced challenges complying with environmental regulations, investing significant resources in environmental management systems and pollution control measures to meet the requirements under the Environmental Management Act (Zimplats, 2020). However, the regulatory framework has been criticised as inadequate and inconsistent, hindering efforts to adopt more climate-responsive practices that could benefit children (Mhlanga, 2018). The lack of a cohesive national policy mandating climate action across all sectors, mainly action centring on children's rights as non-negotiable developmental priorities, allows companies to prioritise economic benefits, sometimes at the expense of environmental sustainability and child welfare (Chikova, 2019). Policy instability and frequent government priority changes create environments where companies are reluctant to invest in long-term climate solutions that protect children.

A significant barrier involves mining and manufacturing companies' tendency to focus on traditional CSR activities, yielding immediate and visible social benefits, infrastructure development, health programmes, and education, without considering how these initiatives protect or advance children's rights in climate contexts or whether they address the structural drivers of climate vulnerability. While beneficial to local communities, these initiatives do not directly address the underlying causes or impacts of climate change, including resource depletion and environmental degradation, nor do they specifically target children's unique vulnerabilities (Tschopp & Huefner, 2015).

Mining companies frequently carry out symbolic CSR activities, exemplified by planting trees and building community schools, without addressing their substantial environmental footprints or considering how environmental degradation specifically and differentially harms children across age groups, developmental stages, and socio-economic positions. Such actions, although positive, often mask ongoing environmental degradation and resource depletion caused by mining activities (Zimbabwe Environmental Lawyers Association, 2022). As CSR remains voluntary mainly in Zimbabwe, companies are not legally obligated to implement stringent climate-responsive measures that prioritise children, creating substantial gaps between CSR ideals and actual practices, affecting children's developmental trajectories and the realisation of their rights (Makumbe, 2021).

14.5.2 Financial, Operational, and Technology Constraints

Financial and operational challenges further limit investment in long-term climate resilience projects. Implementing climate-change-responsive programmes requires substantial financial resources, which many Zimbabwean companies, especially in manufacturing, struggle to secure. The high costs of modernising equipment, adopting cleaner technologies, and investing in sustainable infrastructure often deter companies from making these investments (Moyo, 2020a, 2020b).

RioZim struggled with energy access crises, relying on expensive diesel generators, contributing to greenhouse gas emissions (RioZim, 2020). Despite efforts to invest in renewable energy, regulatory challenges, including the lack of clear policy frameworks for renewable energy development, hindered progress (ZESA, 2020). Delta Corporation faced water management challenges, especially in Bulawayo and Harare, and invested in water conservation measures and waste-treatment systems to reduce environmental impacts (Delta Corporation, 2020). However, these efforts were hindered by regulatory challenges, including a lack of clear policy frameworks for water management (ZINWA, 2020). The National Foods Company struggled with climate-resilient agriculture among smallholder farmers, investing in climate-smart agriculture practices and providing training (National Foods, 2020). However, it was hindered by financial challenges, including the high costs of climate-resilient inputs and the lack of access to affordable finance by smallholder farmers (Moyo, 2019). These examples illustrate regulatory and financial challenges that hinder climate-responsive CSR in Zimbabwe's mining and manufacturing sectors, including fluctuating commodity prices, regulatory uncertainties, and the high costs of transitioning to more sustainable and climate-resilient business models (World Bank, 2020a, 2020b, 2020c).

Technological advancements are crucial for climate change mitigation, yet Zimbabwe faces significant challenges due to limited access to advanced technology and expertise (Chigumira & Kaseke, 2017). In mining, technologies to reduce water and energy consumption and decrease greenhouse gas emissions remain scarce. While companies like Mimosa Mining Company implemented water recycling initiatives, these efforts remain isolated and hindered by the high costs of green technology. The lack of technical expertise further exacerbates these challenges as some of Zimbabwe's educational institutions have not fully integrated climate change, sustainability, and children's rights frameworks into their curricula (Chigumira & Kaseke, 2017). This skill gap limits companies' ability, even those with financial resources, to effectively adopt and operate climate-responsive technologies or to design interventions informed by children's developmental needs and rights entitlements. Addressing these issues requires tackling environmental, economic, and social factors while considering how these barriers prevent CSR from effectively protecting children's rights in climate-vulnerable contexts.

14.6 Climate Resilience Building: Sectoral Capacities and Regional CSR Initiatives

Mining and manufacturing companies are highly vulnerable to climate change impacts, facing risks such as extreme weather events and shifting regulatory landscapes. In the mining sector, floods, droughts, and cyclones can damage infrastructure, disrupt supply chains, and threaten worker safety (Bebbington et al., 2018). Similarly, manufacturing firms contend with rising energy costs, changing carbon regulations, and weather-related disruptions (Sullivan et al., 2020). Building resilience has become a priority. Resilience, the ability to anticipate, prepare for, respond to, and recover from climate-related disruptions, ensures long-term operational continuity. This involves embedding climate risk management into business strategies, adopting resource-efficient technologies, and redesigning business models to mitigate vulnerability (Kolk & van Tulder, 2002). Companies must now demonstrate resilience to regulators and stakeholders, including investors, customers, and the public (UNEP FI, 2020). However, these resilience efforts rarely consider how climate impacts uniquely threaten children or how resilience strategies can advance children's rights, representing a critical analytical and ethical gap in corporate climate responses.

14.6.1 Mining and Manufacturing Sector Opportunities

Financing is crucial for building climate resilience in the mining and manufacturing sectors as adaptation projects often demand substantial investments in infrastructure, technology, and research. These investments, however, are frequently hindered by high upfront costs and uncertain returns, deterring private sector involvement. Zimbabwe's mining sector contributes significantly to the national GDP, with exports primarily comprising platinum, gold, and diamonds. However, mining activities also intensify environmental degradation and contribute to social displacement, exacerbating climate vulnerabilities for nearby communities, especially children (Dube, 2021).

Recognising negative externalities associated with mining, there is an increasing call for mining companies to adopt sustainable practices, including financing resilience measures in affected regions and prioritising children's rights. Mining companies are especially well positioned to contribute to child-centred climate resilience through direct investments in community infrastructure that benefit children, such as constructing water reservoirs, implementing climate-smart agriculture projects, and establishing climate-resilient educational facilities. The Zimbabwean mining sector has initiated corporate social responsibility projects to rehabilitate ecosystems and create alternative livelihoods for displaced populations (Mutenga & Chingodza, 2022). Through enhanced CSR strategies, mining companies can facilitate improved water management, agroforestry projects, and reforestation programmes, helping communities adapt to an increasingly unpredictable climate while protecting children's rights to health, nutrition, and development (Kareem, 2021).

The country's manufacturing sector, including food processing, textiles, and chemical industries, is essential in financing resilience. The sector is energy-intensive and often reliant on imported materials, making it highly vulnerable to climate-induced supply chain disruptions (Gwimbi & Gwimbi, 2021). Manufacturing companies can invest in green technology and support local climate adaptation initiatives designed with children's needs as central design criteria to ensure business continuity and community resilience while protecting children's developmental trajectories. Manufacturers can promote resilience by sourcing local, climate-resilient raw materials, reducing waste, and supporting skills development for communities to diversify income sources. Food processing companies can partner with smallholder farmers to adopt drought-resistant crops, mitigating climate risks and increasing community food security, directly benefiting children (Manduna, 2020). By investing in renewable energy solutions, manufacturing companies can reduce greenhouse gas emissions and serve as models for climate resilience while creating healthier environments for children.

14.6.2 Regional CSR Initiatives for Child-Centred Climate Resilience

CSR within the mining and manufacturing sectors is increasingly recognised as crucial in addressing climate resilience, especially in regions highly vulnerable to climate change, including Zimbabwe and broader sub-Saharan Africa. Sub-Saharan Africa is among the regions most vulnerable to climate change due to a combination of geographic, socio-economic, and environmental factors. This area faces increasing temperatures, fluctuating rainfall patterns, and extreme weather events, including droughts, floods, and cyclones (World Bank, 2021a, 2021b). Due to climate variability, Zimbabwe, situated in the Southern African Development Community (SADC) region, has been substantially impacted by agriculture, water resources, and overall economic stability. Climate shocks have disproportionately affected rural communities, undermining food security, access to water, and livelihoods (UNDP, 2020). Building climate resilience is critical to safeguard livelihoods, protect economic investments, and foster sustainable development (IPCC, 2022), especially for children who simultaneously bear disproportionate climate change impacts across multiple developmental domains.

The mining and manufacturing sectors are major contributors to economic activity in sub-Saharan Africa, but they also exert significant environmental footprints. Industries like mining are water- and energy-intensive, contributing to emissions and environmental degradation, exacerbating climate change vulnerabilities. These sectors, however, are well positioned to support climate resilience, given their substantial resources and influence within the communities where they operate. CSR initiatives can enable these industries to adopt more sustainable practices and directly finance or facilitate community-focused resilience projects that prioritise children's needs, aligning business strategies with climate adaptation goals and children's rights obligations under international and national frameworks.

CSR in climate resilience can take various forms, including community-focused initiatives that benefit children, investments in sustainable infrastructure, and supporting adaptation strategies. Mining companies, for instance, could invest in projects that reduce local communities' dependency on traditional agricultural practices that are highly susceptible to climate variability while ensuring children's nutritional security through diversified, climate-resilient food systems (Chirisa, 2019). The private sector can support infrastructure development to improve water and energy security, which is crucial for community resilience and children's health and development.

Water scarcity remains a critical challenge in many parts of Zimbabwe and the SADC region, compounded by climate change impacts, including prolonged droughts, which threaten children's health and survival. Mining companies can leverage resources and expertise in water management to establish boreholes, dams, and water-harvesting systems for communities. Zimplats has installed boreholes in drought-affected regions of Zimbabwe, providing reliable water sources to local communities (Zimplats, 2022). Although such projects improve resilience by ensuring communities have a sustainable water supply even in times of scarcity, benefiting children's health, hygiene, and educational attendance, critical challenges include limited scaling across other companies and countries in Africa and the SADC region, insufficient attention to maintenance costs and sustainability, and inadequate community involvement, especially children's participation in water resource management decision-making.

The mining sector's energy-intensive nature provides opportunities to invest in renewable energy as part of CSR, benefiting children by reducing air pollution. Anglo American, operating in several SADC countries, has committed to reducing carbon emissions by investing in solar power and other renewable sources to support operations and surrounding communities (Anglo American, 2021). Caledonia Mining is undertaking solar projects in Zimbabwe to power gold mines, reduce reliance on fossil fuels, and promote energy security. Renewable energy projects reduce emissions and offer sustainable power sources to nearby communities, helping build resilience in regions where climate change may impact grid reliability while creating healthier environments for children.

Reforestation constitutes a crucial climate adaptation and mitigation strategy that mining and manufacturing companies can support to benefit children's futures. Reforestation and agroforestry projects sequester carbon, stabilise soil, reduce flooding risks, and diversify income for rural communities. In Mozambique, Vale, a mining company, has engaged in reforestation efforts to offset its carbon footprint while enhancing local environmental resilience (Vale, 2020). Agroforestry projects promoting diverse, climate-resistant crops can provide economic stability to communities, especially those reliant on agriculture affected by erratic weather patterns, directly supporting children's nutritional security.

Climate-smart agriculture (CSA) is a sustainable approach incorporating climate resilience into agricultural practices, essential in a region highly dependent on farming, where children's nutrition depends on agricultural productivity. With significant CSR budgets, mining companies can support local farmers in adopting CSA practices, including drought-resistant crops, soil conservation techniques, and water-efficient irrigation systems. De Beers collaborated with local communities in South Africa to fund agricultural training and technologies that promote sustainable agriculture (De Beers Group, 2021). Similar initiatives could be scaled in Zimbabwe to enhance food security and promote livelihood resilience, benefiting children.

14.6.3 Disaster Preparedness and Financing Mechanisms

Communities in Zimbabwe and the SADC region are often ill-prepared for natural disasters exacerbated by climate change, putting children at heightened risk. The private sector, especially the mining industry, can invest in early warning systems and disaster preparedness programmes that benefit children. Through CSR, companies can fund the establishment of communication systems and training for local communities on disaster response. Mining companies in Botswana and Zimbabwe could extend safety protocols to include community-focused disaster risk management, thus supporting broader regional resilience against climate-related shocks while protecting children.

Financing mechanisms are essential for ensuring sustainable support for climate resilience initiatives that benefit children. Companies can establish dedicated CSR funds or climate resilience financing models, pooling resources from multiple stakeholders, including governments, NGOs, and other private-sector players. The mining sector could co-invest with local governments through public-private partnerships to scale renewable energy and infrastructure projects that benefit children. PPPs not only spread financial risks but also enhance the impact and reach of resilience programmes by leveraging multiple stakeholders' resources (OECD, 2021). Carbon offset programmes could be employed as financing models, whereby companies can mitigate emissions by investing in local climate resilience projects, including reforestation or renewable energy, serving as both mitigation and adaptation measures that address the direct impacts of climate change on children while building resilience.

14.7 Unlocking Private-Sector Resources: Strategies and Implementation Mechanisms

To overcome barriers and specifically address children's rights in climate contexts, several strategies can unlock private-sector resources for climate change resilience in Zimbabwe's mining and manufacturing sectors. Public-private partnerships (PPPs) emerge as promising approaches where mining companies collaborate with government and non-governmental organisations to co-finance climate adaptation and mitigation projects benefiting children. This can involve joint investments in renewable energy infrastructure, reforestation programmes, or sustainable agriculture projects that support environmental sustainability and community resilience while prioritising children's needs (Müller, 2018).

PPPs provide collaborative frameworks where government and the private sector co-invest in resilience-building projects, enabling risk sharing, and combining resources for larger-scale projects, more effectively addressing children's climate vulnerabilities (Tigere & Chigova, 2022). For instance, joint investments in climate-resilient infrastructure, including flood defences, solar energy installations, and water management systems, could alleviate economic burdens on both government and businesses while promoting community welfare and protecting children's rights to safe environments, health, and education.

14.7.1 Policy Incentives and Regulatory Reform

Stronger policy frameworks providing clear incentives for companies to engage in child-centred climate-responsive CSR are essential. These could include tax breaks, subsidies, or preferential access to government contracts for companies investing in climate-resilient projects benefiting children. Tax incentives and financial subsidies for companies investing in resilience projects can effectively encourage private-sector resource channelling towards climate adaptation, prioritising children (Mbaya, 2021). In addition, reduced tariffs on climate-resilient technology and equipment would ease companies' adoption of greener operational practices, protecting children.

Zimbabwe could legislate mandatory CSR standards specifically targeting climate adaptation and resilience investments benefiting children, with requirements for child-rights impact assessments and participatory processes involving children and their caregivers. Such legislation could require mining and manufacturing firms to allocate a percentage of their profits to resilience-building initiatives in communities impacted by climate change, with special attention to children's rights. Similar approaches have been successfully adopted in countries like India, where CSR spending on environmental sustainability is mandated, leading to increased private-sector investment in resilience-building activities (Sharma, 2021).

The introduction of climate-risk disclosure requirements, similar to those implemented in other jurisdictions, could encourage greater corporate transparency and accountability regarding the environmental impacts of business operations on children, requiring companies to report specifically on how their activities and CSR interventions affect children's rights indicators (Sullivan et al., 2020). Regulatory mechanisms aligning corporate interests with climate goals and children's rights would encourage mining companies to take more proactive approaches to climate change adaptation, thereby benefiting children.

14.7.2 Green Finance and Innovative Financial Instruments

Financial instruments, including green bonds or climate adaptation funds, should be explored to mobilise private-sector capital for climate-resilience projects that prioritise children. These instruments can provide companies with the necessary resources to implement large-scale climate adaptation initiatives that protect children while offering investors returns on investment (D'Agostino & McFadden, 2019). Green bonds have emerged as valuable tools to mobilise funds for climate and environmental projects. Zimbabwe could establish a green bond market, enabling mining and manufacturing companies to raise capital earmarked explicitly for climate resilience projects that benefit children (Chirisa et al., 2022). Green bonds would attract local and international investors interested in sustainable development and provide mining and manufacturing firms with accessible funding to invest in adaptation projects. However, operationalising green bonds faces substantial challenges due to Zimbabwe's economic crisis, compounded by poor regulatory frameworks, limited market liquidity, and constrained investor confidence.

Other African countries, including Nigeria, South Africa, Egypt, and Morocco, have successfully implemented green bonds. South Africa was the first African country to issue a green bond in 2017. The City of Cape Town issued the bond, raising US $41 million to finance renewable energy and energy efficiency projects (City of Cape Town, 2017). Since then, South Africa has issued several green bonds, including a US $1.5 billion bond issued by the African Development Bank in 2020 (African Development, 2020). Nigeria issued its first green bond in 2017, raising US $30 million to finance renewable energy and energy efficiency projects (Nigeria Stock Exchange, 2017). Egypt issued its first green bond in 2020, raising US $750 million to finance renewable energy and sustainable infrastructure projects (Egyptian Ministry of Finance, 2020). This bond was listed on the London Stock Exchange and was oversubscribed by 7.5 times (LSEG, 2020).

Creating specific funds dedicated to child-centred climate resilience, with mandatory mining and manufacturing company contributions proportional to environmental impact, would provide structured avenues for channelling CSR resources into climate adaptation efforts benefiting children. The Zimbabwe government has established a climate change fund to finance climate change projects and initiatives (Government of Zimbabwe, 2020), although allocation mechanisms prioritising children's rights remain underdeveloped. Green finance, including tools like green bonds and sustainability-linked loans, has emerged as a key solution in Africa and globally. These instruments direct funding towards environmentally beneficial initiatives, including adopting renewable energy, efficiency, and sustainable mining practices (Zadek, 2020). Governments, development finance institutions, and multilateral organisations further support these efforts by offering concessional finance, risk guarantees, and capacity-building assistance (World Bank, 2021a, 2021b).

The African Development Bank launched the African Climate Change Fund, financing climate change projects and initiatives across the continent (African Development Bank, 2020a, 2020b). Catastrophe bonds (CAT bonds) provide financial protection against natural disasters, including hurricanes or droughts, and are used in countries like Mexico, Jamaica, and the Philippines to manage climate-related risks (World Bank, 2021a, 2021b; Zadek, 2020). The Adaptation Benefits Mechanism (ABM), launched by the African Development Bank, is a non-market model that aims to boost private-sector investments in adaptation projects. It provides a framework for certifying and trading adaptation benefits as credits (African Development Bank, 2020a, 2020b; World Bank, 2021a, 2021b).

14.7.3 ESG Integration and Knowledge Sharing

Transitioning to climate-resilient operations also requires shifts in corporate investment strategies that are aligned with environmental, social, and governance (ESG) criteria. By committing to sustainability, companies enhance their reputations and attract socially responsible investors that prioritise environmental impacts (Eccles & Klimenko, 2019). Adequate resilience financing requires private-sector actors to understand the impact of climate risks on their businesses and surrounding communities, especially on children's developmental rights. Zimbabwe can foster knowledge sharing through partnerships with international organisations, providing companies with training in climate risk assessment and resilience planning (including specific training on child rights frameworks and child-sensitive indicators) (Mupakati & Mutami, 2021).

Several international organisations, including the United Nations Development Programme (UNDP) and the International Finance Corporation (IFC), have promoted knowledge sharing and collaboration in climate adaptation and resilience building through CSR. The UNDP's Adaptation Fund supported several African climate adaptation projects, including a Zimbabwean project, to enhance climate resilience (UNDP, 2020). Governments can catalyse more proactive private-sector involvement in resilience financing by equipping firms with tools to assess climate risks and understand potential adaptation measures. The World Bank's Climate Business Department supported several climate-related projects in Africa, South Africa, and Morocco (World Bank, 2020a, 2020b, 2020c). The African Development Bank's Climate Resilience Infrastructure Financing Facility provides financing for climate-resilient infrastructure projects in Africa, involving knowledge sharing and capacity building (AfDB, 2020). The Mining Association of Canada's Towards Sustainable Mining initiative provides a framework for responsible mining practices, including climate change mitigation and adaptation (MAC, 2020).

The government has launched several knowledge-sharing initiatives in Zimbabwe in partnership with the private sector. The Zimbabwe Climate Change Response Strategy promotes climate resilience and adaptation in various sectors, including mining and manufacturing (Government of Zimbabwe, 2014). The Zimbabwe Chamber of Mines' Environmental and Social Responsibility initiative promotes responsible mining practices, including climate change mitigation and adaptation (Zimbabwe Chamber of Mines, 2020). These initiatives demonstrate the importance of knowledge sharing and collaboration in promoting climate adaptation and resilience building through CSR within Zimbabwe's mining and manufacturing sectors. However, the integration of children's rights perspectives and child-specific outcome indicators remains limited, representing a significant gap in implementation frameworks.

14.8 Children's Rights, Climate Change, and Legal Frameworks

The integration of children's rights perspectives into CSR climate initiatives remains critically limited despite clear legal and policy frameworks establishing children's entitlements. Zimbabwe's Constitution (2013) includes specific protections for children, while the Children's Act (Chapter 5:06) establishes comprehensive legal protections. Zimbabwe has ratified the UNCRC and the ACRWC. Despite these frameworks, children in Zimbabwe face challenges, including limited access to quality education, inadequate health services, child labour issues, and poverty, which affects approximately 70% of children (UNICEF, 2025).

Climate change threatens children's rights in multiple, interconnected ways that exacerbate existing vulnerabilities. These include reduced food insecurity and nutrition, stunting and wasting, and disruption to education when schools are damaged by extreme weather or families cannot afford schooling due to climate-related economic hardship. Other impacts are health issues from malaria, cholera, and other water- or vector-borne diseases expanding their ranges; displacement from homes due to extreme weather events; psychological trauma from disasters and uncertainty; increased child labour when family livelihoods are threatened; and water scarcity affecting sanitation and hygiene, which is crucial for children's health.

While the African Charter and related frameworks provide a normative basis for protecting children's rights, they require operationalisation and adaptation to effectively address climate change challenges through enforceable mechanisms linking corporate environmental impacts to children's rights obligations. CSR initiatives aligned with the Sustainable Development Goals (SDGs) address global sustainability challenges, including climate change, ensuring that social inclusion, environmental preservation, and economic growth are pursued simultaneously (Husainy et al., 2024). Companies are encouraged to adopt renewable energy sources, reduce carbon footprints, and support social justice initiatives, collectively contributing to sustainable futures and improving the quality of life for vulnerable populations, including children (Husainy et al., 2024).

However, significant challenges remain in ensuring that CSR efforts are effectively integrated into broader climate adaptation strategies with measurable, child-specific indicators and accountability mechanisms. The need for collective and inclusive approaches involving governments, international actors, and individuals is emphasised to comprehensively address the socio-environmental crisis in Africa (Roland, 2024). CSR must transition from an altruistic, discretionary perspective to a rights-based imperative within climate change initiatives, especially for vulnerable populations, including children. By fulfilling economic, legal, ethical, and philanthropic responsibilities, businesses can implement programmes protecting the environment and supporting climate change mitigation. This approach not only aids in reducing the adverse effects of climate change on vulnerable child populations but also enhances corporate profitability and competitive advantage (Liedong et al., 2022). However, the subordination of children's rights to business-case justifications risks instrumentalising children's well-being rather than recognising it as an intrinsic obligation under international and domestic laws.

14.9 Discussion

This study exposes a critical disjuncture between normative climate-child rights frameworks and their operationalisation through CSR mechanisms. While international instruments and theoretical discourses increasingly acknowledge children's differentiated climate vulnerabilities, practical integration remains superficial. It is characterised by voluntary engagement, the absence of enforcement architectures, and monitoring systems that systematically render children invisible through aggregate indicators, obscuring age-differentiated impacts.

The study reveals three interconnected failures. First, contemporary CSR frameworks subordinate rights-based obligations to discretionary business-case logics, enabling companies to engage with children's rights considerations only when it is economically expedient rather than recognising them as non-negotiable legal imperatives under Zimbabwe's Constitution, the Children's Act, and ratified international conventions (UNCRC, ACRWC). Second, existing initiatives systematically exclude children's participatory rights under Article 12 of the UNCRC. Third, stakeholder theory applications relegate children to undifferentiated 'community' categories rather than recognising their status as primary stakeholders whose developmental trajectories face disproportionate climate disruptions across physiological, psychological, and social domains.

Zimbabwe's extractive sectors exemplify these structural inadequacies. Despite resource constraints, companies channel CSR towards traditional infrastructure, health, and education initiatives disconnected from climate-child rights intersections. Demonstrated successes in water conservation, renewable energy deployment, and climate-resilient agriculture remain isolated rather than systematised, constrained by non-mandatory CSR frameworks, inconsistent enforcement, financial barriers, and technological deficits. The voluntary-mandatory tension produces regulatory vacuums where environmental degradation compounds children's vulnerabilities without corresponding corporate accountability.

Transformation requires reconceptualising CSR from philanthropic discretion to enforceable rights obligations through coordinated interventions. These can include mandatory child rights impact assessments, child-specific climate indicators in corporate reporting, ring-fenced financing mechanisms, capacity development in child rights frameworks, and participatory governance structures enabling children's authentic engagement. Financial instruments, including green bonds, public-private partnerships, and ESG integration, offer mobilisation pathways, although operationalisation faces Zimbabwe's economic fragility, weak regulatory infrastructure, and compromised investor confidence, revealing how national contexts mediate global climate finance architectures.

This study contributes theoretically by demonstrating how voluntary CSR frameworks structurally reproduce children's marginalisation within climate responses, even as rhetorical commitments proliferate. It advances stakeholder theory by conceptualising children as stakeholder categories requiring recognition rather than subsumption within broader community constructs. Empirically, it maps implementation gaps between Zimbabwe's legal frameworks and corporate practice, identifying specific reform levers.

Critical limitations warrant acknowledgement. The study's documentary analysis cannot capture informal corporate practices or community-level implementation dynamics. Comparative analysis across sectors and jurisdictions would strengthen generalizability. Future research should examine participatory methodologies that enable children's direct voices in evaluating CSR-based climate interventions, assess enforcement mechanisms that translate legal frameworks into corporate compliance, and explore how political-economic contexts shape CSR-climate-rights intersections across differentiated African settings.

The central challenge persists, reconciling voluntary CSR architectures with mandatory rights obligations in contexts where state capacity for enforcement remains constrained. Resolving this tension will determine whether climate-responsive CSR evolves into a substantive mechanism for protecting children's developmental entitlements or remains a symbolic corporate positioning that is disconnected from the realisation of material rights in Zimbabwe's climate-vulnerable landscape.

14.10 Conclusion

This chapter examined the critical nexus between CSR, climate change, and children's rights within Zimbabwe's mining and manufacturing sectors, revealing substantial potential alongside significant implementation gaps. While these sectors contribute over 60% of national exports and are uniquely positioned to address the crisis facing Zimbabwe's 6.5 million climate-vulnerable children, the strategic reorientation of CSR towards child-centred climate resilience represents both a developmental imperative and a rights-based obligation. Key findings demonstrate that climate change poses unprecedented threats to children's rights, yet CSR initiatives traditionally overlook the climate-children's rights nexus. Mining and manufacturing CSR holds substantial promise for resilience building through sustainable agriculture, water conservation, and energy diversification. However, persistent structural barriers, including the lack of policy incentives, regulatory weaknesses, and financial constraints, limit implementation. In addition, innovative financing mechanisms, such as green bonds and public-private partnerships, can unlock private-sector resources when appropriately structured.

Realising CSR's potential requires comprehensive policy interventions. These include mandatory CSR standards targeting climate adaptation with child-rights impact assessments, fiscal incentives such as tax breaks and subsidies for child-benefiting climate projects, and dedicated funds for child-centred climate resilience with mandatory company contributions. Furthermore, enhanced monitoring frameworks incorporating child-specific indicators and capacity-building initiatives are essential. These reforms must recognise children's rights as non-negotiable legal obligations grounded in Zimbabwe's Constitution (2013), Children's Act, and ratified international frameworks (UNCRC, ACRWC). The chapter offers an Africa-centric model for integrating child rights into corporate climate action, with regional precedents from South Africa, Nigeria, and Egypt demonstrating feasibility. Future research should track CSR implementation against child-specific outcomes longitudinally, compare voluntary versus mandatory frameworks, and engage children participatorily in documenting climate impacts and evaluating interventions.

Climate change represents an existential threat to children's rights, demanding the urgent mobilisation of all resources, including private-sector capacity. Zimbabwe's mining and manufacturing sectors possess substantial yet underutilised capacity to advance child-focused climate resilience through strategic CSR investments aligned with national priorities and children's rights legislation. Unlocking this potential requires transcending business-as-usual approaches to recognise children's rights as legal obligations rather than discretionary philanthropy. Mining and manufacturing CSR presents a feasible mechanism for resilience-building financing, capable of contributing to water conservation, renewable energy, sustainable agriculture, and adaptation projects when effectively mobilised. The path forward demands systemic transformation, embedding children's rights centrally within climate governance and corporate accountability frameworks through regulatory reform, fiscal incentives, innovative financing mechanisms, strengthened monitoring with child-specific indicators, and participatory governance structures. Climate-responsive CSR's promise can be realised only through such comprehensive approaches, ensuring Zimbabwe's children can exercise rights to survival, development, health, and education in an increasingly climate-challenged future.

References

African Development Bank. (2020a). *Africa Climate Change Fund*. African Development Bank.

African Development Bank. (2020b). *Climate Resilience Infrastructure Financing Facility*. African Development Bank.

Anglo American. (2020a). *Social and Economic Programme*. https://www.angloamerican.com

Anglo American. (2020b). *Sustainability report*. Anglo American plc.

Anglo American. (2021). *Sustainable mining plan*. Anglo American plc.

Barrick Gold. (2020). *Water Management Programme*. Barrick Gold Corporation.

Bebbington, A., Hinojosa, L., & Bury, J. (2018). Mining and the environment: Challenges for developing countries. *Journal of Environmental Management, 230*, 259–270.

Carroll, A. B. (1999). Corporate social responsibility: Evolution of a definitional construct. *Business & Society, 38*(3), 268–295.

Carroll, A. B., & Shabana, K. M. (2010). The business case for corporate social responsibility: A review of concepts, research and practice. *International Journal of Management Reviews, 12*(1), 85–105.

Chigumira, E., & Kaseke, N. (2017). Technological constraints in climate change adaptation in Zimbabwe's mining industry. *Development in Practice, 27*(6), 874–889.

Chikova, T. (2019). Environmental policy and regulatory compliance in Zimbabwe's mining sector. *Environmental Management Journal, 34*(2), 145–167.

Chirisa, I. (2019). *Urban climate resilience: Lessons for Zimbabwe*. University of Zimbabwe Press.

Chirisa, I., Mutambisi, T., Chigudu, A., Muchini, T., Mukwashi, T., Chirisa, C. J., & Ncube, R. (2022). The green bond market as a vehicle for financing climate change adaptation and mitigation in Zimbabwe. *Journal of Investment and Management, 11*(1), 22–35.

Coca-Cola. (2020). *Replenish Africa Initiative (RAIN)*. The Coca-Cola Company.

D'Agostino, R., & McFadden, B. (2019). Green bonds: Financing climate change mitigation and adaptation. *Environmental Finance Review, 12*(4), 45–58.

De Beers Group. (2021). *Building forever: De Beers Group sustainability report*. De Beers Group. https://www.debeersgroup.com

Delta Corporation. (2020). *Sustainability report 2020*. Delta Corporation.

Dube, K. (2021). Mining and community displacement in Zimbabwe: A social justice perspective. *African Journal of Social Sciences, 15*(2), 89–104.

Eccles, R. G., & Klimenko, S. (2019). The investor revolution. *Harvard Business Review, 97*(3), 106–116.

Egyptian Ministry of Finance. (2020). *Green bond issuance report*. Ministry of Finance.

Environmental Management Agency. (2021). *Environmental Management Act compliance report 2021*. Government of Zimbabwe.

Freeman, R. E. (1984). *Strategic management: A stakeholder approach*. Pitman.

Freeman, R. E., Harrison, J. S., Wicks, A. C., Parmar, B. L., & de Colle, S. (2010). *Stakeholder theory: The state of the art*. Cambridge University Press.

Gold Fields. (2020). *Sustainability report 2020*. Gold Fields Limited.

Government of Zimbabwe. (2014). *Zimbabwe Climate Change Response Strategy*. Government of Zimbabwe.

Government of Zimbabwe. (2020). *Zimbabwe Climate Change Fund*. Government of Zimbabwe.

Gwimbi, P., & Gwimbi, C. (2021). Supply chain vulnerabilities in Zimbabwe's manufacturing sector under climate change. *International Journal of Manufacturing Sustainability, 18*(3), 157–168.

Gwitira, I., Shekede, M. D., & Bhatasara, S. (2024). *Child-centred climate impact, vulnerability, and risk assessment for Zimbabwe*. UNICEF.

Hamann, R. (2003). Mining companies' role in sustainable development: The 'why' and 'how' of corporate social responsibility from a business perspective. *Development Southern Africa, 20*(2), 237–254.

Houghton, R. A. (2018). The environmental impacts of the mining sector in Zimbabwe. *Environmental Policy and Governance, 28*(3), 245–260.

Husainy, S. K., Waheed, H., & Mahmood, F. (2024). Corporate social responsibility and sustainable development goals: A systematic literature review. *Corporate Social Responsibility and Environmental Management, 31*(2), 789–806.

IPCC. (2022). *Climate change 2022: Sixth assessment report*. Intergovernmental Panel on Climate Change.

Jenkins, H. (2004). Corporate social responsibility and the mining industry: Conflicts and constructs. *Corporate Social Responsibility and Environmental Management, 11*(1), 23–34.

Jenkins, H., & Yakovleva, N. (2006). Corporate social responsibility in the mining industry: Exploring social and environmental disclosure trends. *Journal of Business Ethics, 59*(3), 247–268.

Kareem, B. (2021). Mining and climate resilience in Southern Africa. *African Journal of Environmental Economics, 14*(3), 201–218.

Kolk, A., & van Tulder, R. (2002). The effectiveness of self-regulation: Corporate social responsibility and business ethics in the global marketplace. *Business & Society Review, 107*(4), 247–274.

Liedong, T. A., Peprah, A. A., & Amartey, A. O. (2022). Corporate social responsibility and climate change: A systematic review. *Business Strategy and the Environment, 31*(5), 2157–2177.

Linnenlucke, M. K., Griffiths, A., & Winn, M. I. (2013). Firm and industry adaptation to climate change: A review of the literature. *Journal of Management, 39*(5), 1236–1261.

London Stock Exchange Group. (2020). *Egypt green bond listing*. LSEG.

Makumbe, T. (2021). Corporate social responsibility in Zimbabwe focuses on mining and climate change mitigation. *African Journal of Business Ethics, 15*(1), 56–68.

Manduna, R. (2020). *Food security and climate-smart agriculture in Zimbabwe*. Zimbabwe Agricultural Press.

Matten, D., & Moon, J. (2008). "Implicit" and "explicit" CSR: A conceptual framework for a comparative understanding of corporate social responsibility. *Academy of Management Review, 33*(2), 404–424.

Mbaya, P. (2021). Tax incentives as catalysts for corporate investment in climate adaptation projects. *Journal of Development Economics, 20*(5), 105–120.

Mhlanga, N. (2018). Environmental regulations and mining in Zimbabwe. *Journal of Sustainable Mining, 17*(2), 53–62.

Mining Association of Canada. (2020). *Towards Sustainable Mining (TSM) initiative*. Mining Association of Canada.

Mitchell, R. K., Agle, B. R., & Wood, D. J. (1997). Toward a theory of stakeholder identification and salience: Defining the principle of who and what really counts. *Academy of Management Review, 22*(4), 853–886.

Mitchell, T., & Borchard, C. (2014). *Climate finance for children: A child-centred approach to climate change investment*. Overseas Development Institute.

Moyo, D. (2020a). Corporate social responsibility and climate resilience in Zimbabwe's mining industry. *African Journal of Environmental Economics and Policy, 15*(3), 311–329.

Moyo, F. (2020b). Financing sustainable development in Zimbabwe: Perspectives on the manufacturing sector. *Sustainable Development Journal, 12*(1), 24–36.

Moyo, L., & Ncube, M. (2020). The role of CSR in the mining industry in Zimbabwe. *International Journal of Business and Economic Sciences Applied Research, 13*(4), 5–15.
Moyo, S. (2019). Climate-resilient agriculture in Zimbabwe: Challenges and opportunities. *Journal of Agriculture and Rural Development, 8*(1), 1–12.
Müller, A. (2018). Public-private partnerships for climate change adaptation: Insights from the mining sector. *Journal of Environmental Management, 57*(6), 702–719.
Mupakati, L., & Mutami, C. (2021). Corporate engagement in climate resilience in Zimbabwe: Lessons from international partnerships. *Climate Change and Development Journal, 12*(3), 201–214.
Mutambanengwe, B. (2021). Mining sector contributions to Zimbabwe's economy: Opportunities and challenges. *Mining Journal of Zimbabwe, 18*(2), 34–56.
Mutenga, C., & Chingodza, T. (2022). CSR trends in Zimbabwe's mining sector: Opportunities for climate adaptation funding. *Zimbabwe Journal of Corporate Social Responsibility, 7*(1), 41–56.
National Foods. (2020). *Sustainability report 2020*. National Foods.
Nhamo, G. (2018). Climate change policy and practice in Zimbabwe: Role of the private sector. *Climate Policy, 10*(4), 319–329.
Nhamo, G., & Nyikahadzoi, K. (2017). Mining, sustainable development and CSR in Zimbabwe. *Natural Resources Journal, 57*(1), 123–140.
Nigeria Stock Exchange. (2017). *Nigeria's first green bond listing*. Nigeria Stock Exchange.
OECD. (2021). *Public-private partnerships in renewable energy*. OECD Publishing.
Rio Tinto. (2019). *Community Development Programme*. Rio Tinto.
RioZim. (2020). *Sustainability report 2020*. RioZim.
Roland, M. (2024). Corporate social responsibility and environmental sustainability in Africa. *African Development Review, 36*(1), 112–128.
Rugemalira, J. (2018). Corporate social responsibility in Zimbabwe's mining industry. *International Journal of Business Studies, 22*(1), 87–102.
Sharma, N. (2021). Mandatory CSR spending and environmental sustainability in developing economies. *Journal of Environmental Economics and Policy, 13*(2), 150–165.
Sullivan, R., Mackenzie, C., & Fenton, S. (2020). Corporate governance and the integration of climate change risks. *Corporate Governance Journal, 28*(2), 312–328.
Sullivan, R., Purushhothaman, M., & Diez, M. (2018). Stakeholder engagement and the business case for corporate social responsibility. *Journal of Business Ethics, 147*(2), 257–273.
Tigere, R., & Chigova, M. (2022). Public-private partnerships for climate resilience in Zimbabwe. *Southern African Journal of Public Administration, 17*(2), 89–103.
Tschopp, D., & Huefner, R. (2015). The role of corporate social responsibility in environmental management. *Business Strategy and the Environment, 24*(4), 290–306.
UNDP. (2020). *Zimbabwe's Climate Resilience Building Framework*. United Nations Development Programme.
UNEP FI. (2020). *Climate resilience and financial institutions: A guide to action*. United Nations Environment Programme Finance Initiative.
UNICEF. (2021). *The climate crisis is a child rights crisis: Introducing the Children's Climate Risk Index*. UNICEF.
UNICEF. (2025). *When the rains don't come: Climate change through the eyes of Zimbabwe's children*. Retrieved September 29, 2025, from https://www.unicef.org/zimbabwe/stories/when-rains-dont-come-climate-change-through-eyes-zimbabwes-children
UNICEF ESA. (2025). *Turning climate hardship into hope in Eastern and Southern Africa*. Retrieved October 1, 2025, from https://www.unicef.org/esa/reports/turning-climate-hardship-hope-children
Unilever. (2020). *Sustainable Living Plan*. Unilever.
United Nations. (1989). *Convention on the Rights of the Child. Treaty Series, 1577, 3*. UN.
Vale. (2020). *Sustainability and climate actions in Mozambique*. Vale. www.vale.com
World Bank. (2020a). *Climate Investment Fund (CIF)*. World Bank Publications.
World Bank. (2020b). *Global mining industry environmental report*. World Bank.

World Bank. (2020c). *Zimbabwe: Mining sector report*. World Bank Publications.
World Bank. (2021a). *Climate resilience and financing: Opportunities and challenges for the private sector*. World Bank Group.
World Bank. (2021b). *Climate risk profile for Sub-Saharan Africa*. World Bank.
Zadek, S. (2020). *Green finance: Mobilising capital for transitioning to a low-carbon economy*. Harvard Business Review Press.
Zimbabwe Chamber of Mines. (2020). *Environmental and Social Responsibility (ESR) initiative*. Zimbabwe Chamber of Mines.
Zimbabwe Chamber of Mines. (2022). *Zimbabwe mining industry annual report 2022*. Zimbabwe Chamber of Mines.
Zimbabwe Electricity Supply Authority. (2020). *Renewable Energy Policy Framework*. ZESA.
Zimbabwe Environmental Lawyers Association. (2022). *Mining and environmental justice in Zimbabwe*. ZELA.
Zimbabwe National Water Authority. (2020). *Water Policy Framework*. ZINWA.
Zimplats. (2020). *Sustainability report 2020*. Zimplats.
Zimplats. (2022). *Community Investment Report*. Zimplats.

Part V
Conclusions and Policy Recommendations

Chapter 15
The Climate Change–Food System Nexus and Impact on Children in Zimbabwe: Toward Social Policy Interventions for Sustainable Futures

Emmanuel Ndhlovu and Daniel F. Meyer

15.1 Introduction

Zimbabwe has been experiencing worrisome climatic events in recent years. Climate change in Zimbabwe is characterised by significant warming trends, altered rainfall patterns, and an increasing incidence of extreme weather events, which threaten the country's socio-economic stability and development (Chanza, 2018). In recent decades, Zimbabwe's mean annual temperature has soared since 1970, and forecasts indicate a further increase of 1–1.5 °C by 2040, potentially surpassing 3 °C by 2050 under high-emission scenarios (Tirivangasi & Nyahunda, 2025). Mean annual rainfall also exhibits a decreasing trend (Nhara et al., 2020). It is also projected to decrease further (Ministry of Environment, Climate, Tourism and Hospitality Industry, 2020). There are also likelihoods of shorter rainy seasons, with shifts in seasons already reported (Ndhlovu & Dube, 2024). Droughts are also common (rising from once every ten growing seasons to once every four between 1980 and 2011) (World Bank (WB), 2025). Conversely, increases in rainfall amounts are projected, with possibilities of widespread flooding (Ndhlovu & Dube, 2024). Considering Zimbabwe's agrarian nature, with over 80% of the population relying on agriculture for livelihood and income, climate change presents significant challenges, particularly in agriculture and food systems. The impact of climate change on food systems and how this eventually impacts children is an area that has not attracted satisfactory academic attention in Zimbabwe. This chapter contributes to closing this literature and knowledge gap.

The convergence of climate change and vulnerabilities in the food system presents significant challenges to the well-being and rights of children in Zimbabwe,

E. Ndhlovu (✉) · D. F. Meyer
College of Business and Economics, University of Johannesburg, Auckland Park, South Africa
e-mail: dfmeyer@uj.ac.za

E. Ndhlovu, C. Chipenda (eds.), *Climate Change and Children's Rights in Zimbabwe*, https://doi.org/10.1007/978-981-95-6005-9_15

particularly through food insecurity, malnutrition, and exposure to disease. The climate change–food system nexus affects children through many conduits. For instance, climate-change-induced events such as repeated droughts, floods, and erratic rainfall disrupt rain-fed agriculture, the backbone of the economy, particularly in Africa, resulting in extensive crop failure and livestock loss. This leads to reduced food availability, decreased dietary diversity, and lower feeding frequency, aggravating child malnutrition (stunting and wasting) and micronutrient deficiencies (see Chap. 8). Therefore, understanding this nexus is crucial to proposing interventions. Much of the analysis of the impact of climate change in Zimbabwe remains in grey literature, produced mainly by international policy institutions, such as the United Nations Children's Fund (UNICEF, 2024a). Other studies on climate change in Zimbabwe do not specifically focus on children (Moyo, 2017; Muzerengi et al., 2023). Some studies only mention Zimbabwe in passing or discuss it in the context of the broader African region (Mezmur, 2023; Ngwenya et al., 2018). Therefore, the impact of climate change on children in Zimbabwe needs further investigation.

In seeking to close the above gap, this chapter (1) explores climate change trends in Zimbabwe, (2) identifies the conduits through which the impact of climate change affects food systems and children in Zimbabwe, and (3) investigates potential and ongoing social-policy-based interventions to mitigate the impact of climate change on food systems and children in Zimbabwe. This study is vital in providing detailed, context-specific insights that can provide the basis for policy deliberation. Understanding the impact of climate change on children is vital because children are uniquely susceptible due to their developing bodies, dependence on adults, and their lack of agency, facing high risks like malnutrition, disease, and displacement. This knowledge is important to protect their health, support their development, and take action to protect them. This knowledge is also indispensable for designing effective policies and adaptation responses to ensure food safety, improve resilience, and protect vulnerable populations from hunger and malnutrition. Therefore, politicians, the donor community, students, academics, and other stakeholders working on child welfare will find the chapter an important contribution.

This chapter is organised as follows: the next section outlines the research methodology. This is followed by the conceptual framework for the study. After that, the chapter explores Zimbabwe's climate change–food system nexus and how this nexus eventually negatively impacts children. The chapter then outlines existing and potential social-policy-based interventions to address the identified challenges. Lastly, conclusions are drawn from the discussion.

15.2 Materials and Methods

The chapter adopts a scoping review methodology based on the Zimbabwean experience as a case study. This entailed examining climate change and food systems through numerous methods, including desk review and abstraction. Government documents on climate change were reviewed to understand climate change trends. Reports by leading research and policy organisations working together with the government to improve the welfare of children were also reviewed. These organisations include the United Nations Development Programme (UNDP), UNICEF, and the World Bank. This review aimed to determine the trajectory of climate change in the country, how this trajectory affects food systems, and how the impact on food systems eventually affects children. Academic texts on climate change, food systems, and social protection in Zimbabwe were also reviewed to ensure a broader understanding of the impact of climate change on children.

From the identified climate change trends, factors that affected food systems were analysed to determine how they affected food systems and, eventually, children. Weather-related data was obtained from the Zimbabwe Meteorological Department website. Some social-policy-based interventions by various stakeholders were also reviewed to determine effectiveness and challenges. The use of different text formats (official and academic) enabled a detailed reflection on national climate change in Zimbabwe. Using government reports, publications by reputable international organisations, and peer-reviewed academic texts ensured that the information gathered was comprehensive and reputable.

The authors acknowledge the limitations associated with the scoping review as a research methodology. The primary limitations of a scoping review stemmed from its broad scope, lack of critical appraisal, and the narrative nature of its synthesis. However, the authors believe that the method was valuable, enabling them to map the existing literature in the broad fields of climate change, food systems, and social protection. Its benefits were primarily related to identifying and clarifying complex climate change trends, determining the impact of climate change on children, and identifying potential interventions. In essence, a scoping review served as a crucial exercise that provided structure and direction to the study on the impact of climate change on food systems and children in Zimbabwe. It is hoped that future studies will build on the study to conduct more resource-intensive, focused syntheses.

15.3 Conceptual Framework: Climate Change Trajectories in Zimbabwe

The literature on climate change in Zimbabwe has been increasing in recent decades (Gwatida et al., 2023; Nhundu et al., 2021). It is widely agreed that the country is becoming rapidly exceedingly susceptible to climate change (Gwatida et al., 2023; Nhundu et al., 2021). Zimbabwe is already undergoing extreme climate change risks projected to worsen (Chanza & Makombe, 2025). Evidence reveals that since 1900, Zimbabwe has warmed by 1 °C, while precipitation has declined by around 10% (Gwatida et al., 2023). The dominant extreme weather events include droughts, dry spells, floods, storms, temperature extremes, heatwaves, high winds, and cyclones (Mpakairi et al., 2020; Ndhlovu & Mhlanga, 2023). Low-lying areas, such as the Lowveld region, are the worst affected (Government of Zimbabwe (GoZ), 2024).

Zimbabwe's vulnerability to climate change impacts is worsened by its reliance on climate-sensitive livelihoods, such as rain-fed agriculture (Chanza & Makombe, 2025). Extreme weather events deepen vulnerability for communities that are already at risk. Agricultural sensitivity to weather intensifies poor farming output and economic productivity, subsequently aggravating poverty, livelihood, and food insecurity, particularly of smallholders. By 2050, maize and cotton crops are expected to decline by up to 30% due to climate change (GoZ, 2024). Estimates indicate that if, by 2100, no adaptation responses are taken, crop net revenues could decline by up to 90% (Garcia et al., 2023). Reviewed literature shows that since the 1980s, Zimbabwe has been getting warmer (see Fig. 15.1), while rainfall amounts have been falling (Fig. 15.2).

High temperatures and decreases in precipitation negatively impact food security and nutrition, water provision, sanitation, hygiene, and other things. With Zimbabwe being an agrarian country and with 70% of its population engaged in land and agricultural activities either as the primary source of livelihoods or as an additional source of income (Ndhlovu & Dube, 2024), increasing temperatures and reduced rainfall amounts have had disruptive implications for agricultural activities.

Several sources, including the WB (2021) and UNDP (2023), have shown that Zimbabwe has a vulnerability score of 0.54, which is very high. It also has a readiness score of 0.20, which is very low (Table 15.1). These figures suggest weak adaptive capacity. This has resulted in poor development and human welfare outcomes, as demonstrated by the country's position on the Human Development Index—a statistical composite index created by the UNDP to measure a country's average accomplishments in three basic scopes of human development: a long and healthy life, access to knowledge, and a decent standard of living (see Table 15.1).

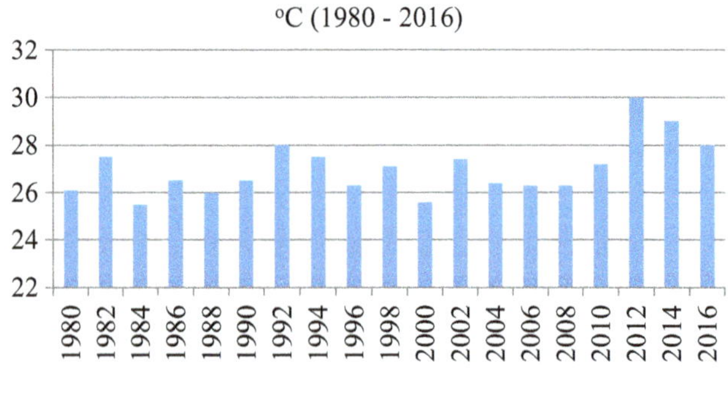

Fig. 15.1 Zimbabwe's mean annual maximum temperature (1980–2016) [Source: Zimbabwe Meteorological Department (ZMD) (2007) and UNDP (2017)]

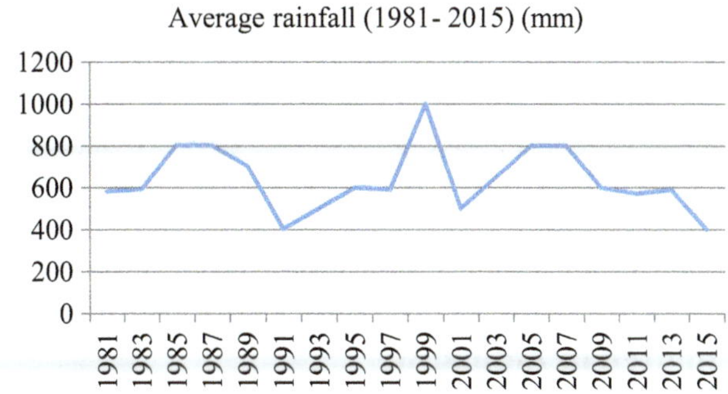

Fig. 15.2 Zimbabwe average rainfall (1981–2015) [Source: ZMD (2007)]

Table 15.1 Zimbabwe: vulnerability and adaptation capacity compared to other selected countries

Country	Income group	Population (millions)	HDI/ rank	GDP per capita (US$)	Readiness score/rank	ND-GAIN vulnerability score/rank
Zimbabwe	Low	15.09	0.57 (146)	1214.51	0.20 (188)	0.54 (147)
Zambia	Low	18.92	0.58 (154)	985.13	0.32 (138)	0.53 (141)
Mozambique	Low	32.16	0.46 (185)	448.84	0.27 (169)	0.52 (137)
Nigeria	Lower middle	211.40	0.54 (163)	2097.09	0.25 (183)	0.50 (128)
Namibia	Lower middle	2.59	0.58 (139)	4157.02	0.38 (106)	0.47 (119)
Botswana	Upper middle	2.40	0.74 (117)	6348.83	0.43 (86)	0.47 (114)
South Africa	Upper middle	60.04	0.71 (109)	5655.87	0.36 (112)	0.41 (82)
United Kingdom	Upper	67.33	0.93 (18)	41098.08	0.68 (16)	0.30 (8)
Germany	Upper	83.13	0.95 (9)	46252.69	0.72 (12)	0.30 (5)

Source: Chanza and Makombe (2025)

Overall, the review literature agrees that Zimbabwe is battling climate change impacts. These impacts significantly negatively affect livelihoods and incomes. Among the most affected and vulnerable, and yet understudied, are children. The next section explores how climate change impacts agriculture and food systems and eventually affects Zimbabwean children.

15.4 Climate Change–Food System Nexus: Impact on Children in Zimbabwe

The review shows that climate change severely impacts food security and nutrition for Zimbabwean children. This is achieved by inflicting a negative impact across the country's food system, from production to consumption. Climate-change-related impacts cause reduced crop yields from droughts and floods, leading to lower food quantity and dietary diversity, and increased food prices (Mpakairi et al., 2020; Ndhlovu & Dube, 2024; Nhundu et al., 2021). Climate-related water shortage further hampers sanitation, increasing waterborne diseases like diarrhoea and cholera, major killers of young children. In addition, climate change contributes to the loss of traditional food sources and impacts household income, forcing families to reduce meal frequency and diversity for their children (Sagomba & Ndhlovu, 2025).

Droughts and floods are now more frequent, particularly in the country's Lowveld region, destroying crops and livestock, leading to low food production and poor harvests (Muzerengi et al., 2023). In Mwenezi, increased pests and diseases for livestock and crops have been reported, negatively affecting productivity and consumption (Muzerengi et al., 2023). In Gwanda, Mbereko et al. (2018) found that due to climate change, households had resorted to strategies such as shifting cultivation practices and informal trading, all of which rarely boosted their food reserves. As food becomes scarcer and expensive, families resort to less diverse, less nutritious diets (Nkonya et al., 2023). This means children receive fewer nutrients essential for growth and development, and families may reduce meal frequency. In the Chipinge District, climate-change-induced food shortages worsened child labour, with some children moving across the border into Mozambique to provide labour as herd boys or working in the fields (Ndhlovu, 2023) as a strategy to boost household food reserves.

Due to climate change, traditional sources of nutrition, such as wild fruits and insects like mopani worms, are becoming unpredictable, further threatening food availability. Chanza and Musakwa (2022) found that in the Mbire District, climate change had severely impacted wild fruits, making them less predictable, smaller, and scarcer due to irregular rainfall, prolonged droughts, and rising temperatures. This directly threatened food security and livelihoods, particularly since the communities in this district relied on these fruits for nutrition and income and as a buffer during crop failure. Specific impacts observed by Chanza and Musakwa (2022) in the Mbire District include delayed flowering, premature withering, and a reduction in the abundance of key species, such as *masau* (*Ziziphus mauritiana*) and *matamba* (*Strychnos cocculoides*), leading to economic hardship and social instability. Reduced agricultural output also negatively impacted household incomes, forcing families to struggle to find enough food (Ndhlovu, 2023). This led women to spend more time searching for food and water, taking time away from childcare practices (Mhembwe, 2025).

Climate change also poses a severe threat to food system infrastructure in Zimbabwe, primarily events like storms and floods. The impacts can span the entire food value chain, from production to consumption. For instance, prolonged droughts, aggravated by events like El Niño, lead to water shortages, critically affecting rain-fed agriculture—the backbone of Zimbabwe's food supply (Ndhlovu & Dube, 2024). This strains existing water infrastructure and limits the viability of non-climate-resilient irrigation systems. Drought is also reducing water levels in dams, rivers, and groundwater, affecting irrigation schemes, livestock watering, and water supply for households (Maphosa & Moyo, 2024). Climate change also deepens aridification in certain regions, rendering previously productive agricultural areas less viable and putting pressure on the infrastructure supporting them (WB, 2025). High temperatures and heat waves also negatively impact crop yields (especially maize, the staple crop) and livestock health, necessitating investment in infrastructure for cooling and heat-stress mitigation (Maphosa & Moyo, 2024).

Climate change also negatively impacts logistics, food storage, and transport infrastructure. Although droughts are the most frequent challenge in Zimbabwe, floods (such as those caused by Cyclone Idai) cause disastrous damage to road networks, bridges, and electric power lines. Cyclone Idai, for instance, disrupted the food supply chain, impeding the transport of agricultural produce to markets and hindering the distribution of food aid and essential inputs like fertiliser and seed to rural communities (Mukurazhizha & Matanga, 2023). In addition, changes in temperature and moisture also affect the quality and safety of stored food, requiring investments in climate-controlled or resilient storage infrastructure to minimise post harvest losses (Mukurazhizha & Matanga, 2023).

In addition, climate-change-related disruptions affect markets and economic infrastructure, resulting in increased food insecurity (Muzerengi et al., 2023). The combined effects of reduced yields and infrastructure damage lead to chronic food deficits, forcing the country to rely on costly food imports. This puts strain on the country's economic stability and trade infrastructure. Infrastructure damage and crop failure also reduce agricultural output, which in turn leads to a reduction in household incomes and a breakdown of local market functions (Ndhlovu, 2024).

The review also reveals significant climate-change-related health risks that affect children in Zimbabwe. Flooding and water scarcity damage water and sanitation infrastructure at home and in public facilities, increasing the risk of water-borne diseases such as cholera and typhoid. Using data from the Zimbabwean National Diseases Surveillance system, Mashe et al. (2023) found that due to increased floods, cholera cases had increased across the country, particularly among children below 15 years. Marumure and Nyila (2024) found that climate change was among the main causes of cholera and typhoid in the country. In the Chiredzi District,

Mavhunga (2025) observed that cholera was affecting children, with poor water and sanitation infrastructure being a primary cause. Efforts to contain the outbreak included mass vaccination campaigns, improving WASH (water, sanitation, and hygiene) services, and community-led initiatives. Children were particularly vulnerable to severe illness from the disease due to overcrowding and limited access to safe water in many communities (Mavhunga, 2025).

Rising temperatures and shifts in ecological zones have also been expanding the habitats for disease-carrying vectors, such as Mosquitoes, in the country. Mosquitoes are malaria vectors. They are known to breed under warm and wet conditions. Increased warming in Zimbabwe has been leading to increased incidence and the geographical spread of diseases like malaria. For instance, Ferriss et al. (2024) found malaria to have spread rapidly in the Mutasa District. Chivasa et al. (2025) reported that climate change is shifting the geographic distribution of malaria transmission in Zimbabwe. Ebi et al. (2005) observed a shift in the country's spatio-temporal patterns of malaria transmission, with longer and less predictable malaria transmission seasons. Malaria emerged in highlands and other previously non-endemic communities, with outbreaks reported after extreme weather events, such as floods. Chapungu and Nhamo (2021) found a positive correlation between malaria occurrence and temperature-related variables in the Masvingo Province. These observations support previous studies, which found that extreme temperatures modified other ecological variables and created conditions favourable for pathogens (Adekiya et al., 2020; Rocklöv & Dubrow, 2020). Therefore, a rise in temperatures can worsen diseases in Zimbabwe.

Heat stress is also negatively impacting children in Zimbabwe. This manifests through direct health effects, such as heat stroke and dehydration, and indirectly through worsened food insecurity and water scarcity associated with climate change. The effects of heat stress include physical health problems, hindered academic performance, and serious long-term consequences for child development. Elevated temperatures and frequent heatwaves put children—who are less equipped to regulate body temperature than adults—at risk of heat stress, resulting in conditions like heat cramps, heat exhaustion, and heatstroke. However, studies exploring the impact of heat stress on children in Zimbabwe are limited. This area, therefore, requires academic and policy attention.

Climate change is also a substantial threat to the mental health and well-being of children and young people in Zimbabwe. Existing social and economic vulnerabilities often compound the impacts. The conduits through which climate change affects children's mental health in Zimbabwe include devastating events such as Cyclone Idai of 2019, floods, and severe droughts, which can be directly traumatic. Children exposed to these events often experience post-traumatic stress disorder (Bhatasara et al., 2025; Ray et al., 2022). Some children can also suffer from anxiety and depression due to the loss of homes, livelihoods, and loved ones and the general fear and distress (Ray et al., 2022). Indirect exposure—through media reports, by witnessing community suffering, or by simply being aware of the ongoing climate crisis and future uncertainty—can lead to chronic fear or worry about the environmental crisis, as well as a sense of hopelessness and vulnerability, particularly among youth who feel they lack the agency to address the threats. Although significantly limited, research consistently points to the need for instant, all-inclusive, and culturally sensitive interventions to protect the psychological well-being of Zimbabwean children under the climate crisis (Chivasa et al., 2025).

15.5 Social-Policy-Based Interventions for Sustainable Futures

The Zimbabwean government and its partners are implementing several interventions to reduce the impact of climate change on food systems, which eventually negatively impact children. This section discusses existing and potential social-policy-based interventions in this regard.

15.5.1 Social Protection and Safety Nets

The impact of climate change on children in Zimbabwe is a major child rights crisis, affecting their survival, development, nutrition, health, education, and protection. Therefore, interventions and responses must be child centred, holistic, and climate resilient, focusing on strengthening children's essential services and empowering them as agents of change. The Government of Zimbabwe, in partnership with international and non-governmental organisations, is already (or considering) implementing and developing several policy and programmatic responses.

One of the interventions the government and its stakeholders are making is strengthening child-sensitive social protection and safety nets. In 2011/2012, Zimbabwe introduced the Harmonised Social Cash Transfer (HSCT). This unconditional cash transfer programme by the Ministry of Public Service, Labour and Social Welfare supports ultra-poor and food-poor households that are labour constrained. The programme aims to increase household consumption, decrease extreme poverty, and prevent negative coping strategies, such as child labour or early marriage, by providing cash payments based on household size. It is jointly funded by the Zimbabwean government, the UK's Department for International Development (DFID), and UNICEF, with the latter also providing technical support. The HSCT programme has positively impacted children by improving their food security, health, and well-being while reducing exposure to violence, early sexual activity, and other risky behaviours (Chikoko et al., 2021; Pace et al., 2022). However, the impact on education is mixed, with a minimal effect on primary and secondary school enrolment (Chikoko & Mavuka, 2025). While the programme seeks to improve child outcomes by providing cash transfers, evidence suggests that the grant amounts and other challenges may limit its effectiveness, particularly for younger children (Pace et al., 2022).

Zimbabwe also implements the Emergency Social Cash Transfer Programme. Implemented in partnership with organisations such as UNICEF, this programme provides timely cash support to communities affected by climate shocks and seasonal food insecurity, enhancing resilience. The programme provides cash to replace food distribution and address basic needs. It targets food-insecure, labour-constrained households and has been shown to improve food consumption and dietary diversity (Marwa et al., 2024). The government and its partners are using cash transfers to address the current complex humanitarian crisis worsened by the El-Niño-induced drought, which has led to water and food shortages (Ndhlovu & Dube, 2024). Challenges of the programme include the need for sustainable, long-term funding and improved coordination among implementing partners to ensure the system is shock responsive. Some studies have also reported inconsistent payments and system downtime (Chikoko & Mavuka, 2025).

There are ongoing efforts to strengthen the national social protection system to be more responsive to future climate shocks, including revising the National Social Protection Policy Framework (NSPPF) and developing guidelines for timely support. Support is being rolled out through the Shock-Responsive Social Assistance (SRSA) programme. Existing cash transfer and food aid programmes are being adapted for rapid, scaled-up delivery to affected households after a climate shock. This entails increasing benefit values (vertical expansion) or adding new, temporarily vulnerable beneficiaries (horizontal expansion). Despite government and partner efforts, Zimbabwe's SRSA framework faces major operational, financial, and political challenges (Ncube et al., 2023). These issues weaken its capacity to scale up effectively and reach those most exposed to economic instability and severe climate shocks, like droughts and floods. In dealing with these challenges, Zimbabwe needs to establish a unified social registry that can quickly identify and target the most vulnerable families, including child-headed households. Social cash transfers must be linked with other services, such as child nutritional support, to improve effectiveness. This can be achieved by scaling up and strengthening school feeding programmes, especially in climate-vulnerable areas, to mitigate malnutrition and encourage school attendance during food-scarce periods.

In addition, Zimbabwe is also implementing the Basic Education Assistance Module (BEAM) programme. This social assistance programme, introduced in 2001, was meant to help exposed children afford education by providing financial grants to cover fees, levies, and examination costs. The programme was designed to prevent children from dropping out of school due to poverty, particularly for orphans, child-headed families, and children from poor households. While the government finances the programme, its donor partners also fund it. The government, therefore, needs to widen the targeting of education subsidy to ensure all children remain in school during extreme climate events, when livelihoods are disrupted and families resort to negative coping mechanisms like child labour or child marriage.

15.5.2 Food and Nutrition Security Policies and Programmes

Zimbabwe has also adopted a Food and Nutrition Security Policy (FNSP), a comprehensive national policy framework designed to address the persistent and growing challenges of hunger and malnutrition across the country. This policy provides an overarching framework to ensure adequate food and nutrition security, explicitly recognising climate change as a significant risk and calling for investment in cost-effective disaster preparedness. To ensure the FNSP prioritises children, the policy must focus on and scale up interventions that specifically target children. Zimbabwe's existing Multi-Sectoral Food and Nutrition Security Strategy (MFNSS) and the role of the Food and Nutrition Council (FNC) already provide a multi-sectoral framework, but prioritising children effectively requires a deliberate concentration of resources, coordinated action, and specific policy directives. The policy must integrate child-specific climate resilience into its core pillars: availability, access, utilisation, and stability. This involves embedding nutrition-sensitive and shock-responsive measures across the agriculture, health, social protection, and water sectors.

The country also implements a Home-Grown School Feeding Programme (HGSFP), which aims to improve nutrition for schoolchildren by providing school meals while creating a market for locally produced, often biofortified, and traditional crops. This links nutrition, agriculture, and local economic development. It has transitioned from emergency food aid to a sustainable, national strategy to improve education, nutrition, and local economies. Zimbabwe adopted the HGSFP approach in 2016, with the government committing to its roll-out. This was a transition from an emergency school-feeding initiative to a long-term, sustainable strategy. As of 2025, legislation (Statutory Instrument 13 of 2025) reportedly mandates all schools to provide at least one hot meal daily, with oversight from the Ministry of Health and Child Care. The HGSFP, often supported by partners such as UNICEF, the World Food Programme (WFP), and the German government (KfW), has demonstrated significant positive impacts, including increased school attendance and enrolment, improved nutrition and health, reduced protection risks, and improved economic support by creating a reliable, local market for smallholder farmers while also providing income-generating opportunities for community groups (Ncube et al., 2023; UNICEF, 2024b).

15.5.3 Climate-Change-Specific Policies

Zimbabwe has adopted child-friendly climate change policies focused on educating young people, incorporating climate change into the school curriculum, and promoting youth engagement in climate action. These initiatives include a grades 6–7 handbook, lessons that integrate climate issues, and programmes that raise awareness and encourage environmentally friendly practices among youth. Developed with UNICEF, this policy is a simplified version of the National Climate Change Policy, ensuring that children's unique vulnerabilities and rights are central to national climate change response strategies.

However, challenges to Zimbabwe's Child-Friendly Climate Change Policy include inadequate funding for climate action and education, poor implementation and coordination, and the lack of integration of child-specific needs into mainstream policies. Other impediments are the limited involvement of children in policymaking, the lack of a specific budget for early childhood development, and infrastructure damage from climate events that directly impact children's access to education and healthcare.

It is vital to ensure that social policy empowers children with the knowledge and capacity to adapt to and mitigate climate change. This should entail mainstreaming climate change into the national education curriculum at all levels, focusing on local-level adaptation strategies, resilience building, and practical components like sustainable agricultural practices. In addition, child participation in policy design should be promoted. It is crucial to ensure the meaningful participation of children and young people in developing and reviewing climate policies, strategies, and disaster response plans, such as the National Adaptation Plan, recognising them as critical actors in climate action. Further, capacity building is also needed. The government and its partners should prioritise providing training for teachers and community leaders on climate change issues, adaptation, and how to support children experiencing climate-related stress. These interventions should be guided by a child-sensitive National Climate Policy and strategy, ensuring dedicated funding and political will for implementation.

Zimbabwe has also adopted Climate-Smart Agriculture (CSA). The programme involves practices like zero tillage, drought-resistant crop varieties, and improved water management to increase productivity and resilience against climate change. The country is developing strategies such as the CSA Investment Plan to support these initiatives to enhance food security and align with global climate goals. Key activities include promoting agroforestry, crop diversification, renewable energy use, and capacity building for farmers and extension officers. The programme also promotes indigenous practices like conservation farming (*Pfumvudza/Intwasa* concept), thus safeguarding the food base for children. However, challenges to CSA in Zimbabwe include a lack of funding, limited access to inputs and information, low farmer knowledge, and technical difficulties with some practices (Mhlanga & Ndhlovu, 2023). High labour costs, the incompatibility of some practices with certain crops, and inadequate support from the government and institutions further hinder adoption (Ndhlovu & Mhlanga, 2023). In addition, sociocultural factors and issues like land ownership, particularly for youth, present obstacles.

15.5.4 Participatory and Rights-Based Approaches

Efforts to reduce the impact of climate change on children must be multifaceted and comprehensive. They should include existing child-centred mechanisms, such as the Child-Centred Climate Impact, Vulnerability, and Risk Assessment, which is conducted to understand children's exposure and vulnerability to climate hazards, ensuring interventions are evidence based and inclusive. Methods through which children should be supported to participate in matters that concern them need to be identified. Efforts should be made to include children's voices in developing climate change policies and action plans, recognising them as agents of change. Policies must also prioritise the protection and continuity of services critical to children's well-being, even during climate-induced disasters.

In addition, the government and its partners must invest in climate-resilient infrastructure. This includes investing in climate-proofed school and health facility infrastructure, especially in flood-prone areas. This entails securing essential utilities like water supply and energy through climate-smart technologies (e.g., solar power, boreholes). They must also increase the supply and upgrade the infrastructure for water and boreholes to ensure reliable, clean water access, reducing the burden on women and girls who typically fetch water and lowering the risk of waterborne diseases exacerbated by climate events. These interventions should reflect a move towards holistic, multi-sectoral approaches that link climate adaptation, food production, social protection, and health/nutrition in order to build resilience and safeguard the well-being of Zimbabwe's children.

15.5.5 Child Protection and Gender-Sensitive Interventions

Policies must also directly address the increased child protection risks (exploitation, violence, abuse) that emerge when climate shocks undermine family livelihoods. The focus should be on preventing families from using negative coping strategies. The government and its partners need to implement gender-sensitive interventions to address the disproportionate impact on girls, such as preventing school dropout and child marriages. This could involve targeted bursaries or conditional cash transfers for girls in vulnerable areas. In addition, the government must strengthen child protection services to thwart and respond to increases in child labour and sexual exploitation, which are often fallback strategies for desperate families (Ndhlovu, 2023). Further, the government should decentralise child welfare services to the local level to enable faster investigation, assessment, and intervention for children needing care during or after a climate crisis.

15.6 Conclusion

This chapter explored the impact of climate change on children in Zimbabwe. It builds on existing studies showing that climate change poses one of the most significant long-term threats to Zimbabwe's socio-economic development, with its effects being acutely felt across critical sectors like agriculture, water resources, and public health. The country is experiencing rising temperatures and increasingly erratic rainfall patterns, which have led to a surge in the frequency and intensity of extreme weather events. This chapter adds the issue of children to this debate, which has not attracted satisfactory scholarly attention. In some instances, it tends to be assumed that adults and children are being affected in the same way. The chapter problematises this approach. Underpinned by a scoping review, the chapter showed that climate change affects food systems, from production to consumption, thereby forcing families to resort to desperate and unsafe adaptation strategies, which include child labour exploitation and early marriages. In addition, climate change affects children through health challenges related to food shortages.

The chapter also outlined several social-policy-based interventions that Zimbabwe and its partners are implementing to reduce the impact of climate change on children. In addition, the chapter proposed some policies that can help fast-track and strengthen existing interventions. Future studies should focus on funding models for social protection programmes that specifically target children.

References

Adekiya, T. A., Aruleba, R. T., Oyinloye, B. E., Okosun, K. O., & Kappo, A. P. (2020). The effect of climate change and the snail-schistosome cycle in transmission and biocontrol of schistosomiasis in sub-Saharan Africa. *International Journal of Environmental Research and Public Health, 17*(1), 1–22. https://doi.org/10.3390/ijerph17010181

Bhatasara, S., Nwosu, C., Macheka, L., & Nyamwanza, A. M. (2025). Narratives of climate adaptation and linkages to psychosocial and nutritional health in a Zimbabwean rural community. *World Development Sustainability, 6*, 100205. https://doi.org/10.1016/j.wds.2025.100205

Chanza, N. (2018). Limits to climate change adaptation in Zimbabwe: Insights, experiences and lessons. In W. L. Filho & J. Nalau (Eds.), *Limits to climate change adaptation* (pp. 109–127). Springer.

Chanza, N., & Makombe, E. K. (2025). Positioning Zimbabwe in the climate change mitigation adaptation discourse: Exploring benefits, barriers and risks. *Environment, Development and Sustainability*. https://doi.org/10.1007/s10668-025-06723-1

Chanza, N., & Musakwa, W. (2022). Indigenous local observations and experiences can give useful indicators of climate change in data-deficient regions. *Journal of Environmental Studies and Sciences, 12*(3), 534–546. https://doi.org/10.1007/s13412-022-00757-x

Chapungu, L., & Nhamo, G. (2021). Interfacing vector borne disease dynamics with climate change: Implications for the attainment of SDGs in Masvingo city, Zimbabwe. *Jàmbá: Journal of Disaster Risk Studies, 13*(1), a1175. https://doi.org/10.4102/jamba.v13i1.1175

Chikoko, W., & Mavuka, A. (2025). Role of social cash transfers among children in child-headed households: A case of *Jacha* area of Epworth in Harare, Zimbabwe, in the face of Austerity era. *Journal of Human Rights and Social Work, 10*, 89–97.

Chikoko, W., Nyabeze, K., Zvokuomba, K., & Mwapaura, K. (2021). The Harmonized Social Cash Transfer Program in Zimbabwe: Achievements and challenges. *Journal of Economics and Behavioral Studies, 13*(5), 12–21.

Chivasa, T., Nunu, W. N., Dhlamini, M., Maviza, A., & Ndagurwa, G. N. (2025). Impact of climate change on Malaria transmission and management in Zimbabwe: A scoping review of the literature. *Health Services Insights, 2025*, 18. https://doi.org/10.1177/11786329251374245

Ebi, K. L., Hartman, J., Chan, N., Mcconnell, J., Schlesinger, M., & Weyant, J. (2005). Climate suitability for stable malaria transmission in Zimbabwe under different climate change scenarios. *Climatic Change, 73*(3), 375–393.

Ferriss, E., Mharakurwa, S., Munyati, S., Gwanzura, L., Hast, M. A., Moulton, L. H., Wesolowski, A., & Moss, W. J. (2024). Malaria transmission at the Zimbabwe–Mozambique Border: An observational study of parasitemia by travel history and household location. *The American Journal of Tropical Medicine and Hygiene, 111*(1), 35–42. https://doi.org/10.4269/ajtmh.23-0466

Garcia, T. F., Madurga-Lopez, I., Liebig, T., Tarusarira, J., Sax, N., Pacillo, G., & Laderach, P. (2023). *How does climate exacerbate root causes of conflict in Zimbabwe?* Climate Security Pathway Analysis. CGIAR FOCUS Climate Security. Retrieved October 17, 2025, from https://cgspace.cgiar.org/server/api/core/bitstreams/8b78ac2c-8053-482a-8663-341c1c8573f2/content

GoZ. (2024). *National climate change adaptation plan*. Ministry of Environment, Climate, Tourism and Hospitality Industry, Government of Zimbabwe (GoZ). Retrieved October 16, 2025, from https://www.scribd.com/document/905611475/Zimbabwe-s-National-Climate-Change-Adaptation-Plan

Gwatida, T., Kusangaya, S., Gwenzi, J., Mushore, T., Shekede, M. D., & Viriri, N. (2023). Is climate really changing? Insights from analysis of 30-year daily CHIRPS and station rainfall data in Zimbabwe. *Scientific African, 19*, e01581. https://doi.org/10.1016/j.sciaf.2023.e01581

Maphosa, M., & Moyo, P. (2024). Assessing climate vulnerabilities of urban food systems and institutional responses: The case of Bulawayo, Zimbabwe. *Frontiers in Sustainable Cities, 6*, 1488144. https://doi.org/10.3389/frsc.2024.1488144

Marumure, J., & Nyila, M. A. (2024). Cholera outbreaks in Zimbabwe: An in-depth analysis of drivers, constraints, and reimagining the use of medicinal plants. *Journal of Tropical Medicine, 24*(1), 1–21. https://doi.org/10.1155/jotm/1981991

Marwa, I., Chen, Y., Pereira, A., Musa, T., Bathia, D., & Handa, S. (2024). The psychology of poverty: A replication based on Zimbabwe's harmonised social cash transfer programme. *Journal of African Economies, 33*(3), 225–239. https://doi.org/10.1093/jae/ejad013

Mashe, T., Chaibva, B. V., Nair, P., Sani, K. A., Jallow, M., Tarupiwa, A., Goredema, A., Munyanyi, M., Chimusoro, A., Mpala, N., Masunda, K. P. E., Duri, C., Chonzi, P., & Phiri, I. (2023). Descriptive epidemiology of the cholera outbreak in Zimbabwe 2018–2019: Role of multi-sectoral approach in cholera epidemic control. *BMJ Open, 13*, e059134. https://doi.org/10.1136/bmjopen-2021-059134

Mavhunga, C. (2025). *Zimbabwe: Cholera outbreak in eight districts*. Retrieved October 17, 2025, from https://www.dw.com/en/zimbabwe-cholera-outbreak-in-al-least-eight-districts/a-71333093

Mbereko, A., Chimbari, M. J., & Mukaratirwa, S. (2018). The political ecology of stakeholder-driven climate change adaptation: Case study from Ntalale ward, Gwanda district, in Zimbabwe. *Jàmbá: Journal of Disaster Risk Studies, 10*(1), a419. https://doi.org/10.4102/jamba.v10i1.419

Mezmur, M. E. (2023). The calm before the storm? Child rights climate change litigation in Africa. *De Jure Law Journal, 56(1)*, 543–568. https://doi.org/10.17159/2225-7160/2023/v56a33

Mhembwe, S. (2025). Climate change and the feminization of poverty in Africa: Insights from rural Zimbabwe. *Journal of Developing Societies, 41*(1), 85–107. https://doi.org/10.1177/0169796X241305062

Mhlanga, D., & Ndhlovu, E. (2023). Digital technology adoption in the agriculture sector: Challenges and complexities in Africa. *Human Behavior and Emerging Technologies, 6951879*, 1–10.

Ministry of Environment, Climate, Tourism, and Hospitality Industry. (2020). *Zimbabwe's first biennial update report to the United Nations Framework Convention on climate change*. https://unfccc.int/sites/default/files/resource/Zimbabwe%20Biennial%20Update%20Report%201.pdf

Moyo, C. (2017). Climate change and health in Zimbabwe: A legal perspective. *Journal of Law, Policy and Globalization, 68*, 7–12.

Mpakairi, K. S., Ndaimani, H., Tagwireyi, P., Zvidzai, M., & Madiri, T. H. (2020). Futuristic climate change scenario predicts a shrinking habitat for the African elephant (Loxodonta africana): Evidence from Hwange National Park, Zimbabwe. *European Journal of Wildlife Research*. https://doi.org/10.1007/s10344-019-1327-x

Mukurazhizha, R. M., & Matanga, S. Y. (2023). The role of women in managing the environmental crisis: A case study of Cyclone Idai in Chipinge, Zimbabwe. *HTS Teologiese Studies/Theological Studies, 79*(3), a8042. https://doi.org/10.4102/hts.v79i3.8042

Muzerengi, F., Gandidzanwa, C. P., & Chirubvu, L. (2023). Impacts of climate change on household food security in Matande communal lands, Mwenezi district in Zimbabwe. *Jàmbá: Journal of Disaster Risk Studies, 15*(1), a1499. https://doi.org/10.4102/jamba.v15i1.1499

Ncube, T., Murray, U., & Dennehy, D. (2023). Digitalising social protection systems for achieving the sustainable development goals: Insights from Zimbabwe. *Communications of the Association for Information Systems, 53*, 138–161. https://doi.org/10.17705/1CAIS.05306

Ndhlovu, E. (2023). Accumulation and livelihoods strategies of the Hlengwe Peasantry in Mahenye, along the Zimbabwe-Mozambique border. In N. Pophiwa, J. Matanzima, & K. Helliker (Eds.), *Lived experiences of borderland communities in Zimbabwe: Livelihoods, conservation, war and Covid-19*. Springer Cham.

Ndhlovu, E. (2024). Extreme weather events and human displacement in sub-Saharan Africa: Toward social policy interventions. *Review of Socio-Economic Research and Development Studies, 8*(2), 70–100.

Ndhlovu, E., & Dube, K. (2024). Contract farming and climate change adaptation in rural Zimbabwe. *Mankind Quarterly, 64*(3), 579–594.

Ndhlovu, E., & Mhlanga, D. (2023). Smart technologies, climate change, and smallholder farmer production in Zimbabwe. In D. Mhlanga & E. Ndhlovu (Eds.), *The fourth industrial revolution in Africa: Exploring the development implications of smart technologies in Africa*. Springer Cham.

Ngwenya, B., Oosthuizen, J., Cross, M., & Frimpong, K. (2018). Emerging heat-related climate change influences, public health challenge to health care practitioners and policy makers: Insight from Bulawayo, Zimbabwe. *International Journal of Disaster Risk Reduction, 27*, 596–601. https://doi.org/10.1016/j.ijdrr.2017.10.012

Nhara, R. B., Halimani, T. E., & Masunda, B. (2020). Impacts of climate change on communal livestock production: Experiences in Chiredzi District. *ACTA Scientific Agriculture, 4*(8), 91–96.

Nhundu, K., Sibanda, M., & Chaminuka, P. (2021). *Economic losses from cyclones Idai and Kenneth and floods in southern Africa: Implications on sustainable development goals. Cyclones in Southern Africa*. Springer International Publishing. https://doi.org/10.1007/978-3-030-74303-1_19

Nkonya, E., Kato, E., Msimanga, M., & Nyathi, N. (2023). Climate shock response and resilience of smallholder farmers in the drylands of south-eastern Zimbabwe. *Frontiers in Climate, 5*, 890465. https://doi.org/10.3389/fclim.2023.890465

Pace, N., Sebastian, A., Daidone, S., Prifti, E., & Davis, B. (2022). Mediation analysis of the impact of the Zimbabwe Harmonized Social Cash Transfer Programme on food security and nutrition. *Food Policy, 106*, 102190. https://doi.org/10.1016/j.foodpol.2021.102190

Ray, S., Goronga, T., Chigiya, P. T., & Madzimbamuto, F. D. (2022). Climate change, disaster management, and primary health care in Zimbabwe. *African Journal of Primary Health & Family Medicine, 14*(1), e1–e3. https://doi.org/10.4102/phcfm.v14i1.3684

Rocklöv, J., & Dubrow, R. (2020). Climate change: An enduring challenge for vector-borne disease prevention and control. *Nature Immunology, 21*, 479–483. https://doi.org/10.1038/s41590-020-0648-y

Sagomba, E., & Ndhlovu, E. (2025). Food system transformation for safe and nutritious diets in Africa. In E. Ndhlovu (Ed.), *African food systems*. Palgrave Macmillan.

Tirivangasi, H. M., & Nyahunda, L. (2025). Determinants of transformative climate change adaptation in rural Zimbabwe: An afrocentric analysis. *Climate Policy*. https://doi.org/10.1080/14693062.2025.2521486

UNDP. (2023). *Coping with drought and climate change*. Retrieved May 25, 2023, from https://www.adaptation-undp.org/projects/coping-drought-and-climate-change-cwdcc-zimbabwe

UNICEF. (2024a). Climate change impact on child health: Perspectives from children and care givers in Zimbabwe. *UNICEF*. https://www.unicef.org/zimbabwe/media/11011/file/Climate%20Change%20Impacts%20on%20Children's%20Health%20Report%202024_designed%20version%20(3).pdf.pdf

UNICEF. (2024b). *Promising practices for integrated school health and nutrition programming: The development of school nutrition guidelines in Zimbabwe*. UNICEF Eastern and Southern Africa Regional Office and World Food Programme (WFP) Regional Bureau for Southern Africa (RBSA).

United Nations Development Programme. (2017). *Zimbabwe human development report 2017: Climate change and human development: Towards building a climate resilient nation*. UNDP.

WB. (2025). Zimbabwe economic update: Improving resilience to weather shocks and climate change. *World Bank*. Retrieved October 16, 2025, from https://www.worldbank.org/en/country/zimbabwe/publication/zimbabwe-economic-update-improving-resilience-to-afe-weather-shocks-and-climate-change#:~:text=The%20World%20Bank's%20Zimbabwe%20Country,seasons%20between%201980%20and%202011

World Bank. (2021). *World development indicators*. Retrieved October 17, 2025, from https://databank.worldbank.org/reports.aspx?source=world-development-indicators

Zimbabwe Meteorological Department (ZMD). (2007). *Climate data, research unit*. Retrieved February 20, 2021, from http://www.fao.org/docrep/x5872e/x5872e04.htm

Chapter 16
Conclusion: Transformative Social Policy—Reimagining Children's Rights in Zimbabwe's Climate Crisis

Emmanuel Ndhlovu and Clement Chipenda

16.1 Introduction

This chapter concludes the book *Climate Change and Children's Rights in Zimbabwe: Towards Social-Policy-Based Interventions*. The intersection of climate change and children's rights in Zimbabwe reveals an essential gap between policy aspirations and implementation realities. It demands the urgent reconceptualisation of how societies protect their most vulnerable members during environmental crises. As Zimbabwe experiences increasingly severe droughts, floods, and extreme weather events, children are confronted with its negative impacts, undermining their rights to health, education, nutrition, and protection (UNICEF, 2022). Zimbabwe's vulnerability is evidenced by its ranking as the 15th most vulnerable country to climate change globally and among the top three in Southern Africa according to the 2021 Global Climate Risk Index, with projections indicating continued warming through 2080, affecting the western and southern provinces, including Masvingo, Matabeleland North and Matabeleland South (GoZ, 2020; UNICEF, 2021, 2022). The scale of this challenge is immense, with all 6.5 million children (0–18 years old) at risk of impact from climate-induced emergencies. This reflects the global reality that every child on earth is exposed to at least one climate and environmental hazard such as heatwaves, cyclones, air pollution, flooding, and water scarcity (UNICEF, 2021, 2022).

It would be argued, however, that existing policy responses have operated within narrow sectoral frameworks, failing to address the structural inequalities that

E. Ndhlovu
College of Business and Economics, University of Johannesburg, Auckland Park, South Africa

C. Chipenda (✉)
South African Research Chair in Social Policy, College of Graduate Studies, University of South Africa, Pretoria, South Africa

E. Ndhlovu, C. Chipenda (eds.), *Climate Change and Children's Rights in Zimbabwe*, https://doi.org/10.1007/978-981-95-6005-9_16

amplify children's climate vulnerabilities while limiting their capacity for meaningful participation in adaptation processes. This failure is concerning given that climate change impacts are deeply intertwined with global patterns of inequality, where the poorest and most vulnerable people, including children, bear the disproportionate burden of climate change impacts despite contributing least to the crisis (World Bank, 2025). Children, alongside female-headed households, persons with disabilities, Indigenous peoples, and other socially marginalised groups, often have fewer financial and other resources to cope with and recover from climate shocks. Their vulnerability is rooted in geographical location, socio-economic status, and limited access to resources, services, and decision-making power (World Bank, 2025).

In this concluding chapter, we argue that protecting children's rights in climate-affected Zimbabwe requires a shift towards transformative social policy (TSP) approaches that challenge existing power structures, redistribute resources, and recognise children as active agents in building resilient communities. Unlike conventional social protection measures that primarily manage the symptoms of climate vulnerability, TSP addresses the root causes of inequality and exclusion that make children susceptible to environmental risks (Ndhlovu, 2024b). This approach is especially relevant in Zimbabwe's context, where decades of economic instability and entrenched inequality have created conditions that now intensify climate change. In this discussion, the COVID-19 pandemic is of importance. It has highlighted the urgency of this paradigm shift by exposing the fragility of existing social protection systems and demonstrating how external shocks can rapidly reverse progress in children's welfare (Chipenda, 2022). Globally, the pandemic has further illuminated the inherent flaws of current economic systems, increased poverty, and created adverse impacts on nutrition, health, education, and employment while also increasing children's exposure to violence (Ndhlovu & Gumede, 2023; UNRISD, 2023). As Zimbabwe navigates post-pandemic recovery while confronting escalating climate impacts, a critical opportunity exists to reimagine social policy architectures that build resilience against multiple, intersecting crises. In addition, a growing recognition of the limitations of conventional development frameworks has created intellectual and policy space for more transformative approaches that directly address questions of power, distribution, and systemic change.

Contemporary social policy scholarship increasingly emphasises the need to move beyond technical solutions towards approaches capable of addressing the challenges of inequality, exclusion, and environmental degradation (Mhlanga & Ndhlovu, 2023; UNRISD, 2023). This scholarly consensus arises from the recognition that the world has entered the Decade of Action for the 2030 Agenda, facing severe crises, broken social contracts, and increasing inequalities, with urgent challenges impeding SDG implementation and undermining efforts towards a just and sustainable world (UNRISD, 2022, 2023). The climate crisis, characterised by biodiversity loss, pollution, and unsustainable resource use reaching dangerous tipping points, is a consequence of an unsustainable economic system that has offloaded costs onto poor countries and people over two centuries (UNRISD, 2022, 2023). This transformative turn aligns with the emerging recognition that climate adaptation requires more robust interventions and changes to social, economic, and political systems (World Bank, 2025). Such transformation necessitates changing relations between states and markets, better governance of global value chains, and new relationships between market actors and communities. It also recognises that economic, social, environmental, and political privileges accumulated at the top often oppose transformative change towards greater social, climate, and economic justice (UNRISD, 2022, 2023). In the context of children's rights, this convergence suggests the need for policy frameworks that can simultaneously build climate resilience while advancing broader agendas of social transformation and rights fulfilment.

Zimbabwe's historical trajectory, marked by colonial exploitation, post-independence redistribution efforts, economic crisis, and ongoing democratisation struggles, provides an essential context for examining how TSP might address climate-children's rights challenges. The country's experience with progressive constitutional provisions on children's rights, alongside persistent implementation gaps, offers critical perspectives (see Chap. 14) into conditions under which transformative approaches might succeed. In addition, Zimbabwe's traditions of community organisation and indigenous knowledge systems provide potential foundations for participatory approaches that centre on children's voices and agency. Two focused research questions and objectives guide the chapter's analysis. The first is: Why do conventional social policy approaches in Zimbabwe have limitations in adequately protecting children's rights in the context of climate change? The objective is to identify the key limitations of current social policy frameworks in addressing climate-induced vulnerabilities affecting children. The second research question is how TSP principles can protect children's rights in climate-affected Zimbabwe. In line with this research question, the second objective is to examine the potential utility of TSP approaches for strengthening children's rights protection in climate contexts.

The chapter is premised on an interpretive approach that seeks to understand the relationship between climate change, social policy systems, and children's rights by critically analysing existing knowledge and policy frameworks. The methodology employs secondary data analysis from academic literature, policy documents, government reports, and grey literature from international organisations and civil society. This approach examines how climate change and children's rights challenges are currently understood and addressed while exploring alternative conceptual frameworks that could enhance policy effectiveness. The chapter contributes to broader debates on the nexus between climate change, children's rights, and social policy by providing a comprehensive framework for understanding how climate change challenges existing social policy paradigms while creating opportunities for more transformative approaches. The chapter bridges theoretical debates with policy design concerns by positioning the TSP as both an analytical lens and a practical framework. In addition, focusing on children's rights within the TSP analysis contributes to discussions about operationalising equity principles in ways that prioritise society's most vulnerable members. The argument proceeds through interconnected stages: firstly, by examining climate impacts on children's rights in

Zimbabwe; secondly, by introducing TSP as a conceptual framework and analysing its utility in addressing intersecting vulnerabilities; thirdly, by exploring how post-pandemic challenges and evolving development paradigms create both vulnerabilities and opportunities; and, lastly, by concluding with implications for policy and practice. Through this analysis, the chapter demonstrates that protecting children's rights in climate-affected contexts requires transformation of social policy approaches, moving beyond technical fixes towards approaches that challenge power structures, redistribute resources, and recognise children as full participants in shaping resilient societies.

16.2 Literature Review

The relationship between climate change and children's rights has emerged as a critical area of scholarly and policy attention, with mounting evidence demonstrating the severe impact of climate change on children globally. This literature review synthesises current research on how climate change affects children's rights and examines the limitations of conventional social policy approaches in addressing these challenges. Special attention will be given to the African context and Zimbabwe as a case study.

16.2.1 International Legal Framework and Children's Climate Vulnerability

The normative foundation for addressing climate change through a children's rights lens is well established in international law. Arts (2019) notes that virtually all states worldwide are bound by both the UN Convention on the Rights of the Child (UNCRC), adopted in 1989 with 196 States Parties, and the UN Framework Convention on Climate Change (UNFCCC), adopted in 1991 with 197 States Parties. This dual obligation creates a compelling legal framework whereby climate change interventions are mandatory and must be child rights based (Arts, 2019). The Committee on the Rights of the Child's General Comment 26 (UN, 2023) provides the most comprehensive articulation of this nexus. It declares that the extent and magnitude of the triple planetary crisis—climate emergency, the collapse of biodiversity, and pervasive pollution—is an urgent and systemic threat to children's rights globally. The General Comment further establishes that a clean, healthy, and sustainable environment is both a human right and a prerequisite for the full enjoyment of a broad range of children's rights. It further emphasises that environmental degradation, including the consequences of the climate crisis, adversely affects the enjoyment of children's rights, especially those in disadvantaged situations (UN, 2023). The general implementation principles of the UNCRC, including child survival and development, non-discrimination, best interests of the child, and participation, provide practical guidance for climate-change-related action (ACERWC, 2025).

The UNCRC provides comprehensive protection for children's rights, with several relevant provisions to address the impacts of climate change. Article 6 guarantees the right to life, survival, and development, which the African Committee of Experts on the Rights and Welfare of the Child (ACERWC) argues is threatened by environmental degradation, including climate change, pollution, and biodiversity loss (ACERWC, 2025). Article 24 addresses health rights by recognising environmental factors and requiring states to combat disease and malnutrition while considering the dangers and risks of environmental pollution (Ndhlovu, 2024a; UN, 1989). The ACERWC (2025) identifies environmental pollution as a significant threat to children's health. Article 27 ensures every child's right to an adequate standard of living for physical, mental, spiritual, moral, and social development (UN, 1989). The ACERWC (2025) clarifies that realising this right requires a clean, healthy, and sustainable environment as a prerequisite. While children's right to a clean, healthy, and sustainable environment is implicit in the UNCRC, it directly connects to other rights, including life, health, adequate standard of living, and education. In this context, the SDGs have emerged as a critical framework linking climate action with children's rights. The ACERWC (2025) emphasises that the SDGs are of cardinal importance because they supplanted the Millennium Development Goals (MDGs) and are intended to achieve sustainable development. The SDGs recognise that ending poverty and other deprivations must go hand in hand with strategies that improve health and education, reduce inequality, and spur economic growth, all while tackling climate change (UNICEF, 2022; ACERWC, 2025). Importantly, the SDGs acknowledge disability as a cross-cutting issue and guide climate-resilient development pathways that heighten social justice and well-being (ACERWC, 2025; UNICEF, 2022).

At the regional level in Africa, the African Charter on the Rights and Welfare of the Child (ACRWC) provides specific protections for children's rights. Ratified by 51 African countries, the Charter is one of the few global human rights instruments that directly addresses environmental concerns, specifically requiring that children's education foster respect for the environment and natural resources (ACERWC, 2025; OAU, 1990). Several key articles within the Charter demonstrate direct relevance to climate change impacts on children's rights. Article 5 mandates that states ensure children's survival, protection, and development to the maximum extent possible (OAU, 1990), an obligation that climate change directly threatens through increased mortality, food insecurity, and developmental challenges (ACERWC, 2025). Similarly, Article 14's guarantee of the best attainable physical, mental, and spiritual health for children is undermined by climate-induced disease burdens, malnutrition, and disaster-related mental health impacts (OAU, 1990; ACRWC, 2025). Article 11's education guarantee becomes compromised when climate disasters damage infrastructure and cause displacement, while Article 20's provisions for parental care suffer when climate impacts reduce parents' capacity to provide adequate care through economic stress and forced migration (ACERWC, 2025; OAU, 1990).

This regional framework gains significance by emphasising climate justice, which reframes global warming as an ethical and political issue rather than an environmental concern (ACERWC, 2025). This perspective proves relevant given that children in the Global South bear disproportionate consequences despite contributing least to the climate crisis. Children's heightened vulnerability to climate change stems from their developmental stage and dependency on adults for protection. The Committee on the Rights of the Child recognises that environmental harm creates discriminatory effects, particularly impacting Indigenous children, those from minority groups, children with disabilities, and those in climate-vulnerable environments (UN, 2023). This vulnerability intensifies when critical biological systems develop during early childhood, making children susceptible to environmental stress and pollution (UNICEF, 2022). Research indicates that up to two-thirds of preventable illnesses and deaths from environmental hazards affect children, predominantly those under 5 years (UN, 2023). Climate change is thus characterised as structural violence against children with poverty, economic inequality, food insecurity, and forced displacement, increasing their risk of violence, abuse, and exploitation (UN, 2023; Bourdillon et al., 2024).

These individual vulnerabilities intersect with broader structural inequalities that compound children's climate risks. The World Bank emphasises that the poorest and most vulnerable populations, including children, female-headed households, persons with disabilities, Indigenous peoples, and ethnic minorities, bear the most significant climate impacts while contributing least to the crisis (World Bank, 2025). This pattern becomes clearer in the African context, where, for example, per capita carbon emissions remain the lowest globally, with average Americans emitting 23 times more carbon than average Nigerians (ACERWC, 2025). These disparities highlight the importance of ensuring that transitions to low-carbon economies do not undermine Africa's development aspirations while protecting children's rights. The justice dimension becomes more important when considering that these vulnerable populations often lack the resources to cope with and recover from climate shocks, creating a cycle where those least responsible for climate change face the most severe consequences.

16.2.2 Climate Impacts on Children's Rights and Well-Being

Climate change directly threatens children's health through multiple interconnected pathways across physiological, developmental, and environmental dimensions. The Committee on the Rights of the Child establishes that environmental pollution constitutes a significant threat to children's health (Committee on the Rights of the Child, 2023). This is recognised in Article 24 of the UNCRC, noting that environmental challenges, which in contemporary times include climate change, biodiversity loss, and ecosystem degradation, create substantial obstacles to realising children's right to health (Committee on the Rights of the Child, 2023). Rising temperatures increase risks of vector-borne and zoonotic diseases while concentrating air pollutants that stunt brain and lung development and exacerbate respiratory conditions. UNICEF identifies environmental risks, including poor solid waste management, indoor and outdoor air pollution, second-hand smoke, unsafe water, inadequate sanitation, and poor hygiene, as causing irreversible and lasting negative impacts on children (UNICEF, 2022). These health implications extend beyond immediate risks as maternal undernutrition, infection, pollution exposure, and illness during pregnancy can cause lifelong damage, including physical stunting, neurological impairments, and immune dysfunction (UNICEF, 2022). Temperature-related health risks prove concerning, with exposure to high temperatures and heatwaves increasing deaths in children aged up to 14. In contrast, children in urban slums face heightened vulnerability due to urban heat island effects and limited access to water, artificial cooling, and green spaces (UNICEF, 2022). Vector-borne diseases present additional threats as rising temperatures and changing weather patterns contribute to the spread of malaria and dengue fever (Zimbabwe, 2025).

Climate change undermines food security for children by directly affecting the underlying determinants for good nutrition, including changing people's food consumption patterns and, therefore, the quality and diversity of diets by influencing local and global food availability (ACERWC, 2025; UNICEF, 2022). In Zimbabwe specifically, seasonal food scarcity remains common. It is a wasting driver, with approximately 1.1 million children at risk of food insecurity due to climate-related factors such as crop failure and water scarcity (UNICEF, 2022; Zimbabwe, 2025). The regional scale of this crisis extends across Southern Africa, where approximately 2.5 million children under five are estimated to be at risk of acute malnutrition due to climate-related food insecurity (UNICEF, 2022, 2025). This nutritional vulnerability intersects with broader developmental challenges as climate change significantly disrupts children's access to education through both direct and indirect mechanisms. The ACERWC recognises education as one of the cornerstones of a child-rights-based approach to the environment while acknowledging that the right to education remains highly vulnerable to environmental harm through school closures, disruptions, dropouts, and the destruction of educational infrastructure (ACERWC, 2025). Direct impacts occur when climate-related extreme weather events destroy educational infrastructure, as evidenced by Cyclone Idai in Zimbabwe, which destroyed schools, roads, and WASH infrastructures for schools (UNICEF, 2022). An estimated 9.5 million children across Southern Africa face the risk of disrupted education due to climate-related disasters (Zimbabwe, 2025). Indirect impacts manifest through economic pressures on families as climate change leads to food shortages that affect children's health and school attendance, with malnutrition and hunger forcing children to drop out of school to seek food or work (Chikoko & Chihiya, 2023; Chipenda & Cochrane, 2024). This educational disruption hampers academic progress and perpetuates poverty and inequality cycles (Chipenda & Cochrane, 2024).

Climate change exacerbates risks of violence and exploitation against children through multiple interconnected pathways that compound existing vulnerabilities (see Chaps. 3, 4, and 5). UNICEF documents how resource scarcity and the resulting increased poverty and stress pose greater risks of violence against girls and women, including increased violence against children due to other's stress, sexual violence as girls are forced to fetch water from greater distances, and risks of transactional sex due to desperation for basic livelihood (UNICEF, 2022). Economic hardships create conducive conditions for exploitation, with climate change increasing instances of child labour, early marriages, and sexual exploitation as families struggle to cope with financial strain (Chikoko & Chihiya, 2023). In Zimbabwe, climate change creates conducive environments for child exploitation and abuse, and this emphasises the tragic irony that while children bear the least responsibility for climate change, they suffer its most significant consequences (Online Reporter, 2024).

16.2.3 Social Policy Architecture and Legislative Frameworks

Integrating climate change considerations into social policy frameworks represents a critical area for protecting children's rights, encompassing the institutional, legislative, and programmatic frameworks through which governments address social welfare, vulnerability, and rights protection. This architecture forms the foundation for how countries respond to climate change impacts on children's rights. At the international level, the UNCRC establishes critical state obligations, requiring that environmental decisions generally concern children and that the best interests of the child constitute a primary consideration in adopting and implementing environmental decisions, including laws, regulations, policies, standards, guidelines, plans, strategies, budgets, international agreements, and development assistance provision (Committee on the Rights of the Child, 2023). The Committee emphasises that states have due diligence obligations to take appropriate preventive measures to protect children against reasonably foreseeable environmental harm, including assessing environmental impacts of policies and projects, identifying and preventing foreseeable harm, mitigating such harm when not preventable, and providing timely and effective remedies. The World Bank emphasises the importance of well-designed and citizen-centred policies in climate responses, noting that, in the absence of such approaches, efforts to tackle climate change can have unintended consequences for specific groups' livelihoods, including placing higher financial burdens on poor households (World Bank, 2025). This challenge is acute for children lacking a direct policy process voice.

Constitutional and legislative frameworks provide the foundation for climate-responsive social policy, with many countries establishing constitutional provisions that create obligations to protect children from environmental threats. These provisions typically encompass environmental rights spanning generations, comprehensive children's rights protections, rights to social security and social care, and family protection obligations. National development strategies and social protection frameworks represent the operational level where climate-children linkages are implemented. Modern social protection systems increasingly recognise climate shocks as key drivers of vulnerability, although mechanisms linking climate resilience to child protection remain limited in many contexts (see Chap. 1). Social protection programmes demonstrate varying degrees of climate-children integration, including cash transfer programmes assisting climate-vulnerable families with children, food security interventions responding to climate-induced shortages, education assistance programmes addressing climate-specific educational needs, and public works programmes incorporating climate adaptation activities. Climate-responsive social service delivery requires integrating climate considerations across health services, education systems, and water and sanitation programmes, with health services needing to address climate-health linkages, including impacts on child health from malaria, malnutrition, and waterborne diseases (UNICEF, 2022).

Disaster risk management policies represent a critical bridge between emergency response and longer-term social policy, with effective disaster risk management acknowledging children's vulnerability through child protection protocols in emergency shelters, continuity of education during climate disasters, psychological support for climate-displaced children, and family reunification systems (UNICEF EAPRO, 2025) Gaps, however, often exist in child-focused disaster management, including delay in resuming education and limited child protection services in displacement settings. The institutional structure for implementing climate-responsive social policy should typically involve multiple ministries and agencies, including social protection agencies, climate policy departments, health- and child-care ministries, civil protection departments, water authorities, and environmental protection agencies. Co-ordination challenges between these entities can result in fragmented approaches to climate-related child protection.

16.2.4 Zimbabwe's Context: Climate Vulnerability and Policy Gaps

Zimbabwe provides a relevant case study for understanding climate change impacts on children's rights in sub-Saharan Africa as the country faces recurrent droughts, erratic rainfall, and extreme weather events that exacerbate existing vulnerabilities and threaten children's rights across the nation (Gwitira et al., 2024; Zimbabwe, 2025). Research in rural Zimbabwe, for example, in Bikita District and Uzumba Maramba Pfungwe (UMP) District, reveals that climate change significantly impacts children's rights, with vulnerabilities including hunger, food insecurity, decreased school attendance, and increased risks of early marriages, sexual exploitation, and child labour (Chikoko & Chihiya, 2023; Gwenzi et al., 2022). Zimbabwe recognises the challenges of climate change and has developed several policies and programmes to address climate change and its impacts on children and vulnerable populations. Zimbabwe's social policy architecture consists of several key components that intersect with climate change and children's rights, with the country's 2013 Constitution providing the legal backbone for social policy by establishing comprehensive children's rights provisions under Section 81, environmental rights spanning generations under Section 73, rights to social security and social care under Section 30, and family protection obligations under Section 27 (GoZ, 2013). These constitutional provisions create binding obligations for the state to protect children from social and environmental threats, including climate change.

Key climate policies include the National Climate Change Response Strategy (NCCRS), developed in 2014, which outlines Zimbabwe's strategic approach to climate change mitigation and adaptation. The NCCRS highlights the need for a multi-sectoral approach and emphasises addressing climate impacts on vulnerable groups, including children and women (GoZ, 2014). The strategy identifies priority areas such as food security, water resource management, health, and disaster risk reduction (DRR), which directly affect children. The National Climate Policy (NCP), launched in 2017, aims to provide a framework for climate governance and guide the implementation of climate change mitigation and adaptation measures across different sectors. The policy recognises the specific vulnerabilities of children and women to climate change impacts and calls for targeted interventions to enhance their resilience (GoZ, 2017). The Government of Zimbabwe has developed Zimbabwe's National Adaptation Plan (NAP). The NAP is said to be an effort to bring about transformative change in the country's capacity to address the challenges of climate change. It seeks to 'strengthen national adaptation efforts by integrating climate change considerations into development planning processes, seek to strengthen institutional structures, co-ordination procedures, research, resource mobilisation and implementation of adaptation options for enhanced climate resilience' (GoZ, 2024a, p. 2). The plan emphasises protecting children and other vulnerable groups from climate-related risks through community-based adaptation strategies and improved access to social services (GoZ, 2024a).

The National Development Strategy 1 (2021–2025) has served as Zimbabwe's primary development blueprint in the past few years, including social policy pillars addressing human capital development, environmental protection, climate resilience, and social protection systems (GoZ, 2020). The NDS1 acknowledges climate change as a cross-cutting challenge affecting social development, though specific child-focused climate provisions remain limited. The National Social Protection Policy Framework, adopted in 2016, coordinates Zimbabwe's social protection interventions, including social assistance programmes, social insurance schemes, labour market interventions, and social care services (GoZ, 2016). The framework recognises climate shocks as key drivers of vulnerability but contains limited mechanisms linking climate resilience to child protection. Zimbabwe's primary social protection programmes demonstrate varying degrees of climate-child integration, with the Harmonised Social Cash Transfer providing cash assistance to ultra-poor and labour-constrained households, often including climate-vulnerable families with children (Gwitira et al., 2024). However, the programme's design does not systematically account for climate risks. Zimbabwe has implemented various social protection programmes targeting vulnerable populations, including children. Programmes aim to provide financial assistance to poor households, enabling them to cope with climate-induced shocks and stresses. The Food Deficit Mitigation Strategy responds to food insecurity, including climate-induced shortages, with children benefiting as household members. The challenge with the programme is that it lacks child-specific nutritional components for climate-change-ravaged contexts.

Zimbabwe's climate-responsive social service delivery shows inconsistent integration of climate considerations, with the National Health Strategy acknowledging climate-health linkages, including impacts on child health. However, rural health centres in climate-vulnerable regions remain under-resourced for climate-related paediatric care. School infrastructure planning rarely incorporates climate resilience despite increasing exposure to floods and extreme heat. The curriculum includes environmental education but has limited practical climate adaptation components. However, the Ministry of Primary and Secondary Education in Zimbabwe has incorporated climate change education into the national curriculum. This integration aims to raise awareness among children about climate change and empower them to contribute to community resilience efforts (Gwitira et al., 2024). The Ministry also developed a Disaster Risk Management and Resilience Plan 2021–2025, which provides step-by-step guidelines on how climate change affects the education sector. WASH programmes acknowledge climate impacts on water security, but implementation in rural areas with high child populations remains inadequate. Zimbabwe's National Disaster Risk Management Policy and Strategy (2018) represents an attempt to bridge emergency response with longer-term social policy, acknowledging children's vulnerability but containing limited child-specific protocols for child protection in emergency shelters, continuity of education during climate disasters, psychological support for climate-displaced children, and family reunification systems. The 2019 Cyclone Idai response revealed significant gaps in child-focused disaster management, including delay in resuming education and limited child protection services in displacement settings.

16.2.5 Limitations of Conventional Social Policy Approaches

Despite established legal frameworks, significant policy implementation and design gaps limit the effectiveness of conventional approaches to protecting children from climate impacts. The Committee on the Rights of the Child identifies critical barriers, including inadequate involvement of children and young people in climate and environment strategies, dialogues, and actions, emphasising that children's voices constitute a powerful global force for environmental protection and that children's views should be proactively sought and given due weight in designing and implementing measures aimed at addressing significant and long-term environmental challenges (Committee on the Rights of the Child, 2023). The Committee requires states to respect and protect children's rights to freedom of expression, association, and peaceful assembly in relation to the environment while acknowledging that children who exercise their right to freedom of expression or engage in environmental protests, including children environmental human rights defenders, often face threats, intimidation, harassment, and other severe reprisals (Committee on the Rights of the Child, 2023). The World Bank emphasises that, in the absence of well-designed and citizen-centred policies, efforts to tackle climate change can have unintended consequences for specific groups' livelihoods, including placing higher financial burdens on poor households, a challenge that is acute for children who lack direct voice in policy processes (World Bank, 2025).

Conventional social policy approaches face several structural limitations in addressing the climate-children nexus due to fiscal and resource constraints that limit social protection spending. In addition, climate adaptation financing is rarely child focused, and donor dependence creates sustainability challenges for climate-resilient social programmes. Policy co-ordination gaps result from limited integration between social welfare and climate change ministries, the absence of dedicated children-climate co-ordination mechanisms, fragmented data systems, and project-based rather than system-based approaches. Implementation capacity challenges include inadequate technical expertise in climate-responsive social policy design, limited monitoring and evaluation systems for climate-related child outcomes, insufficient community-level infrastructure for service delivery, and weak accountability mechanisms for child protection failures. These limitations highlight the need for comprehensive reforms to social policy architecture that integrate climate considerations with children's rights protection. The World Bank emphasises the importance of community engagement in climate responses, noting that communities bring unique perspectives, skills, and knowledge to strengthen resilience and address climate change (World Bank, 2025). This participatory approach aligns with children's rights principles, especially the right to participation enshrined in the UNCRC. However, current approaches remain limited in addressing structural inequalities that amplify children's climate vulnerabilities while constraining their meaningful participation in adaptation processes.

16.2.6 Climate Justice and Equity Considerations

As we discuss Zimbabwe, climate change, children's rights, and social policy context, it is important to consider climate justice and equity considerations, which are of great importance. The concept of climate justice emerges as central to understanding children's rights in the context of climate change, framing global warming as an ethical and political issue rather than one that is purely environmental or physical in nature (ACERWC, 2025). This framing proves relevant given the disproportionate impact on children in the Global South, who are often least responsible for the problem yet face the most severe consequences. The equity dimensions become important when considering emission patterns, with Africa having the world's lowest carbon emissions per person (ACERWC, 2025). This disparity highlights the importance of ensuring that just transition policies to a low-carbon economy do not undermine Africa's aspirations for a better, prosperous future for its people. Climate-induced displacement represents a significant threat to children's rights. Internal Displacement Monitoring Centre data indicate that an estimated 3.3 million people in the region were displaced by climate-related events between 2008 and 2018, with children among those affected (Zinonzwa, 2025). Displacement disrupts family structures and educational continuity while exposing children to heightened risks of exploitation, violence, and psychological trauma. Migration due to environmental stressors disrupts family structures and education, exposing children to violence and xenophobia. In Zimbabwe, specifically, the lack of access to water further exacerbates the issues raised above, forcing families to relocate in search of resources. This negatively affects children's socio-economic rights and overall development (Addaney et al., 2017).

16.3 Theoretical Framework: Transformative Social Policy (TSP)

This study adopts the Transformative Social Policy (TSP) framework as its primary theoretical lens for examining the intersection between climate vulnerabilities and children's rights in Zimbabwe. The selection of TSP as a theoretical foundation stems from its capacity to address the complex, multidimensional challenges that climate change poses to children's welfare and development. The TSP framework emerged from extensive scholarly work conducted by the United Nations Research Institute for Social Development (UNRISD), representing a significant departure from traditional social policy paradigms (Adesina, 2015; Mkandawire, 2004). This theoretical approach was developed to address the limitations observed in conventional social policy models that have been predominantly applied across African and global South contexts. The framework is a critical response to earlier policy approaches, including Social Dimensions of Adjustment, Social Risk Management, and conventional Social Protection systems, which TSP scholars argue were constrained by neoliberal ideological foundations (Tom & Banda, 2023). These preceding approaches have been characterised by their narrow focus on targeted interventions aimed at the 'deserving poor' through restrictive safety net mechanisms, critically failing to interrogate or address the structural causes of inequality, marginalisation, and poverty (Adesina, 2020; Chipenda, 2023). Available evidence demonstrates their inability to generate meaningful developmental transformation and broader societal well-being, especially in contexts where multiple vulnerabilities intersect.

In contrast, TSP adopts a preventative orientation that seeks to address structural vulnerabilities before they manifest as acute social challenges, offering what can be described as a prophylactic perspective on social policy (Adesina, 2007; Chipenda, 2024). This proactive stance is relevant when examining climate-related risks to children's rights as it emphasises building systemic resilience rather than merely responding to climate impacts after they occur. The framework closely relates to Fischer's (2018) analysis to expose how social policy environments in developing contexts often exhibit segmentation, stratification, and segregation characteristics. TSP challenges these fragmented approaches by proposing integrated policy solutions that simultaneously address multiple dimensions of social vulnerability (Adesina, 2020). Central to TSP's analytical power is its conceptualisation of social policy through five interconnected functions: production, reproduction, social protection, redistribution, and social cohesion or nation building (Mkandawire, 2004, 2007). Through these multiple and interrelated functions, TSP extends beyond mere income maintenance and social security to enhance the productive potential of society members while balancing the burden of reproduction with other social tasks. The framework addresses economic inequalities by redistributing resources, protecting individuals against life uncertainties, and contributing to social cohesion and nation-building (Adesina, 2015; Mkandawire, 2004). This multifunctional approach provides analytical tools to understand how climate impacts intersect with children's welfare—from productive opportunities for youth to reproductive care burdens, social protection needs, distributive justice concerns, individual protection, and community cohesion.

Zimbabwe's contemporary social landscape provides a compelling context for TSP analysis, especially given the country's experience with significant social and economic disruptions over the past two decades (Chipenda, 2022). The nation has been plagued by prolonged economic challenges, high unemployment rates, deeply entrenched inequality, poverty, and significant youth marginalisation, creating a composite social ecosystem where climate vulnerabilities intersect with existing structural problems. These conditions have created circumstances where climate change impacts emerge not merely as environmental challenges but as phenomena deeply embedded in economic precarity, social disintegration, and systemic marginalisation. In this context, children's climate vulnerabilities cannot be understood in isolation from broader patterns of structural disadvantage that characterise Zimbabwean society. The TSP framework's emphasis on structural transformation aligns with emerging recognition in climate scholarship that effective adaptation requires changes to underlying social, economic, and political systems rather than merely technical adjustments (UNRISD, 2022, 2023; World Bank, 2025). This perspective recognises that climate change impacts are deeply intertwined with global patterns of inequality, where the poorest and most vulnerable people, including children, bear the disproportionate burden despite contributing least to the crisis. TSP's analytical lens reveals how climate change intersects with existing patterns of disadvantage, creating vulnerabilities that require interventions addressing root causes rather than symptoms.

This study selected TSP because it can integrate multiple dimensions of climate vulnerability affecting children within a coherent analytical framework that moves beyond individualistic explanations. The framework's recognition of social phenomena as deeply embedded in structural conditions, rather than individual pathologies, provides the theoretical foundation necessary for examining how climate change challenges existing approaches to children's rights protection. In addition, TSP's focus on addressing power structures and inequality, combined with its emphasis on preventative intervention and multifunctional integration, makes it suitable for analysing pathways towards more transformative policy responses that can simultaneously build climate resilience while advancing broader agendas of social transformation and children's rights fulfilment.

16.4 Methodology

This study employed an interpretive methodology grounded in TSP analysis to examine why conventional policy frameworks have limitations in adequately protecting children's rights within Zimbabwe's climate crisis context and how TSP principles might enhance this protection. The research design adopted a qualitative secondary data analysis approach, utilising critical discourse analysis and thematic analysis as primary analytical methods to deconstruct existing policy narratives while exploring transformative alternatives. This methodological choice reflected the recognition that climate-children's rights intersections represent a contested terrain where dominant policy discourses may obscure structural inequalities and marginalise alternative approaches to rights protection. The interpretive paradigm acknowledges that social policy responses to climate vulnerability are not neutral technical interventions but rather politically embedded practices that reflect and reproduce power relations and ideological frameworks. This critical orientation enabled the examination of how conventional social protection measures may inadvertently perpetuate the very inequalities they purport to address while creating analytical space for exploring how TSP principles might challenge existing policy orthodoxies and enhance children's rights protection in climate contexts.

Data collection employed purposive sampling strategies to construct a comprehensive corpus of policy-relevant materials spanning government documents, international organisation reports, academic literature, and civil society publications. The selection criteria prioritised materials that directly addressed the intersection of climate change impacts and children's rights in Zimbabwe and broader literature on TSP in the African context. Primary policy sources included national climate policies, development strategies, and constitutional provisions related to children's rights, complemented by sectoral policies addressing education, health, and social protection. International organisation materials encompassed country reports, climate vulnerability assessments, policy briefs addressing climate-children's rights intersections, and the TSP framework. A comprehensive search strategy employed multiple databases, including Web of Science, Scopus, Google Scholar, and institutional repositories, complemented by targeted searches of UNICEF, ACERWC, UN agencies, and civil society organisations. Key search terms included 'climate change', 'children's rights', 'UNCRC', 'ACRWC', 'climate justice', 'Zimbabwe', 'child vulnerability', 'climate adaptation', 'educational disruption', 'food security', 'health impacts', and 'intersectional inequalities', among others. Grey literature from civil society organisations, policy think tanks, and development agencies provided additional perspectives on implementation challenges and alternative approaches. The analytical framework employed thematic analysis structured around the chapter's two core research questions, with analysis organised around TSP's key dimensions: redistributive justice, participatory governance, and rights recognition to evaluate current approaches while exploring transformative alternatives. Triangulation across diverse source types enabled the identification of patterns while maintaining critical distance from government narratives that may minimise structural constraints and international frameworks that may impose external priorities inconsistent with local contexts.

The study maintained rigorous ethical standards throughout the research process, guided by principles of beneficence, non-maleficence, and respect for children's rights as articulated in the UNCRC. Given the focus on children's rights and vulnerabilities, particular attention was paid to ensuring that the analysis did not inadvertently reproduce harmful stereotypes or deficit narratives about children's capacities. The research approach emphasised children's agency and potential contributions while acknowledging their structural vulnerabilities, maintaining ethical commitment to representing children's interests accurately within the constraints of secondary data analysis. All policy documents and grey literature were accessed through legitimate channels, with proper attribution maintained throughout the analysis process. The interpretive methodology acknowledged the inherent power dynamics in policy research and the risk of reproducing adult-centric perspectives that the study critiques. It also sought to maintain reflexivity about these limitations throughout the analytical process.

The methodology's limitations included reliance on textual analysis that necessarily excludes direct engagement with children's lived experiences and perspectives, reflecting broader challenges in policy research where adult-centric documentation may inadequately capture children's understandings of climate impacts and adaptation needs. Focusing on formal policy processes may overlook informal social protection mechanisms and community-based responses that could inform transformative approaches. While enabling comprehensive analysis of existing policy frameworks, the secondary data approach limits the study's capacity to generate new empirical perspectives about implementation challenges or community-level innovations. These limitations highlighted the necessity for future research employing participatory methodologies that genuinely centre children's voices in policy analysis while maintaining a critical analytical orientation towards existing power structures and policy orthodoxies. Despite these constraints, the methodology's focus on policy discourse analysis provides valuable perspectives into how current frameworks construct climate-children's rights challenges and the conceptual space available for transformative alternatives.

16.5 Findings and Discussion

The findings of the review are presented under four subsections focusing on the limitations and challenges of Zimbabwe's current social protection system.

16.5.1 *Fragmented and Sectoral Responses*

The analysis of Zimbabwe's current social policy landscape reveals limitations in addressing climate-induced vulnerabilities affecting children. Despite having what government documents describe as sound policy frameworks that provide for the protection and rights of children and youth (GoZ, 2014), these existing policies demonstrate some gaps when examined through the lens of climate vulnerability. The Government of Zimbabwe acknowledges that current policies do not sufficiently recognise or address children and youth's issues and unique vulnerabilities in relation to the impacts of climate change (GoZ, 2014, p. 54). This admission highlights the inadequacy of sectoral approaches that treat children's rights and climate adaptation as separate policy domains. Contemporary international development practice has increasingly recognised this fragmentation as a barrier to effective climate adaptation. Organisations like UNICEF Zimbabwe have developed a comprehensive Climate, Energy, Environment and Children Strategies that aim to mainstream child-friendly climate, energy, and environmental issues across sectoral policies, plans, and budgets in key sectors including education, WASH, nutrition, health, child protection, and social protection (UNICEF, 2022). Institutional fragmentation is evident in the limited co-ordination across key ministries responsible for children's welfare and climate action. The climate change response framework involves multiple ministries, including the Ministry of Environment, Water and Climate (MEWC); the Ministry of Primary and Secondary Education (MPSE); the Ministry of Higher and Tertiary Education, Science and Technology Development (MHTESTD); the Ministry of Health and Child Care (MHCC); and the Ministry of Youth, Indigenisation and Economic Empowerment (MYIEE) (GoZ, 2014, 2024a). However, these ministries, it can be argued, operate largely in silos, with children's rights policies functioning separately from climate change initiatives, creating protection gaps as responsibilities are divided across different institutional mandates. This challenge is worsened by resource allocation mechanisms that fail to incentivise cross-sectoral collaboration, leading to duplicated efforts and missed opportunities for integrated programming. International development frameworks increasingly emphasise government-led programming principles that work to strengthen policy co-ordination, monitoring, institutional roles and collaboration, and financing mechanisms that enable governments to deliver resilient climate services across multiple sectors simultaneously (UNICEF, 2022).

The fragmentation becomes evident when examining resource allocation and co-ordination mechanisms. While the National Development Strategy 1 (GoZ, 2019) recognises that disasters such as cyclones have had a significant toll on education infrastructure, with schools having roofs blown off, WASH facilities destroyed, and weather-induced droughts leaving many children vulnerable, the policy response remains compartmentalised. The strategy's climate action framework focuses primarily on technical solutions, which include strengthening early warning systems, upgrading meteorological networks, and promoting climate-smart innovations, without adequately addressing how these interventions connect to children's specific vulnerabilities and rights. This technical focus, while important, reflects a broader pattern in climate policy that prioritises infrastructure and technology over social protection and rights-based approaches. Contemporary approaches to climate adaptation increasingly recognise the need for child-sensitive policies that ensure climate frameworks are designed considering children's vulnerabilities and rights, including supporting the development of evidence to strengthen policies and advocating for increased government spending on child-sensitive interventions (UNICEF, 2022).

The country's broader development challenges further complicate this sectoral fragmentation. The NDS1 notes that the COVID-19 pandemic has resulted in the loss of learning time, which will be difficult to make up for, while climate-related disasters continue to undermine educational infrastructure (GoZ, 2019). However, the policy frameworks fail to recognise these as interconnected crises, requiring integrated responses that address structural vulnerabilities rather than managing individual symptoms. The failure to recognise these interconnections reflects deeper limitations in policy frameworks that struggle to address the complex dynamics of contemporary development challenges, where climate change intersects with health crises, economic instability, and social inequality in ways that require different approaches to policy design and implementation. Recent international practice has increasingly emphasised convergent approaches across sectors to develop integrated visions of service provision that address climate needs alongside other development priorities (UNICEF, 2022, 2025).

16.5.2 Reactive Approaches with Limited Child Participation and Agency Recognition

Zimbabwe's conventional social policy approaches demonstrate a predominantly reactive orientation that responds to climate crises, rather than building proactive resilience. The government acknowledges that children are often most vulnerable to adverse health effects from environmental hazards because they are not fully developed physically and psychologically, with preventable and treatable diseases such as diarrhoea and malaria predicted to worsen with climate change (GoZ, 2016, 2024a). However, the policy response framework focuses primarily on emergency response rather than prevention and resilience building. This reactive orientation reflects broader patterns in development policy that prioritise crisis management over structural prevention, despite evidence that preventative approaches are more cost-effective and better aligned with rights-based frameworks that emphasise protecting and fulfilling rights rather than merely responding to rights violations. Zimbabwe's reactive orientation is evident in resource allocation patterns outlined in government strategy documents. The Ministry of Environment, Climate and Wildlife received ZiG 516.8 million in the 2025 National Budget for climate-related activities. Still, these allocations focus primarily on hosting international conferences, restoration projects, and infrastructure upgrades rather than building systematic resilience in communities and households where children live (GoZ, 2024b). While these interventions are essential, they do not address children's immediate and ongoing vulnerabilities from climate variability. The emphasis on high-profile activities and infrastructure reflects a typical pattern in climate finance that prioritises visible, measurable interventions over the longer-term, more complex work of building social and institutional resilience. Contemporary climate adaptation practice increasingly emphasises proactive approaches that focus on protecting children from the impacts of climate change and environmental degradation while working to develop climate-adaptive and -responsive services and climate-resilient facilities that address ongoing vulnerabilities rather than merely responding to crises.

The reactive approach is problematic given the evidence of ongoing climate impacts. Data from the 2024 Zimbabwe Livelihoods Assessment Committee (ZimLAC) Rural Livelihoods Assessment (RLA) shows that climate change effects are already manifesting across all provinces, with children experiencing immediate impacts on food security and nutrition (Food and Nutrition Council, 2024). An essential result of the survey was the impact of climate change on agriculture and water availability, which was negatively impacting livelihoods and reducing food diversity for children (68%), perceived as an immediate consequence of climate change. However, policy frameworks continue to treat climate change as a future challenge rather than a present reality requiring an immediate, comprehensive response. This temporal disconnect between policy framing and empirical reality reflects deeper challenges in climate governance, where the long-term nature of climate change can obscure the immediate needs of vulnerable populations, especially children who may experience climate impacts more acutely due to their developmental needs and limited adaptive capacity. The recognition that climate change represents a present reality has led to emphasis on comprehensive approaches to delivering climate-resilient services across multiple sectors, including WASH, education, nutrition, health, child protection, and social protection. This acknowledges that children are currently experiencing climate impacts that require immediate, integrated interventions.

Perhaps most significantly, conventional approaches demonstrate the limited recognition of children as active agents in climate adaptation processes. While the Government of Zimbabwe acknowledges that children have a major stake in the future and have the right and responsibility to participate in decisions that affect them (GoZ, 2014), the operationalisation of this principle remains weak. The policy framework recognises that children and youth should be actors in the climate change agenda, rather than being treated as passive observers or victims. Yet specific mechanisms for meaningful participation are underdeveloped. This gap between rhetorical commitment and operational reality reflects broader challenges in children's rights implementation, where the formal recognition of children's participation rights often fails to translate into institutional mechanisms that enable meaningful participation in practice. The Government's approach to children's participation appears largely consultative rather than transformative. The climate policy framework and strategies include provisions for promoting the participation of children and youth in climate change policy issues (GoZ, 2014, 2017, 2024a) and building the capacity of children and youth for adaptation. Still, these interventions are conceived within existing power structures rather than as mechanisms for redistributing decision-making authority. The strategy outlines finances for promoting youth participation in policy issues and building capacity, but allocations made over the years suggest limited scope for transformative participation approaches. Compared to infrastructure and technical interventions, the relatively modest financial allocations for participation reflect broader patterns in development policy that undervalue participatory approaches and struggle to recognise participation as both a right and a mechanism for improving programme effectiveness. Contemporary approaches to children's participation increasingly emphasise empowering children and young people by supporting them to have the information, knowledge, and skills necessary to be agents of change in their communities, providing space for their voices, perspectives, and ideas to be heard and addressed and building their capacity to influence national policies and plans (UNICEF, 2025).

This limitation reflects broader challenges in moving beyond tokenistic participation towards approaches that genuinely centre children's voices and agency. The government recognises that the inclusion of children and youth in climate change adaptations and mitigations is not just about consulting them or asking their views, but it also means giving them access to information that they need to comprehensively understand the dynamics of climate change and its impact on their rights, opportunities, and responsibilities (GoZ, 2014, 2024a). However, the implementation mechanisms for this comprehensive approach remain underdeveloped. The challenge of operationalising meaningful participation reflects deeper tensions in development practice between efficiency-driven approaches prioritising rapid implementation and rights-based approaches emphasising process and participation, even when these may slow programme delivery. To address these challenges, there is a need for systematic investment in institutional mechanisms for participation, representing a shift away from ad hoc support towards sustained engagement that provides children with opportunities to learn and educate their peers on climate change while building their capacity to develop solutions.

The new Climate Change Bill (GoZ, 2025) (recently adopted by Cabinet) makes only minimal reference to children, mentioning them once among vulnerable groups such as women, children, the elderly, the sick, and the disabled, who require special consideration in decision-making processes. This limited recognition suggests that, despite rhetorical commitments to children's participation, policy frameworks position children primarily as beneficiaries rather than active participants in shaping adaptation responses. This positioning of children as vulnerable beneficiaries rather than active agents reflects broader patterns in development policy that struggle to reconcile children's needs for protection with the recognition of their capacity for agency and participation. Contemporary approaches to children's rights increasingly emphasise recognising children as agents of change, ensuring that the development processes of climate policies and strategies systematically include children's voices while highlighting the special needs that children and young people have and the importance of safeguarding their rights (UNICEF, 2022, 2025).

16.5.3 Resource Constraints and Implementation Challenges

Zimbabwe's conventional social policy approaches face significant resource constraints that limit their effectiveness in addressing climate-induced vulnerabilities. The economic challenges that have characterised Zimbabwe for decades, including hyperinflation, high unemployment, and political instability, have created conditions where social protection systems are chronically under-resourced (Chipenda, 2022). The government's climate policy framework acknowledges that adequate financing, cross-sectoral co-ordination, climate change science, research, and systematic observations will form the backbone of actions towards a climate-resilient Zimbabwe (GoZ, 2017). However, resource allocations fall short of the comprehensive approach required. These resource constraints reflect broader patterns of development financing that prioritise economic growth and infrastructure over social protection, despite evidence that social protection systems are essential for building climate resilience and protecting vulnerable populations.

While reasonable, the budget allocation of ZiG 516.8 million for the Ministry of Environment, Climate and Wildlife in 2025 represents a fraction of what would be required for comprehensive climate resilience building that prioritises children's rights and welfare (GoZ, 2024b). While important, the Ministry's focus on hosting international conferences such as COP15 of the Ramsar Convention and infrastructure upgrades diverts resources from community-level interventions that could directly address children's immediate vulnerabilities. This allocation pattern reflects common challenges in climate finance, where international visibility and infrastructure projects often receive priority over the less visible but equally important work of building social resilience and protecting vulnerable populations. Addressing resource mobilisation challenges requires innovative approaches to mobilising climate finance while advocating for increased government spending to deliver on child-sensitive policies. This demonstrates how international cooperation can supplement government resources while building local capacity.

Implementation challenges are further worsened by capacity constraints at local government levels, where policy implementation typically occurs. The government's strategy documents acknowledge the importance of local authorities and local leaders in climate adaptation responses but provide limited details on how capacity will be built and sustained at these levels (GoZ, 2014, 2017, 2024a). The involvement of multiple ministries like the Ministry of Environment, Water and

Climate (MEWC); Ministry of Primary and Secondary Education (MPSE); Ministry of Higher and Tertiary Education, Science and Technology Development (MHTESTD); Ministry of Health and Child Care (MHCC); Ministry of Youth, Industry, and Economic Empowerment (MYIEE); and Ministry of Local Government, Public Works and National Housing (MLG) creates co-ordination challenges that are often resolved through fragmented rather than integrated approaches. These capacity constraints reflect broader challenges in decentralised governance systems, where local authorities often lack the technical expertise, financial resources, and institutional capacity needed to implement complex climate adaptation programmes. Addressing these challenges requires systematic approaches to building capacities and systems for government and other partners to scale up solutions while ensuring adequate capacity in local communities to own both the resources and results through sustainable programming.

16.5.4 Limited Climate-Specific Provisions in Child Protection Systems

A limitation of Zimbabwe's conventional approaches is that existing child protection systems were not designed with climate change in mind and lack specific protocols for addressing climate-induced risks to children. The government acknowledges that existing policies do not sufficiently recognise or address children's and youth's issues and unique vulnerabilities in relation to the impacts of climate change (GoZ, 2014). However, the policy response has been slow in developing climate-specific provisions. This gap reflects broader challenges in adapting existing social protection systems to address emerging risks, where institutional structures and professional competencies may not align with the dynamic multi-sectoral nature of climate impacts on children. The evidence of climate impacts on children from the ZimLac RLA 2024 Survey, including reduced food diversity (68%), reduced feeding frequency (67%), and reduced food quantity (67%), requires specialised response protocols that current child protection systems lack (Food and Nutrition Council, 2024). Traditional child protection approaches focus on issues such as abuse, neglect, and exploitation but are not equipped to address the indirect effects of climate change that manifest through food insecurity, displacement, educational disruption, and health impacts. These indirect effects of climate change represent a new category of risk for children that existing child protection frameworks struggle to address, requiring the development of new conceptual frameworks and practice approaches that can recognise and respond to climate-induced dangers to children's welfare. Engaging with and addressing these gaps requires strengthening referral and support systems to protect children and women from violence in areas affected by climate-induced events while ensuring environmental and social safeguards that protect children and communities from negative intervention impacts.

The Climate Change Bill (GoZ, 2025) establishes broad principles requiring that public or private sector programmes or decision-making consider the needs of the most vulnerable to the adverse impacts of climate change, including women, children, the elderly, the sick, and the disabled. However, the Bill provides limited specific guidance on how these principles should be operationalised in child protection systems or how climate considerations should be integrated into existing child welfare frameworks. It remains to be seen how this gap will be covered in practice. The gap between broad principles and operational guidance reflects common challenges in translating policy commitments into practice, especially in areas where different professional domains and institutional mandates must be integrated. Operationalising these principles requires child-centred programming approaches that design solutions with and for children well-being while safeguarding them from violence, abuse, and exploitation.

16.6 The Potential of TSP Approaches

16.6.1 Addressing Structural Determinants of Vulnerability

The limitations of conventional social protection measures point towards TSP approaches that address structural determinants of children's climate vulnerability rather than merely providing *ex post* support following climate shocks. TSP operates as both an analytical lens and a practical framework for simultaneously building climate resilience and advancing social transformation through approaches that challenge power structures, redistribute resources, and recognise children as active participants in shaping resilient societies. This requires confronting how colonial legacies, economic policies, and governance structures create differentiated exposure to climate risks in Zimbabwe. Zimbabwe's 2013 Constitution provides an important legal foundation for TSP approaches, establishing rights to social security and social care (Section 30), family protection obligations (Section 27), and intergenerational environmental responsibilities that create legal space for challenging existing policy orthodoxies (GoZ, 2013). The government's recognition that the impacts of climate change intersect with broader patterns of inequality provides a foundation for TSP approaches, especially through its acknowledgement that child-headed households created by HIV/AIDS are vulnerable to all shocks, including those driven by climate change (GoZ, 2014). However, translating this recognition into transformative policy requires significant shifts that prioritise addressing the root causes of vulnerability rather than managing symptoms.

The ZimLac RLA 2024 assessment's emphasis on comprehensive approaches that tackle poverty, inequality, governance, and sustainability aligns with TSP principles, recognising climate vulnerability as a social and political problem that requires transformation in the relationship between the state, market, and society. Evidence from the survey showing that climate impacts affect 68% of children through reduced food diversity demonstrates the urgency of adopting structural approaches that address the systemic nature of vulnerability (Food and Nutrition Council, 2024). Rather than responding to each manifestation separately, TSP approaches would transform the underlying economic and social structures that make children's basic needs vulnerable to climate variability.

16.6.2 Redistributive and Rights-Based Frameworks

The TSP approach offers potential for developing redistributive responses to children's climate vulnerabilities beyond existing resource allocation frameworks. Rather than providing temporary assistance that maintains existing power structures, transformative approaches operate through redistributive justice dimensions that address wealth and resource distribution patterns, amplifying children's climate vulnerability. They challenge adult and child power relations that exclude children from resource allocation decisions while redistributing material resources and expanding access to information, services, and opportunities for participation. While the government's climate policy commits to supporting climate-sensitive grassroots projects in every district (GoZ, 2014), truly redistributive approaches would examine how resources are distributed within society and how existing mechanisms may perpetuate inequalities, creating differential climate vulnerability for children. The government's analysis reveals that climate impacts affect young people because they lack supportive financial and natural capital (GoZ, 2014, 2017). This suggests the need for redistributive interventions that address structural disadvantages rather than merely providing emergency support.

Provincial variations in climate impacts, as exemplified by the ZimLac RLA 2024 Survey, with children in Masvingo experiencing 76% reduced food diversity compared to 62% in Matabeleland South, demonstrate how geographic location intersects with resource distribution to create differentiated vulnerabilities (Food and Nutrition Council, 2024). A TSP approach would address these disparities through redistributive mechanisms, ensuring all children can access climate-resilient services regardless of location or circumstances. This reflects systematic attention to how development resources are distributed across space and social groups. On the other hand, the rights-based dimensions of TSP are relevant to Zimbabwe's constitutional commitments. The constitutional foundation becomes significant when combined with the international legal obligations under the UNCRC and the regional commitments under the ACRWC, creating multiple legal pathways for advancing transformative approaches. The Climate Change Bill seeks to establish rights to information, participation, and access to benefits from climate programmes (GoZ, 2025). However, realising these rights requires transforming power relations that currently limit children's access, moving beyond formal recognition towards restructuring how climate governance operates to accommodate children's participation and recognise them as legitimate political actors.

16.6.3 *Participatory and Agency-Centred Transformation*

TSP approaches offer frameworks for operationalising meaningful child participation in climate adaptation. Indigenous knowledge systems and community organisation traditions represent untapped potential for participatory approaches that could enhance children's agency in climate adaptation. Traditional ecological knowledge systems rely on intergenerational knowledge transmission, where children play important roles as learners and innovators, while community-based natural resource management practices incorporate children's observations and contributions. While the government recognises that effective adaptation requires giving children comprehensive information about climate change impacts and encouraging creative responses (GoZ, 2014), moving to operational frameworks requires shifts in climate governance, including institutional mechanisms accommodating children's participation. Current instrumentalist approaches view children's involvement primarily as a means to improve programme effectiveness rather than as a rights-based objective, challenging existing power structures.

A TSP approach would position participation as both a right and a mechanism for redistributing decision-making power, moving beyond consultation towards recognising children as legitimate political actors. This requires strengthening already-existing participatory governance mechanisms. These include child-friendly climate vulnerability assessment processes, participatory budgeting mechanisms that enable children to influence resource allocation, establishment of children's climate councils with advisory roles in policy development, and community-based monitoring systems where children track adaptation effectiveness. The government's recognition that children possess energy and enthusiasm for climate responses suggests an understanding of their potential contributions, yet realising this requires transforming institutional frameworks that currently limit children's participation to predetermined roles rather than creating spaces for self-defined engagement. Evidence that children across provinces experience direct climate impacts demonstrates that they possess experiential knowledge that should inform adaptation planning. Using a TSP approach would create mechanisms for this knowledge to influence a policy design rather than treating children as passive recipients of adult-designed interventions, requiring new methodologies and institutional frameworks to accommodate different forms of knowledge and understanding.

16.7 Post-pandemic Opportunities for Transformation

The COVID-19 pandemic has created an important juncture that opens space for TSP approaches in the African context. The pandemic has exposed the fragility of existing social protection systems and demonstrated how external shocks can rapidly reverse progress in children's welfare. This has generated recognition of the need for universal and climate-resilient social protection, acknowledgement of intersecting vulnerabilities that affect children disproportionately, and policy discourse emphasising 'building back better', which could incorporate transformative principles. The intersection of the pandemic and climate impacts has demonstrated inadequacies in sectoral responses and highlighted the need for approaches that simultaneously address multiple, interconnected crises. This intersection creates a policy window where existing approaches are recognised as inadequate, making previously unfeasible alternatives politically possible. Rather than simply rebuilding existing systems, post-pandemic recovery processes could address structural vulnerabilities that both COVID-19 and climate change have exposed. The Zimbabwe government's recognition that COVID-19 contributed to the rapid deterioration of child health outcomes creates opportunities for reimagining social policy architectures and using recovery opportunities to address structural vulnerabilities rather than restoring pre-crisis conditions. The growing recognition of SDG limitations and the need for more transformative sustainable development approaches creates additional TSP opportunities. In Zimbabwe's context, this shift is relevant given experiences with structural adjustment and market-oriented reforms that exacerbated inequality while failing to address structural vulnerabilities. The climate crisis provides an opportunity to move beyond these approaches towards models that prioritise social protection, redistribution, and the realisation of rights as foundations for resilient development.

16.8 Implications for Children's Rights Protection

The findings suggest that protecting children's rights in climate-affected Zimbabwe requires systemic resilience rather than merely responding to individual shocks. TSP offers both an analytical lens and a practical framework for addressing these limitations through approaches that simultaneously build climate resilience and advance social transformation. However, implementing transformative approaches requires political mobilisation and institutional changes that challenge existing power structures. This involves transforming social, economic, and political systems, determining children's exposure and vulnerability to climate impacts. While the government recognises adequate financing, co-ordination, and systematic observation as the backbone of climate resilience, genuine resilience requires transforming power relations and resource distribution patterns that are currently limiting adaptive capacity. Rights recognition requires institutional changes that acknowledge children as full participants in building resilient societies. This includes mechanisms recognising children's differential vulnerabilities while affirming their agency, policy frameworks integrating children's rights across all climate interventions, accountability systems tracking climate impacts on children's rights, and legal reforms strengthening children's access to justice for climate-related rights violations. Integrating children's rights frameworks with climate adaptation planning offers mutually reinforcing potential. Rather than treating these as separate domains, TSP approaches recognise them as interconnected challenges requiring integrated responses. The Climate Change Bills require adaptation responses to consider vulnerable groups, including children (GoZ, 2025), and this creates opportunities for integrating evidence of climate impacts on children into adaptation planning, prioritising their rights and welfare.

TSP-based policy transformation requires immediate institutional integration, the establishment of child-climate co-ordination mechanisms, participatory processes creating formal channels for children's climate engagement, and rights-based monitoring that tracks climate impacts on children's rights. Medium-term interventions should link climate adaptation with inequality reduction strategies, strengthen community-based approaches utilising indigenous knowledge systems, and pursue legal reforms establishing accountability for climate-related rights violations. Long-term systemic change demands paradigm transformation towards development approaches prioritising climate resilience and social justice simultaneously. Finally, meaningful rights protection requires transforming participation frameworks that limit children's engagement. A TSP approach would position children as legitimate political actors with rights to participate in defining problems, designing solutions, and evaluating outcomes. The government's acknowledgement that children should be climate change actors rather than passive observers provides a foundation for approaches that strengthen children's individual and collective agency while addressing structural conditions that limit their capacity to protect themselves and shape their environments. This transformation recognises that children's direct experience of climate impacts provides situated knowledge essential for effective adaptation responses, requiring institutional mechanisms that support genuine partnerships between children and adults in climate adaptation and related processes.

16.9 Conclusion: Towards Transformative Climate Governance for Children's Rights

This chapter concludes the book *Climate Change and Children's Rights in Zimbabwe: Towards Social-Policy-Based Interventions*. The chapter demonstrates that Zimbabwe's climate crisis constitutes an important test of society's commitment to children's rights and social justice. The analysis reveals that conventional social policy approaches, while well intentioned, operate within paradigmatic constraints that render them inadequate for addressing the structural nature of climate vulnerability affecting children. The fragmented, reactive, and adult-centric characteristics of current policy frameworks in Zimbabwe reflect deeper tensions between technocratic climate adaptation approaches and rights-based frameworks that recognise children as active agents in shaping resilient societies. The theoretical contribution lies in establishing TSP as both an analytical lens and a practical framework for understanding how climate vulnerability intersects with inequality patterns to create compound disadvantages for children. By positioning climate impacts as manifestations of structural inequality rather than natural phenomena, the TSP framework reveals how apparently neutral climate risks are mediated by power relations, resource distribution patterns, and institutional arrangements that systematically disadvantage certain populations. This structural understanding challenges dominant narratives framing climate vulnerability as primarily technical problems requiring infrastructure solutions, revealing the inherently political nature of climate impacts and adaptation responses instead.

Findings demonstrate that protecting children's rights in climate contexts requires paradigmatic transformation rather than incremental reform. Zimbabwe's experience illustrates how constitutional commitments create legal foundations for transformation, while persistent implementation gaps reveal the limitations of formal rights recognition absent structural change. Evidence of differentiated climate impacts, for example with children in Masvingo experiencing disproportionate food insecurity, exemplifies how geographic location intersects with existing inequalities to create spatially differentiated vulnerabilities that technical interventions alone cannot address. The policy implications extend beyond Zimbabwe to broader debates about climate governance, suggesting that effective adaptation requires simultaneous attention to redistribution, participation, and rights recognition. These are dimensions that conventional frameworks struggle to integrate coherently.

The study acknowledges formidable challenges facing transformative policy implementation. The TSP approach necessarily challenges existing power structures, creating resistance from beneficiaries of current arrangements. The political economy of transformation requires sustained mobilisation and institutional change beyond policy reform to encompass broader social transformation. This tension between analytical clarity and political feasibility reflects deeper challenges in translating critical scholarship into practical change, especially where structural inequalities are deeply entrenched. While enabling comprehensive policy analysis, the methodological approach highlights urgent needs for research methodologies that genuinely centre children's voices and experiences, positioning them as co-researchers rather than research subjects.

Looking forward, three interconnected areas require sustained attention. These include the institutional development of governance mechanisms that accommodate children's participation while addressing structural determinants of vulnerability; conceptual development integrating climate science, children's rights frameworks, and social policy analysis; and empirical research tracking climate impacts on children's welfare while documenting innovative community responses. The chapter's central argument that protecting children's rights in climate contexts requires transforming social policy approaches rather than technical adaptation extends beyond academic discourse to questions about building societies capable of simultaneously addressing environmental change and social justice. Children's disproportionate vulnerability reflects broader inequality patterns undermining collective resilience, while their capacity for innovation represents untapped potential for developing effective responses to environmental change. TSP offers pathways for harnessing this potential while addressing structural conditions that limit children's capacity to protect themselves and contribute to community resilience.

The Zimbabwe case demonstrates both urgency and the possibility of transformation. While current frameworks remain inadequate, constitutional foundations, emerging policy discourse, and a growing recognition of conventional limitations create space for radical alternatives. The question is not whether transformation is necessary—evidence makes it clear that incremental reform cannot address climate vulnerability's scale and complexity—but whether political will and institutional capacity can mobilise transformative potential. This chapter contributes to broader scholarly debates by demonstrating how climate change challenges existing social policy paradigms while creating opportunities for approaches that integrate environmental sustainability with social justice. Positioning children's rights as both an analytical entry point and a normative foundation offers a framework for climate governance that prioritises society's most vulnerable members while recognising their agency and contribution. The climate crisis demands a fundamental reimagining of how societies protect and empower vulnerable members. For children in Zimbabwe and beyond, TSP offers hope for trajectories that recognise climate action and children's rights protection as mutually reinforcing imperatives in building just and sustainable societies.

References

ACERWC. (2025). *ACERWC study on climate change & children's rights in Africa: A continental overview - 2024*. ACERWC Secretariat.

Addaney, M., Boshoff, E., & Olutola, B. (2017). The climate change and human rights nexus in Africa. *The Amsterdam Law Forum, 9*(3), 5–28. https://doi.org/10.37974/ALF.304

Adesina, J. O. (2007). Social policy in the sub-Saharan African context: In search of inclusive development: Introduction. In J. O. Adesina (Ed.), *Social policy in the sub-Saharan African context: In search of inclusive development* (pp. 1–53). Palgrave Macmillan.

Adesina, J. O. (2015). Return to a wider vision of social policy: Rereading theory and history. *South African Review of Sociology, 46*(3), 99–119. https://doi.org/10.1080/21528586.2015.1077588

Adesina, J. O. (2020). Policy merchandising and social assistance in Africa: Don't call dog monkey for me. *Development & Change, 51*(2), 561–582. https://doi.org/10.1111/dech.12569

Arts, K. (2019). Children's rights and climate change. In C. Fenton-Glynn (Ed.), *Children's rights and sustainable development: Interpreting the UNCRC for future generations* (pp. 216–235). Cambridge University Press.

Bourdillon, M., Driscoll, J., Myers, W., O'Kane, C., & Rink, P. (2024). Climate crisis as a form of structural violence against children and youth. *BMJ Paediatrics Open, 8*(1), e003059. https://doi.org/10.1136/bmjpo-2024-003059

Chikoko, W., & Chihiya, P. (2023). Climate change and vulnerabilities of children in rural Zimbabwe: The case of ward 14 of Bikita District, Zimbabwe. *African Journal of Social Work, 13*(2), 78–86. https://doi.org/10.4314/ajsw.v13i2.4

Chipenda, C. (2022). Comparative perspectives on Zimbabwe and South Africa's social policy response to COVID-19. *Afrika Focus, 35*(2), 235–269. https://doi.org/10.1163/2031356X-35020001

Chipenda, C. (2023). Rethinking the role of social policy in responding to the COVID-19 pandemic in South Africa: Critical reflections using the intellectual contribution of Thandika Mkandawire. In V. Gumede & E. Ndhlovu (Eds.), *Development in Africa: Remembering Thandika Mkandawire*. Africa Century Editions (ACE) Press.

Chipenda, C. (2024). A transformative social policy perspective on land and agrarian reform in Zimbabwe. *Africa Spectrum, 59*, 89–118.
Chipenda, C., & Cochrane, L. (2024). Out of school children in the context of new policy trajectories and interlocking crises in Zimbabwe: A transformative social policy perspective. *SN Social Sciences, 4*, 131. https://doi.org/10.1007/s43545-024-00938-1
Committee on the Rights of the Child. (2023). General comment No. 26 (2023) on children's rights and the environment, with a special focus on climate change: Committee on the Rights of the Child. *International Human Rights Law Review, 12*(2), 322–355. https://doi.org/10.1163/22131035-12020006
Fischer, A. (2018). *Poverty as ideology: Rescuing social justice from global development agendas*. Zed Books.
Food and Nutrition Council. (2024). *Zimbabwe Livelihoods Assessment Committee (ZimLAC) rural livelihoods assessment (RLA)*. FNC Zimbabwe.
Government of Zimbabwe. (2013). *Constitution of the Republic of Zimbabwe*. Government Printers.
Government of Zimbabwe. (2014). *Zimbabwe National Climate Change Response Strategy*. Ministry of Environment, Water and Climate.
Government of Zimbabwe (2016). *Zimbabwe's National Climate Change Response Strategy*. Government of Zimbabwe.
Government of Zimbabwe. (2017). *Zimbabwe National Climate Policy*. Ministry of Environment, Water and Climate.
Government of Zimbabwe. (2019). *National Development Strategy 1: Towards a prosperous and empowered upper middle-income society by 2030*. Ministry of Finance and Economic Development.
Government of Zimbabwe. (2020). *Understanding climate risks in Zimbabwe*. Ministry of Environment, Climate, Tourism and Hospitality Industry.
Government of Zimbabwe. (2024a). *The 2025 National Budget Speech: "Building resilience for sustained economic transformation"*. Ministry of Finance and Economic Development.
Government of Zimbabwe. (2024b). *Zimbabwe National Climate Change Adaptation Plan*. Ministry of Environment, Climate and Wildlife.
Government of Zimbabwe. (2025). *Climate Change Management Bill*. https://www.hevacraz.co.zw/sitepad-data/uploads/2024/06/DRAFT-Climate-Change-Bill-Review-_Pamuzinda-Mazowe_24-May-2024.pdf
Gwenzi, J., Mafongoya, P. L., & Mashonjowa, E. (2022). Effects of climate change on food production in semi-arid areas: A case study of Uzumba Maramba Pfungwe district, Zimbabwe. In *Handbook of climate change across the food supply chain* (pp. 451–465). Springer. https://link.springer.com/chapter/10.1007/978-3-030-87934-1_26
Gwitira, I., Shekede, M. D., & Bhatasara, S. (2024). *Child-centred climate impact, vulnerability, and risk assessment for Zimbabwe*. UNICEF.
Mhlanga, D., & Ndhlovu, E. (2023). Goals of social policy in the fourth industrial revolution from a developmental context in Africa. In D. Mhlanga & E. Ndhlovu (Eds.), *The fourth industrial revolution in Africa: Exploring the development implications of smart technologies in Africa*. Springer.
Mkandawire, T. (2004). Introduction: Social policy in a development context. In T. Mkandawire (Ed.), *Social policy in a development context*. UNRISD/Palgrave Macmillan.
Mkandawire, T. (2007). Transformative social policy and innovation in developing countries. *The European Journal of Development Research, 19*(1), 13–29. https://doi.org/10.1080/09578810601144236
Ndhlovu, E. (2024a). Extreme weather events and human displacement in sub-Saharan Africa: Toward social policy interventions. *Review of Socio-Economic Research and Development Studies, 8*(2), 70–100.
Ndhlovu, E. (2024b). Social protection instruments and strategies in southern Africa. *International Journal of Innovation in Management Economics and Social Sciences, 4*(2), 44–59.

Ndhlovu, E., & Gumede, V. (2023). Reflections on South Africa's social policy response to the COVID-19 pandemic. In V. Gumede & E. Ndhlovu (Eds.), *Development in Africa: Remembering Thandika Mkandawire* (pp. 128–155). Africa Century Editions Press.

Online Reporter. (2024, March 28). NEW: 'Children vulnerable to climate change'. *The Sunday Mail*. https://www.heraldonline.co.zw/new-children-vulnerable-to-climate-change/

Organisation of African Unity. (1990, July 11). *African Charter on the Rights and Welfare of the Child*. OAU.

Tom, T., & Banda, R. (2023). Women farm workers in Zimbabwe: The social policy outcomes two decades after the transformative fast track land reform. *Feminist Africa, 4*(1), 75–102.

United Nations. (1989, November 20). *Convention on the Rights of the Child*. Treaty Series, vol. 1577. UN.

UN. (2023). *United Nations Committee on the Rights of the Child*. General Comment No. 26 on Children's Rights and the Environment with a Special Focus on Climate Change. UN.

UNICEF. (2021). *The climate crisis is a child rights crisis: Introducing the Children's Climate Risk Index*. UNICEF.

UNICEF. (2022). *UNICEF Zimbabwe climate, energy, environment and children strategy*. UNICEF.

UNICEF. (2025). When the rains don't come: Climate change through the eyes of Zimbabwe's children. https://www.unicef.org/zimbabwe/stories/when-rains-dont-come-climate-change-through-eyes-zimbabwes-children

UNICEF East Asia and Pacific Regional Office. (2025). *Climate-resilient child protection systems in East Asia and the Pacific: Technical brief*. UNICEF.

UNRISD. (2022). *Crises of inequality: Shifting power for a new social contract. UNRISD Flagship Report 2022*. UNRISD.

UNRISD. (2023). Crises of inequality shifting power for a new eco-social contract. *Research and Policy Brief 39*. UNRISD.

World Bank. (2025, April 9). *Social dimensions of climate change*. https://www.worldbank.org/en/topic/social-dimensions-of-climate-change#:~:text=Transitioning%20to%20low%2Dcarbon%2C%20climate,jobs%20are%20all%20critical%20components

Zimbabwe. (2025). *Environmental child rights: A call to action*. https://zimbabwenow.co.zw/articles/8843/environmental-child-rights-a-call-to-action

Zinonzwa E. (2025). *Environmental Child Rights: A call to action*. https://zimbabwenow.co.zw/articles/8843/environmental-child-rights-a-call-to-action#:~:text=In%20terms%20of%20displacement%20and,education%20for%20thousands%20of%20children.

GPSR Compliance
The European Union's (EU) General Product Safety Regulation (GPSR) is a set of rules that requires consumer products to be safe and our obligations to ensure this.

If you have any concerns about our products, you can contact us on

ProductSafety@springernature.com

In case Publisher is established outside the EU, the EU authorized representative is:

Springer Nature Customer Service Center GmbH
Europaplatz 3
69115 Heidelberg, Germany

www.ingramcontent.com/pod-product-compliance
Ingram Content Group UK Ltd.
Pitfield, Milton Keynes, MK11 3LW, UK
UKHW020631260926
475829UK00003BA/26

* 9 7 8 9 8 1 9 5 6 0 0 4 2 *